LAW AND SOCIETY

The law is not an abstraction
nor an end in itself,
but the means to an end;
and that end is justice

(Lloyd P. Stryker)

L. C. GREEN

University Professor
University of Alberta

—

LAW
AND
SOCIETY

1975

A. W. Sijthoff—Leyden

Oceana Publications, Inc.—Dobbs Ferry, N.Y.

ISBN 90 286 0235 6 (Sijthoff)
ISBN 0-379-00307-4 (Oceana)

Printed in The Netherlands.

TO
LILIAN

For some time now, colleagues and students have suggested that it would be useful if I were to bring together
some of the papers that I have written or delivered over
the years touching on various aspects of the interplay
of law and society. The purpose of this volume is to
meet this suggestion and at the same time provide an
opportunity to bring the material up to date.

The aim of each of these essays has been to draw
attention to some of the sociological problems that
arise when the law is confronted with problems of modern
life.

The emergence of the new states has called for a
re-examination of the relationship of so-called primitive
peoples and the law that has been evolved and applied by
their rulers, on both the national and the international
level. Modern societal trends, together with medical
advances, have cast doubt on the validity of customary
concepts of law and morality, and investigation of the
extent to which traditional views of marriage and sexual
behaviour remain relevant. To some extent, this revolution reflects current interest in individual freedom and
human rights, which the United Nations and the World
Court have sought to raise to the level of general
principles of law. Of recent floutings of such
principles, among the most glaring perhaps was the
massacre of civilians at My Lai in Vietnam, but it is
difficult to expect ordinary soldiers to abide by the

laws of war if they do not know what those laws are. Almost as disruptive of the rule of law has been the crop of terrorist acts which have taken place in recent years in the name of national liberation. These have aroused renewed interest in both the right of asylum and proposals for an international criminal law.

In discussing some of these problems it is inevitable that arguments, cases, quotations, and the like, are relevant to more than one issue. There must, therefore, be some repetition, but this has been kept to a minimum and to those instances where to omit a reference, because of its relevance elsewhere, would inhibit proper appraisal of the matter under discussion. Moreover, it is this very duplication which helps to illustrate the social function and wholeness - or, in Smuts' term, holism - of law, explaining why a comment or principle in one field is significant in another.

Throughout, the underlying thread connecting these essays is the extent to which the law operates on a functional level in answering the needs of the society it is called upon to govern and serve.

In preparing this collection in its present form, I have been greatly assisted by the patience and encourage-ment of my wife, to whom the volume is dedicated. I should also like to thank the University of Alberta and Dr. Kreisel its Vice President Academic for the grant given me to cover some of the typing expenses. Finally, I must thank Mrs. Jill Murray of Ottawa who has proved an absolute marvel in putting a scissors-and-paste manuscript together in a form that the publishers are able to reproduce.

L.C.G.
1975

CONTENTS

TABLE OF CASES

* Since the footnotes do not appear at the bottom of the page, footnote numbers have been given when the case is not identified in the text

xii

J. v. J. (1947) 471 n 475
Joana-Vapor v. Anton Susami and Agnes-Deporobu (1967)
    90 n 96, 116 n 38
John Calder (Publications) Ltd. v. Powell (1965) 40
Jones v. Fraser (1886) 121
Jones v. Meehan (1899) 124 n 52
Joyce v. D.P.P. (1946) 157 n 71

Kahan v. Pakistan (1954) 166
Karadzole v. Artukovic (1957) 329, 382 n 36
Kaur v. Ginder (1958) 121 n 48
Kavic, Bjelanovic and Arsenijevic, Re (1952) 330 n 26,373
Kay, Re (1973) 375
Kerr v. Illinois (1868) 245 n 14
Keyling v. Keyling (1942) 444 n 40, 471
Khoo Hooi Leong v. Khoo Hean Kwee (1926) 55 n 55, 112
Knott v. Knott (1955) 467
Kobogum v. Jackson Iron Co. (1889) 16 n 46, 78 n 61
Kolczynski, Ex p. (1955) 248 n 27, 288 n 29, 326 n 16,
    328, 329, 330, 382, 383, 384, 385, 386, 388
Konty v. U.T.C. (1934) 105 n 15
Koykoy Jatta v. Menna Camara (1961) 84
Kyper case (1974) 32 n 99

L. v. L. (1922) 471
L. v. L. (1949) 26, 478
La Jeune Eugénie (1822) 287
Lawrance v. Lawrance (1950) 465
Le Louis, The (1817) 286
Leong v. Lim Beng Chye (1955) 88, 108
Llandovery Castle, The (1921) 135, 136, 420
Loss of Nationality (Germany) Case (1965) 242 n 2
Lotus, The S.S. (1927) 168 n 109, 184, 187, 258 n 59
Lowenthal v. A.G. (1948) 242 n 2

M. v. K. (1968) 15 n 44, 77 n 59, 122
Maclennan v. Maclennan (1958) 26, 478 n 141
Magayi v. Uganda (1965) 104
Magellan Pirates (1853) 248 n 26
Malatesta, Re (1891) 326 n 15, 380
Mangold's Patent, Re (1951) 242 n 2
Mapolisa v. R. (1965) 86
Mavrommatis Palestine Concessions (1924) 274 n 99
Mawji v. The Queen (1957) 114
McCall v. McDowell (1867) 47 n 139, 411
McCarthy, ex p. (1924) 418 n 28
McNaughten (1843) 168
Menkes, ex p. (1953) 245 n 15
Melaksultan v. Sherali Jeraj (1955) 114
Mensah v. Winabob (1925) 69, 107 n 20
Mergé Claim (1955) 245 n 15
Mersah v. Konongo Gold Mines Ltd. (1948) 66 n 22, 71
Meunier, Re (1894) 325 n 10, 379, 384, 385

LAW AND MORALITY IN A CHANGING SOCIETY*

> Morality wherever met
> Is merely local etiquette.
> The habits of the Eskimo
> Appear peculiar in Bordeaux;
> St James' Street might well object
> To language Limehouse deems correct...
> What Petersburg considers mean
> Seems generous in Aberdeen.   (Henry Graham)

> The state has no place in the bedrooms of the nation.
> (Pierre Elliott Trudeau)

In any study of the relationship between law and
morality, perhaps one of the most difficult issues is
that of terminology. It is often implied that since
English is the language of Shakespeare and the King
James Version it is the richest and most fluent language
in the world. In fact, this is far from being true, at
least in so far as law is concerned. The word law
itself presents a problem. Whereas the French speak of
loi and droit, the Spanish of ley and derecho, and the
Germans of Gesetz and Recht, we have but the one word
'law', which we are compelled to use whether we are
referring to the law against murder, the criminal law
of which that law is part, or of the law of Canada of
which the criminal law is but a portion, or of law in
its abstract sense, of which the other three are but
emanations. A similar problem arises in connection with
many of our legal concepts. Perhaps as good an example
as any is to be found in the way in which Lord Lindley
used the terms 'right' and 'liberty' in Quinn v Leathem:[1]

'The plaintiff had the ordinary rights of a British subject. He was at liberty to earn his living in his own way, provided he did not violate some special law prohibiting him from doing so, and provided he did not infringe the rights of other people. This liberty involved the liberty to deal with other persons who were willing to deal with him. This liberty is a right recognized by law; its correlative is the general duty of everyone not to prevent the free exercise of this liberty except so far as his own liberty of action may justify him in so doing. But a person's liberty or right to deal with others is nugatory unless they are at liberty to deal with him if they choose to do so.' Similarly, what could be more confusing than the legal idea of 'sanction'? This term may be used in two completely conflicting meanings. According to Blackstone,[2] 'human legislators have for the most part chosen to make the sanction of their laws rather <u>vindicatory</u> than <u>remuneratory</u>, or to consist rather in punishments, than in actual particular rewards.' This use of the term was raised almost to the level of a divine ordinance by Austin,[3] although by 1720 it had already been used to indicate 'express, authoritative permission or recognition.'[4]

For the 'English' lawyer the only way of ascertaining what he means by the term 'law' is to adopt a functional approach directed to the purpose he wishes the term to serve. In order to do this it is necessary to free oneself of the shackles of Austinian positivism. Austin was a typical product of his time: a Victorian <u>paterfamilias</u> whose disciplinarian authoritarianism and egocentricity were only emphasized by his experience in the army, and his definition of law reflects these characteristics. 'A law, in the most general and comprehensive acceptation in which the term, in its

literal meaning, is employed, may be said to be a
rule laid down for the guidance of an intelligent being
by an intelligent being having power over him ...
Every law or rule (taken with the largest signification
which can be given to the term properly) is a command.
Or, rather, laws or rules, properly so called, are a
species of commands ... [A] law, properly so called ...
is a command which obliges a person or persons, and
obliges generally to acts or forbearances of a class...
[that is to say] to a course of conduct ... [T] he term
superiority(like the terms duty and sanction) is implied
by the term command ... Strictly speaking, every law
properly so called is a positive law. For it is put or
set by its individual or collective author ... Laws
properly so called are a species of commands. But,
being a command, every law properly so called flows
from a determinate source, or emanates from a determinate author ... If a determinate human superior, not
in a habit of obedience to a like superior, receive
habitual obedience from the bulk of a given society,
that determinate superior is sovereign in that society,
and the society (including the superior) is a society
political and independent.'[5]

Such a view of law is a reflection of society as it
existed in Victorian England and may, to a great extent,
be viewed not merely as a criterion of legal validity -
which it tends to be rather than a definition of law -
but as based solely on consideration of the nature of
criminal law. Generally speaking, matters relating to
commercial law, the law of property, family law, and
the like, do not require a determinate superior for their
existence, nor do they require any sanction in the
punitive sense. Moreover, a demand for a legislator,
enforcement authority, and penalty would quite clearly
exclude from the ambit of the law what had only just

become known in Austin's day as international law,[6] and which he regarded as law improperly so called or positive morality.[7] For modern purposes, and in assessing the true role of law in society, which is to facilitate the maintenance of peace, order, and reasonable existence within the group, Austin's views may be dismissed somewhat peremptorily. 'Austin defined what the word [law] meant for him, which he was entitled to do, but he was not entitled to adopt a legislative attitude and declare what the word should mean for other people. The power that Austin assumed for himself, to define the words he used, he should have accorded to others.'[8] Exercising such freedom, there is no reason why international law, for example, should be considered any less law than any other branch of law, for it is nothing but that system of laws and regulations which those who operate on the international scene recognize as being necessary for their orderly conduct, and which they recognize as being binding upon themselves in order to achieve that orderly conduct.[9]

Similar problems of definition arise in connection with morality. The conflict between Devlin[10] and Hart[11] on this matter has tended to obscure the situation.[12] Devlin first propounded his views in his Maccabean Lecture in Jurisprudence at the British Academy in 1959[13] and elaborated them somewhat in his Presidential Address to the Holdsworth Club two years later.[14] While he affirmed that 'the original law of England was based on the moral law, although in many respects it lagged behind it, for there were many sins which were not punishable as crimes,'[15] his insistence on the difference between offences which were mala in se and those created by law which were only mala prohibita, creating a quasi-criminal law, has resulted in a general view that morality is the opposite of sin, and concepts

4

of morality tend to be confined to the sphere of sex,
and particularly to what the law regards as sexual
offences. His analysis bears repetition.'

The distinction between the real criminal law and the
quasi-criminal in their relationship to morals is that
in the former a moral idea shapes the content of the
law and in the latter it provides a base upon which a
legal structure can be erected. In the former the law
adopts a particular moral idea, usually taken from a
divine commandment. In the latter no more is required
of the law than that it should maintain contact, more
or less remote, with the general moral idea that a
man, if he cannot reach the perfection of loving his
neighbours, should at least take care not to injure
them and should not unfairly snatch an advantage for
himself at their expense.

Real crimes are sins with legal definitions. The
criminal law is at its best when it sticks closely
to the content of the sin ...

The basis for the distinction between mala in se and
mala prohibita, between what one might call a crime
and an offence ... is that crime means to the ordinary
man something that is sinful or immoral and an offence
at worst a piece of misbehaviour ...

.. [H] istory shows that the loosening of moral bonds
is often the first stage of disintegration, so that
society is justified in taking the same steps to
protect its moral code as it does to preserve its
government and other essential institutions. The
suppression of vice is as much the law's business as
the suppression of subversive activities ...

Immorality then, for the purpose of the law, is what
every right-minded person is presumed to consider to
be immoral. Any immorality is capable of affecting
society injuriously and in effect to a greater or
lesser extent it usually does, this is what gives the
law its locus standi ...

... [T] he free-thinker and the non-Christian can
accept, without offence to his convictions, the fact
that Christian morals are the basis of the criminal law
and that he can recognize, also without taking offence,
that without the support of the churches the moral
order, which has its origin in and takes its strength
from Christian beliefs, would collapse ... [Neverthe-
less,] I do not think that you can equate crime with
sin. The divine law and the secular have been disunited,

5

but they are brought together again by the need which
each has for the other ...

...[T]he law must base itself on Christian morals
and to the limit of its ability enforce them, not
simply because they are the morals of most of us, nor
simply because they are the morals which are taught
by the established Church ... but for the compelling
reason that without the help of Christian teaching the
law will fail.[16]

   Much of Devlin's argument is concerned with such
matters as abortion, homosexuality, and fornication.
It must not be forgotten, however, that important though
sexual matters and their regulation may be, sex is not
the only force in societal life, nor is sexual conduct
the only manifestation of human relations with which
society must concern itself. While the general public
has largely appeared to accept the view that one
measures morality and moral conduct in sexual terms,
morality is wider than this. Just as a functional
view of law must be adopted, a similar approach is
necessary in this field. From this point of view,
morality is to be equated with the ethic or mores of
society which, for the sake of convenience, may be
described as society's idea of what is right and
wrong. It cannot be denied that, to some extent,
society tends to adopt a particular standard in so far
as sexual conduct is concerned, and uses the term
immorality to indicate sexual activity which deviates
from the norm, as well as to describe conduct which
it regards as contrary to its idea of rightness. This
means that a man whose sexual activities do not coincide
with those generally accepted by the society in which
he lives - he may for example reject monogamy or
matrimony and may even enjoy pornography, a right which
the Supreme Court of the United States has recognized[17]-
may nevertheless have so high a concept of right-living,

in the sense of working for the welfare of his society
and abstaining from any conduct which may harm his
neighbours, that his life may serve as a model of the
good life for those around him. This view is conceded
even by Devlin, although he tends to persist in viewing
morality in its narrow sense: 'Society cannot live
without morals. Its morals are those standards of
conduct which the reasonable man approves. A rational
man, who is also a good man, may have other standards.
If he has no standards at all he is not a good man ...
If he has standards, they may be very different; he
may, for example, not disapprove of homosexuality or
abortion. In that case he will not share in the
common morality; but that should not make him deny
that it is a social necessity.'[18] Mr. Justice Cusack's
view of morality is much wider and, in an address to
the Oxford University Newman Society, he did not
hesitate to condemn the law with regard to the legal
liability imposed upon one in possession of dangerous
drugs, who has no defence even if he is unaware of the
contents of a parcel containing such drugs: 'In such
circumstances I regard the law as immoral, because it
is unjust and immoral to convict the innocent. Criminal
responsibility should be excluded where there is no
moral responsibility.'[19]

Acceptance of the 'right-wrong' view of morality
clearly indicates the relation between it and law,
especially in the light of the definition of law based
on its function to preserve peace and good order in
society. For then, from the functional point of view,
law may be regarded as the means by which society
ensures that its _mores_ are protected by its institutions.
Perhaps one of the easiest ways to illustrate this
proposition is to be found by reference to the transition from primitive law to modern society. Primitive

7

man defended the ethos of his society by the blood
feud and expulsion. Likewise with organized religion.
Those heretics whose views were considered so dangerous
that tolerance towards their holders would threaten
the very basis of the religion were burned, while those
whose deviation from the current beliefs were not so
fundamental were merely subjected to excommunication.
With the development of the secular state both of these
penalties have faded and the nearest that remains is
the private boycott and the sending of a man to
Coventry. It is only in more 'backward' areas like
Sicily that the blood feud remains, although with the
increasing recourse to violence that is being experienced today we see something closely akin to it in
the gang warfare of the underworld in the modern city.
In more developed societies, custom, which may well be
regarded as the hardening of society's concepts of
right and wrong into the accepted code of behaviour,
has developed more sophisticated methods of ensuring
compliance with society's mores, often under the
pressure of religious ideology. The blood feud,
together with the hue and cry of outlawry, gave way to
the idea that social institutions should exact
penalties for breaches of society's rules, even when
the offender's conduct was directed against the very
basis on which that society rested. Long before there
was any statutory definition of murder, homicide was
treated as an offence which merited punishment, and
the same is true of lesser offences like theft.

Even ideas as to the nature of God over which
societies have fought and destroyed each other came to
be tolerated and the sceptic derived as much protection
from the law as did the ardent believer who attended
church regularly. Sunday Observance laws are merely
the legacy of the period when churchgoing was

compulsory and those who failed to attend church were punished in the ecclesiastical courts. Gradually the situation changed. The pressures were off and non-attendance was no longer accompanied by a sanction. From this, it was but a short step to religious toleration in respect of those who not merely did not attend, but those who did not believe. The history of Catholic[20] and Jewish[21] emancipation shows how the law in this field did not always keep in touch with society's morality. In so far as the former was concerned, public opinion imposed limits upon parliamentary action. Thus, the Act of 1829 which was directed to removing all disabilities from Roman Catholics sought to banish Jesuits and all members of Catholic religious orders from Great Britian. 'How does it happen that a law restoring to Roman Catholics the rights of citizenship, contained penal laws against Jesuits and monks? The answer lies close at hand. The general scope of the Act represents the enlightenment of a governing class which, by favour of peculiar circumstances, carried through a scheme of religious toleration opposed to the prejudices of the people. Penal enactments threatening Jesuits and monks with a banishment, which had never in a single instance been put in force, are the monument of a concession made by parliamentary statesmanship to vulgar bigotry.'[22]

The raising of political restrictions upon Jews shows public morality running ahead of the law. Lionel Rothschild was elected to the House of Commons by the City of London in 1847, but he was refused his seat because he declined to take the oath as it then was framed. He was constantly re-elected, but the House of Lords just as constantly refused to agree to any amendments in the law. It took eleven years before Parliament caught up with the public sentiment and amended the law, enabling a Jew to sit.[23]

Today the clock has come full circle. Not only are
religious minorities normally granted equal rights with
majorities among whom they live,[24] but little attempt
is made anywhere to enforce the legislation originally
enacted to protect the Lord's Day while more and more
people to whom it is directed seem to be determined
to show that they are no longer interested in the
purpose of the legislation. They also seem determined
to defy the law-enforcement agencies to give effect
to a law which has lost touch with the current ethos
of the society whose morality it is intended to
preserve.

This statement of the situation concerning religion
and religious toleration is evidence of the fact that
man's views are not static and the society in which
he lives is one of constant progress or regression,
depending on one's views of moral conduct. It is
clear, therefore, that, just as there cannot be one
concept of law good for all men, in all places, at
all times, so there cannot be one everlasting view of
morality. As society has developed, so have its needs
and with them there have been changes in the concepts
of law and the relationships of those concepts to
prevailing moral considerations.

Perhaps family law is a useful example. The institution of marriage, beginning with marriage by capture
and purchase, is closely interwoven with that of
property, and many of the legal consequences of
marriage reflect this fact. In Rome, the paterfamilias
was not merely head of the family but at first the only
member to enjoy legal rights, possessing virtually the
power of life and death. Gradually, the sons acquired

10

legal status, although one of the methods of granting it to them was that of manumission, the same process by which the slave received his freedom. In so far as the wife and daughters of the marriage are concerned, the property characteristic is even more marked. That the wife was a mere chattel becomes clear from the history of the development of her separate property,[25] the demand for damages of a monetary character from her paramour in a divorce action, the enticement or 'Helen of Troy' cases,[26] and the common law view that since husband and wife were but one flesh no action for tort could lie between them. The property character of the daughter is indicated by the action for seduction. A father is entitled to recover damages in respect of the seduction of his daughter provided he is able to prove some loss of service as a result of the seducer's activity. Thus, no action will lie if the child is too young to render any services, and 'the quasi fiction of servitium amisit affords protection to the rich man, whose daughter occasionally makes his tea, but leaves without redress the poor man whose child ... is sent, unprotected, to earn her bread among strangers.'[27] Despite this emphasis on the property significance of the family, and although even pickpockets were liable to the death penalty, child-stealing did not become an offence until 1814.[28] Public opinion concerning the rights of man, accompanied by the struggles of the suffragettes and in respect of women's rights, have, in the Anglo-American world at least, effected a situation whereby the rights of the father have been diminished almost to vanishing point[29] and the marriage relationship has been reduced almost to that of contract, with each of the persons affected enjoying a legal capacity of his own dependent rather on age than on status. Similar manifestations are to be found in the family law of Japan, with the defeat of 1945 constituting

11

the watershed[30] - although to some extent it may be
argued that in this case the traditional law has been
modified by the standards of morality belonging to
another, alien people.

The marriage relationship per se illustrates the
inter-connection of law with the ethos of society.
While Blackstone states that 'our law considers
marriage in no other light than as a civil contract.
The holiness of the matrimonial state is left entirely
to the matrimonial law; the temporal courts not having
jurisdiction to consider unlawful marriage as a sin,
but merely as a civil inconvenience,'[31] they have
nevertheless used the current views of religion as
their measuring rod. Thus, in Hyde v Hyde[32] the
House of Lords referred to 'marriage as understood
by Christendom,' and of this Devlin has said:

> In England we believe in the Christian idea of
> marriage and therefore adopt monogamy as a moral
> principle. Consequently the Christian institution of
> marriage has become the basis of family life and so
> part of the structure of our society. It is there not
> because it is Christian. It has got there because it
> is Christian, but it remains there because it is
> built into the house in which we live and could not
> be removed without bringing it down. The great
> majority of those who live in this country accept it
> because it is the Christian idea of marriage and for
> them the only true one. But a non-Christian is bound
> by it, not because it is part of Christianity but
> because, rightly or wrongly, it has been adopted by
> the society in which he lives.[33]

The first inroad into the Christian concept of marriage
was made by granting a right of civil divorce. Even
in countries like Italy where the power of the church
is still strongly enshrined, the ethos of modern society
has brought about demands for legislation to permit
divorce and a most bitter election was fought over
the issue. Even in a country where divorce has been

12

possible for a long time, the cleavage between the
religious and civil concepts of marriage, and the
dichotomy of law and morals have to be recognized.
'The law of the land cannot be coextensive with the
law of morals, nor can the civil consequences of
marriage be identical with its religious consequences.
The solution to the question which arises for determination in a divorce case cannot be settled on a consideration of the Christian doctrine of marriage as laid
down in the <u>Book of Common Prayer</u>, but on a true
construction of the relevant Acts of Parliament.'[34]
For many years it was thought, in accordance with the
injunction 'Be fruitful and multiply, and replenish
the earth,'[35] that procreation was one of the ends of
marriage. In <u>G.</u> v <u>M.</u> in 1885, Lord Fitzgerald stated
that 'the procreation of children being the main object
of marriage, the contract contained by implication, as
an essential term, the capacity for procreation,'[36]
and this view was still being adopted by the English
courts as recently as 1946. In <u>Cowen</u> v <u>Cowen</u>[37] the
question was whether an annulment was possible on the
grounds of nonconsummation when the husband refused
to have intercourse without the use of a contraceptive
or by way of <u>coitus interruptus</u>. The Court of Appeal
was of opinion that 'sexual intercourse cannot be said
to be complete when a husband discontinues the act of
intercourse before it has reached its natural termination
or when he artificially prevents the natural termination...
To hold otherwise would be to affirm that a marriage is
consummated by an act so performed that one of the
principal ends, if not the principal end, of marriage
is intentially frustrated.' Such a view was completely
out of line with the prevalent morality on the use of
contraceptives, and only two years later a marriage
was considered consummated even though the wife would

not permit intercourse without the use of a condom.
On this occasion, Lord Jowett LC declared that 'it
is indisputable that the institution of marriage generally is not necessary for the procreation of children,
nor does it appear to be a principal end of marriage
as understood in Christendom.'[38] The current situation
in Canada where dissemination of contraceptive information was until recently an offence, as was the open
sale of contraceptive appliances, although some stores
did in fact have them on their open shelves, reflects
a similar change in morality. Not only were no
prosecutions brought, but public institutions assisted
in the spreading of family planning information, and
the government took advantage of the new morality to
introduce amendments which brought the Penal Code into
line with practice and the general attitude. Similarly
the United States Supreme Court has held that statutes
banning the use of contraceptives are unconstitutional
as an invasion of marital privacy, and in words
reminiscent of those of Mr. Trudeau Justice Douglas
condemned such laws as offensive to 'the sacred precinct
of marital bedrooms'[39]. Even Eire has upheld the
constitutional right of a married woman to obtain
contraceptives, although they may still not be sold in
Ireland. In Canada, on the other hand, as in a number
of other countries, the new attitude has resulted in
the opening of a plethors of 'love' or 'sex' shops
selling sex aids of various kinds.

The requirement of monogamy as a <u>sine qua non</u> for a
marriage to be recognized has also come under attack.
The idea that English law will only recognize a
marriage which is monogamous stems from the decision
in <u>Hyde</u> v <u>Hyde</u>,[40] but there has been a gradual acceptance of the fact that potentially polygamous marriages
can create the relationship of husband and wife,[41] a

modern application of the old common law concept that,
in the absence of impediments, public repute can create
a marriage.[42] Strange consequences can result from
the activities of the courts. Such a case was
Ochochuku v Ochochuku,[43] the parties to which, though
Christians, had gone through a customary form of
marriage in Nigeria in 1949, at which time Nigeria
permitted polygamy. In 1963, in order to obtain a
certificate, they entered into an English registry
office marriage. Wrangham J held: 'Whatever might be
the effect on the marriage for other purposes and in
other courts of the parties being Christians, in this
Court and for this purpose the Nigerian marriage must
be regarded as a polygamous marriage over which this
court does not exercise jurisdiction. I therefore
pronounce a decree nisi for the dissolution not of the
Nigerian marriage but of the marriage in London. I
am told that, in fact, that will be effective by
Nigerian law to dissolve the Nigerian marriage, but
that forms no part of my judgment. That is for someone else to determine and not for me.'

A judgment which probably more closely reflects
today's morality was delivered in England in March
1968.[44] Justices had committed a fourteen-year-old
Nigerian girl to the care of a local authority as
being exposed to moral danger and in need of care,
protection, and control. She was living with a twenty-
eight-year-old Nigerian male, to whom she was married
in accordance with Nigerian law in Nigeria where they
were both domiciled. The magistrates wrongly concluded
that since the marriage was potentially polygamous
it could not be recognized in England; but the Queen's
Bench Divisional Court held that, in so far as the
girl's status was concerned, the marriage would be
recognized so that she would be a wife. The Lord Chief

15

Justice pointed out that

the question was whether the evidence justified such
an order [of protection]. The justices had found that
before the marriage the [man] had lived with a woman
and had had three illegitimate children, and that after
the marriage at a time when his wife had almost certainly not reached puberty, he had had intercourse with
her. After the marriage he had contracted gonorrhoea
from a prostitute, but he was now cured and intended
to resume intercourse with his wife. The justices
had found that the continuance of the association
between the girl and the appellant would be repugnant
to any decent minded English person ... They had
misdirected themselves and were considering the
reactions of an Englishman regarding an English man
and woman in the western way of life. A decent Englishman realising the way in which a Nigerian man and woman
were brought up would not say it was repugnant. They
developed sooner and there was nothing abhorrent in a
girl of 13 marrying a man of 25. To say the girl was
in moral danger would be ignoring the way of life in
which she and her husband had been brought up. It
had been suggested that every time the appellant slept
with his wife in England, he was committing a criminal
offence under the Sexual Offences Act, 1956, s. 6[45]
which made it an offence for a man to have unlawful
intercourse with a girl between 13 and 16 ... [Lord
Parker did] not think the police could properly
prosecute cases where a foreign marriage was recognized
in England ... Intercourse between a man and wife was
lawful ... Where a husband and wife were recognized
as validly married according to the laws of England,
His Lordship would not say the wife was exposed to
moral danger because she carried out her wifely duties.

It may happen that the law will give effect to a
local concept of morality even where it appears to
deviate from the general law. This type of situation
frequently occurs in Canada's Northwest Territories
when questions arise concerning Indian marriages,
contracted in a form which would have been valid before
the introduction of English law in 1870. In such a
case, Witman J asked:[46]

[A]re the laws of England respecting the solemnisation
of marriage applicable to these Territories quoad the

16

Indian population? I have great doubt if these laws
are applicable to the Territories in any respect.
According to these laws marriages can be solemnised
only at certain times and in certain places or buildings.
These times would be in many cases most inconvenient
here and the buildings, if they exist at all, are often
so remote from the contracting parties that they could
not be reached save with the greatest inconvenience.
I am satisfied however that these laws are not applicable to the Territories quoad the Indians. The Indians
are for the most part unchristianised; they yet adhere
to there own particular marriage customs and usages.
It would be monstrous to hold that the law of England
respecting the solemnisation of marriage is applicable
to them ... A marriage between Indians by mutual
consent and according to Indian custom since 15th
July 1870, is a valid marriage, providing that neither
of the parties had a husband or wife, as the case might
be, living at the time.

In modern times there has been some evidence of
retreat from marriage. Not only have the divorce rates
gone up, but there appears to have been an increase in
irregular unions of long or short duration and there
have even been attempts in the United States and
elsewhere to create a legally recognized marriage
relationship between persons of the same sex. In
addition, while the illegitimacy rate throughout the
world seems to be increasing, there is a growing public
feeling that the illegitimate child is not to blame
for his predicament and so should not be subjected to
any form of legal discrimination. In some places, this
has now been recognised by the law.[47]

Probably the portion of the law which is most constantly present in the minds of the members of society is
criminal law, and it is in this field that the effect
of morality upon law - and perhaps vice versa - is
most evident. When he is hurt man's most primitive
urge is to retaliate, and this urge finds Divine
Sanction in the Bible: 'And, if any mischief follow,
then thou shalt give life for life. Eye for eye,

tooth for tooth, hand for hand, foot for foot'[48] and
this view is reflected in Lord Denning's evidence
before the British Royal Commission on Capital Punishment: "The punishment for grave crimes should
adequately reflect the revulsion of the majority of
the citizens for them. ... The ultimate justification
of any punishment is not that it is a deterrent, but
that it is the emphatic denunciation by the community
of a crime." In his lex talionis Henry I carried this
to its logical conclusion, so that if a man fell from
a tree injuring another who was beneath him, then that
other could climb a tree in order to fall therefrom and
injure the original wrongdoer.[49] This idea of equal
retaliation was not confined to humans. Animals, too,
were liable to be killed if they were responsible for
the death of a person. Once again the source was
Exodus,[50] and even as late as 1595 a dog was sentenced
to death by a court at Leiden, Holland, for having
caused the death of a child:[51]

The Schepenen of Leiden, having seen the claim and
conclusion made and taken by Lot Huygens Gael, Schout
of this town [as prosecutor], against and to the charge
of the dog of Jan Jansse van der Poel, named Provetie,
or by whatsoever other name or surname he may be known,
the prisoner being present, having seen, moreover, the
information obtained by the prosecutor for the purpose,
besides the prisoner's own confession made without
torture or being placed in irons, doing justice and in
the name of, &c, &c, have condemned and hereby do
condemn him to be led and taken to the plain of
Gravesteijn in this town, where evildoers are custom-
arily punished, and that he be there hanged by the
executioner to the gallows with a rope until death
ensues, that further his dead body be dragged on a
hurdle to the gallowsfield, and that he there remain
hanging to the gallows, to the deterring of other dog.
and to all as an example; moreover, they declare all
his goods, should he have any, to be confiscated and
forfeited for the benefit of the countship ...

Inanimate objects, too, were liable to answer for

injury they caused to human beings or their goods.
Pausanias records, in the second century AD, that at
Prytaneum there was a court to which 'iron and all
lifeless things are brought to trial,' and he refers
to the acquittal of an axe.[52] In Norman England the
law required that any thing causing death was to be
handed 'to the king and devoted by his almoner to pious
uses, "for the appeasing" says Coke "of God's wrath."'
The 'pious purpose' was determined by the justice in
eyre, and 'the sister of a man who has been run over
obtains the value of the condemned cart, since she is
poor and sick.'[53] According to Blackstone, the deodand
'seems to have been originally designed, in the blind
days of popery, as an expiation of the souls of such as
were snatched away by sudden death; and for that purpose
ought properly to have been given to holy church ...
And this may account for that rule of law, that no
deodand is due where an infant under the age of discretion is killed by a fall from a cart, or horse, or
the like, not being in motion; whereas, if an adult
person falls from thence and is killed, the thing is
certainly forfeited ... [T]he child, by reason of its
want of discretion, was presumed incapable of actual
sin, and therefore needed no deodand to purchase
propitiatory masses: but every adult, who died in
actual sin, stood in need of such atonement, according
to the humane superstitions of the founders of the
English law.'[54] It was not until 1846[55] that deodands
were abolished, and the reason is to be found in the
capitalist morality of the day - in 1842 a steam engine
responsible for causing death had been forfeited!

   Today the death penalty, in those countries which
still retain it, tends to be confined to murder and
treason. But this has not always been the case. Once
again, economic interests have been responsible for

giving property both protection and a sanctity,[56] and
by the end of the seventeenth century stealing from
the person as well as sheep-stealing above the value of
one shilling[57] were punishable by death, a punishment
that was extended to all felonies in 1826.[58] These
penalties extended not only to adults, but to small
children too, and it was perhaps small wonder that a
revulsion began to set in. In 1748 William York, aged
10, was sentenced to death at Bury Assizes for the
murder of a five-year-old girl. The judges thought that
'it would be a very dangerous consequence to have it
thought, that children may commit such atrocious crimes
with impunity. There are many crimes of the most heinous
nature, such as in the present case the murder of young
children, poisoning parents or masters, burning houses,
etc., which children are very capable of committing ...
Therefore, though the taking away the life of a boy of
10 years old may savour of cruelty, yet as the example
of this boy's punishment may be a means of deterring
other children from the like offence.' The boy was
pardoned in 1757.[59] At the turn of the century a boy
of the same age was similarly sentenced for secreting
notes at Chelmsford Post Office. Baron Hotham wrote:

All the circumstances attending the transaction
manifested art and contrivance beyond his years, and
I therefore refused the application of his Council to
respite the Judgment on the ground of his tender years,
being satisfied that he knew perfectly what he was
doing. But, still, he is an absolute Child, now only
between 10 and 11, and wearing a bib, or ... a Pinafore.
The scene was dreadful, on passing sentence, and to
pacify the feelings of a most crowded court, who all
expressed their horror of such a child being hanged,
by their looks and manners, after stating the necessity
of the prosecution and the infinite danger of its going
abroad into the world that a Child might commit such a
crime with impunity, when it was clear that he knew
what he was doing, I hinted something slightly of its
still being in the Power of the Crown to interpose in
every case that was open to Clemency.

The sentence was commuted and the child was transported for fourteen years, an arrangement having been made with one of the grand jurors to accept him on his plantation.[60]

It is small wonder that juries were prepared to perjure themselves and find that stolen articles were of infinitesimal value in order to ensure that the accused was not sentenced to hang. Thus, during a debate in the House of Lords in 1833 Lord Suffield stated: "I hold in my hand 555 perjured verdicts delivered at the Old Bailey in 15 years, beginning with the year 1814, for the single offence of stealing from dwellings, the value stolen being in these cases sworn above 40/-, but the verdicts returned being to the value of 39/- only...It deserves remark that when the legislation raised the capital indictment to £5 in June 1827, the juries at the same time raised their verdicts to £4.19s; still keeping it low enough to save the offender's life."[61] In fact, it has been notorious in recent years that juries have been increasingly unwilling to sentence to death even in murder cases. Acceptance in some jurisdictions of the crime passionel and of justifiable and excusable homicide in others recognizes this. Further, frequently juries have returned a verdict of manslaughter when the lex lata demands one of murder. Introduction of the defence of diminished responsibility is an acknowledgment of current morality. Opposition to the carrying out of the death penalty has often meant that in practice the law had become a dead letter and the United States Supreme Court has held in fact that as the sentence had been rendered in the past, by verdict of the jury and so not consistently or even-handedly, it was unconstitutional constituting cruel and unusual punishment.[62] The way was, however, left open for state legislatures to word their capital legislation in a way which could not be construed as infringing the constitution, and this has been done in a number of instances. Nevertheless, there is in most countries a strong body of opinion, among women, police, and judicial officers in particular, which maintains that morality demands the reintroduction of the penalty and its enforcement. In their view, it is perhaps even more immoral not to carry out the penalty.

Agitation against the death penalty is a concomitant of the current arguments concerning the purpose of punishment. It is becoming increasingly contended that the desire for retribution is immoral and the law should recognize criminality as a sickness and should seek to rehabilitate the offender. However much one might sympathise with this view, care must be taken that 'featherbedding' of prisoners does not become so extreme that a moral backlash sets in resulting in a risk that society will again resort to such things as the blood feud, outlawry, and the hue and cry. Should this happen, there is grave risk that by the time the machinery of the law has been set in motion, there will be no point in starting it up since society will have taken the law into its own hands and proclaim once again that morality demands punishment and that the interests of the victim, particularly of violent crime, and his relatives are of greater concern for both law and morality than those of the criminal.[63]

Perhaps one of the most outstanding examples of morality modifying the rigours of the law is to be found in the judgment of Lawton J in England, when accepting Mrs. Harrison's plea of not guilty of the murder of her baby. Mrs. Harrison was a West Indian who, because of housing difficulties had had to place her young baby with a white foster mother; on being returned to its mother, the child had rejected her

black face. In finding her guilty of manslaughter and
placing her on probation for three years, the learned
Judge said: 'Judges in the past during my 30 years of
being concerned with the administration of justice have
thought that the right way of dealing with women who
caused the death of their children by loss of temper
was a long term of imprisonment. Judges nowadays
appreciate that women living in the sort of circumstances that you were in, and the family problems you
were having do get depressed and in their depression
lose their tempers. But we can only be merciful once.'[64]

Morality also plays a major part in the attitude of
society towards suicide. Although the ancients seemed
to tolerate suicide, and there is general praise of
Socrates for the manner of his going, the common law
regarded felo de se as a crime as heinous as any other
form of culpable homicide. While the mores of some
societies enjoin suicide as an expression of public
feeling as well as of private sentiment, as is the case
with Japanese hara kiri, western Christian nations
have taken an opposite attitude. So much is this so
that while English imperial policy generally refrained
from interfering with the local religious customs of
those they governed, this was not so in the attitude
towards suttee, the self-immolation of a Hindu widow
upon her husband's funeral pyre, which was formally
abolished in British India in 1829. In so far as the
Englishman was concerned, Christian sentiment was interwoven with more practical rationalism. The suicide was
regarded as breaking his duty of fealty to the crown
and his liability to service if called upon. His goods,
therefore, were forfeited to the king. At the same
time, the suicide was considered guilty of a spiritual
offence 'in invading the prerogative of the Almighty,
and rushing into his immediate presence uncalled for.'[65]

23

For this blasphemy the corpse of a suicide was buried ignominiously at the crossroads with a stake through the heart. In Blackstone's view, the reason for this type of punishment was to disparage the reputation of the suicide for the heinous act committed immediately prior to his death, which act and not the death was the cause of the forfeiture. He was aware of the severity of the penalty of forfeiture and that it worked against the welfare of the innocent survivors, but he derived some consolation from the fact that the king possessed the power of mitigation.[66] Juries, however, sometimes considered as the true exponents of accepted public opinion,[67] were apparently not so sanguine about the king's generosity and, perhaps recognizing the possibility that they or their relatives might be potential suicides, adopted a somewhat different attitude. Since the ignominy of burial in unconsecrated places and the disaster of forfeiture were reserved for felons, and since felonies could only be committed with malice aforethought, it was but a simple matter to declare that the suicide was insane at the time he committed the act. This practice became so common that it incurred the wrath of Blackstone. He deplored the fact that juries were acting as if 'the very act of suicide is an evidence of insanity; as if every man who acts contrary to reason, had no reason at all: for the same argument would prove every other criminal non compos, as well as the self-murderer ... [Further] if a real lunatic kills himself in a lucid interval, he is a felo de se as much as another man.'

Juries persisted in their evil ways even after burial at the crossroads was abolished in 1823 and forfeiture in 1870.[68] In practice it appeared as if suicide was accepted as evidence of insanity unless there was the clearest evidence to the contrary, and the Coroners'

Rules of 1953 suggested that the usual verdict should
be 'while the balance of his mind was disturbed.' The
type of circumstances that indicated sanity is illustrated by Beresford v Royal Insurance Co.[69] in which a
man who was unable to pay further premiums on his
policies shot himself outside the insurance company
office immediately prior to the expiry of the policies.
He was considered sane for no man can benefit from his
own wrongdoings and it was only proper that the company
should win as against his dependants. This situation
has been changed with the passing of the Suicide Act,
1961,[70] which declared that suicide would no longer
be considered a crime, so that 'benefits under policies
of assurance will no longer be unenforceable on the
grounds of public policy' - unless the House of Lords
decides that such an attitude would be contra bona
mores.[71]

In view of the temporary insanity verdict, anomalies
of an immoral character frequently arose. In the first
place, the unsuccessful suicide was tried for attempting
to commit a crime and treated as sane, although had he
succeeded in his attempt he would almost certainly have
been regarded as insane. Similarly, in the case of a
suicide pact juries would invariably hold both the
victims to have been insane. If one survived, however,
he was treated as if he were sane and tried for murder.
The law went some way towards recognizing the immorality
of its stance when, in the Homicide Act, 1957,[72] it
provided that the survivor of such a pact would in future
be guilty of manslaughter instead of murder. The 1961
Act carried matters a little further by providing that
the survivor would only be guilty of aiding, abetting,
or counselling and liable to a penalty of fourteen
years' imprisonment. In some ways this has become a
strange offence. The act, in the complicity of which

the survivor was a participant, is, to the extent that it was successful, no longer a crime. The survivor - or both of them - cannot be tried for any offence in respect of the attempt, although each of them presumably could be tried for having counselled the other to commit or attempt to commit suicide. It is perhaps doubtful whether, in the end, the law has in fact been made that much more moral.

Modern medical advances have created new legal and ethical problems in relation to the sanctity of life. Reference has already been made to the use of contraceptives. Closely related is the problem of artificial insemination. To the older generation this smacks of interference with nature and is, for those who believe in the absolute sanctity of marriage and of the husband/wife relationship, highly immoral. In the earliest case in English law confusion reigned supreme. Mrs. L. had been artificially inseminated by her husband, but she nevertheless secured a decree of nullity on the ground of non-consummation.[73] On the other hand, the Scottish courts refused to give Mr. Maclennan a divorce based on the allegation that his wife had committed adultery, having conceived a child as a result of artificial insemination by a donor, while separated from her husband.[74] Perhaps the Englishman's concept of morality in this field was best demonstrated in the evidence given to the Feversham Committee[75] which was set up after this decision, and in its Report.[76] One of the commentators on this Report has found it useful to introduce his remarks with Macaulay's comment: 'We know no spectacle so ridiculous as the British public in one of its fits of morality.'[77] In view of the finding that there can be 'no doubt' that a child born of AID is illegitimate, that a woman bearing such a child does not commit adultery, but that resort to AID

probably amounts to an unlawful and indictable conspiracy
to produce an illegitimate child, one can understand his
sarcasm, particularly as the Report indicates that the
Committee was doubtful whether a charge would ever be
brought or whether, if brought, a conviction could be
secured. No prosecution has been brought, and the
relative silence of the divorce reports on this matter
since 1960 suggests that public opinion has come to
accept the position and no longer considers such
practices as immoral. Similar problems have arisen in
the United States where, according to the Feversham
Report, 10,000 AID children had been born by 1960, and
which according to The Times of London numbered 100,000
by mid-1963.[78]

American judicial decisions are inconsistent. In
Strnad v Strnad[79] a New York court held that, where AID
had taken place with the husband's consent, the child
would not be illegitimate. However, in 1963 the New
York Supreme Court ruled[80] that such a child was a
bastard, but Justice Constantino held that since the
husband had given consent he was liable to support the
child so born. He took the traditional stand - also
to be found in English law[81] - that a child begotten by
a father not the woman's husband was illegitimate, for,
as he pointed out, the state legislature has never
modified this concept, in spite of the many problems
that have arisen in the field of artificial insemination.
On the other hand, the California District Court of
Appeal has ruled the other way, holding that a husband
who gave his consent to AID and then held out that the
child was his own was nevertheless not criminally
liable for failing to support someone else's child.[82]

The changes in the ethical approach to this issue
over the years are such that we will probably never
again come across the repulsion felt and expressed by

Orde J of the Ontario Supreme Court in what must have been the first instance of AID to be judicially examined. In Orford v Orford, in 1921,[83] he appeared to depend largely on the Mosaic law in holding that AID constituted adultery. He was of opinion that 'had such a thing as "artificial insemination" entered the mind of the [Mosaic] lawgiver, it would have been regarded with the utmost horror and detestation as an invasion of the most sacred of the marital rights of husband and wife, and have been the subject of the severest penalties ... Adultery ... involves the possibility of introducing into the family of the husband a false stream of blood.' Not only has there been a change in the attitude to artificial insemination, but morality now seems increasingly to suggest that adultery is not nearly so destructive of the marriage tie as once was thought, and the general view seems to be that any modern law of divorce which is to coincide with society's ethos should be based rather on the concept of marriage breakdown.

Artificial insemination is only possible when the woman is fertile. Experimentation with the creation of life, however, raises the possibility of fertilisation outside the human and then engrafting into the uterus to enable birth to take place. While at one time such action might have been considered immoral and conducive to the production of a monster, recent success with the creation of life in test-tubes indicates that here too society's concepts of morality are changing. Not very long ago an English legal journal discussed the problem of the effect in the law of divorce of the grafting of an ovary upon a sterile woman whose ovaries had already been removed. It was pointed out that counsel had advised the Medical Defence Union that a child so born would be a bastard, since no ova were produced by the ovaries after birth and therefore the

ovum that had been fertilised would have come from the
donor. The author queried whether this would imply
that a husband was committing adultery with his own
wife,[84] while a later correspondent made the issue more
involved by suggesting that the ovary could in fact
come from the husband's mistress.[85] Public opinion
would today probably find nothing immoral in accepting
this type of transplant, just as it has accepted
transplants from both living and dead donors, although
it should be borne in mind that when in 1974 an English
doctor claimed to have produced babies by uterine
implantation the criticism was sufficiently intense for
him to announce the abandonment by him of any such
experiment in the future.

In so far as the dead are concerned, a number of
countries have introduced legislation similar to the
British Human Tissues Act, 1961,[86] but the real
ethical problems concern the transplantation of such
organs as the heart or other vital parts from those who
are legally dead, although there may be some doubt
whether society at large would always agree that the
donor is in fact deceased, regardless of what the
medical verdict may be. The law became entangled with
this problem in 1963. John Potter received severe
head injuries as the result of a brawl and was kept
alive for 24 hours in a respiratory machine in order
that a kidney might be removed for transplant purposes.
At the inquest into his death, the coroner's jury held
that death had resulted from the brain injuries, that
the removal of the kidney had in no way contributed to
his death, and a verdict of manslaughter was returned
against Henry Hall, the other party to the brawl. The
medical evidence was to the effect that the victim had
ceased breathing and was virtually dead, 'though from
the legal point of view it would be correct to say that

he died when the heart ceased beating and the circula-
tion ceased to flow' a day later. The Coroner stated
that he had supposed that [it] would be taken after
the man's death.'[87] Since then we have become hardened
to every type of transplant and those who now question
whether it is proper to keep a dying person 'alive'
for this purpose are the ones who tend to be regarded
as immoral. As a result, those who advocate euthanasia
are no longer regarded as moral outcasts and in 1969
the House of Lords debated a private bill on the
subject. It is, in fact, now becoming questionable
whether it is more moral to allow the incurably and
painfully sick to die or to struggle unconscionably
to keep them alive, and various medical associations
have expressed themselves in support of graceful death.
It might also be questioned whether, in view of the
population explosion, the law which permits transplants
to the chronically sick is moral in the light of social
needs. Either way, we have come a long way since the
time when Byron's physician refused with horror his
Lordship's request to remove the club from his foot,[88]
an operation that has become so common that to deny it
to a child might almost be considered immoral.

Another operation in this field to which reference
might be made as illustrating the way in which the law
has been compelled to give way to the needs of society
and remain in accord with public concepts of morality
is that for voluntary sterilisation.[89] It is only two
hundred years since castration was considered a maim
and a felony,[90] for it was believed that this would
decrease a man's bodily vigour and thus make him less
capable of fulfilling his military duties, and such
action is still criminal in some United States'
jurisdictions.[91] Under pressure of public opinion,
partly conditioned by the struggle for women's rights

and partly by the population explosion, many countries now have legislation expressly granting the right to obtain voluntary sterilisation,[92] while in others, notably India, vast government inspired sterilisation programmes are in progress. The United Nations has sponsored aid programmes to encourage sterilisation in underdeveloped areas, and, except in the most ortho- dox of religious circles, there no longer seems to be any thought that such activities are immoral or that they should be treated as illegal.

A similar change in legal attitudes based on a developing societal morality is to be seen in the current attitudes towards such matters as abortion and homosexuality - although in many countries it would seem as if male homosexuality, at least at the time the law developed, was more immoral and repulsive than lesbianism. Thus, under the British criminal law, which is reflected in most Commonwealth countries, only the former has been regarded as criminal.[93] Gradually, there has been a change in the moral attitudes to sexual deviations. In 1947 the English divorce court granted a decree to a husband on the grounds of his wife's cruelty, as evidenced by the effect upon him of her unnatural sexual activities with other women,[94] while in 1965 equality between the sexes was carried still further. In Coffer v Coffer[95] a man was granted a divorce in respect of his wife's lesbian activities with the resident au pair girl, the court having exercised its discretion in respect of his admitted adultery with the same person. It is difficult to see the moral justification of this judgment. With this trend towards equality as between married men and women, a new sense of morality was developed in England and by the Sexual Offences Act, 1967,[96] the law was brought into line with the view that in the criminal

field as well as in others men and women should be
treated equally, so that homosexual acts between consenting adult males in private will no longer be
regarded as criminal. Similar changes in the moral
regard for male homosexuality are being experienced in
other parts of the world, and are being accompanied by
a similar reassessment of the public view concerning
abortion. In England, for example, the law has been
brought up to date on abortion too,[97] as it has been in
a number of states in the United States with the Supreme
Court ultimately holding that legislation forbidding
abortion or treating it as criminal was contrary to the
constitutional rights of the woman concerned.[98] In
Canada both topics were dealt with among the recent
amendments to the Criminal Code, with most of the
opposition coming from the Creditiste Party on religio-
moral grounds. While the Criminal Code was amended to
permit homosexual acts between consenting adult males,
the rules concerning immigration were not altered. As
a result, any intending entrant who confesses to being
a homosexual, or who is, it would appear, in possession
of homosexual literature is denied admission under the
Immigration Act, s. 5 of which covers such other
undesirables as prostitutes, pimps, chronic alcoholics,
drug addicts and traffickers, subversives, epileptics
and the insane.[99] It is of interest to mention here
that, according to Mr. Stephen Brown, Q.C., prosecuting
in R.v. Lindsay[101], arising from the production and
publication of obscene films, in England it would seem
that while sexual acts of any kind between consenting
adult males are no longer criminal, "sodomy with a
woman is still a criminal offence". If this be true,
the situation as to discrimination has been reversed,
not so as to make lesbianism criminal, but to the effect
that anal intercourse between a consenting man and
woman, even a married couple, is criminal, while similar

32

acts between men are not.

Perhaps the most fundamental revolution in societal
moral standards has taken place with regard to sexual
entertainment, literature, and language. While the
ancient Greek and Latin classicists are famous for their
bawdy, and Shakespeare and the Restoration playwrights
are not far behind, and Inigo Jones was designing
costumes for Queen Henrietta Maria to wear at royal
masques which would have made a modern liable to
prosecution for indecent exposure, by the latter part
of the eighteenth century things had changed. By the
time of Victoria, rigid regulation of language, movement, and dress had become general - and the legs of
even grand pianos had to be draped in pantalettes.
The pendulum now seems to have swung full circle. It
is almost true to say that, on the Anglo-American stage
at least, complete freedom of movement, dress, and speech
has come to be almost de rigueur and the law seems for
the main part hesitant to take any steps towards
restraint. When it does move there is an outcry, just
as there is when art exhibitions are closed down for
indecency. An interesting example of the change in
morality concerning art is the painting of a mother and
child of the school of Cima de Conegliano recently
exhibited at the Agnew Gallery in London. As a result
of x-ray examination this picture was restored. It has
now become clear that both sexual and religious morality
have been responsible for censorship. The picture is
now shown to have originally included a second child,
while the mother's dress had been painted over to
obscure the fact that she was suckling the infant on
her lap. In its restored condition, the picture is
identified as a 'Madonna and Child and Infant St.John.[101]

In so far as literature is concerned, the history of

both law and morality have been somewhat chequered.
During the eighteenth century pornographic writing,
including Cleland's Fanny Hill, circulated fairly freely
in England. In 1787 George III issued a proclamation
against vice exhorting the suppression of such publications and the punishment of their publishers. In 1802
the Society for the Suppression of Vice was founded
and pursued a consistent policy of prosecuting publishers. As literacy spread, the establishment became more
concerned about the moral welfare of the lower classes,[102]
and in 1857 Lord Campbell's Act[103] was passed and the
test that came to be accepted in Anglo-American law was
laid down in R. v Hicklin:[104] 'The test of obscenity
is to deprave and corrupt those whose minds are open to
such immoral influences, and into whose hands a publication of this sort might fall.' As the years passed,
judges appeared to assume that the test of obscenity
was measured not by ordinary adults, but by pubescent
girls, especially those belonging to the servant class,
and no evidence by experts as to the literary or social
merit of the work was tolerated. The first breakthrough
occurred when the Americans recognised the literary
worth of James Joyce's Ulysses in 1933 and 1934,[105]
but this was by no means a general permission to publish.
It was not until the mid-sixties that the United States
reached what appears to be full freedom with the lifting
of bans on Lady Chatterley's Lover, Henry Miller's
Tropics and Fanny Hill.[106] Today, in the United States
the law seems to have recognised a morality in this
field in which established publishers like the Grove
Press appear to compete with the purveyors of Grub
Street as to who can produce more epics of the 'underground'. It would almost look as if authors count the
four-letter Anglo-Saxon words in their rivals' writings
in order to ensure that their own work goes one better.
However, the Supreme Court has recently held by a

majority that complete freedom is not tolerable and has introduced the concept of local morality[107], so that what might be published and sold freely in one village might well be considered obscene and suppressed in the next.

In other countries, perhaps because Victorian traditions and the impact of Lord Campbell's Act went deeper, the relaxation has not been so rapid or complete. While the ban on Ulysses was being evaded in England by the issue of a limited and expensive edition in 1936, by the following year an unlimited edition was available, but at a price that was beyond the bulk of the population. After the war, individual publishers were taking chances, although the more timid among them were put off by prosecutions like that at Swindon of The Decameron.[108] The first indication that an English judge was prepared to approach a publication in accordance with modern standards of morality came from Stable J in 1954,[109] when he was judging whether or not Stanley Kauffman's The Philanderer was obscene. In his charge to the jury he stated:

Remember the charge ... that the tendency of the book is to corrupt and deprave. ... 'Well, corrupt or deprave whom?' and again the test: those whose minds are open to such immoral influences and into whose hands a publication of this sort might fall. What exactly does that mean? Are we to take our literary standards as being the level of something that is suitable for a fourteen-year-old school girl? ... Of course not. A mass of literature, great literature, from many angles is wholly unsuitable for reading by the adolescent, but that does not mean that the publisher is guilty of a criminal offence for making those works available to the general public.

This is a book which obviously and admittedly is absorbed with sex, the relationship between the male and the female of the human species. I, personally, approach that great mystery with profound interest and at the same time a very deep sense of reverence ... Speaking, as I am sure I do, to a representative group

of people, nine men and three women, each one of you,
I am sure, is of good will and anxious that in the
solution of this great mystery today we should achieve
some conception which will lead to great personal
happiness between individuals of the opposite sex in
millions of homes throughout this island ...

Rome and Greece, it is not uninteresting to reflect,
elevated human love to a cult, if not a religion, but
when we reach the Middle Ages we find an entirely
different approach. The priesthood was compelled to
be sexless, and a particular qualitative holiness was
attached to the monks and the nuns who dedicated
themselves to cloisters and sheltered lives ...

When you approach this matter ... you get two schools
of thought ... At one extreme you get the conception...
of the medieval church, that sex is sin; that the whole
thing is dirty ... let it be covered up and let us
pretend that it does not exist ... I suppose the high
tide was obtained in the Victorian era, possibly as a
reaction against the coarseness of the Georges and the
rather libertine attitude of the Regency, when I understand that in some houses legs of tables were actually
draped and rather stricter females never referred as
such to gentlemen's legs but called them their 'under-
standings'.

At the other extreme you get the line of thought
which says that nothing but mischief results from this
policy of secrecy and covering up, that the whole thing
is just as much a part of God's universe as anything
else and the proper approach to the matter is one of
frankness, plain speaking and the avoidance of any sort
of pretence. Somewhere between these two poles the
average, decent, well-meaning young man or woman takes
his or her stand.

... [W]hat are the functions of the novel? ... The
only real guidance we get of how people thought and
behaved over the ages is in their contemporary literature.

It is equally important that we should have an understanding of how life is lived and how the human mind
is working in those parts of the world which, although
not separated from us in point of time, are separated
from us in point of space. At a time like today, when
ideas and creeds and processes of thought seem ... to
be in the melting pot, this is more than ever necessary,
for people are bewildered and puzzled to know in what
direction humanity is headed ... This is an American
novel ... purporting to depict the lives of people

living today in New York, to portray their speech and
their attitude in general towards this particular aspect
of life. If we are going to read novels about how
things go on in New York, it would not be of much assistance, would it, if contrary to the fact, we were led to
suppose that in New York no unmarried woman of teenage
has disabused her mind of the idea that babies are
brought by storks or are sometimes found in cabbage
plants or under gooseberry bushes?

    ... You may think that if this [book] does reflect
the approach on that side of the Atlantic towards this
great question, it is just as well that we should know
it and that we must not close our eyes or our minds to
the truth because it might conceivably corrupt or
deprave any somewhat puerile young mind ...

It is probably not surprising, in view of this summing
up, that the jury found the novel innocent. Three
months later, however, Sir Gerald Dodson, Recorder of
London, was turning the clock all the way back. He and
his jury were concerned with Connell's September in
Quinze, and in his summing up 'the Recorder suggested
that a book which would not influence the mind of an
archbishop might influence the minds of a callow youth
or a girl just budding into womanhood.' He remarked:
'I should have thought any reader, however inexperienced,
would have been repelled by a book of this sort, which
is repugnant to every decent emotion which ever concerned man or woman. That it could ever have been in
doubt is difficult to understand.' The jury apparently
agreed and was congratulated by Sir Gerald, for '... it
was a comforting thought that juries from time to time
took a very solid stand against this sort of thing, and
realised how important it was for the youth of this
country to be protected, and that the fountain of our
national blood should not be polluted at its source.'[110]

At this time there was a veritable rash of prosecutions
of British publishers and often concerning books that
were freely available elsewhere - and sometimes in parts
of England other than that in which the particular court

was sitting. The occasion that showed how far the
administrators of the law were from current views of
morality was the trial of Penguin Books for publishing
a cheap edition of Lawrence's Lady Chatterley's Lover,[111]
which followed enactment of the Obscene Publications
Act, 1959,[112] permitting the use of literary experts and
the defence that publication was for the public good or
in the interest of science, literature, art or some
other public concern. There may be many people who
would find it difficult to accept the morality of those
witnesses who went so far, in their expert evidence, as
to consider Lawrence's descriptions of coitus as
equivalent to holy communion. Byrne J not only found
this impossible to concede, but he was seriously
concerned that the low price would put the book within
reach of the mass of the population - presumably
wealth indicates a tendency against becoming depraved -
and was equally worried about its availability to the
young. The whole tone of his summing up was against
the book. The jury, however, upheld its publication.
The Supreme Court of India, untrammelled by a jury,
agreed with the views of Byrne J and suppressed the
book.[113] The Supreme Court of Canada has also dealt
with this book, in the first case after the enactment
of the Criminal Code which introduced the test of
'undue exploitation.' By a majority of five to four the
book was held not obscene,[114] and and the Hicklin test
was expressly rejected. The influence of current
standards of morality is brought out in the course of
Judson J's remarks: 'Surely the choice of courses is
clear-cut. Either the Judge instructs himself or the
jury that undueness is to be measured by his or their
personal opinion - and even that must be subject to
some influences from contemporary standards - or the
instruction must be that the tribunal of fact should
consciously attempt to apply these standards. Of the

38

two, I think that the second is the better choice.'

Despite the Lady Chatterley case, prosecutions in England continued. Regardless of the general feeling that freedom should be complete - which had resulted in the abolition of stage censorship - Fanny Hill as a paperback was condemned by a magistrate without reasons given, in 1964,[115] and a hardback edition of Selby's Last Exit to Brooklyn was condemned by a jury in 1967.[116] Although the Judge instructed them that they were only concerned with depravity and corruption and not with questions of taste, but were to use their common sense and experience, he nevertheless did emphasise that price should be taken into consideration. As if to prove the truth of Macaulay's comment about British hypocrisy, a deluxe edition of Fanny Hill has been published in England without prosecution, the publisher explaining that 'this is a deluxe edition intended for people who like good books,'[117] although paperback editions are now freely available.

In the Chatterley case constant reference was made to the use of Anglo-Saxon four-letter words and there was a time when any book containing such language was likely to be suppressed, while the use of such language in public could result in prosecution.[118] Today, the language has become generally acceptable and has even appeared in school collections of short stories. Moreover, graffiti nowadays seem to be confined to racial and political comments rather than coarse sexuality. Any prosecution based on such language would almost certainly be ridiculed as belonging to an out-of-date morality. This is particularly true now that the Anglo-Saxon term for coitus has even appeared in a legal autobiography, that of Sir James Watson, a former Chief Magistrate of the Juvenile Courts.[119]

It must not be thought that the courts have regarded only sex novels as being likely to deprave or corrupt and therefore obscene. In John Calder (Publications) Ltd. v Powell,[120] despite the evidence of the experts to the contrary, the justices held that Trocchi's Cain's Book was obscene in that its description of the life of a 'junkie' was likely to deprave and corrupt. It is likely that with the new attitude of society towards drugs, such a decision would probably not be given today, and many American novels are at least as explicit.

A nice problem arises in connection with obscenity prosecutions. If books are considered obscene because they are likely to deprave and corrupt those into whose hands they might fall, why are juries considered as being so pure that they may read such material without fear? Or are they of a higher moral standard than ordinary readers? In 1963 this question became real. A bookseller had been charged on the basis of books purchased from him by police officers who were members of the Vice Squad. The charge was dismissed on the bases that it was the job of the officers to purchase such materials and their evidence showed that they were not affected by them in any way.[121] This type of reasoning is both paternal and out of date. Far preferable is the comment of Porter J in the Ontario Court of Appeal when it was decided that Fanny Hill was not obscene under Canadian law.[122] 'The freedom to write books, and thus to disseminate ideas, opinions and concepts of the imagination - the freedom to treat with complete candor of an aspect of human life and the activities, aspirations and failings of human beings - these are fundamental to progress in a free society. In my view of the law, such freedom should not, except in extreme circumstances, be curtailed. The difference

between Fanny Hill and Lady Chatterley's Lover is that
Fanny Hill is more candid. In my view, people in Canada
today who read books generally prefer candor.' However,
an unsuccessful attempt was made in Edmonton, Alberta,
in 1974 to secure the suppression of Dr. Alex Comfort's
Joy of Sex, but the shallowness of the prosecution was
illustrated by the fact that the Crown only called one
witness whose expert evidence contained comments to the
effect that the work was clearly obscene in that it had
no footnotes, contained too many semi-colons and had been
printed in Amsterdam!

In his remark just quoted, Porter J shows both a
trust of the general public and an appreciation of its
morality. The same cannot be said of Lord Simonds
delivering judgment on The Ladies' Directory.[123] Shaw
published a small pamphlet giving details of prostitutes,
their names, addresses, specialities, and the like, and
was charged with obscene publication, living off the
earnings of prostitutes who had paid him for the entries,
and conspiracy to corrupt public morals. The jury
found him guilty on all counts, a verdict that was
confirmed by the Court of Criminal Appeal and upheld
by the House of Lords, although one might have thought
that those who subscribed to the Directory, either by
providing information or by purchase, were already
depraved and corrupt. The comments of Viscount Simonds
with regard to the common law offence of conspiracy to
corrupt public morals - the very existence of which
was doubted by Lord Reid - have become significant:

In the sphere of criminal law I entertain no doubt that
there remains in the courts of law a residual power to
enforce the supreme and fundamental purpose of the law,
to conserve not only the safety and order but also the
moral welfare of the State, and that it is their duty
to guard it against attacks which may be the more
insidious because they are novel and unprepared for...

It matters little what lavel is given to the offending
act. To one of your Lordships it may appear an affront
to public decency, to another considering that it may
succeed in its opposite intention of provoking libid-
inous desires, it will seem a corruption of public
morals. Yet others may deem it aptly described as the
creation of a public mischief or the undermining of
moral conduct. The same act will not in all ages be
regarded in the same way. The law must be related to
the changing standards of life, not yielding to every
shifting impulse of the popular will but having regard
to fundamental assessments of human values and the
purposes of society. Today a denial of the fundamental
Christian doctrine, which in past centuries would have
been regarded by the ecclesiastical courts as heresy and
by the common law as blasphemy, will no longer be an
offence if the decencies of controversy are observed.
When Lord Mansfield ... said[124] that the Court of King's
Bench was the custos morum of the people and had the
superintendency of offences contra bonos mores, he was
asserting, as I now assert, that there is in that court
a residual power, where no statute has yet intervened
to supersede the common law, to superintend those
offences which are prejudicial to public welfare. Such
occasions will be rare, for Parliament has not been
slow to legislate when attention has been sufficiently
aroused. But gaps remain and will always remain since
no one can foresee every way in which the wickedness of
man may disrupt the order of society ... Let it be
supposed that at some future ... date homosexual practices between adult consenting males are no longer a
crime. Would it not be an offence if even without
obscenity, such practices were publicly advocated and
encouraged by pamphlet and advertisement?

One hates to think that Lord Simonds would do to the
editors, publishers, printers, and vendors of the
'underground' press in North America which seems to
specialise in homo-and heterosexual advertisements of
the kind he was condemning, while 'gay' societies
announce their dances and other functions without let
or hindrance.

At the time of this judgment, Lord Simonds was already
80, and it indicates how far from current morality the
organs of an establishment may be. It should be compared, however, with the comment of Davey JA of British

Columbia in <u>Crickney</u> v <u>Crickney</u>:[125]

> The belief that a person should not marry the brother
> or sister of a deceased spouse seems rooted in archaic
> ecclesiastical doctrine, and common law; it is contrary
> to prevailing social and ethical opinion, as evidenced
> by Imperial and Canadian legislation on the subject.
> It may be well to recall the words of Sir Frederick
> Pollock[126]... quoted by Judson J in <u>G.</u> v <u>G.</u>[127] ...
> 'the duty of the courts is to keep the rules of law
> in harmony with the enlightened common sense of the
> nation.' Too much reliance on that injunction will
> lead to judicial legislation and a usurpation of the
> authority of parliament, but it is a proper reminder
> that judges by slender reasoning and rigid interpret-
> ation ought not to extend the language of statutes of
> bygone ages to bind contemporary society in a manner
> out of keeping with current notions.

Viscount Simonds, himself, showed a more enlightened
awareness of modern sentiments when delivering the opinion
of the Judicial Committee of the Privy Council in
<u>Overseas Tankship (U.K.) Ltd.</u> v <u>Morts Docks and Engin-
eering Co. Ltd.</u> (The Wagon Mound), rejecting the rule
relating to direct consequential damage:[128]

> It did not seem consonant with current ideas of
> justice and morality that for an act of negligence,
> however slight or venial, which results in some trivial,
> foreseeable damage the actor should be liable for all
> the consequences however unforeseeable and however
> grave ... It is a principle of civil liberty ... that
> a man should be responsible for the natural or necessary
> consequences of his act ... the answer is ... because,
> since they have that quality, it is judged by the
> standard of the reasonable man that he ought to have
> foreseen them ... Why should that test (reasonable
> foreseeability) be rejected which, since he is judged
> by what the reasonable man ought to have foreseen,
> <u>corresponds with the common conscience of mankind</u> ...

This decision is fully in line with the trail blazed
some twelve years earlier by the then Denning J [129]
when considering the validity of a Bristol housing
scheme directed to the benefit of all classes, when the
permissive statute[130] referred to accommodation for the

working classes:

'Working classes' fifty years ago denoted a class which
included men working in the fields or the factories, in
the docks or the mines, on the railways or the roads,
at a weekly wage. The wages of people of that class
were lower than those of most of the other members of
the community, and they were looked upon as a lower
class. That has now all disappeared. The social
revolution in the last fifty years has made the words
'working classes' quite inappropriate today. There is
no such separate class as the working class ... Nor is
there any social distinction between one or the other.
No one of them is of a higher or lower class.

Denning J could also have pointed out that, in view of
the extensive bombing of Bristol that had taken place,
it would have been considered immoral for the local
authority to rehouse only one class of the injured
community.

Nearly every western country is now going through a
moral crisis in regard to its treatment of coloured
minorities. It will suffice to refer to the great
revolution, both legal and moral, that has taken place
in the United States, revolving round the concept of
'separate but equal.'[131] Starting with Plessy v
Ferguson[132] the Supreme Court held that segregation was
tolerable so long as it was based on reasonableness
'with respect to the established usages, customs and
traditions of the people, and with a view of their
comfort, and the preservation of the public peace and
good order,' so long as civil and political equality
exists. In application of this reasoning, the state
of Missouri was considered as satisfying legal requirements when it opened a law school for one Negro
student,[133] and nobody seemed to consider it immoral
when this student was denied debating or sports facilities, and even though its peak attendance was only 35,
and in 1943 no students were enrolled.[134] The ethical

attitude of the United States, particularly in the
north, was changing after the second world war and
public pressure was building up to achieve full equality.
The 'separate but equal' doctrine was expressly rejected
by the Supreme Court in <u>Brown</u> v <u>Board of Education</u>,[135]
at least in the field of education: 'Does segregation
of children in public schools solely on the basis of
race, even though the physical facilities and other
"tangible" facilities may be equal, deprive the children
of the minority group of equal educational opportunities?
We believe that it does ... We conclude that in the
field of public education the doctrine of "separate but
equal" has no place. Separate educational facilities
are inherently unequal.' The Court, however, in a
decision delivered a year later which tends to be overlooked, recognised that the morality of some parts of
the United States might not be as advanced as in others,
and therefore accepted that change could not take place
all at once.[136] It recognised that a number of obstacles
might be involved, and 'Courts of equity may properly
take into account the public interest in the elimination
of such obstacles in a systematic and effective manner.
But it should go without saying that the vitality of
these constitutional principles cannot be allowed to
yield simply because of disagreement with them. While
giving weight to these public and private considerations,
the courts will require that the defendants make a
prompt and reasonable start toward full complience ...
Once such a start has been made, the courts may find that
additional time is necessary to carry out the ruling in
an effective manner. The burden rests upon the defendants to establish that such time is necessary in the
public interest and is consistent with good faith
compliance at the earliest practicable date.' While
there have been complaints as to the way in which southern
states have sought to evade this judgment, the over-all

impact has been to bring the legal rights of American Negroes, broadly speaking, into line with those of the white majority. However, a backlash has set in and in many instances busing efforts to effect the integration of school children have been met with violence and even been stopped by presidential order. To some extent white morality is becoming reactionary, while the Negro population is itself demanding 'equality through seg- regation.'

The problem of the treatment of political and racial minorities has also proved of major significance in international law since the end of the second world war. Hitler's racial policies had created a moral revulsion in the peoples of the United Nations which expressed itself in large scale campaigns on behalf of human rights, as well as in demands for the punishment of those Nazis who had been responsible for the holocaust. Moral feeling was concerned with what became known as crimes against humanity, rather than with war crimes in the traditional sense or the crime against peace, regardless of the fact that the Nuremberg judges and the politicians tried to elevate the latter into a moral offence. The law recognised the sentiments of morality when it rejected the defence of superior orders while allowing it to be pleaded in mitigation of punishment.[137] The test that has been traditionally applied in this field is sub- jective in so far as the accused is concerned, while at the same time demanding of him that he act in a reasonable way. The basis for this seems to be the view that no man should obey orders which are 'grossly', 'palpably,' or 'manifestly' illegal. In 1779 Lord Mansfield con- sidered that the test depended on how the heart stood:[138] 'If the heart is wrong, if cruelty, malice and oppression appear to have occasioned or aggravated the ... injury ... they shall not ... escape, under the cover of a

46

justification the most technically regular, from that
punishment which it is ... your duty to inflict ..."
A similar opinion, but even more conscious of moral
implications, was expressed by a New York court concerning an order 'so palpably atrocious as well as illegal
that one ought instinctively feel that it ought not to
be obeyed by whomever given.'[139] Morality is clearly
evident in the words of Judge Halevy when sentencing
an Israeli officer for his part in the Kafr Kassim
tragedy:[140] '... a flagrant and manifest violation of
the law, a definite and incontrovertible unlawfulness
apparent on the face of the order itself, the clearly
criminal character of the order or the acts ordered,
an unlawfulness glaring to the eye and repulsive to the
heart, provided the eye is not blind and the heart not
stony and corrupt ...' Even under the strains of the
operations in Vietnam, the United States military courts
apply the same principles limiting the validity of orders,
so that 'the act of a subordinate, done in good faith
in compliance with the supposed order of a superior, is
not justifiable when the order is such that a man of
ordinary sense and understanding would know it to be
illegal ... Also, there are strong moral, religious,
and legal prohibitions in our society against killing
others which should arouse the strongest scruples against
killings of this kind. In fact, it is difficult to
conceive of a military situation in which the order
of a superior would be more patently wrong. Accordingly,
we view the order as commanding an act so obviously beyond
the scope of authority of the superior officer and so
palpably illegal on its face as to admit of no doubt as
to its unlawfulness to a man of ordinary sense and
understanding.'[141]

The aspect of modern war which probably has aroused
the greatest moral indignation relates to the use of

nuclear weapons.[142] The difficulties that confront both
the moralist and the lawyer in this field are perhaps
best illustrated by the words of the late Judge
Lauterpacht:

It is difficult to express a clear view as to whether
an explicit prohibition of the use of the atomic weapon
in warfare would be merely declaratory of existing
principles of International Law ... There must be
envisaged the possibility of its being resorted to in
contingencies not amounting to a breach of International
Law ... Its use must be regarded as permissible as a
reprisal for the actual prior use by the enemy or his
allies. Secondly, recourse to the atomic weapon may be
justified against an enemy who violates the rules of the
law of war on a scale so vast as to put himself altogether outside the orbit of considerations of humanity
and compassion ... Moreover as laws are made not only
for the preservation of ultimate values of society, it
is possible that should these values be imperilled by
an aggressor intent upon dominating the world, the
nations thus threatened might consider themselves bound
to assume the responsibility of exercising the supreme
right of self-preservation in a manner which, while
contrary to a specific prohibition of International Law,
they alone deem to be decisive for the ultimate vindication of the law of nations.143

This was published in 1952, yet, in a paper of his
published but a year later, he wrote that 'there is
difficulty in accepting the suggestion ... that the
State which is the victim of aggression should be
entitled to resort to weapons the use of which might
otherwise be illegal ... There is superficial attract-
iveness in the notion that hostilities conducted for
the collective enforcement of peace should be governed
by a code of rules different from those obtaining in
ordinary wars and that efforts of international lawyers
ought to be directed towards that end. The attractive-
ness of that idea tends to diminish as we realise that
the practical scope of its application is insignif-
icant.' [144]

As already indicated, the main legacy of the war on

the interrelation of law and morality lies in the field
of human rights. According to classical international
law, and expressive of the morality of empire, a state
is entitled to treat its nationals as it pleases, and
the concept of nationals is delimited by its own municipal law so that, normally speaking, the inhabitants of
colonial territories are amenable to equal or discrimin-
atory treatment, to the rule of law or to the rule of
tyranny. So embedded is this principle in international
law, that it finds recognition in article 2(7) of the
Charter of the United Nations. The Charter did, however,
pay some measure of lip service to morality in that it
called upon the member states 'to promote and encourage'
respect for human rights and fundamental freedoms for
all, although no attempt was made to define what these
terms meant, nor what rights were envisaged. The first
step towards giving substance to such moral principles
came with the adoption of the Universal Declaration of
Human Rights in 1948,[145] although this was a document
of pious hope which lacked legal significance. It was
accompanied by the Genocide Convention[146] which recognised that this crime should be internationally punished,
although until such time as an international criminal
tribunal was established, punishment was to be effected
by the authorities of the state in which it was committed.
Since genocide is not a crime which can easily be
committed by private enterprise, it would follow that
in time of peace it would be committed by state authorities or with their consent within the territory of the
state. It is hardly likely that one branch of the executive would authorise the prosecution of another branch
for this offence.

The strongest moral condemnation was reserved for the
Union of South Africa with regard to its policy of
apartheid which controverted everything in the Universal Declaration and all that the United Nations

purported to believe in. As a result, a number of
resolutions were passed condemning the government of that
country for its treatment of Africans and for denying
them political and civil rights, culminating in the
Resolution of 6 December 1971[147] condemning apartheid
as "a total negation of the purposes and principles of
the Charter ... and [as] a crime against humanity."
While these condemnations were being recorded, the
nature of international society was changing, as were
its moral standards. The 1945 world which drew up the
Charter was almost entirely devoted to the Judaeo-
Christian ethic, believed in laissez-faire economics
and liberal democracy and, despite the existence of
empires, owed some allegiance to the principles of
the French Revolution, the dignity of man, and the rule
of law insofar as it protected these principles. But
as the retreat from empire gathered pace, and the new
states were admitted to the United Nations, the balance
of tradition changed. The new states did not have the
same religious ethic, were prone to accept socialism
rather than free enterprise, and were more concerned
about self-determination and anti-colonialism than they
were about individual rights, as is clear from the first
article of each of the international Covenants on Human
Rights.[148] Further, they were aware that law is invariably the protector of those who enact it and the guaran-
tor of their vested interests, and were therefore not
over-willing to accept what was proclaimed as being
international law unless they felt this to be in their
own interests.[149]

These states were very happy to push the older members
of the United Nations into condemnation of the South
Africans, and so long as it suited their purpose were
prepared to co-operate in condemnations of a denial of
what were originally regarded as fundamental human

rights. Gradually, as their number increased and with
it the desire to balance one side of the cold war
against the other, this interest in the individual
declined. The new morality apparently is only concerned
with the rights of peoples rather than single individuals, with the right of self-determination rather than
the right of individual protest, with anti-colonialism
instead of local democracy, with national ownership of
natural resources as distinct from the right of
property, and so forth.[150]

The changes that are taking place on the international
scene merely emphasise that law is but a reflection of
the beliefs and needs of the community it is intended
to serve. It is neither rigid nor sacrosanct and as
those needs and beliefs change, so the law, if it is
to be observed, must change with them. It is difficult
to be certain at any time whether the law indicates the
current morality or whether the few who have secured an
amendment of the law are responsible for the development
and raising of moral standards. It depends upon one's
own subjective approach whether, for example, the
campaign for the abolition of the death penalty was
truly an expression of the morality of an individual
society, or merely that of a small group of reformers
within that society, who eventually persuaded the legislators to abolish the punishment in the hope that
societal morality would catch up with the reform. On
the other hand, the attitude of society towards obscenity and sexual deviations tends to suggest that in this
case morality has been running ahead of the law, and the
law is only gradually catching up. What is certain is
that if the law lags too far behind current trends in
morality, the law will become obsolescent and fall into
desuetude. If the legislators allow this to happen too
frequently, they can only have themselves to blame if the

society they serve appears to have abandoned respect
for the law.

* Based on a paper published in 20 University of
Toronto Law Journal (1970).

1 [1901] A.C. 495, 534. See also Williams, Salmond
on Jurisprudence (1957) 269ff.

2 1 Commentaries on the Laws of England (10th ed.,
1787) 56.

3 Brown, The Austinian Theory of Law (1906) 6, 7.

4 Oxford English Dictionary. This dictionary defines
the verb: '1. To ratify or confirm by sanction or
solemn enactment; to authorize; to countenance.
2. To enforce (a law etc.) by attaching a penalty
to transgression.' The Random House Dictionary of
the English Language (1966) states: 'sanction
1. authoritative permission ... solemn ratification...
4. Law, a. a provision of a law enacting a penalty
for disobedience or a reward for obedience ...
6. to authorize, approve or allow ... 7. to ratify
or confirm, to sanction a law.'

5 Brown, supra note 3, at 1, 4, 16-17, 21, 34, 40,97
(italics in original).

6 Bentham, Principles of Morals and Legislation,
(1789), reproduced in 1 Bowring Works of Jeremy
Bentham (1843) 149.

7 Brown, supra note 3, at 3.

8 Williams, 'International Law and the Controversy
concerning the Word "law"' (1945), 22 Brit. Yearbook
Int'l Law, 146, 148.

9 See IV below.

10 Devlin, The Enforcement of Morals (1965).

11 Hart, Law, Liberty and Morality (1963); The Morality
of the Criminal Law (London, 1965).

12 Mitchell, Law, Morality and Religion in a Secular
Society (1967).

13 Devlin, supra note 10, at 1.

[14] Ibid., at 26.

[15] The Times (London), 18 March 1961.

[16] Devlin, supra note 10, at 27, 33, 13-14, 15 (italics added), 23, 25.

[17] Stanley v Georgia (1969), 394 U.S. 557.

[18] Devlin, supra note 10, at 24.

[19] The Times (London), 19 February 1968.

[20] Papists Act, 1778, 18 Geo. III, c. 60; Roman Catholics Relief Act, 1791, 31 Geo. III, c. 32, 1829, 10 Geo. IV, c. 7.

[21] Jewish Relief Acts, 1858, 21 & 22 Vict., c. 48, 49; 1860, 23 & 24 Vict., c. 63 (A General Relief Act, repealing a number of disabling measures had been passed in 1846, 9 & 10 Vict., c. 59). See also Oaths Acts, 1866, 29 & 30 Vict., c. 19; 1868, 31 & 32 Vict., c. 72.

[22] Dicey, Law and Public Order in England (1914) 13.

[23] For a summary of these events, see Sacher, The Course of Jewish History (1958), 115.

[24] See Green, 'The Protection of Minorities in the League of Nations and the United Nations,' in Gotlieb, Human Rights, Federalism and International Law (1970), 180.

[25] See, e.g., Married Women's Property Act, 1882, 45 & 46 Vict., c. 30.

[26] Winsmore v Greenbank (1745), Willes 577; a similar right was not granted to the wife in respect of the enticement of her husband until Gray v Gee (1923), 39 T.L.R. 429. In England, this type of action is no longer possible.

[27] Note to Grimmell v Wells (1844), 7 Man. & G. 1033, 1044.

[28] 54 Geo. III, c. 101.

[29] For a recent rejection of the Victorian concept of paternal rights, see Lord Denning MR in Hewer v Bryant, [1969] 3 W.L.R. 425.

[30] Watanabe, 'The Family and the Law: The Individual-

istic Premise and Modern Japanese Law,' in Von Mehren, Law in Japan (1963) 364.

31 1 Commentaries, supra note 2, at 433.

32 (1866), L.R. 1 P. & D. 130, 133.

33 Devlin, supra note 10, at 9.

34 Weatherley v Weatherley, [1947] A.C. 628, 633 per Jowett LC.

35 Genesis 1: 28; see also causes for matrimony in Book of Common Prayer. See XI below.

36 (1885) 10 A.C. 171, 204.

37 [1946] p. 36, 40.

38 Baxter v Baxter [1948] A.C. 274, 286.

39 Griswold v Connecticut (1965) 381 U.S. 479, see Zellick, 'An Uncommonly Silly Law' (1969) 119 New Law J. 332.

40 See n. 32 above.

41 Baindail v Baindail [1946] P.122; Thynne v Thynne [1955] P.272; see Hartley, 'Polygamy and Social Policy', (1969) 32 Modern Law Rev. 155.

42 Rumsey v Sterne (1967) 111 S.J. 113, The Times (London) 12 Jan. 1967.

43 [1960] 1 W.L.R. 183, 185.

44 M. v K. The Times, 29 Mar. 1968 - sub nom. Mohamed v Knott [1968] 2 W.L.R. 1446, 1457 (the quotation is taken from The Times).

45 4 & 5 Eliz. II, c. 69

46 R. v Nan-E-Quis-A-Ka (1885), 1 Terr. L.R. 211, 215; see, for a similar United States decision, Kobagum v Jackson Iron Co. (1889), 45 N.W. 602, even though such marriages have been polygamous, 605.

47 See, e.g., (U.K.) Law Reform (Miscellaneous Provisions) (Scotland) Act, 1968, c. 70, and Family Law Reform Act, part II, 1969, c. 46.

48 Exodus 21: 23, 24.

[49] Lex talionis 'Si homo cadat ab arbore vel quolibet mechanico super aliquem, ut inde moriatur vel debitetur; si certificat valeat, quod amplius non potuit, antiquis institucionibus trabeatur innoxias; vel si quis obstinata mente, contra omnium estimacionem, vindicare vel weram exigere presumpserit, si placet, ascendat, et illum similiter obruat' (Leg. Hen. I, 2 Holdsworth, A History of English Law (1911), 473.

[50] 21: 28, 29.

[51] (1907), 24 South African L. J., 232-4; see also 22 ibid., 290-3.

[52] 1 Frazer, Pausanias's Description of Greece (1913) bk. 1, c. 28, s. 11.

[53] 2 Pollock and Maitland, The History of English Law (1911), 473.

[54] 1 Commentaries, supra note 2, at 300-1.

[55] 10 Vict., c. 62.

[56] See Tawney, Religion and the Rise of Capitalism (1926).

[57] 3 Stephen, A History of the Criminal Law of England (1883) 467.

[58] 7 & 8 Geo. IV, c. 29.

[59] 1 Radzinowicz, A History of the English Criminal Law and its Administration (London, 1948), 12-3; this should be compared with the Canadian case of Steven Truscott, see LeBourdais, The Trial of Steven Truscott (1966).

[60] J.L. and B. Hammond, The Town Labourer (1941) 75.

[61] Calvert, Capital Punishment in the Twentieth Century (1930) 15-16.

[62] Furman v Georgia (1972) 408 U.S. 238.

[63] See, e.g., Williams, supra note 1, at 115-24, and Denning above.

[64] The Times (London), 4 October 1969.

[65] 4 Commentaries, supra note 2, at 189.

[66] Ibid., at 190.

[67] See, however, comment of Maule J, in sentencing: 'Prisoner, your counsel thinks you innocent, the prosecution thinks you innocent, and I think you innocent. But a jury of your own fellow-countrymen, in the exercise of such common sense as they possess, have found you guilty, and it remains that I should pass sentence on you. You will be imprisoned for one day, and as that day was yesterday, you are free to go about your business.' Andrews, The Lawyer in History, Literature and Humour (1896) 240-1.

[68] 4 Geo. IV, c. 52; 33 & 34 Vict., c. 23.

[69] [1937] 2 K.B. 197.

[70] 9 & 10 Eliz. II, c. 60

[71] Downey, Note in (1962), 25 Modern Law Review 60, 61 (in n. 12 he raises the possible application of the decision in Shaw v D.P.P. see infra note 123).

[72] 5 & 6 Eliz. II, c. 11.

[73] L. v L., [1949] P. 211. See also XI below.

[74] Maclennan v Maclennan, [1958] S.L.T. 12.

[75] See Bartholomew, 'The Report of the Feversham Committee: A Sterile Solution', (1962), 2 University of Malaya Law Review, 201; Pollard, Note in (1961), 24 Modern Law Review, 158.

[76] Cmnd. 1105 (1960).

[77] Bartholomew, supra note 73, citing Essay on Moore's Life of Byron, 1830.

[78] 8 August 1963.

[79] (1948), 78 N.Y.S. 2d 390.

[80] Gursky v Gursky (1963), 242 N.Y.S. 2d 406, 409-10.

[81] 3 Halsbury's Laws of England (3rd ed., London, 1953) 86: 'the child of a woman who is lawfully married, but upon whom he is begotten by another than her lawful husband.'

[82] People v Sorensen (1967), 66 Cal. Rptr 7, 13.

[83] (1921), 58 D.L.R. 251, 258.

[84] Note, (1962), 106 Solicitors' Journal, 741.

[85] Ibid., 797.

[86] 9 & 10 Eliz. II, c. 54.

[87] The Times (London), 26 July 1963

[88] Minty, 'Unlawful Wounding: Will Consent Make It Legal?' (1954), 24 Medico-Legal Journal, 54, 58.

[89] See XI below.

[90] Hawkins, Pleas of the Crown (1739), 107.

[91] 1 Anderson, Wharton's Criminal Law (1957) 733.

[92] E.g., Singapore - Sterilisation Bill, 1969.

[93] Offences Against the Person Act, 1861, 24 & 25 Vict., c. 100.

[94] Gardner v Gardner (1947), 1 All E.R. 630.

[95] The Times (London), 16 May 1964; 108 S.J. 465.

[96] 1967, c. 60.

[97] Abortion Act, 1967, c. 87.

[98] Roe v Wade (1973) 410 U.S. 113; Doe v Bolton (1973) ibid., 179.

[99] R.S.C. 1970, I-2; see Globe and Mail (Toronto), 21 Sept. 1974, re John Kyper.

[100] The Times (London), 22 Oct. 1974.

[101] Ibid., 4 Mar. 1969.

[102] A History of Pornography (1964), 163.

[103] Obscene Publications Act, 20 & 21 Vict. c. 83.

[104] (1868) L. R. 3 Q. B. 360.

[105] U.S. v Ulysses 5 F. Suppl. 182 and 73 F. (2d) 705.

[106] See Rembar, The End of Obscenity (1968).

[107] Miller v California (1973) 413 U.S. 15.

[108] Hyde, supra note 102 at 71.

[109] R. v Martin Secker & Warburg Ltd., [1954] 1 W.L.R.

1138, 1139-40.

[110] Manchester Guardian, 18 September 1954. Cf. Comments by Dato Sir James Thomson, Chief Justice Malaya, in condemning Miller's Tropic of Cancer as a paperback: 'It is thus on sale at a price which brings it within the reach of the great majority of the reading public, that is to say a public which includes not only the old and the learned but also the young and the thoughtless, those who read books for pleasure and not for moral edification or for intellectual improvement. It is the effect on the minds of such persons that is to be considered': Straits Times, 19 January 1963.

[111] Rolph, The Trial of Lady Chatterley (1961).

[112] 7 & 8 Eliz. II, c. 66.

[113] Ranji Udeshi v Maharashtra, The Times (London), 20 August 1964.

[114] R. v Brodie (1962), 32 D.L.R. (2d) 507, 529.

[115] Hyde, supra note 192 at 233.

[116] R. v Calder & Boyars Ltd., [1968] 3 W.L.R. 974.

[117] The Times (London), 30 November 1963.

[118] See, for parody of operation of Profane Oaths Act, 1745, Herbert, 'Rex v Haddock: Is a Golfer a Gentleman?' Uncommon Law (1935) 18.

[119] Which is the Justice? (1969) 153.

[120] [1965] 1 Q.B. 509.

[121] R. v Clayton and Halsey, [1963] 1 Q.B. 163.

[122] R. v C. Coles Co. Ltd. (1964), 49 D.L.R. (2d) 34, 40.

[123] Shaw v D.P.P., [1962] A.C. 220, 267-8. For a scathing attack on this judgment, see Davies, 'The House of Lords and the Criminal Law' (1961), 6 J. Society of Public Teachers of Law, 104, esp. 108fl.

[124] R. v Delaval (1763), 3 Burr. 1434, 1438, 1439.

[125] (1967) 58 W.W.R. (n.s.) 577, 578

126 'Judicial Caution and Valour' (1929), 45 Law Quarterly R. 293, at 295.

127 [1943] S.C.R. 527 (sub nom. Gracie v Gracie, 1943 4 D.L.R. 145).

128 [1961] A.C. 388, 422-3 (italics added).

129 Green & Sons v Minister of Health, [1948] 1 K.B.34, 38.

130 Housing 'Act, 1936, 26 Geo. v & 1 Edw. VIII, c.51.

131 See, e.g., Blaustein and Ferguson, Desegregation and the Law (1962) ch. 7.

132 (1896) 163 U.S. 537, 550.

133 Missouri ex rel. Gaines v Canada (1938), 305 U.S. 337.

134 Wheildon, 'Negro Segregation' (1947), 11 Editorial Research Reports 822.

135 (1954) 347 U.S. 483, 491-2.

136 (1955) 349 U.S. 294, 296.

137 Green,'Legal Issues of the Eichmann Trial' (1963), 37 Tulane Law Review, 641, 673ff.;'Superior Orders and the Reasonable Man' (1970), 8 Can. Ybk Int'l Law (1970) 61.

138 Wall v M'Namara (1779), 1 Term Rep. 537.

139 McCall v McDowell (1867), 15 Fed. Cas. 1235,1240.

140 Chief Military Prosecutor v Melinki (1958), 13 Piskim Mehoziim 90 (c. Att. Gen., Israel v Eichmann (1961) 36 Int'l L. Rep., al 257).

141 U.S. v Griffen (1968), 3 C.M.R. 586, and see X below.

142 See, e.g., Schwarzenberger, The Legality of Nuclear Weapons (1958); Singh, Nuclear Weapons and International Law (1959).

143 2 Lauterpacht, Oppenheim's International Law (7th ed., 1952) 350-1.

144 'The Limits of the Operation of the Law of War' (1953), 30 Brit. Yearbook Int'l Law 206, esp. 220.

[145] United Nations, <u>Yearbook on Human Rights for 1948</u> (1950) 466.

[146] <u>Ibid.</u>, at 484.

[147] G. A. Res 2786 (XXVI), 11 Int'l Legal Materials (1972), 212.

[148] 1966, Res. 2200A (XXI) 6 <u>ibid.</u>, 1967, 360, 368.

[149] Sinha, <u>New Nations and the Law of Nations</u> (1967) 59, 137.

[150] For a fuller discussion of this attitude, see V below.

II

NATIVE LAW AND THE COMMON LAW:

CONFLICT OR HARMONY[*]

When I reflect upon the spread and acceptance of
our common law principles throughout the United
States and Canada and Australia and New Zealand,
may I not say that nothing has left a deeper or
more beneficient impression upon the Western
World than the Common Law of England. Its work
can never be undone. Its spirit and its ideals
must ever live. If this country were to sink
tomorrow beneath the waves, the record of the
Common Law of England would stand forever on the
noblest pages of history.

> Mr. Justice McCardie, The Law, The
> Advocate and the Judge (1927) 17.

With such content as we may, we must even believe
that our lady the Common Law, like many other
good-natured people busied with more matters than
they can attend to in person, allowed herself to
be put upon and her customers harassed by fussy,
greedy and sometimes dishonest underlings.

> Sir Frederick Pollock, The Genius
> of the Common Law (1912), 37.

Perhaps one of the least objectionable features of

British imperialism has been the introduction into

colonial territories of the English concept of the rule

of law. This stems from the fact that, as is probably

known to the veriest tyro in the legal world, when an

Englishman goes abroad he takes his law with him. As

long ago as 1693 Holt C.J. pointed out: "In case of an

uninhabited country newly found out by English subjects,

all laws in England are in force".[1] The extent of this

incorporation was reduced somewhat by the Master of the

Rolls thirty years later:

If there be a new and uninhabited country found out
by English subjects, as the law is the birthright of
every subject, so, wherever they go, they carry their
law with them, and therefore such new found country is
to be governed by the laws of England; though, after
such country is inhabited by the English, acts of
parliament made in England, without naming the foreign
plantations, will not bind them.[2]

Basing himself upon these two judgments, but at the
same time restricting the scope of English law still
further, Blackstone wrote that:

Colonists carry with them only so much of the English
law as is applicable to their own situation and the
condition of an infant colony; such, for instance, as
the general rules of inheritance, and of protection
from personal injuries. The artificial refinements
and distinctions incident to the property of a great
and commercial people, the laws of police and revenue,...
the jurisdiction of spiritual courts, and a multitude
of other provisions, are neither necessary nor convenient for them, and therefore not in force. What shall
be admitted and what rejected, at what times, and under
what restrictions, must, in case of dispute, be decided
in the first instance by their own provincial judicature,
subject to the revision and control of the king in
council.[3]

As Blackstone pointed out, this situation only prevailed in territories which had not been formerly
occupied by a recognised sovereign. In so far as ceded
or conquered territory was concerned, English Common Law
recognised that the already-existing law prevailed until
such time as it was amended by the King. This practice
reflected convenience, for an immediate abrogation of
existing law could easily produce anarchy. Moreover,
where a lex loci already existed, the local residents,
unlike their English conquerors, would be unacquainted
with English law, but would be accustomed to a legal
system that was already operating.[4] This attitude

underlays the judgment of Chief Justice Marshall in
Worcester v Georgia[5] in so far as the North American
Indians are concerned: "America, separated from Europe
by a wide ocean, was inhabited by a distinct people,
divided into separate nations, independent of each
other and of the rest of the world, having institutions
of their own, and governing themselves by their own
laws". This approach was confirmed by the Supreme
Court in Ex parte Crow Dog,[6] holding that an Indian who
had murdered another Indian on a reservation was not
amenable to federal criminal law, but only to tribal law,
although this was altered by statute two years later.[7]
Further, in most cases conquered territories were
acquired from Christian rulers, and a different approach
was adopted to fellow-Christians as distinct from Barbarians.[8] Newly-discovered territories possessed no
recognised legal system; it was therefore obvious that
the new settlers would apply the law to which they were
accustomed, although some of its manifestations might
differ from the law known and practised in the Royal
Courts of Justice. It was unlikely, for example, that
the settlers would be unduly concerned with the intric-
acies of land law as it had developed in England
expressing itself in such rules as that in Shelley's
case, for this rested on "reasons affecting the land
and society in England and not reasons applying to a
new colony".[9]

It should not be thought that it was only the English
who took their law with them when they went into
foreign climes. A somewhat similar practice operated
in ancient Rome, for in classical law the inhabitants
of conquered territories did not become citizens: "The
vast majority of Roman subjects are, so far as her law
is concerned, peregrini, 'foreigners', outside the pale
of the strict law and only entitled to such rights as

all free persons have under the _ius gentium_", with the
ius civile applying only to citizens.[10] Bryce's
description of the situation is similar to that of
Blackstone concerning English possessions and the
rights of the inhabitants:

[peregrini] had their own laws or tribal customs, and
to them Roman law was primarily inapplicable, not only
because it was novel and unfamiliar, so strange to their
habits that it would have been unjust as well as
practically inconvenient to have applied it to them,
but also because the Romans, like the other civilized
communities of antiquity, had been so much accustomed
to consider private legal rights as necessarily
connected with membership of a city community that it
would have seemed unnatural to apply the private law
of one city community to the citizens of another ... .
Each province was administered by a governor ... . The
governor's court was the proper tribunal for those
persons who in the provinces enjoyed Roman citizenship,
and in it Roman law was applied to such persons ... .
No special law was needed for them. As regards the
provincials, they lived under their own law, whatever
it might be, subject to one important modification.
Every governor when he entered his province issued an
Edict setting forth certain rules which he proposed to
apply during his term of office ... .

but when the distinction between citizens and provincials
disappeared, Roman law became applicable throughout the
Empire and to all its inhabitants.[11]

   The Dutch, too, took their law with them and the
principles of Roman-Dutch law were introduced into their
territories. Thus, "when Van Tiebeck and his band of
pioneers settled at the Cape in 1652, they introduced
the general principles and rules of law prevailing at
that date in the Netherlands",[12] but "the first
settlers carried with them only those laws which were
applicable to the circumstances of this country".[13]
The purity of Roman-Dutch law as the common law of those
Dutch colonies which were conquered by the British was
affected by the fact that, for the main part, it was

English-trained judges and lawyers who were called upon to apply it. In so far as Ceylon is concerned, it has been said that "the Roman-Dutch law, as applied by the British, was like an old kadjan roof; as it got older it let in the outside elements, and they were mainly English law."[14] The same criticism has been made by the courts in South Africa:

Here we have a phenomenon that appears all too often in our jurisprudence. A Roman-Dutch legal rule is compared with its English counterpart; with pleasure, if indeed not with joy, it is stated that there is no difference, and then the door is wide open for the reception of English law .... Gradual adaptation to new circumstances and problems is a type of development that leads to strength; uncontrolled development on the other hand leads to malignant growths and decay.[15]

In fact, it has been stated that it was because of the wrong interpretation of Roman-Dutch law and the grafting thereon of English principles by the Judicial Committee of the Privy Council in Pearl Assurance Co. v Union Government[16] that South Africa abandoned appeals to that body.[17]

Apart from the introduction of some system of common law - for in South Africa, Southern Rhodesia, Basuto-land and Ceylon, Roman-Dutch law is the common law - by settlers or conquerors, it may happen that a terri-tory expressly adopts an alien system of common law. Thus, in British Guiana "An Ordinance to codify and to substitute the English common law and principles of equity for the Roman-Dutch common law" has been enacted. In Liberia, which has never been a British colony, similar legislation was passed. In 1820 "the common law, as in force and modified in the United States and applicable to the situation of the people" was intro-duced, but in 1824 this was widened to include "the common law and usages of the courts of Great Britain

and the United States", to which there was added in
1839 "such parts of the common law as set forth in
Blackstone's Commentaries as may be applicable to the
situation of the people." Finally, the 1956 Code
provides:[18]

> Except as modified by laws now in force and those which
> may hereafter be enacted and by the Liberian common law,
> the following shall be, when applicable, considered
> Liberian law: (a) the rules adopted for chancery
> procedure in England, and (b) the common law and
> usages of the courts of England and of the United States
> of America, as set forth in case law and in Black-
> stone's and Kent's Commentaries and in other authorit-
> ative treaties and digests.[19]

In so far as British colonial territories are concerned,
after the initial introduction of the English common law,
legislation has tended to be introduced specifying what
parts of English law are to be applied in the territory
in question, and indicating an operative date. In the
Gold Coast, for example, the relevant ordinance provides
that "the common law, the doctrines of equity, and the
statutes of general application, which were in force
in England at the date when the Colony obtained a local
legislature, that is to say, on the 24th day of July,
1874, shall be in force within the jurisdiction of the
court",[20] together with the law and practice in divorce
which is in force in the Probate, Divorce and Admiralty
Division of the English High Court.[21] This has resulted
in the invidious consequence that "when a principle or
doctrine of the English common law has been abolished
by a post-1874 British statute of general application
in the United Kingdom, but which has not been expressly
or implicitly applied to Ghana, the old principle or
rule must still be followed in Ghana until altered by
local legislation."[22]

There are some colonial territories where no calendar

date is specified, reference being made merely to the coming into force of the particular ordinance, and occasionally it is specified that the common law is only introduced into a specific field of law. In so far as Malaysia is concerned, the Civil Law Enactment of 1937[23] provided that the "common law of England, and the rules of equity as administered in England at the commencement of this enactment, other than any modifications of such law or any such rules enacted by statute, shall be in force." This was amended some twenty years later, so that

save in so far as other privision has been made or may hereafter be made by any written law in force in the Federation or any part thereof, the Court shall apply the common law of England at the date of the coming into force of this Ordinance; provided always that the said common law and rules of equity shall be applied so far only as the circumstances of the States and Settlements comprised in the Federation and their respective inhabitants permit and subject to such qualifications as local circumstances render necessary.[24]

It is further provided that in commercial cases "the law to be administered shall be the same as would be administered in England."[25] A somewhat similar situation prevails in Singapore, where,

in all questions or issues which arise or which have to be decided in the Colony with respect to the law of partnership, corporations, banks and banking, principals and agents, carriers by air, land and sea, marine insurance, average, life and fire insurance, and with respect to mercantile law generally, the law to be administered shall be the same as would be administered in the like case, at the corresponding period, if such question or issue had arisen or had to be decided in England, unless in any case other provision is or shall be made by statute.[26]

In the case of Papua and New Guinea, the situation is somewhat mixed due to the way in which the two parts of this Territory came under 'British' control. In 1888

Papua, then known as British New Guinea, became a
British settlement, and in the following year it was
enacted that "the principles and rules of common law
and equity that for the time being shall be in force
and prevail in England shall so far as the same shall
be applicable to the circumstances of the Possession be
likewise the principles and rules of the common law and
equity ... of the Territory of Papua".[27] The Territory
of New Guinea came under Australian control in 1921 and
was administered separately from Papua until the Second
World War, and there "the principles and rules of common
law and equity that were in force in England on the
ninth day of May, 1921 ... so far as the same are
applicable to the circumstances of the Territory" shall
be effective.[28]

It may also happen that the system of prevailing law
to which reference is made is not English alone, but
also the law which operates in some other part of the
Commonwealth. This is the position in Kenya, where the
civil and criminal jurisdiction is, so far as circumstances allow, in conformity with Indian Acts in force
in East Africa, and,

so far as the same shall not extend or apply, shall be
exercised in conformity with the substance of the common
law, and doctrines of equity, and the statutes of
general application in force in England on August 12,
1897 .... Provided always that the common law,
doctrines of equity and statutes of general application
shall be in force in the protectorate so far only as
the circumstances of the protectorate and its inhabitants and the limits of H.M.'s jurisdiction permit and
subject to such qualifications as local circumstances
render necessary.[29]

This provision was commented upon by Denning L.J. in
Nyali Ltd. v. Att. Gen.[30] after he had pointed out that
the Crown's perogatives applied within the protectorate

since they were "the very substance of the common law":

Just as with an English oak, so with the English common law. You cannot transplant it to the African continent and expect it to retain the tough character which it has in England. It will flourish indeed but it needs careful tending. So with the common law. It has many principles of manifest justice and good sense which can be applied with advantage to peoples of every race and colour all the world over; but it also has many refinements, subtleties and technicalities which are not suited to other folk. These off-shoots must be cut away. In these far off lands the people must have a law which they understand and which they will respect. The common law cannot fulfill this role except with considerable qualifications. The task of making these qualifications is entrusted to the judges of these lands.

This realistic approach should be compared with Welbeck v. Brown[31] in which the Chief Justice of the Gold Coast held that "according to the principles of English jurisprudence" a local custom must date back to 1189, a view which was rejected in Mensah v. Winabob,[32] and which had never operated in Singapore, for "the history of Singapore began in 1819, more than 600 years after 1189, and that in itself concludes the matter."[33] In New Guinea the situation concerning custom has been statutorily regulated preventing any reference to 'time immemorial', and allowing the judicial declaration and recognition of recent and altered custom, and since native custom means local custom it may vary from place to place.[34]

The tendency to apply principles of English law because they are those best known to English judges is well-illustrated by the award of Lord Asquith of Bishopstone in Petroleum Development (Trucial Coast) Ltd. v. Sheikh of Abu Dhabi.[35] The learned arbitrator had to determine the proper law of a contract, conceding that, if any municipal system of law were applicable, it would <u>prima facie</u> be that of Abu Dhabi. But no such law can reasonably be said to exist .... Nor can I see any basis upon which the municipal law of England could apply .... The terms of [the contract] .... prescribe the application of principles rooted in the good sense and common practice of the generality of civilized nations - a sort of 'modern law of nature' .... But, albeit English municipal law is inapplicable <u>as such</u>. some of its rules are in my view so firmly grounded in reason, as to form part of this broad body of juris- prudence - this 'modern law of nature'... [while] the rigid English rules have been disregarded,... the English rule which attributes paramount importance to the actual language of the written instrument in which the negotiations result seems to me no mere idio- syncracy of our system, but a principle of ecumenical validity. Chaos may obviously result if that rule is widely departed from: and if, instead of asking what the words used mean, the inquiry extends at large to what each of the parties meant them to mean, and how and why each phrase came to be inserted.

The desire to apply and occasionally to limit English common law doctrines in a foreign environment may be illustrated by reference to India and Ghana. Ever since the Charter given by Charles II to the East India Company in 1683, judges in India have interpreted their function as being to judge in accordance with "justice, equity and good conscience". These concepts were "generally interpreted to mean the rules of English law if found applicable to Indian society and circumstances,"[36] and in 1937[37] Stone C.J. was of the opinion that

in considering what is today consonant to justice, equity and good conscience, one should regard the law as it is in England today, and not the law that was part of England yesterday. One cannot take the common law of England divorced from the statute law of England and argue that the former is in accordance with justice, equity and good conscience .... The doctrine of common employment would not apply, not because the case would fall outside the common law doctrine of common employment, but because it would fall inside the Employer's Liability Act.[38] What I desire to point out is that when I find a rule has been abrogated by legislation, that rule becomes an unsafe guide. Even when, as in this case, the rule remains but its practical applicability is by statute very greatly reduced, one is entitled and bound to view it more critically than would be the case if it remained in full force and effect. When one finds it criticised by competent jurists in the country of its origin and followed not because of its infrangible logic but because of its authority, an authority derived from an earlier age when circumstances were different, one is also justified in treating it as an unsafe guide.

No such hesitation was shown in Ghana in 1948 when the doctrine was accepted in Mersah v. Konongo Gold Mines; Ltd.[39]

The courts in Ghana have also shown a conservative attitude in connection with contributory negligence. In Amoabeng v. Mills[40] contributory negligence was held to be a complete defence, and despite the passage in England of the Law Reform (Contributory Negligence) Act, 1945,[41] the court followed Radley v. London and North Western Railway.[42] The law was however changed by the Ghana Civil Liability Act, 1963. The Privy Council, too, has felt constrained to apply the common law rule to an overseas territory even though it has been abrogated in England. When dealing with a case concerning wagering in India, Lord Campbell said:[43]

We are bound to consider the common law of England to be that an action may be maintained on a wager, ... and I rejoice that it is at last constitutionally abrogated by the Legislature ... . The Statute does not extend to India, and although both parties on the record are Hindoos, no peculiar Hindoo law is alleged to exist upon the subject: therefore this case must be decided by the common law of England.

A case in which English law applied despite the existence of native law was decided in Uganda in 1920. Guthrie Smith J. was dealing with succession to immovables and held[44] that,

in the absence of any enactment we must fall back on
what English law decided as to its own application to
newly acquired territories ... . Taking into consideration the general effect of the Uganda Act, 1900,
I think I may say we adopted much the same course as
was done in the settlement of India which is described
in Freeman v. Fairlie[45] as follows: 'The course
actually taken seems to have been to treat the case in
a great measure like that of a newly discovered country
for the Government of the Company's servants, and other
British or Christian settlers using the laws of the
mother country, so far as they were capable of being
applied for the purpose and leaving the Mohammedan and
Gentoo inhabitants to their own laws and customs but
with some particular exceptions that were called for by
commercial policy or the convenience of mutual intercourse.' If we substitute 'Natives of the Protectorate'
for the words 'Mohammedans and Gentoo inhabitants' ...
we shall have a correct description of how the matter
has been treated in Uganda. Therefore, apart from the
Succession Ordinance, 1906, the law of inheritance for
immovables was English law ... as far as regards
foreigners and native customs as far as regards
Natives of the Protectorate. There is no room anywhere
for the application of Mohammedan law to land and it
would lead to hopeless confusion if the course of
descent of land depended both on tribe and religion.
The conclusion is that this case falls to be determined
according to the English rules of succession.

The learned judge made no attempt to explain why
confusion would be caused by deciding succession cases
affecting Mohammedans in accordance with Mohammedan law,
while it would apparently not be so caused by applying
native custom in the case of Natives. This decision
was not cited in Re Abdulhusen Abhai Decd.[46] nor in
Re Cookman Nugnal Imam Din decd.,[47] in which it was
pointed out that it was "unreasonable to suppose that if
the legislature had seen fit to exempt Muslims from
an alien system of intestate succession under the Act,
it had done so only to make them subject to an equally
alien system under the law of England." On the other
hand, while local custom is recognised in New Guinea,
this does not allow expatriates, be they Chinese,
Australians or other Pacific Islanders, to plead a

specific deviation from the local law in their favour. By the Native Custom (Recognition) Ordinance such privilege is reserved to the "aboriginal inhabitants of the Territory."[48]

It is particularly in the field of public policy, and especially with regard to morality and marriage, that the strange consequences of the interplay between common and native law become most marked, with judges waxing almost lyrical on repugnancy, barbarism and civilization. An example of this arose before an English court. The parties, although Christians, had gone through a customary form of marriage in Nigeria in 1949, and in 1953, in order to obtain a certificate, had followed it by an English registry office marriage. At the time of the marriage, Nigeria permitted polygamy and Wrangham J. held:

Whatever might be the effect on the marriage for other purposes and in other courts of the parties being Christians, in this court and for this purpose the Nigerian marriage must be regarded as a polygamous marriage over which this court does not exercise juris- diction. I therefore pronounce a decree nisi for the dissolution not of the Nigerian marriage but of the marriage in London. I am told that, in fact, that will be effective by Nigerian law to dissolve the Nigerian marriage; but that forms no part of my judgment. That is for someone else to determine and not for me.[49]

The learned judge did not deal with the situation that would have arisen had Nigeria not recognized the validity of the English decree. In such a case the parties would have been in the strange position of finding that though the English marriage had been dissolved, since English law recognizes a polygamous marriage as creating the status of husband and wife, an attempt by either to enter into a second monogamous marriage in England would have produced a null effect,[50] though it might not have grounded an action for bigamy.[51]

A case in which English colonial judges approached native custom in a similarly cavalier fashion, and one which is still being applied by the courts of the territory in question, is the Six Widows case.[52] Here, English judges introduced into Singapore a concept of Chinese law not previously known and which is still not recognized in China.[53] The case concerned the status of Chinese "concubines", and Hyndman Jones C.J. accepted that,

the evidence is very contradictory, but I am disposed to think that when it is intended to take a woman into a man's household as a concubine for the purpose of securing a succession, or at all events as more than a temporary mistress, there are some sort of ceremonies; although these ceremonies, in some districts and among some classes are of a more or less perfunctory character, and always much less elaborate than those adopted in the case of taking a t'sai [principle wife].

Braddell J., whose knowledge of Chinese law was no better than that of the Chief Justice, declared

I entirely adopt the exposition of the Chinese law given in the judgment of the Chief Justice and concur with him in the conclusion to which he has arrived, namely, that concubinage is recognized as a legal institution under the law, conferring upon the t'sip [secondary wife] a legal status of a permanent character.

The anxiety of Singapore judges to assert the existence of the marriage bond was recognized by the Privy Council in affirming Penhas v. Tan Soo Eng[54] in which a form of ceremony was conducted by a Chinese between a Chinese Christian woman and a Jewish man in a house before witnesses, with each of the parties offering prayers in his own way. In the view of the Privy Council, although,

it is not suggested that either of the parties is a
Christian [,] ... the evidence as it stands sufficiently
proves a common law monogamous marriage. The wishes
expressed by the respondent and her mother for a Church
marriage, the reason why a modified Chinese ceremony
was substituted, the presence of Jewish friends at the
ceremony, the words spoken by the Chinese gentleman who
performed the ceremony as to a lifelong union, the
cohabitation as man and wife which followed and continued
until the husband's death, and the introduction to a
Christian pastor of the respondent as his wife, and last
but not least the baptism of their children as Christians,
with the approval of their father, all indicate that
the spouses intended to contract a common law marriage.

While it may be true that the parties did indeed intend

to effect a lifelong marriage and that this was rendered

respectable by the common law being introduced to

modify the rigours of the local law, a similar effect

might have been obtained had the court adopted the words

of Lord Phillimore, that "in deciding upon a case

where the customs and the laws are so different from

British ideas a Court may do well to recollect that

it is a possible jural conception that a child may be

legitimate, though its parents were not and could not

be called legitimately married."[55]

    It should not be thought that the desire to sustain a

marriage if that should be possible has been confined

to native systems of law. In January 1967 Brown J. was

called upon to decide upon the validity of a will and

his decision turned on the question of the subsistence

of a marriage put forward by a surviving husband who

could not remember the name of the Scottish town in

which the ceremony was performed. Mr. S. stated that

when he returned from a walk,

he was informed by the deceased that she had arranged
a marriage for the following morning. The next morning
they went to a chapel which was in a village hall. The
interior resembled a church, with pews, altar rail, dais,
combined lectern and pulpit, and a table with a candle
and Bible upon it. The priest, who had been expecting

them, wore black and conducted a very short service during which S. and the deceased agreed to take each other as husband and wife respectively. Both signed a large book and the deceased was given a certificate which some years later she destroyed after a row with her family. That account of the ceremony was highly improbable, the arrangements were incredibly casual, and grave doubts were necessarily aroused by the failure to remember the date or place of the ceremony, the absence of any record, and the account of the destruction of the certificate. It was clear that if S.'s case rested on his own account alone the Court would have no hesitation in holding the marriage was not proved. [In Penhas v. Tan Soo Eng, however, the Court accepted equally questionable proof]. On the other hand, the Court was satisfied from independent evidence that for the 14 years after the marriage the defendant and deceased had lived together, and were known as Mr. and Mrs. S. and accepted as a married couple. The deceased always wore a wedding ring and there was strong evidence to suggest that it was not in keeping with the deceased's character to be living in sin.

Since, however, a common law marriage will today only be assumed to exist by the English courts in exceptional circumstances, the marriage was upheld on the basis of repute from cohabitation.[56]

An up-to-date attitude to marriages performed in accordance with native law was shown by a Queen's Bench Divisional Court in March 1968. Justices had committed a 14-year old Nigerian girl to the care of a local authority as being exposed to moral danger and in need of care, protection or control. The girl was living with a Nigerian male aged 28, having married him by Nigerian law in Nigeria where they were both domiciled. The magistrates wrongly concluded that since the marriage was potentially polygamous it could not be recognized in England. The Court held that in so far as the girl's status was concerned, the marriage would be recognized and she would, therefore, be a wife. The Lord Chief Justice accepted the decision in Baindail v. Baindail,[57] and recognized the

possibility that even a wife might be the subject of
a fit person order. "The question was whether the
evidence justified such an order. The justices had
found that before the marriage the man had lived
with a woman and had had three illegitimate children,
and that after the marriage at a time when his wife
had almost certainly not reached puberty, he had had
intercourse with her. After the marriage he had contracted gonorrhoea from a prostitute, but he was now cured
and intended to resume intercourse with his wife. The
justices had found that the continuance of the association between the girl and the appellant would be
repugnant to any decent minded English person." Lord
Parker was convinced that "they had misdirected
themselves and that they were considering the reactions
of an Englishman regarding an English man and woman in
the western way of life. A decent Englishman realizing
the way in which a Nigerian man and woman were brought
up would not say it was repugnant. They developed
sooner and there was nothing abhorrent in a girl of 13
marrying a man of 25. To say the girl was in moral
danger would be ignoring the way of life in which she
and her husband had been brought up. It had been
suggested that every time the appellant slept with his
wife in England, he was committing a criminal offence
under the Sexual Offences Act, 1956, s. 6,[58] which made
it an offence for a man to have unlawful intercourse
with a girl between 13 and 16 ... [The Lord Chief
Justice did] not think the police could properly
prosecute in cases where a foreign marriage was recognized in England ... Intercourse between a man and
a wife was lawful ... Where a husband and wife were
recognized as validly married according to the laws of
England, His Lordship would not say the wife was exposed
to moral danger because she carried out her wifely
duties."[59]

An enlightened approach to the native law of marriage
and the consequential rejection of English law was
shown by Witman J. when called upon to decide whether
a marriage between Indians in Canada's North West
Territories, and contracted in a form which would have
been valid before the introduction of English law in
1870, was to be recognized. He asked,

[A]re the laws of England respecting the solemnisation
of marriage applicable to these Territories quoad
the Indian population? I have great doubt if these
laws are applicable to the Territories in any respect.
According to these laws, marriages can be solemnised
only at certain times and in certain places or buildings.
These times would be in many cases most inconvenient
here and the buildings, if they exist at all, are often
so remote from the contracting parties that they could
not be reached save with the greatest inconvenience.
I am satisfied however that these laws are not
applicable to the Territories quoad the Indians.
The Indians are for the most part unchristianised;
they yet adhere to their own particular marriage customs
and usages. It would be monstrous to hold that the law
of England respecting the solemnisation of marriage is
applicable to them .... A marriage between Indians by
mutual consent and according to Indian custom since
15th July 1870, is a valid marriage, providing that
neither of the parties had a husband or wife, as the
case might be, living at the time ....[60]

The learned judge could have reached the same conclusion
by holding that a common law marriage had been created,
but he preferred to apply the native law, even though
he insisted on monogamy.

In the case of American Indians, marriages contracted
in accordance with native custom have been upheld, even
though they have been polygamous:[61]

[A]mong these Indians polygamous marriages have always
been recognized as valid, and have never been confounded
with such promiscuous or informal temporary intercourse
as is not reckoned as marriage. While most civilized
nations in our day very wisely discard polygamy, and
it is not probably lawful anywhere among English

speaking nations, yet it is a recognized and valid institution amony many nations, and in no way universally unlawful. We must either hold that there can be no valid Indian marriage, or we must hold that all marriages are valid which by Indian usage are no regarded .... We have here had marriages between members of an Indian tribe in tribal relations, and unquestionably good by the Indian rules. The parties were not subject in those relations to the laws of Michigan .... We cannot influence or interfere with such marriages without subjecting them to rules of law which never bound them.

A similar view of the inapplicability, if not irrelevance, of the technicalities of English law was taken by the Privy Council in <u>Amodu Tijani</u> v. <u>Secretary, Southern Nigeria</u>:[62]

In interpreting the native title to land, not only in Southern Nigeria, but in other parts of the British Empire, much caution is essential. There is a tendency, operating at times unconsciously, to render that title conceptually in terms which are appropriate only to systems which have grown up under English law. But this tendency has to be held in check closely. As a rule, in the various systems of native jurisprudence throughout the Empire, there is no such full division between property and possession as English lawyers are familiar with.

The Privy Council's attitude had, however, been inconsistent when dealing with terms in colonial legislation which are the same as or similar to terms in English law. Thus, in <u>Nadarajan Chettiar</u> v. <u>Walaawa Mahatmee</u>[63] the Council pointed out that s. 2 of the Ceylon Moneylenders' Ordinance was the equivalent of s. 1 of the Moneylenders' Act, 1900, and commented that,

it is one thing to presume that a local legislature, when re-enacting a former statute, intends to accept the interpretation placed on that statute by local courts of competent jurisdiction with whose decision the legislature must be taken to be familiar; it is

quite another thing to presume that a legislature, when
it incorporates in a local act the terms of a foreign
statute, intends to accept the interpretation placed
on those terms by the courts of the foreign country with
which the legislature may or may not be familiar.
There is no presumption that the people of Ceylon at
the relevant date knew, or must be taken to have known,
decisions of the English courts under the Moneylenders' Acts, there is no basis for imputing to the
legislature an intention to accept those decisions ....
In Trimble v. Hill[64] the Board expressed this opinion
'... in colonies where a like enactment has been
passed by the legislature the Colonial Courts should
also govern themselves by it [a decision of the Court
of Appeal].' This, in their Lordships' view, is a
sound rule, though there may be in any particular case
conditions which make it inappropriate. It is not
suggested that any such conditions exist in the present
case, and the Courts in Ceylon acted correctly in
following the decision of the English Court of Appeal.

Local conditions were recognised, however, in Adegbenro
v. Akintola[65] for,

while it may well be useful on occasions to draw on
British practice or doctrine in interpreting a doubtful
phrase whose origins can be traced or to study decisions
on the Constitution of Australia or the United States
when federal issues are involved, it is in the end the
wording of the Constitution itself that is to be interpreted and applied, and this wording can never be
overridden by the extraneous principles of other Constitutions which are not explicitly incorporated in the
formulae that have been chosen as the frame of this
Constitution.

Once again the position concerning Indian custom in
the United States is more enlightened than tends to be
usual with the interplay of English and local law.
The Supreme Court refused to uphold a South Dakota
prosecution for adultery when the parties were Sioux
and the offense was alleged to have taken place on a
Sioux reservation. In U.S. v. Quiver[66] Justice Van
Devanter stated,

At an early period it became the settled policy of
Congress to permit the personal and domestic relations
of the Indians with each other to be regulated, and
offences by one Indian against the person or property
of another Indian to be dealt with according to their
tribal customs and laws .... [T]he act of June 30, 1834,
ch. 161, sec. 25, 4 Stat. 729, 733, while providing
that 'so much of the laws of the United States as
provides for the punishment of crimes committed
within any place within the sole and exclusive jurisdiction of the United States shall be in force in the
Indian country', qualified its action by saying, 'the
same shall not extend to crimes committed by one
Indian against the person or property of another Indian'.
That provision with its qualification was later carried
into the Revised Statutes as Secs. 2145 and 2146 ....
There is [no statute] dealing with bigamy, polygamy,
incest, adultery or fornication, which in terms
refers to Indians, these matters always having been
left to the tribal customs and laws and to such preventive and corrective measures as reasonably could be
taken by the administrative officers.

Problems sometimes arise when common law courts
exist side by side with Native courts. While the
jurisdiction of the two systems is never identical, it
may happen that both are competent to deal with certain
aspects of the same factual situation. This occurred in
Nyasaland in 1962. A 'crocodile man' named Elland
brought an action before a Native authority court
seeking payment from one Odrick who had engaged to pay
him £4 10s. if he killed a girl suspected of witchcraft.
Elland fulfilled his part of the bargain, but only
received 10s. from Odrick, whom he sued for non-payment
of debt. The court ordered the latter to pay £2 10s.
into court in settlement and gave him a receipt. Both
men were both subsequently indicted before the
Nyasaland criminal court for murder.[67]

It is perhaps unfortunate that judges in colonial
territories, who are called upon to apply native law
and to examine its interconnection with the common
law far more frequently than the Privy Council, appear

to be more reticent in recognizing local needs and abandoning English concepts. This is the case with Wilson J. in Tanganyika, who held[68] that,

a Turu custom whereby the property of a father might be seized in compensation for a wrong done by his son was so repugnant to British ideas of justice and morality that it should not be endorsed in the High Court. It would, however, almost certainly have succeeded in a local court, to which such ideas of vicarious liability would not be so difficult to accept.[69]

Similar attitudes are evident in Nigerian decisions, where,

the repugnancy doctrine has also been applied in the field of customary family law. In Joshua Chawere v. Hannah Aihenu[70] it was held that any native custom to the effect that a wife who committed adultery ipso facto of the adultery became the wife of the male adulterer would be repugnant and unenforceable. And in this same field, the English common law concept of "public policy", which would forbid the encourage- ment of promiscuous intercourse,[71] has been suggested[72] as capable of striking down the now well-established[73] customary rule that an originally illegitimate child whose paternity is acknowledged and recognized by its father thereby acquires the same status as a child born legitimate.[74]

Perhaps one of the most glaring instances of trimming native customary law to the moral code of the English common law is to be seen in Re GM (An Infant).[75] A Kikuyu orphan child had been placed by the local author- ities in a state of de facto adoption with a respect- able woman, against whom the deceased father's brother brought an action on the ground that by Kikuyu law and custom he had "the right of custody as against all strangers." Miles J. found that it was in the infant's interest to stay with the respondent, and that by English law this was the test to apply in a

contest between strangers or between parents. As
between a parent and a stranger, however, he held that
the parent must prevail unless this would be inimical
to the child. He decided that English law applied,
but that in determining the child's welfare it was
necessary to look to native custom and habits:

I am entitled to inquire what the position of the
applicant is under native law and then to inquire what
would be the rights of a person in that position under
English law .... The applicant cannot be said to be a
"parent". It is also clear on the evidence that the
applicant is, under Kikuyu law, in the position of a
guardian with surely all the obligations of a parent.
He has greater obligations than a guardian under
English law who is not bound to support a child except
out of the child's estate. [Since the respondent was
a stranger, and the applicant a blood relation] under
English law the latter would be held to have a legal
right as against all strangers.

It would seem that the learned judge assimilated a
"guardian" in Kikuyu law with a "parent" under English
law.[76]

It is decisions like this which make one feel that
Maine's comment in 1871[77] is still valid:

The higher courts, though they openly borrowed the
English rules from the recognized English authorities,
constantly used language from which it implied that they
believed themselves to be taking them from some
abstract body of legal principles which lay behind all
law; and the inferior judges, when they were applying
some half-remembered legal rule learnt in boyhood, or
culling a proposition of law from a half-understood
English textbook, no doubt honestly thought in many
cases that they were following the rule prescribed for
them, to decide "by equity and good conscience"
whenever no native law or usage was discoverable.

One would like to hope that judges faced with assessing whether native customary law was applicable despite
its apparent inconsistency with the common law would

adopt the reasoning of Lord Atkin:[78]

> The more barbarous customs of earlier days may under
> the influence of civilization become milder without
> losing their essential character as custom, so as in
> that form to regulate the relations of the native
> community _inter se_. In other words, the court cannot
> itself transform a barbarous custom into a milder one.
> If it still stands in its barbarous character it must
> be rejected as repugnant to "natural justice, equity
> and good conscience." It is the essence of a native
> community that gives a custom its validity, and,
> therefore, barbarous or mild, it must be shown to be
> recognized by the native community whose conduct it
> is supposed to regulate.

The Chief Justice of Gambia has recently shown that
the concept of "barbarism" is relative and that customs
which might not be approved by Christian missionaries
are not necessarily contrary to "natural justice".
Thus, in _Koykoy Jatta_ v. _Menna Camara_[79] he held that
female circumcision "is your custom but can only be
your custom in your own tribe and applied to your own
people."

A similar enlightened approach is to be found in the
attitude of Bennan A. J. in the Supreme Court of Papua
and New Guinea, when called upon to decide whether
insulting words could provoke the ordinary person to
kill. The words were spoken by a woman to a man who
had used a coarse expression to the woman's daughter;
she said "You cannot find a woman to marry, and if you
talk like that to a girl child you will die still
unmarried." The learned judge thought that in
"western communities which apply common law principles,
the view that words alone cannot be relied upon as a
provocation has hardened since the seventeenth century.
As a general proposition that thesis is hardly open
to dispute, but it does not necessarily follow that
the same principle should apply in a native community

where sophistication does not approach to that of, say, seventeenth century England, where a type of insult such as the one here in question is calculated and not infrequently intended to throw a man into an ungovernable rage."[80] A somewhat similar attitude is evident in the approach of Smithers J. in R. v Rumints-Gorok,[81] who considered that "for the exemplification of the ordinary man [in the Territory] one must take the ordinary native living the rural life of low standard led by the accused and his relatives and similar lines."

The problems involved when an outsider is called upon to assess native customary law are also evident in the attitude of India Bureau officials of the United States,

who disapproved of the 'uncivilized' practices of the Indians and sought to substitute a 'civilized' system of 'courts of Indian offenses' in which the superintendent of the reservation claimed the right to act as lawmaker, chief of police, prosecutor, witness, and court of appeal. This allegedly 'civilized' system of justice was in force on a number of reservations from 1884 until 1935, when it was superseded by a more liberal system which made the so-called Courts of Indian Offenses responsible to the Indian tribes and terminated the reservation superintendent's power to control proceedings in these courts.[82]

In Ceylon, Roman-Dutch common law has had to give way before the customary law of a particular community, for while,

no court would recognize as reasonable a custom which deprived a section of the community of its common law rights in the freedom which the custom is supposed to regulate,[83] it must be remembered that in Ceylon there are customary laws governing people, and if it could be proved that such customary laws enunciate principles which are in derogation to the general principles of Roman-Dutch law, it is the customary law which would govern such a matter to the exclusion of Roman-Dutch law.[84]

Where Roman-Dutch law happens to be the common law, problems sometimes arise not only because of the relevance of native law, but also because the concept being examined is also known in England and the judges are frequently English trained. Mr. De Silva, delivering judgment on behalf of the Privy Council, dealt with this problem in so far as it affected accessories after the fact of murder:[85]

Under section 2 of the General Law Proclamation[86] the common law of Basutoland "shall,as nearly as the circumstances of the country will permit, be the same as the law for the time being in force in the Colony of the Cape of Good Hope".... The determination of the question before their Lordships depends on the Roman-Dutch common law, which is the common law of the Cape of Good Hope and is also the common law in force in South Africa .... It does not necessarily follow from the fact that the term 'accessory after the fact' has been adopted from the English law that it has the same meaning in the law of South Africa as it has under the English law. No doubt it would retain much of the connotation which it possessed under the English law, but its meaning in the country of its adoption could naturally and properly be influenced by the system of law prevailing in that country, namely the Roman-Dutch law. This was almost inevitable, as the term had to be used in relation to, and in the course of administration of that law.

In the instant case, while the accused was not guilty under English law, he was guilty under the Roman-Dutch common law by which the case was governed.

The importance of South African decisions in determining the meaning of Roman-Dutch law for those areas in which it is the common law remains, even though South Africa has become a Republic outside the Commonwealth. This is illustrated by the comments of Lord Donovan on behalf of the Privy Council in Mapolisa v. R.[87]

The common law in force in the Cape of Good Hope (now

part of the Republic of South Africa) on the date specified [by the High Court Act of Southern Rhodesia, 1893] was, and remains, Roman-Dutch law. Under the law a socius criminis [accomplice] is not regarded as committing the self-same crime as the principal perpetrator but as committing instead the offence of aiding and abetting that crime .... Even if the Roman-Dutch common law regarded the socius criminis as committing the very crime perpetrated, it did so only in relation to crimes which were offences created by that common law. Since Roman-Dutch law is the common law of Southern Rhodesia, judicial decisions given in the courts of what is now the Republic of South Africa have relevance in Southern Rhodesia and are applicable subject to any statutory modification of the law in Southern Rhodesia. The Appellate Division of the Supreme Court of South Africa served until recent times as a Court of Appeal for Southern Rhodesia. During that period its decisions were binding in Southern Rhodesia, and while this is technically no longer so, those decisions continue to have persuasive authority.

It is to be hoped that the reduction of South African appellate decisions to a level of persuasive rather than binding authority, will not result in the elevation of decisions of the English Court of Appeal on similar causes to the level of compulsive authority.

From what has been said it is clear that while the introduction of the common law into native societies has undoubtedly led to some modification of local native customs which were not acceptable to western Christian society, and has resulted in the expansion of the scope of the rule of law as understood in such society, it remains true that too often the judges called upon to apply the one or the other or an admixture of the two have tended to disregard local conditions or susceptibilities, and have frequently stretched English concepts as if their task lay in creating replicas of the English legal system wherever English-trained judges held sway. This situation was condemned by Sir Frederick Pollock in so far as India was concerned in 1912:

One may find indeed that imitation is now and then
carried to excess. Not only the decisions of Indian
superior courts and of the Judicial Committee on appeal
therefrom, but those of English courts, are cited
wholesale throughout British India, frequently by
advocates who cannot know much of the common law and by
judges or magistrates who may know as little; and the
citations, one suspects, are too often not even from the
report but at second hand from textbooks. Even
technical rules of English real property law have been
relied on by Indian courts without considering whether
they had any reasonable application to the facts and
usage of the country. Some Indian judges, even in the
superior judgment seats of the High Courts, have
forgotten that the law they administer .... is not
English law as such, but 'justice, equity and good
conscience' interpreted to mean as much of English
jurisprudence as appears to be reasonably applicable,
and no more. Bland following of English precedents
according to the letter can only have the effect of
reducing the estimation of the common law by intelligent
Indians to the level of its more technical and less
fruitful portions and making those portions appear, if
possible, more inscrutable to Indian than they do to
English lay suitors.[88]

It would appear that the underlying basis of these

comments was true in so far as the Privy Council is

concerned even as recently as 1955. In Leong v. Lim

Beng Chye[89] the issue concerned the validity of restraints

on marriage in Penang, and the opinion on the Board

was delivered by Lord Radcliffe:

The considerations which have influenced the Court of
Appeal can be plausibly restated in the proposition that
the rule of English law ought not to be applied by the
courts in Malaya, having regard to the differences of
race and social custom that separate the one country
from the other. Something like this proposition was
indeed advanced by the respondent's counsel in his
argument on the appeal. The rule in question, it was
said, was a rule of construction only, which, originating
in an attempt to correct a social malady that prevailed
in one period of the Roman Empire, had found an ambig-
uous and rather restricted lodging in one part of the
law of England. It would be wrong to resort to it
when dealing with the construction of wills made by
residents of Malaya, many of whom inherit customs and
traditions very different from those of the English

race. Their Lordships are far from denying that there
is force in an argument on these lines. It is very
natural to see something anomalous in the introduction
into Malaya of a special rule of English law of this
kind. But English law itself has been introduced
into Penang ... 'so far as it is applicable to the
circumstances of the place';[90] and while so much of
that law as can be said to relate to matters and
exigencies peculiar to the local condition of England
and to be inapplicable to the conditions of the overseas territory is not being treated as so imported,
their Lordships are of opinion that the process of
selection cannot rest on anything less than some solid
ground that establishes the inconsistency; it is any
solid ground of that sort which is lacking in this
case; not the less when it is recalled that the
testator made the will in the English language, and
employed in it forms and legal conceptions that are
wholly derived from English law [-this is to ignore the
fact that the language of the testator was almost
certainly English as it is with so many Straits Chinese;
that the lawyer who drafted the will was English-
trained; and that the language of the law in Malaya
at that time was English]. In fact, if the English law
was so far imported into Penang as to nullify through
the rule against perpetuities a Chinese lady's
testamentary disposition relating to a family burying
place and a house for performing religious ceremonies
to the memory of her dead husband,[91] it would be very
hard to say why there was not also imported the English
rule as to the effect of conditions of partial restraint
of marriage .... This rule ... is not merely a rule
of construction, since its history shows that it owes
its existence to a particular conception of what public
policy required, even though that conception never
prevailed in the English law as a whole. Yet there is
nothing that is peculiar to the local conditions of
England or, for all that appears, anything necessarily
inappropriate to the circumstances of Malaya, in a
reluctance on the part of the courts of law to allow a
person's decision whether or not to enter the state of
matrimony to be overhung by [such] a condition.[92]

A somewhat different approach by non-native judges is

to be found in the treatment of North American Indians:

"Where [federal] statutes do not reach, Indian custom

is the only law. As a matter of convenience, the regular

courts (white men's courts) tacitly assume that the

general law of the community is the law in civil cases

between Indians; but these courts will apply Indian custom whenever it is proved."[93]

It is perhaps unfortunate that not enough colonial legal officers have been prepared to follow the lead of such persons as Sissons J. in Canada's North West Territories[94] and depart from the rigorous application of legal rules when they consider justice and native interests required such action. Among those who have may be numbered Mr. Austin Coates, a former Special Magistrate in Hong Kong who never became legally qualified, and therefore found it comparatively simple to apply rough justice in accordance with local Chinese custom.[95] Others have recognized that the judicial process itself is likely to lead to injustice and have found their true role to be that of a mediator, even though the 'case' before them may appear as a formal legal process. This is likely to be more successful if the judicial officer is aware of native suscepti- bilities, reactions and habits. Such a case came before a native 'specialist' local court magistrate in Wewak, New Guinea, in 1967.[96] Joana claimed that Anton had married her at Rabaul, paying the requisite bride-price. She contended that the custom of her people was 'one man and one wife'. A child had been born, but she sought dissolution of the marriage on the grounds that Anton was interested in Agnes, whom he regarded as his second wife, and as he had told Joana to return to Rabaul. Anton complained of Joana's conduct towards him and his relatives and pointed out that she could not work because of the child and so he had to get another wife, but "I have not paid Agnes's bride-price yet. However, since she has been in my village for one week, we claim it is a marriage by native custom. I believe her parents would not dispute her marrying me." The magistrate advised them that in

his view "a valid marriage obtained between Joana and
Anton by native custom, bride-price having paid; the
'marriage' between Agnes and Anton was not a valid
marriage according to native custom, no bride-price
having been paid to Agnes's parents and no celebrations
held by way of recognition of marriage in accordance
with the local custom; Joana would be entitled to have
her marriage dissolved by native custom since in her
community there should be only one woman and one man
in a marriage." Joana thereupon agreed to withdraw
her application for dissolution, provided Anton would
send Agnes away. Since he agreed, the magistrate
succeeded in preserving a marriage in circumstances
where had there been a formal local court hearing he
would almost certainly have found it necessary to
issue an order for dissolution in accordance with the
Local Courts Ordinance, 1963, s. 17.

Addressing the International Commission of Jurists
in 1966, Judge Vivian Bose remarked that "in developing
countries the rule of law is often being equated with
the former foreign domination ... These new nations
must be shown that law was not a western product,
but something grounded in their own traditions.
Institutions rooted in their own custom could be raised
and moulded to modern forms."[97] An early recognition
of the need to acknowledge the existence of native
institutions of law was shown by Lord Sumner[98] who
pointed out in 1919 that

the estimation of the rights of aboriginal tribes is
always inherently difficult. Some tribes are so low in
the scale of social organization that their usages
and conceptions of rights and duties are not to be
reconciled with the institutions of the legal ideas of
civilized society. Such a gulf cannot be bridged.
It would be idle to impute to such people some shadow
of the rights known to our law and then to transmute
it into the substance of transferable rights of

property as we know them .... On the other hand,
there are indigenous peoples whose legal conceptions,
though differently developed are hardly less precise
than our own. When once they have been studied and
understood they are no less enforceable than rights
arising under English law.

With the rise as new independent States of territories
which were formerly colonies, and the feelings of
national pride which their people enjoy, together with
the gradual replacement of expatriate lawyers and
judges and the retreat from the Judicial Committee of
the Privy Council as the supreme court of appeal, we
are on the threshold of a new relationship between
the common law and native systems. Those English
judges who remain, and the English lawyers who have
gone out to staff the law schools, are conscious of
the realities that surround them. While there is still
the need to supplement the law and realization that
what has been past practice cannot be abandoned, there
is growing recognition that the local people will not
be satisfied with the example of their former rulers
and that, in any case, local needs require more than
a slavish adoption of the common law. Further, the
principles of public policy and concepts of civilization understood in such native societies are no longer
seen as inferior to those of another legal system as
realized in the United States in so far as Indians on
the reserves are concerned a generation ago.[99] The
common law has served the purpose of making the basic
principles of a western view of the rule of law
understood and appreciated. If it is to continue to
play a role, (English) common lawyers must be prepared
to see its adaptation and rejection in issues where,
in the past, it might have been adopted either in full
or in amended form. It may well be true that "the
only realistic course [is] one that leads towards some

kind of association or synthesis of western-derived law and custom and procedures of the villages."[100] If common lawyers do not adapt themselves to this view and continue to look down upon "barbaric" and "uncivilized" systems, they may find that there is a reaction which results in a total rejection of the influences of the common law, instead of this being but one of the various systems of law that nationalist lawyers and judges seeking to serve the needs of their people are prepared to investigate and adapt as their requirements demand.

* Based on a paper, 'The Common Law and Native Systems of Law', prepared for a Duke University Symposium, International and Comparative Law of the Commonwealth, ed. R. R. Wilson (1968), 81.

[1] Blankard v. Galdy, 2 Salk 411.

[2] Anon. (1722), 2 P. Wms. 75.

[3] 1 Commentaries (10th ed., 1787), 108.

[4] Freeman v. Fairlie (1828), 1 Moo. Ind. App. 305,324.

[5] (1832) 6 Pet. 515, at 542.

[6] (1883) 109 U.S. 556.

[7] 1885, 18 U.S.C.A. sec. 548.

[8] See, e.g., Calvin's Case (1608), 7 Co. Rep. 1a; Campbell v. Hall (1774), 1 Cowp. 204; Adv.-Gen. of Bengal v. Ranee Surnanoye Dossee (1883), 9 Moo. Ind. App. 391.

[9] In re Simpson's Estate [1927] 3 W.W.R. 534, 539.

[10] Jolowicz, Historical Introduction to Roman Law (1961), 71, 101.

[11] Bryce, Studies in History and Jurisprudence (1901), 77-78.

[12] Wille, Principles of South African Law (1961), 38.

13 Seaville v. Colley (1891), 9 S.C. 39, per de
    Villiers C.J., at 42. See also Wijekoon v.
    Gunawardena (1892), 1 S.C.R. 147, 149.

14 Jennings and Tambiah, The Dominion of Ceylon
    (1952), 198.

15 Preller v. Jordaan (1956) (1) S.A. 483 (A.D.) per
    van den Heever J.A. at 504.

16 [1934] A.C. 570, per Lord Tomlin at 585.

17 Aquilius, "Immorality and Illegality in Contract",
    So. Afr. L.J., LX (1943), 468, 476.

18 Title 16, Chap. 3, s. 40.

19 Allott, Essays in African Law (1960), 12.

20 Sup. Ct. Ord. No. 4, 1874; Cts. Ord. 1951, s.83.

21 Elias, Ghana and Sierra Leone (1962), 116.

22 Ibid. (citing Mersah v. Konongo). See also
    Brand v. Griffin (1908), 9 W.W.R. 427, in which it
    was held that since the operative date in Alberta
    is 1870, a statute of 1874 is inapplicable.

23 F.M.S. No. 3, s 2(1).

24 Civil Law Ord. 1956 (no. 5 as amended by No. 41),
    s. 3(1).

25 S. 5.

26 Civil Law Ord., S. 5.

27 Courts and Laws Adopting Ordinance 1889 (amended),
    s. 4.

28 Laws Repeal and Adopting Ordinance 1921 (amended),
    s. 16.

29 E. Africa O. in C., 1902 (S.R. & O. 1902, No. 661,
    amended 1911, No. 243). For the position in
    W. Africa see Daniels, The Common Law in West Africa
    (1964), chs. 4, 6.

30 [1955] 1 All. E.R. 646, 652, 653 (affirmed [1956]
    3 W.L.R. 541).

31 (1882) Sar(bah) F(anti) C(ustomary) L(aws) 172.

[32] (1925) Div. Ct. Judgments 1921-5, 172 (Elias, op. cit., p. 119).

[33] Anguillia v. Ong Boon Tat (1921), 15 S.S.L.R. 190, 193.

[34] Native Custom (Recognition) Ordinance, 1963), s. 4.

[35] (1951) 18 Int. Law Rep. 144, 149.

[36] Waghela Rajsanji v. Shekh Masludin (1887), 14 Ind. App. 89, per Lord Hobhouse, at 96.

[37] Sec.of State v. Rukhminibai, A.I.R. [1937] Nag.354.

[38] 1880, 43 & 44 Vict. c. 42.

[39] Unreported (cited in Daniels, op. cit. p. 240).

[40] [1956] 1 W.A.L.R. 210.

[41] 8 & 9 Geo. 6, c. 28.

[42] (1876) 1 App. Cas. 754.

[43] Ramloll Thackoorseydass v. Soojanmull Dhoondumull (1848), 4 Moo. Ind. App. 339, 348-349.

[44] Re Mohd Habash, Vasila v. Worsta Sophia (1920), 3 U.L.R. 20, 26.

[45] See note 4, above.

[46] (1941) 6 U.L.R. 89.

[47] (1949) cited in Moriss and Read, Uganda (1966), 401.

[48] See above, n. 34. s. 4.

[49] Ohochuku v. Ohochuku [1960] 1 W.L.R. 183, 185.

[50] Baindail v. Baindail [1946] P.122. See also Thynne v. Thynne [1955] P. 272.

[51] R. v. Sarwan Singh [1962] 3 All E.R. 612.

[52] (1888), 12 S.S.L.R. 120, 187, 209.

[53] Information supplied to the writer by senior Chinese members of the Supreme Courts of Singapore and Malaya.

54 [1953] A.C. 304, 318, 319-320

55 Khoo Hooi Leong v. Khoo Hean Kwee [1926] A.C. 529, 543.

56 Rumsey v. Sterne (1967), The Times (London), 12 Jan. 1967.

57 See note 50 above.

58 4 & 5 Eliz. 2, c. 69.

59 M. v. K., The Times (London), 29 March 1968 (reported as Mohamed v. Knott [1968] 2 W.L.R. 1446 1457). (Italics added).

60 Reg. v. Nan-E-Quis-A-Ka (1885), 1 Terr. L.R. 211, 215.

61 Kobogum v. Jackson Iron Co. (1889), 43 N.W. 602, at 605 (per Justice Campbell). (For a novel based on this case, see Traver, Laughing Whitefish,1965.)

62 [1921] 2 A.C. 399, 402-3 (per Lord Haldane).

63 [1950] A.C. 481, 491-2 (per Sir John Beaumont).

64 (1879) 5 App. Cas. 342, 244 (per Sir Montague Smith).

65 [1963] A.C. 614, 632 (per Lord Radcliffe).

66 (1916) 241 U.S. 602, 603-5.

67 The Times, 25 August 1962.

68 Gwao bin Kelimo v. Kisunda bin Ifuti (1938), 1 T.L.R. (R) 403.

69 Cole and Denison, Tanganyika (1964), 131.

70 12 N.L.R. 4.

71 See "The Ladies' Directory Case" (Shaw v. D.P.P. [1961] 2 W.L.R. 897).

72 In re Sarah Adadevoh (1951), 13 W.A.C.A. 304, per Verity C.J., at 310.

73 Savage v. Macfay (1909), Ren. 504; Re Sapara (1911), Ren. 605.

74 Ajayi, "Interaction of English Law with Customary Law in Western Nigeria, II", Jour. of Afr. Law,

IV (1960), 98, 104-5.

75 [1957] E.A. 714, 716.

76 Allott, note, Jour. of Afr. Law, III (1959), 72, at 74.

77 Maine, Village Communities in the East and West (1871), 298-9.

78 Eshugbayi Eleko v. Govt. of Nigeria (Officer Administrating) [1931] A.C. 662, 673.

79 (1961), Jour. of Afr. Law, VII (1964), 35.

80 R. v. Awabe (1960) unreported (c. Hookey, 'The "Clapham Omnibus" in New Guinea', in Brown, Fashion of Law in New Guinea (1969), 117, 126).

81 [1963] P. & N. G.L.R. 81, 83. See also R. v. Zariai-Gavene [1963] P. & N. G.L.R. 203, in which the judge expressly took into consideration the effect of the words spoken upon a Giolala villager, of whom the accused was one.

82 Cohen, "Indian Rights and the Federal Courts", Minn. L.R., XXIV (1939-40), 145, 153.

83 See, also, Att. Gen., Canada v. Lavell (1973) 38 D.L.R. (3d) 481, in which the Supreme Court of Canada held that the Canadian Bill of Rights did not invalidate s.12 of the Indian Act (R.S.C. 1970, I-6), which removed Indian status from an Indian woman marrying a non-Indian, while not treating Indian men marrying out in the same way.

84 Fernando v. Fernando (1920), 22 N.R.R. 260, per Bertram C.J.

85 Nkau Majara v. The Queen [1954] A.C. 235, 240-1.

86 Laws of Basutoland, cap. 26.

87 [1965] A.C. 840, 857-8.

88 Genius of the Common Law, (1912), 92. On the position of Indian law generally, see Setalvad, The Common law in India (1960), ch. 1. See, however, Setalvad, The Role of English Law in India (1966), in which the learned author examines the suitability or otherwise of English law under Indian conditions, and forecasts the emergence of Indian legal thought as a contributing force to Anglo-Saxon jurisprudence.

89   [1955] A.C. 648, 665-6.

90   Yeap Cheah Neo v. Ong Cheng Neo (1875), L.R. 6
     P.C. 381, 393.

91   Ibid., p. 393.

92   See, however, Adeyinka Oyekan v. Musendiku Adele
     [1957] 1 W.L.R. 876, in which Lord Denning remarked
     that in Nigeria Government grants of land "do not
     convey English titles or English rights of owner-
     ship. The words 'his heirs, executors, administ-
     rators and assigns forever' are to be rejected as
     meaningless and inapplicable in their African
     setting" (p. 882).

93   Rice, "The Position of the American Indian in the
     Law of the United States", J. Comp. Leg. (3rd Ser.),
     XVI (1934), 78, 90.

94   Sissons, Judge of the Far North (1968).

95   Coates, Myself a Mandarin (1968), esp. 22-5,
     204-12.

96   Joana-Vapor v. Anton Susami and Agnes-Daporobu,
     reported in Brown, op. cit., n. 80 above, 209.

97   The Times (London), Oct. 1, 1966.

98   In re Southern Rhodesia [1919] A.C. 211, 233-4.

99   See note 82 above.

100   Brown, 'Justice and the Edge of Law: Towards a
      "People's" Court', in Brown, op. cit., n. 80
      above, 181, 183.

III

"CIVILIZED" LAW AND "PRIMITIVE" PEOPLES

On July 16th 1974, Judge King-Hamilton sitting in
the Central Criminal Court, London, found Felicia
Foluke Adesanya, a Yoruba, guilty of assaulting her
sons, Roufemi, aged 14, and Lanre, aged 9, occasioning
bodily harm, having cut their faces with a knife. For
Mrs. Adesanya it had been pleaded that the boys had
agreed to her actions, which after all only involved
tribal scarification during new year celebrations. The
learned judge felt he was able to take a lenient view
of the case and order her absolute discharge, for "this
is a test case, the first of its kind, and ... I am
convinced you did not realize you were breaking the
law."[1] This case immediately throws into profile a
fundamental issue of anthropological jurisprudence -
the conflict and the interplay as between 'civilized'
systems and concepts of law and the 'primitive' people
to whom such systems seek to apply.

In order to avoid unnecessary semantic disputation
as to the meaning of words, it is as well that we
define how the terms 'civilization' and 'primitive'
are being used in this paper. Civilization is a
relative term depending upon the ethos, beliefs, culture
and background of the person using it, and that
person's concept of the primitive condition is formed
on exactly the same basis. According to Article 38
of the Statute of the International Court of Justice,
one of the 'sources' of international law consists of

general principles of law recognized by civilized nations,[2] although the Court has never found it necessary to decide a case on these alone. This inability is by no means surprising, for it would be well-nigh impossible to decide what constituted general principles of law, other than perhaps that unjustifiable homicide constitutes a punishable offence. Moreover, who is to decide which are the civilized nations? Every member of the United Nations, which is automatically also a party to the Statute of the Court, regards itself as 'civilized' and would contend that if it did not recognize any particular legal principle, that principle could not therefore be a general principle of law for if it were, it would obviously be recognized by the state in question since that state is, as the whole world knows, civilized. All that one can say of this concept is that general principles of law recognized by civilized nations are nothing but those principles of law which are generally recognized by us and those nations which we consider to be civilized. For our purposes, therefore, the term civilization will be used to connote a state which possesses a sophisticated legal system in the common and civil law traditions. It is equally difficult to define 'primitiveness', and we will use the term to connote a people which is not sophisticated in the above sense, which is regarded as primitive by the ordinary lay person, and which has found itself in a special relationship with one of the more sophisticated groups which latter has attempted to impose, graft or adapt its system of law on to such primitive society.[3]

The interplay between a civilized and a primitive people requiring some examination of the legal framework may arise in one of two ways. On the one hand, the sophisticated may arrive and take over the territory

inhabited by the primitives, establishing themselves
and their own government, making the territory in
question their own country, as happened in such places
as Australia, New Zealand, North America and South
Africa. In other places, the invaders took the
territory but did so only as a colony or a protectorate, establishing their alien order, but not intending
to make the land their own home, for they sent their
children 'home' to school and themselves hoped to
'return home to die'. In the former case, there was no
hesitation about imposing their own system of law,
especially when the settlers were English, for, as
Blackstone pointed out,[4] an Englishman took his law
with him. This is only true, however, to the extent
that English law was applicable to their situation and
the condition of the colonists. This was made clear in
an Albertan case concerning the validity of a judgment
delivered by a female police magistrate, it having
been alleged that a woman could not be appointed to
such a post. In R. v. Cyr[5] Stuart J. stated: "We
are at liberty to take cognizance of the different
conditions here, not merely physical conditions, but
the general conditions of our public affairs and the
general attitude of the community in regard to the
particular matter in question." He also cited an
earlier decision of the Supreme Court of the State of
Washington:[6] "The common law grew with society not
ahead of it; as society became more complex and new
demands were made upon the law by reason of new circumstances the courts originally in England out of the
storehouse of reason and good sense declared the
'common law'. But since courts have had an existence
in America they have never hesitated to take upon themselves the responsibility of saying what is the common
law, notwithstanding current English decision [even
to the contrary], especially upon questions involving

new conditions."

This comment is only concerned with rights of the settlers, ignoring completely the problem of the already indigenous inhabitants. The reason for this is that, so far as the established states of the time were concerned, newly-discovered territories were considered uninhabited, regardless of the size of the aboriginal population, and therefore there was no existing legal system which could conflict with that known to the settlers and which they took with them. Perhaps the most extreme example of this is to be found in the attitude of the Permanent Court of International Justice, when it held in the <u>Eastern Greenland</u> case[7] that "conquest only operates as a cause of loss of sovereignty when there is war between two States and by reason of the defeat of one of them sovereignty over territory passes from the loser to the victorious State. The principle does not apply in a case where a settlement has been established in a distant country and its inhabitants are massacred by the aboriginal population." In those cases where there was already an established state which had been conquered or ceded, the newcomers recognized that the already-existing law prevailed until amended by the new sovereign, although all repugnant laws, especially those based on religious or ethical principles inconsistent with European civilization, are <u>ipso facto</u> abrogated. Tredgold C.J., Southern Rhodesia, sought to explain the meaning of this concept by saying: "Whatever these words [- repugnant to natural justice and morality -] may mean, I consider that they should only apply to such customs as inherently impress us with abhorrence or are obviously immoral in their incidence."[8]

In so far as English settlements have been concerned,

the local judges have had power, until such time as new
laws have been introduced, to administer justice in
accordance with the concepts of natural equity.[9]
This was a matter of necessity and convenience, for if
the existing laws were abrogated immediately anarchy
would probably ensue. At the same time, it was recognized that the local population would not be any more
familiar with the new law being introduced than the
conquerors would be with the one already existing.
Sometimes this meant that the two systems could continue
to survive side by side, operating independently with
each controlling its own community. This was what
happened in the case of the North American Indians in
the United States until the situation was changed by
statute in 1885.[10] This was never the case in Canada,
although it tended to prevail in some British colonies.
Thus, in Bechuanaland native law continues, but in
matters affecting Europeans the Roman-Dutch law of the
Cape is applicable as common law. The most complex
situation prevailed in Ceylon where Roman-Dutch law is
also the common law. However, the Hindu inhabitants
of the northern province are governed by Tesawalamai
customs, and where these are silent by Roman-Dutch law;
the Mohammedans have their own laws and usages; while
the Kandyans are governed by their own laws, with
Roman-Dutch operating when these are silent.[11]

In some instances attempts have been made not merely
for the two systems to exist side by side independently,
but for them to work cooperatively, although this may
produce strange and even contradictory results,
especially if the native system involves the application of principles which may be considered as contrary
to doctrines of humanity, such as slavery, in which
case they are likely to be suppressed by prohibitive
legislation or by the refusal of the courts to give

effect to the offending practice. In recent years
there has been much criticism of South Africa for
allowing native chieftain courts in Namibia (Southwest
Africa) to inflict floggings, especially in cases
involving women or for offences considered trivial by
the critics, such as criticism of the chiefs. The
rejection of local practices by the courts in some
African territories may be illustrated by Magayi v.
Uganda[12] which arose from the killing of a prisoner
under escort. The accused was a member of the escort
who, under orders from a chief, another member of the
escort, had beaten a suspected thief to death. In the
view of the court, "although it is the custom in Uganda
and elsewhere in East Africa to beat thieves [,] the
appellants cannot shelter behind the ... order of the
chief. It was not a lawful order which they were
bound to obey and they must have known as much."
On the other hand, s.52 of the 1960 Ghana Criminal Code
provides that "a person who intentionally causes the
death of another person by unlawful harm shall be guilty
only of manslaughter, and not of murder ... if ...
in causing the death, he acted on the belief, in good
faith and on reasonable grounds, that he was under a
legal duty to cause the death or to do the act which he
did..." Perhaps one of the most incongruous issues of
all is that of the 'crocodile man' in Nyasland whose
contractual arrangement to kill was recognized by the
native court in 1962, while the act carried out in
accordance with that arrangement was punished by the
ordinary criminal court.[13]

Occasionally, there have been instances when even the
foreign settler has been subjected to the local customary law. This happened in the Gold Coast in 1956
when it was held that a European father was liable to
maintain his child[14], for "there is a customary law in

this country that a father maintains his child. This
is the effect of the common law of this country. ...
I should be particularly reluctant to subscribe to the
view that in one country one law should exist for one
man and a different law for another, merely on a
question of race. To hold so would be a retrogressive
step in the law and the principles of natural justice
in this country." Some twenty years earlier, however,
Kingdon C.J., Gold Coast, had held[15] that "... where
one party is a native and one a non-native, the native
customary law only applies where it shall appear to the
Court that substantial injustice would be done to any
party by a strict adherence to the rules of any other
law. In other words, it is a condition precedent of
the application of the native customary law at all
that there would be substantial injustice if it were
not applied." While the Chief Justice apparently had
a predilection for non-native law, the Acting Justice
appears to have been completely unaware of the problem
of minority rights.

The clash between the two systems often becomes
evident when an issue affecting the public policy of
the ruler is involved. While the tendency in the period
of English settlement abroad was not to interfere with
local customs, this was only true when those customs
were not completely repugnant to English concepts of
morality and ordre public. Thus, although England
rejected any system of polygamous marriage and refused
to recognize as a marriage one that was performed in
accordance with the personal law of the parties if it
was potentially polygamous, it nevertheless continued
to recognize the right of Mohammedans living in India
to have more than one wife for their personal law - for
the settlers recognized that there was an established
system of law already in existence governing at least

the personal relations of the indigenous population at
the time of the British conquest - recognized polygamy.
On the other hand there was complete rejection of the
Hindu custom of <u>suttee</u>. The problem facing a judge
who is a member of a colonial legal service and whose
natural tendency is to look to the concepts of his own
system is illustrated by the comments of Wilson J. in
the Tanganyika High Court, which he insisted on describ-
ing as a British court. The case[16] concerned the
attachment of cattle, not belonging to the judgment
debtor, but to the debtor's father, on the ground that
this was in accordance with native customary law.
While the Subordinate Court had found this to be the case,
Wilson J. considered it doubtful, and asked whether,
even had this been so, "a British Court should be
guided by and should apply this native 'law' as part of
its own procedure," in accordance with the 1920 Order
in Council which recognized such native custom so
long as it was not repugnant to justice and morality:

As regards its applicability, I am not prepared to say
definitely that, other things being equal, the 'law'
in question would not be applicable to the present
circumstances, though in such matters one must be
mindful of the dangers and disadvantages of putting new
wine into old bottles.

But on the other question - as to whether the application
of the 'law' in question to the present case would be
'repugnant to justice and morality' - I hold more to
the present views, that I am far from unmindful of the
difficulty of construing the meaning of that phrase.
Morality and justice are abstract conceptions and every
community probably has an absolute standard of its own
by which to decide what is justice and what is
morality.[17] But unfortunately, the standards of
different communities are by no means the same. To what
standard, then, does the Order in Council refer - the
African standard of justice and morality or the British
standard? I have no doubt whatever that the only
standard of justice and morality which a British court
in Africa can apply is its own British standard.
Otherwise we should find ourselves in certain circumstances having to condone such things, for example,

as the institution of slavery.

On this basis, then, the justice of applying to the
present circumstances the native 'law' which has been
postulated in this case must be decided. Is it just
according to our ideas to take away a man's property
in order to compensate a party who has suffered injury
at the hands of the man's son, the son being of full
age and fully responsible in law for his own actions?
I hold most strongly the opinion that it is not just.

In Nigeria a somewhat similar attitude of superiority
was adopted in rejecting the native custom that the
wife who committed adultery became thereby the wife of
her paramour.[18] This rejection of a local practice
has about as much validity as the view adopted by the
Chief Justice of the Gold Coast in 1882[19] that for a
local custom to be accepted it must, "according to the
principles of English jurisprudence", date back to
1189, when 'time immemorial' begins at common law.
This decision was rejected some forty years later,[20]
perhaps in the light of Anguillia v. Ong Boon Tat[21]
in which it had been held only shortly before that such
a rule could never have operated in Singapore, since
"the history of Singapore began in 1819, more than
600 years after 1189, and that in itself concludes
the matter." In some cases, legislation has been
enacted making it clear that local customs do not
depend in any way upon the rules of English law.[22]

It has already been shewn that a judge sitting in a
colonial court has on occasion been prepared to apply
the native concept of law to the general population.[23]
A somewhat similar situation has arisen in Nigeria,
for it has been held[24] that Crown grants of land in
Lagos in English form and using English terms "do not
convey English titles or English rights of ownership",
but must be interpreted in accordance with local
indigenous law. This indicates a much more sensible

approach to the law than is to be found in _Leong_ v. _Lim Beng Chye_[25] when a restraint upon marriage effected by a Straits Chinese testator in Penang was construed by the Judicial Committee of the Privy Council in accordance with the rules applicable in England, partly on the ground that "the testator made the will in the English language, and employed in it forms and legal conceptions that are wholly derived from English law" - this is to ignore of course that the will was drafted by a practitioner who had been trained in England and called to the English bar, and was not spelled out by the testator _ipsissima verba_ at all.

Occasionally, a courageous judge has been prepared to disregard the general law and apply local custom, even when it would appear that by so doing he was going against the general law. Perhaps the best known practitioner in this field was Sissons J. in Canada's North West Territories when dealing with the Inuit (Eskimos),[26] although it might be argued that all he was doing was continuing along the path marked out by his predecessor Witman J., who had already decided as long ago as 1885[27] that Native marriages might be valid even though not contracted in forms recognized in England or prescribed by law.

The case that came before Sissons J. in 1962 was not directly concerned with the validity of a marriage. _Re Noah Estate_[28] turned on the application of the Northwest Territories Intestate Ordinance and this depended on whether the claimants were in fact the 'widow' and 'issue' of the deceased. To decide this, the Inuit marriage in question had to be examined to see whether it satisfied the conditions of a 'Christian' marriage as required by English law.[29] The suggestion that cohabitation and marriage in accordance with Inuit custom was mere concubinage was dismissed by the judge as

'fanciful and scandalous', since "marriage according
to Eskimo custom is not 'the Eskimo custom of concubinage'." Sissons J. considered that the Inuit system
of trial marriage was as separate from marriage proper
as is the Western system of 'engagement' or 'going
steady'. He pointed out that the relationship in
question complied

in every respect with the requirements of what was
known, according to the old law of England, as a
consensual marriage, that is formed or existing by
mere consent. The old law of England recognized a
consensual marriage. The general law of Europe
apparently also recognized a consensual marriage as
being in all respects perfect .... The Marriage
Ordinance has no provision stating that a native
marriage is invalid and no statement that a marriage
carried out on the basis of common law is null and
void. ... This Ordinance is misnamed. In spite of its
title, this is not a Marriage Ordinance but a
Solemnization of Marriage Ordinance .... I think there
was considerable solemnization of this marriage, even
if tinged with irregularity. The solemnization of an
Eskimo marriage follows pretty well that of the
Anglican Church, or rather the Anglican Church's
solemnization seems to follow that of the Eskimos. In
Christian countries marriage did not become a religious
ceremony before the ninth century, when newly-wed
couples began coming to the church door to have their
union blessed by the priest. The marriage had already
taken place and was generally a family and community
affair ...

as was the case with the instant marriage, where
everybody knew of the union and accepted it.

The marriage custom of the Society of Friends (Quakers)
seems very much like that of the Eskimos. The Friends
marry at a special meeting called for the occasion,
the only formality being a public declaration of the
marriage by the couple and the signing of a certificate
by all present as witnesses .... [As for the Intestate Succession Ordinance, t]his Ordinance does not
apply to Indians. The Indian Act has its own provisions
for intestate succession .... The rights and customs
of the Indians have not been completely ignored. They
have their treaties and their Indian Act, codifying

some at least of their rights and customs. The Eskimos
have no treaty. They have not given the covenant
appearing in the Indian treaties, whereby 'they promise
and engage that they will, in all respects, obey and
abide by the law'. They have no Eskimo Act ....
[T]hey have no one to represent them in Parliament.
They have no representation on the Territories Council
of the Northwest Territories. This Court must guard
their rights, when it can, and sometimes must write
upon a clean slate. While I think that generally the
Intestate Succession Ordinance has no application to
Eskimos, I think there are times and circumstances
when these provisions are applicable to an Eskimo
estate ...

and among such circumstances was the instant case

where the deceased had gone to live in white society

and had become part of that society and economy.

   A somewhat similar approach to a native 'marriage',

in this case an allegedly unrecognized union in Nigeria,

is to be found in the judgment of the Privy Council in

Bamgbose v. Daniel[30] which, like Noah, concerned

intestate succession. The deceased had been born of a

marriage contracted under the Lagos Marriage Ordinance,

1884, by which the disposable estate of an intestate

was distributed according to the laws of England, any

native law or custom to the contrary notwithstanding.

The deceased, who had died domiciled in Nigeria and

intestate, was alleged to have entered into nine

polygamous marriages in Nigeria in accordance with

native law and custom, and there was no suggestion

that he was incapable of so doing by his local law.

The appellant, a lawful nephew of the deceased claimed

to succeed to the whole estate, while the respondents

claiming as legitimate children born in Nigeria of the

polygamous marriages sought to exclude him. The

Judicial Committee pointed out that everything depended

on the direction that intestate distribution was to be

in accordance with the law of England, and

the relevant law of England in 1884 is to be found in
the Statute of Distributions, 1670 and the Act of
1685. ... The appellant's contention is that this
law precludes the succession on intestacy of children
or others who cannot claim kinship with the deceased
through monogamous marriage ....

The contention for the respondent children is that by
the law of their domicile of origin they are legitimate
children of the deceased and accordingly come within
the class of persons entitled to succeed under the
English Statute of Distributions. ...

Their Lordships would observe that no question can
arise as to the capacity of the deceased to enter into
polygamous marriage by his local law. He himself was
the child of a monogamous marriage, but that was no
impediment to his contracting a marriage by native law
and custom. ... If, then, the respondent children are
found to have been from birth legitimate children of
the deceased the only question with which their
Lordships are concerned is whether they are entitled to
share in the succession of the deceased under the
Statute of Distributions.

Their Lordships entertain little doubt that under what
are now well-accepted principles recognized by the
English courts, no grounds exist, in circumstances
like the present, for excluding the respondents from
taking their rights of succession if they are legitimate
children of the deceased under the law of their
domicile. ... [A]ll the circumstances concur to fix
Nigeria as the domicile of the parents, the place of
their marriages, and the place of birth of their
children ....

In their Lordships' opinion the West African Court of
Appeal upholding the claims of the children has
reached a right conclusion on the law applicable in
this case. In re Goodman's Trusts[31], on which that
court ... largely proceeded, ... held ... that a child
born in Holland, where her parents were at that time
domiciled, who had been legitimated under Dutch law by
the subsequent marriage of her parents there, was
entitled to share as a 'brother's child' under the
Statute of Distributions. ... [T]heir Lordships
cannot hold that the principle of this decision is
restricted to the case of monogamous marriage. Cotton
L.J. said: '... I am of opinion that if a child is
legitimate by the law of the country where at the time
of its birth its parents were domiciled, the law of
England, except in the case of succession to real
estate in England, recognizes and acts on the status

thus declared by the law of the domicile.' And James
L.J. said: 'It must be borne in mind that the Statute
of Distributions is not a statute for Englishmen only,
but for all persons, whether English or not, dying
intestate and domiciled in England, and not for any
Englishman dying domiciled abroad ... And as the law
applies universally to persons of all countries,
races, and religions whatsoever, the proper law to be
applied in determining kindred is the universal law,
the international law, adopted by the comity of
States. The child of a man would be his child so
ascertained and so determined.' ... ... [T]he Statute
of Distributions is a statute applying to a limited
class of persons domiciled in Nigeria ... [and] cannot
... be limited in its local application to children
who are the issue of monogamous unions. The effect
of the application of the statute in the cases to which
it applies is to fix the order of succession according
to a table different from that prevailing under
native law and custom, leaving it to the courts to
determine ... who are the particular individuals who
fall within any particular class in the succession
table.

It was contended for the appellant that the Statute of
Distributions could not be applied to polygamous unions
because of the difficulty of applying its provisions
to a plurality of wives ... [but] no claim had been
put forward ... by any person as a widow of the
deceased .... Whatever difficulties may arise in the
case of the mothers of the children, the claims of the
children as lawful children of the deceased must ...
be considered independently. This may be so in some
cases even in questions of status. In ... Khoo Hooi
Leong v. Khoo Hean Kwee[32], where the claim of a child
to be legitimate by the law of a community in which
polygamy was recognized and practised was considered,
Lord Phllimore [speaking for the Judicial Committee]
said: 'In deciding upon a case where the customs and
the laws are so different from British ideas a court
may do well to recollect that it is a possible jural
conception that a child may be legitimate, though its
parents were not and could not be legitimately
married. This principle was admitted by the canon law
which governed western continental Europe till about
a century ago and governed still later, if it does
not govern still, the countries of South America.' ...
[Moreover, i]n Seedat's Executor v. The Master (Natal)[33],
the Supreme Court of South Africa held ... that they
could not recognize as valid in Natal a polygamous
marriage of the deceased entered into in India before
he became domiciled in Natal, but that the children
of this marriage, who were all born in India while

112

their parents were domiciled there, were entitled to be treated as legitimate children. Accordingly, while the widow was not entitled to exemption in the matter of exemption duty but ... was liable to the rate appropriate to a stranger in blood, the rate of duty attributable to the children's share of the succession was held to be that borne by lawful children of a testator. ... It would be a strange result that ... where a marriage of the parents was recognized as valid the children should be deprived of their rights of succession because of a difficulty in working out the rights of the wife ....

In view of the dates of enactment of the relevant legislation, preceding the establishment of British rule in Nigeria, it might be argued that this case illustrates how unwise it is to introduce legislation extending to a native territory English law with regard to so technical a matter as the distribution of an estate on intestacy, particularly as this is so closely connected with the English ethos and social conditions. It might be possible to defend the application of these rules to the estate of an English settler or of an alien claiming in England, but there appears to be little ground for its extension to a locally domiciled Nigerian. While it is true that the Court construed the legislation in a way that upheld the claims of the deceased's children and may have been consistent with native ways and customs, it might easily have decided contrariwise. However, care must always be taken to ensure that when colonial judges think that they are applying native customs of marriage and concubinage, they do not in fact introduce conceptions that are unknown to the native system they purport to be interpreting, especially when their knowledge of the local language is rudimentary to say the least. This appears to have been what happened in Singapore in the Six Widows case[34] when, in their desire to uphold the principles of Victorian morality and the sanctity

of the marriage relationship, an unfortunate legacy
has been left which should, perhaps, never have been
bestowed.

Before leaving the issue of monogamy and the validity
of polygamous marriages, perhaps it might be worthwhile
to refer to <u>Melaksultan</u> v. <u>Sherali Jeraj</u> in which it
was necessary to consider English views on monogamy
in the light of the 1920 Tanganyika Order in Council
which extended English law 'subject to such qualifications as local circumstances may render necessary.'
Briggs J.A. said: "I cannot think that it would be a
reasonable application of the common law to the circumstances of this territory and its numerous Asian
inhabitants to refuse recognition of those marriages
which alone would accord with the requirements of
their personal law and religious beliefs, or to refuse
recognition of divorces which in accordance with such
personal law and religious beliefs would validly
determine such marriages." Concordant with this and
of perhaps equal importance is <u>Mawji</u> v. <u>The Queen</u>[36]
where problems concerning the status of the partners
to a polygamous marriage became important from the point
of view of the criminal law. By the Tanganyika Penal
Code conspiracy to obstruct the course of justice is
a misdemeanour, and by s.4 the Code is "to be interpreted in accordance with the principles of legal
interpretation obtaining in England, and expressions
used in it shall be presumed ... except as may be
otherwise expressly provided, to be used with the
meaning attached to them in English criminal law and
shall be construed in accordance therewith." The
appellants were Shia Mohammedans living together in a
matrimonial home under conditions similar to a monogamous union, although the marriage was potentially
polygamous. Both the High Court and the Court of Appeal

for Eastern Africa agreed with the magistrate that the
rule of English law that husband and wife were one and
so could not be guilty of conspiracy did not apply to
a potentially polygamous union. The Judicial Committee
of the Privy Council disagreed:

... [T]he rule is an example of the fiction that
husband and wife are regarded for certain purposes,
of which this is one, as in law one person. Some of
the consequences of the fiction have been removed or
modified by statute. In the criminal law of Tanganyika
the words husband and wife if unqualified are not
restricted to monogamous unions. If it is desired to
deal with monogamous as distinct from other marriages
express words are used ....

It is clear, of course, that the marriages primarily
contemplated by the rule in England were monogamous
marriages, but the rule being now part of the criminal
law of Tanganyika, their Lordships are of opinion that
it applies to any husband and wife of a marriage valid
under Tanganyika law.

It was submitted for the respondent that the rule
could not apply to the appellants unless it would apply
to them if the alleged conspiracy had taken place in
this country. Their Lordships do not accept this
submission. Potentially polygamous marriages have been
recognized for various purposes in this country ....
It may be that such a marriage would be recognized
for the purpose of this rule. Their Lordships express
no opinion on that point. The rule plainly applies
here at least to marriages recognized as fully valid,
and it should therefore apply in Tanganyika to marriages
recognized as fully valid there. It was not suggested
that the appellants' marriage was not in this category...

The need to recognize potentially strange jural
conceptions because of basic deviations from the British
way of life is to be seen in the memoirs of Austin
Coates, a former Special Magistrate in Hong Kong who
never qualified legally and perhaps, therefore, found
it comparatively simple to apply rough justice in
accordance with local Chinese custom and predilections[37].
In fact, there may be much to be said for appointing

non-home trained personnel or non-lawyers to deal with
issues among 'primitive' peoples, for even though the
'case' may appear as a formal legal process, the person
hearing it has often to act as a 'Dutch uncle' or a
mediator rather than a judge. Such mediation is likely
to be far more successful if the officer involved is
aware of or amenable to native susceptibilities,
reactions and habits. Such is in fact sometimes the
case in New Guinea where native 'specialists' may
serve as local court magistrates.[38]

As long ago as 1919 Lord Sumner recognized the need
to acknowledge the existence of native institutions
of law and the limitations inherent in seeking to
impose 'civilized' law upon 'primitive' peoples[39]:

The estimation of the rights of aboriginal peoples is
always inherently difficult. Some tribes are so low
in the scale of social organization that their usages
and conceptions of rights and duties are not to be
reconciled with the institutions or the legal ideas
of civilized society. Such a gulf cannot be bridged.
It would be idle to impute to such people some shadow
of the rights known to our law and then to transmute it
into the substance of [e.g.] transferable rights of
property as we know them .... On the other hand,
there are indigenous peoples whose legal conceptions,
though differently developed are hardly less precise
than our own. When once they have been studied and
understood they are no less enforceable than rights
arising under English law.

Unfortunately, however, judges from the colonial powers
or from among settlers who have become the establishment are rarely prepared to study or understand such
local legal systems.

On the other hand, recent trends in the recognition
by the law of the significance of psychology have often
resulted in local judges taking a special - and often
more lenient - view of the law when a 'primitive' is

involved.[40] Evidence of this is to be found in a wide variety of jurisdictions. Thus, in 1951 the Appellate Division of the South African Supreme Court heard the appeal of Mrs. Mkize[41] who had been found guilty of murder, having placed arsenic, which she believed to be a love potion, in her husband's beer. In substituting a finding of culpable homicide for the murder conviction, the Court stated:

The belief which the accused says she had in the results of administering the potion ... may appear to educated minds to be absurd but it must be borne in mind that the accused is an illiterate native woman living in a native kraal and that it is well known that Natives genuinely believe in magic and witchcraft.

The question of native beliefs was equally important in an earlier case in which a murder verdict had been reduced to culpable homicide. Some Native children thought they had seen a tikoloshe in a hut, and since it would be fatal for humans to look such an evil spirit in the face they summoned the accused, a Native youth of 18, to deal with it. Like them, he thought it was a tikoloshe and struck it with a hatchet. When he dragged the 'tikoloshe' from the hut, he found that he had killed his nephew who had been sleeping there. In the course of its judgment, the Appellate Division held[42] that the standard of reasonableness in such a case was "not that of an ordinary 18-year-old native living at home in his kraal, but that of a reasonable person of his age."[43]

A somewhat more reasonable approach to the idea of legal reasonableness has been adopted by judges dealing with Papuan Natives and Australian aborigines. It is a well-established rule of 'civilized' law that words alone are not sufficient to ground a defence based on provocation. However, judges in Papua and New Guinea

have not been hesitant in adopting a more lenient
approach, recognizing that the standards demanded from
sophisticated inhabitants of the western world cannot
be expected from less sophisticated native communities,
where the words provoking the violence have constituted
an insult "calculated and not infrequently intended to
throw a man into an ungovernable rage".[44] In other
words, what is necessary in such circumstances is to
construe as the 'reasonable man' not 'the man on the
Clapham omnibus', but "the ordinary native living
the rural life of low standard led by the accused and
his relatives .... The man in the lap lap takes the
place of the man on the Clapham omnibus."[45]

   Perhaps one of the most enlightened judgments in this
field is that of Bright J. of South Australia in
R. v. Gibson, 1973.[39] The accused, an aborigine
living on the Yalata reserve, was charged with killing
another aborigine, and as soon as the case came for
trial the judge was faced with a problem that is more
likely to affect 'primitive' rather than 'civilized'
defendants. It was argued on behalf of the defendant
that the case concerned 'men's secrets' and therefore
no woman should be allowed on the jury or in the court-
room, for if any were present witnesses would refuse
to give evidence and the defendant would be denied the
opportunity of a fair trial. This request was acceded
to by the learned judge, and one cannot help but wonder
what might have happened in a similar case in Canada
affecting an Indian or an Inuk in view of the Bill of
Rights and the ban on discrimination against women -
although it must be remembered that a Canadian judge
has the right to order a hearing in camera if he
considers that justice so demands. The killing arose
out of a quarrel occasioned by insulting remarks
concerning aboriginal circumcision at a time when both

the deceased and the accused were somewhat the worse for liquor. During his judgment, Bright J. soon made it clear that he was aware of the peculiar problems confronting him because aborigines were involved, for one of the preliminary issues related to the accused's statement to the police. It was pleaded that Natives tended to say what they thought the authorities wished them to say, and while the judge agreed

... that there is a distinction to be made between white persons who have been brought up in the concepts of society and ideas (including the idea of independence of authority) prevalent in Europe and Australia on the one hand, and indigenous persons who not only have a limited command of English but whose whole culture differs radically from the white culture ,... and if the accused had been able to express his state of mind he might have said, 'Yes, I know that you have told me that I don't have to answer, but I am an uneducated black man from my tribe and you are white men in authority over me and I am frightened of you; so when you ask me a question I answer you because I can't exercise my right to keep silent when people like you ask me questions.'

[But i]f I were to exclude the statement on that ground I should be creating a different law for Aborigines from the law applicable to white men. And I should be overlooking the fact that many white accused persons who are cautioned are ignorant, simple minded and scared....

In the course of his address to the jury, Bright J. constantly indicated his awareness that the accused was an Aborigine:

The accused, like the deceased, is a member of the Pitjantjajara tribe living in a tribal environment. From the foundation of the Province of South Australia black people and white people have lived under the same laws of the country. The tribesman is more immediately aware of the laws of the tribe which preserve his culture and ensure his survival in the arid conditions of outback Australia. In the same way a nun in a convent may be more aware of the laws of the convent. I must hasten to add that I should regard a

nun as being much less remote from the general white
culture than a Pitjantjajara tribesman. Perhaps it
is unnecessary for me to add that I am in no way
talking of relative intelligence. Indeed, I do not know
what is the measure of intelligence. If it be an
ability to survive and to thrive in the environment
in which one finds oneself, and I would think that this
is the proper test, then the Pitjantjajara Aboriginal
displays an ability to do both, according to his own
lights, in his own environment. I am not prepared
to say that white persons in general, display a greater
ability to thrive according to white concepts in a
white environment than black persons, in general, do
according to black concepts in theirs. In each case
one must apply not absolute standards but standards
of achievement capable of attainment in the particular
environment.

..What the rules of a convent or a tribe may do by way
of retribution to a member who broke the criminal law
is no concern of ours at present. ... A nun might
be shocked more readily and more deeply than many members   of the general public by a blaspheming of the
Christian faith. And a tribesman would be more shocked,
disturbed and aroused by an improper disclosure of the
sacred mysteries of tribal lore than you or I would
be. The law is not foolish. It takes account of these
matters. ... We shall often have more difficulty in
understanding black men's ways than white men's ways
for we are ignorant in these matters. ...

Your task is to determine whether it is reasonably
possible that a tribal Aboriginal who took a reasonable
view of the matter - if you like, a reasonable tribal
Aboriginal - might have been so provoked by the things
that the deceased said and did, that when he struck ...
the deceased he was so carried away that he was not the
master of his mind but had lost control of himself,
that at the most. he is guilty of manslaughter. ...

... It is true that the blows were heavy, but we are
not dealing with dainty members of society. We are
considering tribal Aborigines living in the desert...

...[H]e had been provoked by violence himself and by
the insulting and terrifying use of ritual references.
These ritual references, if he heard them without
protest, might expose him to punishment, and punishment
in the tribe might go as far as death.

... Not every form of provocation is of effect in the
criminal law. The provocation is usually said to be
such as would cause a reasonable man to lose control

of himself. Where tribal lore in a tribal setting is
improperly referred to by an initiated tribesman to an
uninitiated tribesman <u>it is useless to think of a</u>
<u>reasonable white man. One must think of a reasonable</u>
<u>man having the awareness, the timidity, the ordinary</u>
<u>reactions of a Pitjantjajara tribesman, viewing the tribe</u>
<u>as a social group and the accused as a member of the</u>
<u>group</u>. . . .

<u>In fine</u>, the jury found the accused not guilty of
murder or manslaughter.

Even when courts in 'civilized' countries have had
to deal with 'primitive' people, not aboriginals or
other indigenous groups, but alien persons coming from
less sophisticated cultures, they have in recent years
adopted a more reasonable attitude than was formerly
the case. Marriage is probably as good an example as
any to take, and these cases differ from the marriage
cases already considered in that a court is now being
called upon to recognize as a marriage a union that has
been entered into under some alien system of law which
is recognized as valid by that system, notwithstanding
that it runs counter to principles of local public
policy. The earlier cases, on the other hand, were
concerned with marriages which were, for the main part,
entered into locally. The general rule of the common
law is that marriage as understood by Christendom is
monogamous,[47] although in Canada this seems not to have
been the case, at least in so far as Indian marriages
were concerned, for as was pointed out by Monk J. in
<u>Jones</u> v. <u>Fraser</u>[48]

It has been said that polygamy existed among the
Indian tribes of the North-West and that the marriage
invoked by the respondent could not therefore be
supposed to possess the character required for marriage
in all Christian countries, that is unity and perpet-
uity. ... [P]olygamy did not exist as a rule among
those who married Indian women, but only among the
Indian tribes. A marriage which took place there
according to the local usage was considered as an

ordinary marriage.

Today, even jurisdictions which applied _Hyde_ rigorously have moved away from so narrow an approach. An example is _Ochochuku_ v. _Ochochuku_[49]. The parties, though Christians, had entered into a marriage in accordance with Native custom in 1949 in Nigeria, at which time Nigeria permitted polygamy. While in England they went through a register office marriage and subsequently the wife sued for divorce, which was granted. However,

> Whatever might be the effect on the marriage for other purposes and in other courts of the parties being Christians, in this Court and for this purpose the Nigerian marriage must be regarded as a polygamous marriage over which this court does not exercise Jurisdiction. I therefore pronounce a decree nisi for the dissolution not of the Nigerian marriage but of the marriage in London. I am told that, in fact, that will be effective by Nigerian law to dissolve the Nigerian marriage, but that forms no part of my judgment. That is for someone else to determine and not for me.

By 1968 the English courts were adopting a far more liberal attitude to unions which were valid according to the law of the domicile of the parties at the time of the marriage, not only recognizing potentially polygamous marriages, but even those where one of the parties was under age and where, if there had not been a valid marriage, the male partner would have been guilty of a criminal offence by virtue of his having had sexual relations with an 'infant' whom he claimed was his wife. This was the situation in _Mohamed_ v. _Knott_,[50] the 'marriage' in question having taken place in Nigeria at a time when the girl was only 13. An attempt had been made to place the 'wife' under a protection order, but the Lord Chief Justice pointed out that the relationship was not to be considered by "the reactions of an Englishman regarding an English man and woman in the western way of life." He was of opinion that,

recognizing the background and the way in which the
parties had been brought up, a 'decent Englishman'
would consider the relationship to be repugnant. In
his view this was a foreign marriage recognized in
England, and since "intercourse between a man and wife
was lawful, ... where a husband and wife were recognized as validly married according to the laws of
England, he would not say that the wife was exposed to
moral danger because she carried out her wifely
duties," nor the husband exposed to the rigours of the
criminal law for exercising his marital rights. If
this decision is followed and rendered any more liberal,
it would seem that the English courts have, in so far
as concerns marriages valid according to the law of the
domicile of the parties, abandoned the view that local
rules of public policy and morality are to be the
deciding factor.

Within the last ten years or so a new issue as between
'civilized' law and 'primitive' people has arisen in
some countries possessing indigenous populations. This
concerns the meaning of the relationship established
between the original inhabitants and the invaders on
the basis of treaties drawn up between them. This is
not the place to discuss whether these documents are
'treaties' in the technical sense of that term or what
their exact legal significance and import may be.[51]
What is important, however, is that these documents
were drafted by sophisticated lawyers operating within
their own legal _milieu_ and that the terms they used
were the technical terms known to them and probably
impossible of translation into the language of the
aboriginals with whom they were negotiating. This is
largely true whether the invaders were government
spokesmen or the representatives of such trading
companies as the British and Dutch East India Companies

or the Hudson Bay Company, or whether the Natives with
whom they were dealing were North American Indians,
Malay or east Indian princes, Australian Aborigines,
Javanese or Sumatrans, or New Zealand Maoris. In
none of these cases could it be said that the parties
were operating on a basis of true equality, and it is
doubtful whether the Native negotiators were at any
time really ad idem with the westerners. Problems
therefore arise with regard to the true meaning of
these documents which were held out to be legally
binding arrangements and requiring legal interpretation. Recognition of this fact is to be found in the
judgment of the United States Supreme Court at the end
of the nineteenth century, when Justice Gray commented:[52]

in construing any treaty between the United States and
an Indian tribe, it must always ... be borne in mind
that the negotiations for the treaty are conducted on
the part of the United States, an enlightened and
powerful nation, by representatives skilled in diplomacy,
masters of a written language, understanding the modes
and forms of creating the various estates known to their
law, and assisted by an interpreter employed by themselves; that the Indians, on the other hand, are a
weak and dependent people, who have no written language
and are unfamiliar with all the forms of legal expression, and whose only knowledge of the terms in which the
treaty is framed is that imparted to them by the United
States; the treaty must therefore be construed not
according to the technical meaning of the words to
learned lawyers, but in the sense in which they
would naturally be understood by the Indians.

When looking at the treaties made with the Canadian
Indians it is equally necessary to bear this comment
in mind, particularly in the light of the historical
background of the treaties. Thus, in a despatch relating
to the North-West Angle Treaty negotiations, 1873,
Lieutenant-Governor Morris reported[53] that

the principal [Indian] spokesman, Mawedopenais, came
forward and drew off his gloves, and spoke as follows:
'Now you see me stand before you all. What has been

124

done here today, has been done openly before the Great
Spirit, and before the nation, and I hope that I may
never hear any one say that this treaty has been done
secretly. And now, in closing this council, I take
off my glove, and in giving you my hand, I deliver over
my birthright, and lands, and in taking your hand I
hold fast all the promises you have made, and I hope
they will last as long as the sun goes round, and the
water flows, as you have said.' To which I replied as
follows: 'I accept you hand, and with it the lands,
and will keep all my promises, in the firm belief that
the treaty now to be signed will bind the red man and
the white man together as friends forever.'

The Manitoban, in reporting the meeting, stated[54] that
Morris also told the Indians:

You ought to see by what the Queen is offering you
that she loves her red subjects as much as her white...
[T]hat which I offer you is to be while the water flows
and the sun rises. You know that in the United States
they only pay the Indians for twenty years ....
I only ask you to think for yourselves, and for your
families, and for your children and children's children.

Again, when negotiating with the Cree at Forts
Carlton and Pitt,[55] Morris gave assurances:

I told you that what I was promising was not for today
or tomorrow only, but should continue as long as the
sun shone and the river flowed. My words will pass
away and so will yours, so I always write down what I
promise, that our children may know what we said and
did. Next year I will send copies of what is written
in the treaty, printed on skin, so that it cannot run
out or be destroyed, and one shall be given to each
Chief so that there may be no mistakes.

This was also the understanding of the Indians, as is
shown by the comment of Chief Mis-tah-wah-sis:

What we speak of and do now will last as long as the sun
shines and the river runs, we are looking forward to
our children's children, for we are old and we have but
few days to live.

Apparently not all the agreements were made in this
way, at least in the case of British Columbia:

The practice was to pay the Indians the purchase price
against their signature by mark on blank paper to be
filled in later as a deed. In 1854 the Saalequun tribe
so surrendered their lands on Commercial Inlet, 12
miles up the Nanaimo River. For that surrender no
deed was made up but the signatures or marks were
obtained on blank paper against payment.[56]

Recognizing the disproportionate relationship between
the parties and the peculiarities of language used, as
well as the need to uphold the dignity of the Crown in
whose name these arrangements were made, Canadian
judges have, for the main part, accepted the need for a
uberrima fides interpretation of the rights of the
Indians under these treaties. Thus, when holding that
the Alberta Game Act did not interfere with the right
to hunt embodied in the relevant treaty, McGillavray
J.A. held[57] that the latter must be interpreted:

with the exactness which honour and good conscience
dictate .... It is satisfactory to be able to come to
this conclusion and not to have to decide that 'the
Queen's promises' have not been fulfilled. It is
satisfactory to think that the legislators have not
so enacted but that the Indians may still be 'convinced
of our justice and determined resolution to remove all
reasonable cause of discontent'

as stipulated in the Royal Proclamation of 1763[58]
guaranteeing their rights against encroachment.

A somewhat similar approach is to be found in a
judgment of Patterson (Ag) co. Ct. J. :[59]

... Having called the agreement a treaty, and having
perhaps lulled the Indians into believing it to be a
treaty with all the sacredness of a treaty attached
to it, it may be the Crown should not now be heard to
say it is not a treaty. ... That is a matter for
representations to the proper authorities - representations which ... could hardly fail to be successful.

This view, however, may be regarded as somewhat sanguine,
for in 1964 when construing Morris's promises and

126

their interminability, McGillavray J.A. said that at the time of drafting the legislation being interpreted, and which was alleged to be inconsistent with treaty promises, it appeared "likely that these obligations under the treaties were overlooked."[60]

There can be little doubt that the legislative body of any of the countries alleged to be bound by such treaties is competent to pass legislation abrogating, controverting or disregarding these alleged undertakings. However, it should be borne in mind that equity and morality demand a modicum of good faith even, or perhaps especially, in the relations between 'civilized' and 'primitive' peoples. Moreover, the political framework of the present era suggests that one can no longer ride roughshod over the rights of people and that aborigines have their rights as well as others. Moreover, there are plenty of bodies, some truly altruistic and others perhaps with an ideological axe to grind, who will publicize what they consider to be disregard or abuse of such rights. However, there is a limit to the extent to which modern and newly discovered or invented rights can be used in order to interpret documents and undertakings that were entered into before such concepts were even dreamed of. This is true of, for example, aboriginal rights in the sense of continued ownership or independence and self-determination.[61]

It is perhaps inevitable that difficulties and controversies arise when a 'civilized' system of law attempts to deal with the problems, rights and status of 'primitive' peoples, and it may well be that complete elimination of such confrontation is beyond human reach. However, it may be possible to reduce the contretemps and effect a more congenial modus vivendi.

In so far as arrangements like treaties are concerned, an attempt should be made on both the political and judicial level to recognize the extent to which the 'primitives' were misled into certain beliefs and the 'civilized' took advantage of those beliefs. So far as possible the arrangements should be interpreted in the sense in which the 'primitives' were led to understand them and, in accordance with the principle of normal interpretation, contra proferentem the party responsible for putting forward the particular terms or holding out particular promises. When a legislature wishes to abandon its undertakings towards the 'primitives' and effect a state of affairs which appears to be contrary to the anticipations of those 'primitives', care should be taken to ensure that these people are not given the impression that their rights are being disregarded under the guise of 'civilized' legality. Effort should be exercised to ensure that the reason for change is fully explained, some quid pro quo extended, and the participation of the representatives of the 'primitives' arranged for.

In so far as the situation relates to the judicial application of 'civilized' law, it is perhaps time that we start teaching the magistrates who will be called upon to judge such cases some of the folk lore and folkways of the people concerned. It might also be wise to encourage the use of mediators rather than judges. Perhaps, best of all would be to encourage members of the 'primitive' community to make themselves acquainted with the requirements of the 'civilized' system of law and enable them to qualify for judicial office or appointment as mediators, recognizing that they will be called upon to temper this 'black letter' law with an equitable understanding of native needs. There is not really any reason why even a sophisticated society should not be willing to recognize the special needs of a particular group, in much the same way as customs of a particular trade are recognized and accepted. It is all very well to say that the law must be obeyed and its grandeur upheld. To do this, however, sometimes entails injustice and denial of the rule of law. Writing in 1851, John Ruskin said:[62]

All things are literally better, lovelier, and more beloved for the imperfections which have been divinely appointed, that the law of human life may be Effort, and the law of human judgment, Mercy.

* Based on a paper delivered at the Christmas 1973 Conference of the Western Association of Anthropologists and Sociologists.

1 The Times (London) 16, 17 July 1974.

2 See, e.g., Cheng, General Principles of Law as applied by International Courts and Tribunals, 1953; Herczegh, General Principles of Law and the International Legal Order, 1969.

3 See, e.g., II above.

4 1. Blackstone, Commentaries on the Laws of England, 10th ed., 1787, p. 108, see II above, n.3.

5 (1917) 38 D.L.R. 601, 610.

6 Daywood v. Carlson, 30 Am. and Eng. Ann. Cases 1223.

7 (1933) Series AB, No. 53, 47.

8 Tabitha Chiduka v. Chidano 1922 S.R. 55, 56.

9 5 Halsbury, Laws of England, 3rd (Simonds) ed. (1953) 693, c. Calvin's Case (1608) 7 Co. Rep. 1a, 17.

10 See e.g., Worcester v. Georgia (1832) 6 Pet. 515, 542; Ex parte Crow Dog (1883) 109 U.S. 556; 18 U.S.C.A. sec. 548 (II above, nn. 5, 6, 7).

11 Halsbury, op.cit., 695.

12 [1965] E.A. 667, 670.

13 See II above, n.67.

14 Adjei and Dua v. Ripley (1956) 1 W.A.L.R. 63, per
    Smith Ag.J.

15 Konty v. U.T.C. (1934) 2 W.A.C.A. 188, 191.

16 Gwao bin Kilimo v. Kisunda bin Ifuti (1938)
    1 T.L.R. (R.) 403.

17 See II above.

18 Joshua Ghawere v. Hannah Aihenu 12 N.L.R. 4.

19 Welbeck v. Brown (1882) Sar. F.C.L. 172.

20 Mensah v. Winabob (1925) Div.Ct.Judgments 1921-5,
    172.
21 (1921) 15 S.S.L.R. 190, 193.

22 E.G., New Guinea, Native Custom (Recognition)
    Ordinance, 1963, s.4.

23 Adjei and Dua v. Ripley, n.14 above.

24 Oyekan v. Adele [1957] 1 W.L.R. 876.

25 [1955] A.C. 648, 665 (see II above, n. 89).

26 See his Judge of the Far North (1968).

27 Reg. v. Nan-E-Quis-A-Ke (1885) 1 Terr.L.R. 211
    (see II above, n.60).

28 (1962) 32 D.L.R. (2d) 185, 197-8, 199, 200, 203,
    205-6 (It was in connection with this case that
    Sissons J. is alleged to have said: "I am not
    going to have a lot of bastards in Ottawa tell me
    that my people here are a lot of bastards").

29 It may perhaps be not irrelevant to point out that
    Mrs. Adesanya, the defendant mentioned in n.1 above,
    was formerly a Muslim who had become a Christian.

30 [1955] A.C. 107, 115, 116-7, 118-20, per Lord Keith
    of Avenholm.

31 (1881) 17 Ch,D. 266, 292, 300.

32 [1926] A.C. 529, 543.

33 [1917] S.A.L.R. (A.D.) 302.

34 (1888) 12 S.S.L.R. 120 (see II above, nn.52 et seqq.).

35 [1955] E.A.C.A. 142, 148.

36 [1957] A.C.126, 135-6, per Lord Somervell of Harrow.

37 Myself a Mandarin (1968), esp. 22-5, 204-12.

38 Joana-Vapor v. Anton Susami and Agnes-Daporobu (1967 - c. Brown, Fashion of Law in New Guinea (1960), 209; see II above, n.96).

39 In re Southern Nigeria [1919] A.C. 211, 233-4.

40 See, e.g., n. 1 above.

41 R. v. Mkize [1951] (3) S.A.28 (A.D.)33, per Centlivres C.J.

42 R. v. Mbombela [1933] A.D.269, at 271 (per de Villiers J.A.).

43 For consideration of the concept of the 'reasonable man' in relation to the armed forces, see Green, 'Superior Orders and the Reasonable Man', 8 Can.Y.B. Int. Law (1970), 61.

44 R. v. Awabe (1960 - unreported, c. Hookey, 'The "Clapham Omnibus" in New Guinea', in Brown,op.cit., n.38 above, 117, 126; see also R. v. Zariai-Gavene [1963] P. & N.G.L.R. 203; see II above, nn.80, 81).

45 R. v. Rumints-Gorok [1973] P. & N.G.L.R. 81,83.

46 Judgment No.1810, delivered 12 Nov. 1973 - the writer is indebted to Bright J. for having supplied him with a transcript of the judgment (italics added).

47 Hyde v. Hyde (1886) L.R. 1 P.& D. 130.

48 (1886) 12 Q.L.R. 327, 335. See also his decision in Connolly v. Woolrich (1867) Lower Can.Jur.197, and Bartholomew, 'Recognition of Polygamous Marriages in Canada',(1951) 10 Int.& Comp.Law Q. 305. See, also, Kaur v. Ginder (1958) 13 D.L.R.(2d)465 in which the court upheld a valid polygamous marriage in India by an east Indian domiciled in British Columbia to an Indian woman domiciled in India, as barring a subsequent monogamous marriage.

49 [1960] 1 W.L.R. 183,at 185 (per Wrangham J.). See, also, Hartley,'Polygamy and Social Policy',32 Modern Law Rev (1969) 155.

50 [1968] 2 W.L.R.1446,1457 (See I above, n.44,II, n.59).

51 See Green, 'The Legal Significance of Canada's Indian Treaties', 1 Anglo-American Law Rev. (1972), 119.

52 Jones v. Meehan (1899) 175 U.S. 1 at 11.

53 Morris, The Treaties of Canada with the Indians (1880 - reprinted 1971), 51.

54 18 Oct. 1873 (c., ibid., 61).

55 Op.cit., 208, 213.

56 R. v. White and Bob (1964) 50 D.L.R. (2d) 513, 622, per Sheppard J.A.

57 R. v. Wesley [1932] 2 W.W.R. 65, 69-70.

58 R.S.C. 1970, App. II, No. 1.

59 R. v. Syliboy [1929] 1 D.L.R. 307, 313-4.

60 R. v. Sikeya (1964) 46 W.W.R. 65, 69-70.

61 See, e.g., Green, 'Tribal Rights and Equal Rights', 'Aboriginal Rights or Vested Rights', 22 Chitty's Law Journal (1974), 97, 219, resp.

62 The Stones of Venice, vol. 2, ch. 6, s. 25.

IV

IS INTERNATIONAL LAW LAW?

International Law is that thing which the evil
ignore and the righteous refuse to enforce.
(Leon Uris, Exodus).

One of the most frequent assertions made among lawyers
who are not specialists in the field is that there is
no such thing as international law. Then, remembering
their background as civil lawyers, they fall back on
the "rolled-up plea" and assert that even if there is
such a thing, it is not law and is wrongly described
as such. It is not only the lawyers, however, who
regard international law as something of a pretence.
The man on the Clapham omnibus, too, in so far as he
thinks about the subject at all, tends to regard international law as something that statesmen talk about,
but which none of them has any intention of regarding,
a view which is not far removed from that of the character in Leon Uris's Exodus who described international
law as a thing which the evil ignored and which the
righteous refused to enforce.

The blame for the development of such attitudes
may, largely, be placed at the door of international
lawyers themselves. Too many of them, accepting the
"academic" nature of their subject, have adopted for
themselves an egocentric ipse-dixitism that may have
served their own ideas of self-aggrandizement, but that
has done nothing but harm to the subject they profess
to serve. There is a tendency for such "authorities"

to postulate a principle as law, and to maintain it is such regardless of evidence that states in their practice have consistently behaved in a contrary fashion, without any allegations being made that such conduct constitutes a breach of the law.

As an example of this type of reasoning reference may be made to what is recognized as one of the leading works in the English language in the field of international law. In the first edition of Oppenheim,[1] it is stated that "a Federal State is a perpetual union of several Sovereign States which has organs of its own and is invested with a power, not only over the member-States, but also over their citizens. The union is based, first, on an international treaty of the member-States, and, secondly, on a subsequently accepted constitution of the Federal State." The learned author listed the United States, Switzerland, Germany, Mexico, the Argentine, Brazil, and Venezuela as the federal states then in existence. In the eighth edition of the same work (1955, s.89) these two sentences are preserved in toto, although Australia, the Soviet Union, Pakistan, India, and Indonesia have been added to the list of the "principal" federal states. At no time is it conceded that any of these federations was born in a way different from that indicated, or that the method of birth given might not be the only creative process in so far as federations are concerned. A casual glance at Table II of the 2nd edition of Peaslee's Constitutions of Nations[2] indicates that the list is far from complete, and that Oppenheim's comments would hardly apply to, for example, Austria, Burma, Libya, Malaya, South Africa, Viet Nam, Western Germany, or Yugoslavia. The revised and enlarged edition of the third edition contains no such table, but an examination of the texts shows that Oppenheim's statement has become even more unreal.

Another and even more glaring example from the same
author refers to the problem of superior orders as a
defence to a charge of war crimes. In his first edition
Oppenheim stated: "Violations of rules regarding warfare are war crimes only when committed without an order
of the belligerent Government concerned. If members
of the armed forces commit violations by order of their
Government, they are not war criminals, and may not be
punished by the enemy."[3] These words are repeated in
every edition until the fifth (1935), which was the last
to appear before the outbreak of the Second World War.
From the third edition (1921) on, a note appears which
recognizes that "the contrary is sometimes asserted.
But ... the law cannot require an individual to be
punished for an act which he was compelled by law to
commit." Although the German Supreme Court in the
Llandovery Castle[4] expressly rejected the plea as a
defence when the act was clearly contrary to international law, it was not until the fifth edition that
any of Oppenheim's editors mentioned it, and then the
case is only added to the footnote as part of the
evidence put forward to the contrary.

None of the pre-war editions of Oppenheim refers to
past practice in so far as the defence is concerned.
As long ago as 1474, at the trial of Peter of Hagenbach,[5]
the defence was expressly rejected in a war crimes
trial. During the trials of the regicides after the
restoration of Charles II it was pointed out that an
order to participate in the execution of one's king
could never be a legal order and provide a defence to
a charge of treason.[6] In so far as war crimes are
concerned, the defence had been invoked at least twice
before the decision in the Llandovery Castle. In the
Trial of Wirz[7] - the so-called Andersonville trial -
the defence was rejected when put forward by the

commandant of a Confederate prisoner-of-war camp charged with responsibility for ill-treating some 30,000 Federal prisoners, of whom about 10,000 died. On the other hand, during the Boer War the defence was recognized in R. v. Smith.[8] Solomon J. pointed out, however, that "it is monstrous to suppose that a soldier would be protected where the order was grossly illegal." During the First World War French courts consistently disregarded the plea when put forward by German prisoners of war.

None of this evidence had any effect on the views of Oppenheim or his pre-war editors. In the sixth edition, revised, which appeared in 1944, an entirely different view of the position is to be found for the first time:

> ... the fact that a rule of warfare has been violated in pursuance of an order of the belligerent Government or of an individual belligerent commander does not deprive the act in question of its character as a war crime; neither does it, in principle, confer upon the perpetrator immunity from punishment by the injured belligerent. ... The question is governed by the major principle that members of the armed forces are bound to obey lawful orders only and that they cannot therefore escape liability if, in obedience to a command, they commit acts which both violate unchallenged rules of warfare and outrage the general sense of humanity.[9]

The decision in the Llandovery Castle is cited in support of this latter statement, while the argument in favour of superior orders as a defence is dealt with as summarily as was the opposite view in earlier editions: "A different view has occasionally been adopted ... by writers [fn.: See, e.g. s. 253 of the previous editions of this volume.], but it is difficult to regard it as expressing a sound legal principle".[10]

It is this type of attitude that is criticized by C.C. Hyde in the Foreword to his study of the practice of the United States in international law.

To mirror the views of his own country on international law is the chief endeavour of the author .... In the course of so doing he has been forced to observe how States act, and may be expected to act, under certain conditions that confront them; how fantastic and unscientific are statements or conclusions which ignore such expectations or probabilities; and how unconvincing it is to the layman to hear proclaimed as the law rules which States under certain well-defined circumstances may be expected habitually to ignore. Such proclamations suggestive of preachments of what States should or should not do, shed little light on what they may at the time accept as correct standards of conduct to be respected as such. The thing to which they ascribe the quality of law contrasts sharply with a body of principles serving in fact to regulate inter-State conduct; it projects itself rather as a detached collection of precepts variously expressed, reflecting, moreover, no oneness of thought, and impervious to the possible contempt of States for what is laid down.[11]

More recently, a somewhat similar view has been expressed in more behavioural terms:

... the critics of 'law' who use the word to refer merely to authoritative rules or formal doctrine, policy crystallizations of the past, and who focus too sharply upon naked force as sanction may conceal from both themselves and others the true nature of the decision-making process. It is not suggested that past authoritative formulations of policy do not greatly influence decision-makers. Such formulations play varying roles in the perspectives of decision-makers and it is only rational for present decision-makers to seek guidance from the experience of their predecessors. Decision-making is also forward-looking, however, and decision-makers respond in fact not alone to prior prescriptions but to a great many environmental and predispositioned variables, including doctrines which formulate the effects of alternative decisions upon the groups which they represent or with which they identify and which state objectives and policies for the future. The process of decision-making is indeed ... one of continued redefinition of doctrine in its application to ever-changing facts and claims. A conception of law which focuses upon doctrine to the exclusion of the pattern of practices by which it is given meaning and made effective is, therefore, not the most conducive to understanding. It may be emphasized, further, that official decision-makers, the people who have formal authority and are expected to make important

decisions, may or may not make the decisions in fact.
Effective control over decisions may be located in
governmental institutions, but it may also be located
in political parties and pressure groups or private
associations and the people exercising control may
rely for their power not upon formal authority but upon
wealth, enlightenment, respect, or other values. ... A
realistic conception of law must, accordingly, conjoin
formal authority and effective control and include
not only doctrine, but also the pattern of practices of
both formal and effective decision-makers.[12]

The trouble is that critics and, too often, apologists
alike start by attempting to define law or international
law and then seek to measure the conduct of a state by
this definition. This type of definition is to be found
in the writings of both democratic and socialist lawyers,
classicists and official spokesmen. As good an example
as any of the former is the late Judge Lauterpacht[13]:

International law is the body of rules of conduct,
enforceable by external sanctions, which confer rights
and impose obligations primarily, though not exclusively,
upon sovereign States and which owe their validity both
to the consent of States as expressed in custom and
treaties and to the fact of the existence of an international community of States and individuals. In that
sense international law may be defined, more briefly
(though perhaps less usefully), as the law of the
international community. ... [It] is the law of the
individual and collective units comprising the international society,[14] particularly and predominantly as
organized in the form of independent States. The
international society is the totality of human beings
inhabiting the earth. ... [This necessitates] the
assumption that the final purpose of that legal order
is to secure the well-being of its ultimate units,
namely, of individuals. This applies to all law ...
its rules emanate not only from the consent of States
as expressed in customary and conventional rules,
but from the paramount fact of the existence of an
international community of States by an ultimate solidarity of interests transcending any immediate conflict
of aims and interests.

In so far as the socialist States are concerned, reference may be made to the official text[15] issued by the
Institute of State and Law of the Soviet Academy of

Sciences, according to which international law is the

aggregate of rules governing relations between States
in the process of their conflict and cooperation,
designed to safeguard their peaceful coexistence,
expressing the will of the ruling classes of these
States and defended in case of need by coercion applied
by States individually or collectively.... Although
International Law, like any other branch of law, has a
class character and pertains to the superstructure, it
cannot express the will of the ruling class of any
particular State. It is the expression of the agreed
will of a number of States in the form of an international
agreement or custom which has grown up over a period.
The purpose of present-day International Law is to
promote peaceful coexistence and cooperation between
all States regardless of their social systems.

Given this particular class-oriented definition, it is

perhaps not surprising that the Soviet Union was able

to invoke what has become known as the 'Brezhnev

Doctrine'[16] to provide a legal basis for the 1968

invasion of Czechoslovakia:

... We cannot ignore the assertions, made in some
places, that the actions of the five socialist countries
ran counter to the Marxist-Leninist principle of
sovereignty and the rights of nations to self-determination.

The groundlessness of such reasoning consists primarily
in that it is based on an abstract, nonclass approach
to the question of sovereignty and the rights of nations
to self-determination.

The peoples of the socialist countries and Communist
parties certainly do have and should have freedom for
determining the ways of advance of their respective
countries.

However, none of their decisions should damage either
socialism in their country or the fundamental interests
of other socialist countries, and the whole working class
movement, which is working for socialism.

This means that each Communist party is responsible not
only to its own people, but also to all the socialist
countries, to the entire Communist movement. Whoever
forgets this, in stressing only the independence of

the Communist party, becomes one-sided. He deviates
from his international duty ....

The sovereignty of each socialist country cannot be
opposed to the interests of the world of socialism, of
the world of revolutionary movement....

The socialist states respect the democratic norms of
international law. They have proved this ... by coming
out resolutely against the attempts of imperialism to
violate the sovereignty and independence of nations.

It is from these same positions that they reject the
leftist, adventurist conception of 'exporting revolution',
of 'bringing happiness' to other peoples.

However, from a Marxist point of view, the norms of
law, including the norms of mutual relations of the socialist countries, cannot be interpreted narrowly,
formally, and in isolation from the general context of
class struggle in the modern world. The socialist
countries resolutely come out against the exporting and
importing of counter-revolution.

Each Communist party is free to apply the basic principles
of Marxist-Leninism and of socialism in its country,
but it cannot depart from these principles ....

Concretely, this means, first of all, that, in its
activity, each Communist party cannot but take in account
such a decisive factor of our time as the struggle
between two opposing social systems - capitalism and
socialism.

This is an objective struggle, a fact not depending on
the will of the people, and stipulated by the world
being split into two opposite social systems....

... The weakening of any of the links in the world system
of socialism directly affects all the socialist countries,
which cannot look indifferently upon this.

The anti-socialist elements in Czechoslovakia actually
covered up the demand for so-called neutrality and
Czechoslovakia's withdrawal from the socialist
community with talk about the right of nations to
self-determination.

However, the implementation of such 'self-determination',
in other words, Czechoslovakia's detachment from the
socialist community, would have come into conflict
with its own vital interests and would have been
detrimental to the other socialist states.

140

Such 'self-determination' ... in effect encroaches upon
the interests of the peoples of these [socialist]
countries and conflicts, at the very root of it, with
the right of these people to socialist self-determination.

Discharging their internationalist duty toward the
fraternal people of Czechoslovakia and defending their
own socialist gains, the Soviet Union and the other
socialist states had to act decisively....

People who 'disapprove' of the actions of the allied
socialist states are ignoring the decisive fact that
these countries are defending the interests of all of
world socialism, of the entire world revolutionary
movement....

Formal observance of the freedom of self-determination
of a nation in the concrete situation that arose in
Czechoslovakia would mean freedom of 'self-determination'
not of the popular masses, the working peoples, but of
their enemies....

Those who speak about the 'illegal actions' of the
allied socialist countries in Czechoslovakia forget that
in a class society there is not and there cannot be
nonclass laws.

Laws and legal norms are subjected to the laws of the
class struggle, the laws of social development....

Formally juridical reasoning must not overshadow a class
approach to the matter....

Such an approach to the question of sovereignty means
that, for example, the progressive forces of the world
would not be able to come out against the revival of
neo-Nazism in the Federal German Republic,

although it is possible that action against the latter
might well be covered by the reservations in Article
107 of the United Nations Charter permitting action
against ex-enemy States.

This societal approach is not, if one discards the
Marxist ideological terminology, so very different
from that of Roberto Ago[17]:

Law, as a social phenomenon, is manifested and operates
in the life of society and therefore one must look for

it in society and in relation to society and its needs.
... Legality is an attribute conferred, not by society
or by any other real or fictitious creating body, but
by some human thought which reflects on social phenomena;
it is an attribute which is reserved for a certain
category of norms, for a given group of judgments which
it meets in social life, because they, and they alone,
are found to possess as a whole definite objective
characteristics. In other words it is a legal science
which, by discovery of these characteristics and observ-
ing how they differ from those of other categories of
judgments, which are also social, and present, and
operating in the life of society, picks out the
category of judgments in which it finds these characteristics and qualifies it as legal. The reason for their
legality and being qualified as norms of law lies in
the objective presence of these characteristics,
which legal norms reveal in their structure and in their
common functioning: not in imaginary 'laying down' or
'creation' or 'formulation' by 'society'....

Ago's reference to legal science reminds one of the
view of Vattel in the middle of the eighteenth century
that "the Law of Nations is the science of rights which
exist between Nations or States, and of the obligations
corresponding to these rights."[18]

It is not only the socialist states which express
their view of the meaning of international law in
ideological terms. While Whiteman's Digest of International Law, which is primarily concerned with the
practice and views of the United States, states that
"international law is the standard of conduct, at a
given time, for states and other entities subject
thereto,"[19] the Legal Adviser to the United States
Department of State put the matter more subjectively.[20]
International law comprises

Those rules for international conduct which have met
general acceptance among the community of nations.
It reflects and records those accommodations which,
over centuries, states have found it in their interest
to make. It rests upon the common consent of civilized[21] communities. It is not to be found in any code.

It is made up of precedent, judicial decisions, treaties, arbitrations, international conventions, the opinions of learned writers in the field, and a myriad of other acts and things which represent in the aggregate those rules which _enlightened_ nations and their people accept as being appropriate to govern international conduct. It is constantly changing, and expanding, as modern technology shrinks the world and brings its peoples into ever closer contact....

In view of the complex form in which so many of these attitudes to international law find expression, it is refreshing to turn to Article 5 of the Charter of the Organisation of American States which puts it simply:[22]

International law is the standard of conduct of States in their reciprocal relations.

If, as is so often the case, state conduct does not conform to this postulated definition, there is a tendency for commentators, instead of examining their definitions to see whether they may be incorrect, to assert instead that the state concerned has broken the law. This is the attitude, for example, of those who maintain that the individual is a subject of international law and is entitled to protection against all states, including even his own.[23] As shown by article 2, paragraph 7, of the Charter of the United Nations, as well as the need to make express provision for such a right in the European Convention on Human Rights, the treatment by a state of its own nationals is a matter of domestic jurisdiction and, unless a threat to the peace is concerned, is beyond the scope of United Nations action. The fact that the politicians who make up the United Nations, which is itself a political organization, decide for political reasons[24] to interpret the concept of domestic jurisdiction in a political rather than a legal fashion does not alter the position one iota. Again, some of those who seek to elevate international law to a point beyond which realism counsels caution make use of non-binding manifestos like the Universal Declaration of Human Rights to assert, for example, that, even in the absence of any treaty conferring it, every man has a right to seek asylum from political persecution.[25]

It is not only writers who bring international law into disrepute by claiming for it what is not its own. Courts, too, bear a share of responsibility. Thus, in _Fujii_ v. _California_[26] the California District Court of Appeals held that the provisions of the Charter of the United Nations concerning human rights, statements by the President of the United States, and the Universal Declaration of Human Rights were all sufficient to invalidate the Californian Alien Land Law, 1920. It did not advance the cause of international law or of human rights in any way when the Californian Supreme Court,[27] upholding the decision on the basis of the Fourteenth Amendment of the United States Constitution, said:

The humane and enlightened objectives of the United Nations Charter are, of course, entitled to respectful consideration by the courts and Legislatures of every member nation, since that document expresses the universal desire of thinking men for peace and for equality of rights and opportunities. The Charter represents a moral commitment of foremost importance, and we must not permit the spirit of our pledge to be compromised or disparaged in either our domestic or foreign affairs. We are satisfied, however, that the Charter provisions relied on by plaintiff were not intended to supersede existing domestic legislation, and we cannot hold that they operate to invalidate the Alien Land Law.

As regards the critics of international law, for the main part they take as their starting point Austin's definition of law. Austin, a true representative of the Victorian middle class, defined law as a "rule laid down for the guidance of an intelligent being by an

intelligent being having power over him," with every
law, properly so called, a species of command, which
command is obeyed because of the sanction attending its
breach. Such a definition of law has as a prerequisite
the existence of a sovereign, and for Austin the
sovereign is "a determinate human superior, not in a
habit of obedience to a like superior, [who] receive[s]
habitual obedience from the bulk of a given society."
Inherent in such a view of the law there is a clearly
observable legislative authority whose commands tend
to be obeyed, and when they are not there is a law-
enforcing authority which takes the necessary steps
to ensure that the non-observance of the law is visited
by punishment. If one looks at international law in the
light of this definition it soon becomes clear that
international law does not measure up to the tests
postulated for law by John Austin, who described
international law as "law improperly so called." It
would be open to us to terminate the discussion by
accepting Austin's view or, with Glanville Williams,
we could assert that Austin's definition was one
intended to suit "his purpose." "Austin defined what
the word meant for him, which he was entitled to do,
but he was not entitled to adopt a legislative attitude
and declare what the word should mean for other people.
The power that Austin assumed for himself, to define
the meaning of the words he used, he should have
accorded to others."[28] Unfortunately, many lawyers
since Austin's day, particularly practitioners of the
common law, have glibly followed the path he blazed and,
secure in the protection of Austin's name, solemnly
declare that, whatever else international law may be,
it is not law.

It ill behoves any international lawyer to disregard
this challenge. While there is nothing sacrosanct

about the Austinians, it is not enough just to dismiss
their criticisms. These views must be examined and
assessed and, in the light of the findings, it might
well transpire that while international law does not
fit the Austinian concept of law, it is nevertheless
law. On the other hand, one does not need to go as
far as James Brown Scott in the first volume of the
American Journal of International Law, seeking to prove
that international law did in fact largely satisfy
Austin's definition:[29]

> Admitting for a moment Austin's strictures, it is
> evident that a great deal of the body of international
> law would be law in the strict sense of the term; for
> a nation may and does bind itself by treaty, a positive
> agreement, and a violation of rights under the treaty
> would lead to a 'command' from the injured state to the
> state guilty of the infraction. It would likewise seem
> to follow that if nations should recognize a custom or
> the body of customs which make up the law of nations,
> and give full effect to this custom, when rights depend-
> ing upon the custom arise and enforce through municipal
> courts the so-called law, the principle of decision
> might claim in such a case the epithet of law. The law
> administered in the various prize courts in civilized
> states is universal, practically identical and is
> enforced by process of court. Each specific instance
> would make this law, at least for the purposes of the
> case, municipal law and the sanction required by Austin's
> definition would clearly be present. Austin would
> indeed allow the quality of positive law to these
> various instances, but he maintains that the law so
> applied becomes municipal or national law and loses
> the character of international law.
>
> ... the presence of a sanction is not essential to the
> quality of law, for law as such is simply a rule of
> conduct, and is neither self-applying nor self-executing.
> The rule of conduct exists, and in a perfect state,
> whether it be enforced or not...
>
> If, then, the recognition of the body of usages and
> customs forming the bulk of international law involves
> their adoption both by the state so recognizing,
> subjects and citizens thereof, it follows... that the
> usages and customs of international law become, for the
> purpose of state and citizen, municipal law of such
> state and citizen, and that such usages and customs

become the common law of each and every state so
recognizing and adopting. There then present itself
a body of fixed and binding law - the common law of
nations - just as clearly and surely as the common
customs and usages of England become the common law
of that realm.

International law has no legislative assembly.
Despite attempts to elevate it into something which it
was never intended to be, it is now generally recognized that the draftsman of the Charter never intended
the United Nations to be the medium for the realization
of Tennyson's Vision:[31]

[When] the war drum throbbed no longer, and the battle
  flags were furled
In the Parliament of man, the Federation of the world.
There the common sense of most shall hold a fretful
  realm in awe,
And the kindly earth shall slumber, lapt in universal
  law.

The limitations of the United Nations were fully
appreciated by the International Court of Justice when,
in the course of its Advisory Opinion on the Bernadotte
Case, it made clear that while, like states, "the
organisation is an international person [,] that is not
the same thing as saying that it is a State, which it
certainly is not. ... Still less is it the same thing
as saying that it is a 'super-State', whatever that
expression may mean."[32] It is true that the Security
Council has power to make decisions, and that by
article 25 of the Charter the members of the United
Nations agree to accept and carry out those decisions.
This gives the appearance of a binding law-making
authority to the Security Council. However, one cannot
overlook the fact that by article 27, paragraph 3, it
only requires the dissident vote of one permanent
member of the Council to prevent any decision being

reached, or to prevent the sanction of "enforcement
measures" being taken against a member of the United
Nations which declines to carry out such a decision.
Nevertheless, it must not be thought that resolutions
of the Security Council are completely without effect.
As was pointed out by the World Court when dealing with
the status of <u>Namibia</u>[33], Council resolutions are binding
when the council is

acting in the exercise of what is deemed to be its
primary responsibility, the maintenance of peace and
security, which, under the Charter, embraces situations
which might lead to a breach of the peace. ... When
the Security Council adopts a decision under Article
25 in accordance with the Charter, it is for member
States to comply with that decision, including those
members of the Security Council which voted against it
and those Members of the United Nations who are not
members of the Council .... The qualification of a
situation as illegal does not by itself put an end to
it. It can only be the first, necessary step in an
endeavour to bring the illegal situation to an end.
... A binding determination made by the competent organ
of the United Nations that a situation is illegal
cannot remain without consequence. Once the Court is
faced with such a situation, it would be failing in the
discharge of its judicial functions if it did not declare
that there is an obligation, especially upon Members of
the United Nations, to bring that situation to an end.
... The Member States of the United Nations are
[therefore] under obligation to recognize the illegality
and invalidity of South Africa's continued presence
in Namibia...

The situation is not changed in any way by Article 2(6)
of the Charter which purports to impose upon non-members
an obligation to abide by the purposes and principles
of the Charter. Recognizing the validity of the
principle that agreements do not affect third parties -
<u>pacta tertiis nec nocent nec prosunt</u> or, as it is
expressed in municipal law, <u>res inter alios acta</u> -
this can only mean that the members of the United
Nations have assumed an obligation whereby, if a non-
member does not abide by the Charter or ignores Security

Council instructions, and refuses to alter its conduct when called upon to do so, the members will carry out such instructions as are directed to them in order to bring the non-member into line. In view of the well-nigh universal character of the Organization's member-ship it may be anticipated that the non-member will in fact conform. This was the view of the Court in the Namibia opinion, when it pointed out that non-members were "not bound by Articles 24 and 25", but since it considered the South African illegal occupation of the area opposable erga omnes non-members should act accordingly, and "no State which enters into relations with South Africa concerning Namibia may expect the United Nations or its Members to recognize the validity or effects of such relationship, or the consequences thereof."[34]

It might be as well to cite here the views of leading Soviet lawyers on this issue. Koretsky when a member of the International Law Commission stated:[35] "... the Charter of the United Nations, ... which laid down new principles of international law, was essentially a treaty." His successor Tunkin appears to differ:[36] "... the new principles of the United Nations Charter were binding on non-members as an expression of customary law." The Soviet Union, however, only joins international organizations "to the extent that this promotes peace and the development of international cooperation [and the] decisions of international organ-izations and organs can ... be considered as sources of international law if they receive international recognition."[37] These seeming discrepancies have led one commentator to remark:[38]

Principles and norms of the Charter are binding on the U.S.S.R. as a signatory of the treaty. The same principles and norms are binding on non-signatories as custom.

One cannot help but feel that the Soviet Union would
rapidly assert the traditional view if it were at any
time to withdraw from the United Nations.

The General Assembly is even less of a legislative
body. It is true that the General Assembly "decides"
to admit new members; to suspend those against which
preventive or enforcement action has been taken; to
expel those which persistently violate the principles
of the Charter; and to elect a secretary-general of the
organization - all upon the "recommendation" of the
Security Council, which recommendation must be positive,[39]
for "nowhere has the General Assembly received the power
to change, to the point of reversing, the meaning of a
vote of the Security Council. In consequence, it is
impossible to admit that the General Assembly has the
power to attribute to a vote of the Security Council
the character of a recommendation when the Council
itself considers that no such recommendation has been
made." The Assembly does possess the sole power of
decision on such matters as the budget of the organization; the election of Ecosoc and the Trusteeship
Council; the establishment of subsidiary organs;
the terms of employment of the international civil
service; and the regulation of its own procedure. It
cannot really be said that any of these matters is
truly fundamental to the maintenance of international
peace and security. For the main part, and particularly
when issues of international strain are likely to be
involved, the powers of the General Assembly are limited
to discussion, consideration, calling attention, initi-
ating studies, receiving and considering reports, and,
especially, making recommendations. None of these
functions can be described as legislative and the fact
that the General Assembly expresses its views in the
form of a decision is merely United Nations shorthand

for "decides to recommend."[40] The most important, and
potentially legislative, of these functions is the
recommendation. When an attempt was made in the
Corfu Channel Case (Preliminary Objection)[41] to give
obligatory force to a recommendation of the Security
Council, seven of the fifteen judges delivered a Joint
Separate Opinion rejecting this contention, and referred[42] "to the normal meaning of the word recommendation,
a meaning which this word has retained in diplomatic
language, as is borne out by the practice of the
Pan-American Conferences, of the League of Nations,[43]
of the International Labour Organization , etc."
However, it must be borne in mind that the dissenting
judges (Tanaka, Jessup and Padilla Nervo) in the 1966
Southwest Africa judgment[44] regarded constant reiteration
of the same assertions in Assembly resolutions as
evidence of generally accepted customary law, or of
such law in embryo,[45] although in 1971 Judge Gros,
dissenting in the Namibia advisory opinion[46] bluntly
stated that "resolutions have no binding force on
member States of the Organization."

Perhaps the readiest confirmation of the non-legis-
lative function of the General Assembly lies in the
status of the Universal Declaration of Human Rights.
Of this, Kelsen has pointed out: "It stands to reason
that the resolution of the General Assembly on Human
Rights has no legal effect whatever,"[47] a view which
accords with that of Mrs. Roosevelt as chairman of the
Commission on Human Rights which drafted the Declaration:
"In giving our approval to the declaration today,
it is of primary importance that we keep clearly in
mind the basic character of the document. It is not
and does not purport to be a statement of law or of
legal obligation. It is a declaration of basic
principles of human rights and freedoms, to be stamped

with the approval of the General Assembly by formal
vote of its members, and to serve as a common standard
of achievement for all peoples of all nations."[48]
The same attitude to the work of the General Assembly
was shown by Mr. Attlee, as prime minister of a member
state which had voted in favour of the adoption of
the Declaration, when asked, some four weeks after its
adoption, whether he intended amending English law in
order to make it conform with the Declaration: "There
is no question ... of an obligation to give early
legislative effect to any provision with which United
Kingdom or Colonial laws may at the moment be at
variance."[49] In so far as national constitutions may
have embodied the Declaration into their texts, as has
been done by a number of the new states, although these
constitutions are often more honoured in their breach
than their observance, or municipal courts have referred
to the Declaration and made it part of their judgments,
this is because the Declaration has, for the countries
or courts in question, been made part of the municipal
law. It is only as such, and not as international law
per se, that any form of legal recognition or protection
is given to the individual in question, and this remains
true despite the efforts of Judge Tanaka in the
Southwest Africa Cases.

Since it is clear that the United Nations and its
two principal organs do not constitute a legislative
body, there seems little prospect of any of the subsidiary organs constituting a legislature. This is true,
for example, of the International Law Commission whose
task it is to promote the progressive development of
international law and its codification, as was made
clear by Lord Asquith as umpire in Petroleum Development
Ltd. v. Sheikh of Abu Dhabi.[50] He refused to accept as
binding statements of the law on the continental shelf

the proposals made by the Commission in the report of its third session.[51] The latest proposals of the Commission on this and related questions on the law of the sea[52] were shown in their true light at the Geneva Conferences on the Law of the Sea, 1958 and 1960, when they were treated as no more than bases of discussion. What is more, as was made crystal clear by the World Court in the North Sea Continental Shelf Cases,[53] the conventions[54] on the subject drawn up by a diplomatic conference summoned in the name of the United Nations in no way constituted law for any party until they were ratified by that party, save in so far as, in the words of the Preamble to the Convention on the High Seas, they constituted provisions "generally declaratory of established principles of international law" - in which case they were law without any legislative action by the conference.

The deficiencies of the United Nations as a legislative body have led to suggestions, particularly from American lawyers, that the Charter be amended in order to remedy the defect. Thus, at the Dubrovnik Conference of the International Law Association,[55] Eagleton, on behalf of the American Branch of the Association, proposed that the Charter be amended so as to grant "to the General Assembly the power to adopt rules of international law which would become binding upon each member which does not, within a specified time, notify the United Nations of its rejection of the rule." Such a proposition would not only constitute a fundamental amendment of the Charter, it would also be directly contrary to what has until now been regarded as a basic rule of international law - that written changes in the law are only binding on those states which clearly indicate their acceptance of them, a principle which is already embodied in a report by the

King's Advocate in 1796,[56] which finds judicial support
in the Advisory Opinion of the World Court on the Status
of Eastern Carelia,[57] and as we have seen, was reiterated by it in the Namibia opinion. The conference did
not accept this proposal, but referred it to its
Committee on the Review of the Charter for further
consideration, and it has not been seriously discussed
at any conference since.

A more far-reaching proposal to transform the General
Assembly into an international legislature suggests
the replacement of article 13 of the Charter, which
permits the Assembly to discuss any matter within the
scope of the Charter and to make recommendations, by
one giving it power "to enact legislation binding upon
member Nations and all the peoples thereof, within the
definite fields and in accordance within the strictly
limited authority herein delegated."[58] Such powers
are to relate to the maintenance of international
peace and security, disarmament and armed forces. Such
a proposal, it is submitted, is, in the present tri-
polarized world,[59] even more unrealistic and impossible
of achievement than those for enlarging the Security
Council or abolishing the veto.

Closely connected with the idea of legislation in the
positivist theory is the concept of sovereignty,
requiring both a superior and an inferior. It is
inherent in the very nature of internation life that
all states are equal, or as it is sometimes expressed,
par in parem non habet imperium.[60] This is merely a
more elaborate form of expressing Vattel's famous
statement that "Since men are by nature equal, and their
individual rights and obligations the same, as coming
equally from nature, Nations, which are composed of
men and may be regarded as so many free persons living
together in a state of nature, are by nature equal and

154

hold from nature the same obligations and the same rights.
Strength or weakness, in this case, counts for nothing.
A dwarf is as much a man as a giant is; a small Republic
is no less a sovereign State than the most powerful King."[61]
Such an idea is the very antithesis of the existence of
a sovereign and is contained in article 2, paragraph 1,
of the Charter of the United Nations which postulates
the sovereign equality of all members as the principle
upon which the organization is based. Even a cursory
glance at the Charter, and particularly the preferential
position of the "Big Five" with permanent seats and a
veto in the Security Council, gives the lie to this
assertion. It is true that the member states by accepting
the Charter have freely exercised their sovereignty so
as to place these powers in a privileged position. But,
as Senator Connally on behalf of the United States
reminded Committee 1 of Commission III of the San Francisco Conference during the discussion on the veto:
"The sponsoring governments and France had gone as far
as they could go with respect to the voting procedure
of the Security Council.... [C]ould delegates face
public opinion at home if they reported that they had
killed the veto but had also killed the Charter."[62] It
is put even more picturesquely in Connally's autobiography: "You may go home from San Francisco - if
you wish, I cautioned the delegates, and report that you
have defeated the veto .... But you can also say 'We
tore up the Charter.' At that point I sweepingly ripped
the Charter draft in my hands to shreds and flung the
scraps upon the table."[63]

That the Great Powers intended to keep the other
members in their proper place, and bring home to them
the reality of Orwell's comment that "all animals are
equal, but some animals are more equal than others,"[64]
has constantly been made clear in the period since the
San Francisco Conference. From the very first election

of the non-permanent members of the Security Council,[65] when it appeared that China and France had been dropped from the inner caucus,[66] until the "secret" discussions in 1961 concerning a successor to Secretary-General Hammarskjold, the hierarchic meaning of "equality" in the United Nations has been unceasingly emphasized. On the other hand, it is as well to point out that if one accepts the view of sovereignty put forward by Leibniz,[67] that "a sovereign in international law is a ruler whose armed strength counts in international relations, and who cannot be compelled to adopt any course of conduct except by measures amounting to war," the situation appears in a different light. In accordance with this view there may be more than one sovereign. Even Austin, for whom sovereignty was indivisible, might perhaps have found it difficult to maintain this rigidity had he been called upon to analyse the position under modern English constitutional law[68] or, even more so, in the relation of the dominions inter se[69] - a relationship in which it would not be impossible for the "personal" sovereign to find that in her capacity as "legal" sovereign she is at war with herself-or in a federation like Canada or the United States.

The third positivist precondition for law is observance. In so far as international law is concerned, it has almost become a music-hall joke that this is a system which everybody talks about, but of which nobody takes the slightest notice or, as it is so dramatically expressed by one of the characters in Leon Uris's Exodus, "that thing which the evil ignore and the righteous refuse to enforce." Even legal practitioners tend to vent their cynical spleen by conceding that the arrangements for the delivery of air or surface mail tend to work satisfactorily under the auspices of the Universal Postal Union. There is no doubt that we tend

to take for granted such services as the cheap
air-letter-card and that the "man on the Clapham
omnibus" would never believe that this particular
service depends on complex international agreements
involving limitations on state sovereignty. Nor does
he recognize that his movement by air from one country
to another, across the territory of a third, depends
on arrangements like the Chicago Convention establishing
the International Civil Aviation Organisation as well
as numerous bilateral transit agreements.[70] He accepts as
his right the fact that he may visit a foreign state and
regards his passport as a vade-mecum guaranteeing him
protection and security.[71] What the ordinary man
accepts as part of his everyday existence, the cynic seeks
to reduce to complete insignificance: "I find no
consolation in the fact that the International Postal
Union works successfully in time of peace. The rule of
law internationally has got to control states more
effectively than merely by furthering commercial
correspondence, or facilitating love letters to their
girls from soldiers exiled far from home."[72]

Despite such remarks as this, the cynics are invariably
among the first to cry out if what they have thus
described as matters of insignificance are disrupted.
Should a passport not be recognized, or a diplomat not
be granted access to an arrested national, much is heard
of the denial of the rule of law. This attitude is
similar to that shown by the press and other organs of
popular opinion when breaches of municipal law occur.
There is no news value to be derived from the fact that
the majority of people sleep safely in their beds.
There is great news value in the fact that one old lady
was brutally done to death by an intruder. Law-abiding-
ness is newsless. The difference is that on the international level breaches of the law have grave and far-
reaching effects, often involving the peace of the world

and the lives of millions. To a certain extent, it
is the press and the cynics who are responsible for
the sneering disrespect afforded to international law.
In the name of world order and the rule of law, they
seem to take a perverse delight in drawing attention
not to the instances, often involving state prestige,
when the law is observed, but to the rarer though more
spectacular breaches. Perhaps it might be opportune to
reproduce here the comments of two former judges of
the World Court. In John Bassett Moore's view:[73]

Nor is international law in ordinary times badly
observed. It is, in fact, usually well enforced; and
any differences in regard to its interpretation and
enforcement are, except in matters of a political
nature, commonly left to international tribunals for
determination, in connexion with individual claims.

For Lauterpacht:[74]

A system of law in which duties of secondary importance
are broken with impunity partakes of a high degree of
unreality. There is no reason for impatience on the
ground that public opinion concentrates on violations
of political treaties and on resort to war in disregard
of existing obligations. When viewed against the background of transgressions of that magnitude, the normal
observance of other rules of international law can
only imperfectly maintain the authority of the system
shaken by major exhibitions of lawlessness.

With this in mind, it is necessary to see whether
states do in fact observe any rules of conduct in
their relations with each other. Before doing so,
however, it is as well to see whether the final hallmark
of law in the Austinian system - a judicial authority -
has any counterpart in international life. Most people
nowadays have heard of the World Court at The Hague,
and even some of the cynics are prepared to concede that
here is a judicial body which may be called upon to
decide disputed issues with all the care, reasoning,
and objectivity which one associates with any judicial

tribunal. In fact, some take their belief in the value
of the Court so far that they ignore the limitations
of the statute defining its jurisdiction and elevate
it into a panacea for all the evils of the world.
Thus, Mr. Harvey Moore deplored the fact that his
challenge to test his view as to the illegality of
nuclear weapons by asking the Court for an advisory
opinion had been taken up by "no one."[75] This ignores
the fact that "no one" can ask the Court for an advisory
opinion. By its statute, "the Court may give an
advisory opinion on any legal question at the request
of whatever body may be authorised by or in accordance
with the Charter of the United Nations to make such a
request."[76] It must also be borne in mind that the
bodies so referred to are made up of the representatives
of states, who vote on any question being considered
by the body in accordance with the instructions they
receive from their governments. According to the
latest edition of the British Manual of Military Law
"there is no rule of international law dealing specifically with the use of nuclear weapons ... In the absence
of any rule of international law dealing expressly
with it, the use which may be made of a particular
weapon will be governed by the ordinary rules and the
question of the legality of its use in any individual
case will, therefore, involve merely the application
of the recognised principles of international law."[77]
The United States Army Field Manual[78] adopts a similar
stand and, in the light of their own experiments with
nuclear devices, it may be presumed that both China
and the Soviet Union also regard such weapons as legal.
In view of this, it may be doubted whether any of
these powers would support a request for an advisory
opinion on the matter. Moreover, France has refused
to recognize the jurisdiction of the Court to decide,
at the request of Australia and New Zealand, on the

legality of her explosions in the Pacific.[79]

The primary function of a court is to settle disputes, not to give declaratory judgments on abstract points of law, and the chief role of the World Court, which consists of persons "who possess the qualifications required in their respective countries for appointment to the highest judicial office, or are jurisconsults of recognized competence in international law," is to adjudicate upon controversies between states. Unfortunately, however, even the Court is obliged to recognize the realities of sovereignty and, therefore, jurisdiction only arises when the parties to an issue agree to submit the matter to the Court. Like all state decisions this, too, is one that is made for political reasons.[80] The statute does allow for states to limit their discretions in this field by way of article 36, which permits a state to declare its option for accepting compulsory adjudication of future disputes affecting itself. However, declarations under the "Optional Clause" may be made subject to reservations, and it has become popular for states, when reserving from jurisdiction matters which are essentially within their domestic jurisdiction, to reserve to themselves the sole power to decide on the domesticity of any issue. Although, "In the event of a dispute as to whether the Court has jurisdiction, the matter shall be settled by the decision of the Court," the Court has, with what at times appeared to be almost indecent haste, given an impression of its unwillingness to assume jurisdiction whenever this should prove possible. Some states, following the example set by the United States in what is known as the Connally Amendment, have excluded from jurisdiction matters falling within their domestic jurisdiction as determined by themselves, and in the <u>Norwegian Loans Case</u>[81] the Court went so far

as to uphold the validity of this reservation to protect
a defendant which had accepted the jurisdiction of the
Court with the sole reservation of "reciprocity,"
the plaintiff, having made such a domestic jurisdiction
reservation, found the Court in agreement with Hamlet
that "'tis the sport to have the engineer hoist with his
own petar. "

In recent years we have seen states go so far as to
refuse to recognize the Court's jurisdiction on the
ground that the law it would be called upon to enforce
was out of date or alien, or that there was in fact no
law. Thus, in 1961 at the time of India's invasion of
Goa, her representative in the Security Council said:[82]

Who gave Portugal sovereign rights for any part of India
they occupied illegally and by force? Who gave them
that right? Not the Indian people. There can be no
question of aggression against you own frontier. ...
If any narrow-minded, legalistic considerations -
considerations arising from international law as
written by European international law writers - should
arise, those writers were, after all, brought up in
the atmosphere of colonialism. I pay all respect due
to Grotius, who is supposed to be the father of international law, and we accept many tenets of international
law. They are certainly regulating international life
today. But the tenet ... quoted in support of colonial
powers having sovereign rights over territories which
they won by conquest in Asia and Africa is no longer
acceptable. It is the European concept and must die...

More recently, on introducing her anti-pollution
legislation, Canada added a new reservation to her
acceptance of the Court's jurisdiction to exclude its
authority in thie field. Prime Minister Trudeau
explained:[83]

The way international law exists now, it is definitely
biased in favour of shipping in the high seas in various
parts of the globe. And in the past this has probably
been to the benefit of the states of the world because
there has been, because of this bias in international
law, a great deal of the development of commerce in all

parts of the globe.... This was fine in the past, but
now with the advance of technology and the importance
which is coming forth to us in all parts of the world -
of not only thinking of commerce, but also of quality
of life. We're saying international law has not
developed in this direction .... [Canada is willing]
to participate in every aspect of the development of
international regimes which would prevent pollution
of coastal states. But until this international regime
has developed we are stuck with the law as it has
developed in the past centuries and the centuries before
when ... there was no danger of pollution, and it was
important for commercial and other reasons that the
nations could communicate on the high seas.... Where
no law exists, or where law is clearly insufficient...
we're saying somebody has to preserve this area for
mankind until the international law develops and we are
prepared to help it develop by taking steps on our own.
... There is no law so we can't be taken to the courts.

Nevertheless, Canadian delegates to the United Nations
have constantly proclaimed their belief in the value
of the Court and called for wider recognition and
acceptance of its jurisdiction.[84]

   As with the decisions of other courts, those of the
World Court are binding and final. Likewise, unsuccessful parties will occasionally seek to avoid carrying
out the judgment. Here a line must be drawn between
the attitude of the Court and those responsible for
establishing the Court. In the S. S. Wimbledon an
attempt was made to persuade the Court to award a
higher rate of interest "in the event of the judgment
not being complied with at the expiration of the time
fixed for compliance. The Court neither can nor should
contemplate such a contingency."[85] The draftsmen of
the Charter were more realistic. In article 94 they
provided that "if any party to a case fails to perform
the obligations incumbent upon it under a judgment
rendered by the Court, the other party may have recourse
to the Security Council, which may, if it deems necessary, make recommendations or decide upon measures to

be taken to give effect to the judgment." Here, for
the first time, is an attempt to provide a means of
law enforcement on the international plane. There is
no appeal from the decisions of the Court, but this
article may be used for the same purpose. It author-
izes the Countil to decide upon the measures necessary
to give effect to the judgment, provided the Council
deems it necessary to do so. In other words, the
Council has discretion to do nothing and, by its
default, allow the party found in breach of law by the
Court to continue in its breach. The draftsmen,
recognizing that legal and political realities do not
necessarily coincide, have provided a political
authority which can act as an appellate tribunal on the
decisions of a judicial body - although, unlike the
normal situation in municipal law, it is the successful
party to the proceedings which has the right of appeal.
Another concession to reality is the recognition that a
judicial decision which seeks to upset the territorial
status quo may endanger the maintenance of international
peace and security, the preservation of which always
depends on the goodwill of the Big Five. Article 94
therefore allows the operation of the veto, where
necessary, to prevent a judgment from being made
effective.

It should not be thought that judgments exist only
so that they may be disregarded. Generally speaking,
states go to Court because they wish to settle their
dispute and are agreeable to do so on an objective
level, without political emotions being allowed to
obscure the true nature of the issue. Normally speaking, once states have agreed to take their issue to
Court, they intimate their willingness to carry out
any judgment that may be delivered. It is only in
rare circumstances, as in the Sabotage Claims[86] and

the Corfu Channel Case,[87] that the losing party refuses to comply. Sometimes, as in the case of the Aerial Incident of July 27th, 1955,[88] a defendant will admit its liability and undertake to "identify and punish the culpable persons and pay compensation," but will do nothing to this end nor agree to an international tribunal adjudicating the issue. Of late, however, there seems to be an increasing number of instances of states which have accepted the Court's jurisdiction refusing to acknowledge its authority when matters come to the crunch, as happened with Iceland in its dispute with Britain[89] and with France concerning nuclear testing in the Pacific.[90]

It is one thing to talk of compliance with and observance of the law, but this still leaves for consideration the issue of enforcement. In the municipal sphere one is accustomed to seeing judicial decisions being enforced. As has just been pointed out, while the Statute of the Court and the Charter of the United Nations provide for Security Council action to this end, there are real political reasons why this is unlikely to be common. Moreover, there are methods of enforcement and sanction which do exist. Obviously, the ultimate sanction which is available to a victim of a breach of law is recourse to armed force or war. Apart from philosophical debate as to whether a legal system can be truly such if it depends on a breakdown of every basis of the rule of law for its enforcement, it must be recognized that there are now, at least on paper severe legal restrictions on the right to resort to war. In so far as the individual state is concerned, the Pact of Paris (the Kellogg-Briand Pact)[90] and the Charter of the United Nations have sought to make this unlikely. However, it is still open to the United Nations as the organized institution of the world

community to take sanctions, which may amount to armed
intervention or be merely economic in character as they
are in the case of Southern Rhodesia and South Africa.
The United Nations can also resort to expulsion,
although this may be self-destructive. If a member has
refused to abide by the law despite the obligations of
membership, it is hardly likely that it will do so when
it has been ejected, and is no longer entitled to the
rights nor subjected to the obligations of membership.
In addition, it should not be overlooked that municipal
courts are frequently called upon to carry out and
enforce rules of international law and do so effectively,
while the members of the European Communities have
undertaken to give full recognition and effect to the
decisions of the European Court. In fact for these
countries this court has become, within its own sphere,
the supreme court of the land with its judgments as
much entitled to enforcement as any municipal court,[92]
although here it may be suggested we have passed from
the field of inter, through intra, to supranational
law.[93] Finally, one should not overlook the possibility
of the eventual evolution of an international criminal
law with a court for its own enforcement,[94] although
all that we have witnessed so far has related to the
punishment of war criminals, either by municipal
tribunals or by specially created international military
tribunals as at Nuremberg and Tokyo after the Second
World War. However, one must remember that in the field
of criminal law it is the individual rather than the
state that suffers. As Westlake pointed out at the
end of the nineteenth century:[95]

The State is, other than by occupation or seizure of its
treasures, only punished indirectly, and even then the
true losers or victims are the nationals of the state.
In so far as punishment in its popular meaning is
concerned, this can only be directed against individuals.
... The men who form a state are not allowed to disclaim

their part in the offences alleged against it, whether those on account of which the war was begun or those charged as having been committed by it in the course of the war, or therefore to claim that hostile action shall not be directed against their State through them in their respective measures. And this is just. Whatever is done or committed by a State is done or committed by the men who are grouped in it, or at least the deed or the commission is sanctioned by them. The state is not a self-acting machine.... [And] if we look more closely at the facts, we shall probably find that in the foreign affairs of a state the rulers oftener act under the impulse of the mass than by its tacit permission, and that tacit permission is seldom conceded by the mass except to those who embody and represent the national character.

When criticism is levelled at international law in this field, two things should be remembered. In the first place, it is wrong to criticize the courts or the law for the failings of those who are subject to them. Secondly, weaknesses in law enforcement are by no means unknown on the municipal level. It has never been suggested that the English rules regarding the rights of diplomats are not legal rules, and the courts not true courts because of the principle of diplomatic immunity. Thus, in <u>Taylor</u> v. <u>Best</u>[96] it was indicated that acknowledgement of jurisdiction did not amount to acknowledgement of liability to execution, while in <u>Kahan</u> v. <u>Pakistan</u>[97] a statement recognizing English law as the law of the contract was held not to amount to the recognition of English law and English courts as governing the contract. Further, in municipal law, for every case that goes to court, twenty or more are settled amicably. The same is true in international life, and when the Chinese People's Republic shot down a British aircraft, apologies were expressed and compensation paid without any recourse to court.

Enough has been said to indicate that although the international scene does not present the characteristics

which Austinians regard as essential for law, states -
and for that matter international institutions too -
do regard themselves as bound to obey certain rules of
conduct in their relations one with another. Reference
to any collection of state papers or such works as
Lord McNair's International Law Opinions,[98] the
various Digests of United States practice by Wharton,[99]
Moore,[100] Hackworth[101] and Whiteman,[102] of British
practice by Parry[103] and Lauterpacht,[104] the French
Repertoire by Kiss,[105] the newly instituted Prassi
Italiana by Ago[106] and the state practice sections in
the various international law periodicals all show
how regularly states use legal language for communic-
ating with each other, while the terminology used in
connection with breaches of the law only has meaning
within the context of a legal system.[107] It is perhaps
for this reason that, when they indulge in an economy
drive involving cuts in the size of the civil service,
states but rarely make any reduction in the size of the
legal department attached to their foreign offices.
Amidst all the talk of the expense involved in maintaining the United Nations, there is no suggestion that
the International Court of Justice be closed down.
Instead, efforts are being made to widen its jurisdiction and the Legal Committee of the General Assembly has,
for some years now, been concerned with the role of
the Court, seeking ways to promote its wider use.
Moreover, the International Law Commission has been
enlarged to afford representation to the new members
of the United Nations.

When contemplating whether law exists or not, it is
necessary to see whether those who are supposed to be
governed by the rules regard those rules as being legal
in character. In municipal law we are accustomed to
distinguish between legal custom and non-binding usage.

The same is true of the position in international law. Lord Alverstone C.J. in <u>West Rand Central Gold Mining Co., Ltd.</u> v. <u>The King</u> expressed it as follows:[108]

> There is an essential difference, as to certainty and definiteness, between municipal law and a system or body of rules in regard to international conduct, which, so far as it exists at all - <u>and its existence is assumed by the phrase 'international law'</u> - rests upon a consensus of civilised States, not expressed in any code or pact, nor possessing, in case of dispute, any authorised or authoritative interpreter; and capable, indeed, of proof, in the absence of some express international agreement, only by evidence of usage to be obtained from the actions of nations in similar cases in the course of their history."

In order to satisfy the World Court, such usages only amount to law if they are "generally accepted as expressing principles of law and established in order to regulate the relations between these co-existing independent communities [States] with a view to the achievement of common aims."[109] The view that habit is insufficient, but that there must be a "constant and uniform usage, accepted as law," was reiterated in the <u>Asylum Case</u> when it was pointed out that "the party which relies on a custom ... must prove that this custom is established in such a manner that it has become binding on the other party. [It] must prove that the rule invoked by it is in accordance with a constant and uniform usage practiced by the States in question, and that this usage is the expression of a right appertaining to the State [putting it forward] and a duty incumbent on the [other] State."[110]

In the municipal sphere it is a well-established rule that ignorance of the law is no defence. So much is this so, that the legal test of insanity as expressed in the <u>McNaughten Rules</u>[111] regards a man as not liable for his acts in law only if he did "not know the nature or quality of the act he was doing, or if he did know it, that he did not know he was doing wrong." A similar test may be applied in the field of international law. In certain circumstances, particularly in the event of piracy or war crimes, it is recognized that states are able to try persons who, but for the commission of these offences, would not normally be amenable to their jurisdiction. If those who are accused of breaches of international law may be shown to have been aware that they were in fact committing such infringements, this may be used as some evidence to suggest, on a level below that of state practice, that, whatever the Austinians may think, there is in fact something known as international law which ought to be obeyed. It is sufficient for our purpose to refer to the attitude adopted by certain war criminals. Thus Keitel agreed at the Nuremberg Trial[112] that he was aware of and "really agreed" with the view of Canaris that the regulations concerning the treatment of Soviet prisoners of war were contrary to international law, but "the objections arise from the military concept of chivalrous warfare. This is the destruction of an ideology. Therefore, I approve and back the measures." According to documents published by the Soviet Union in 1961,[113] he went even further: "This struggle has nothing to do with military chivalry or with obligations of the Geneva Convention.... The troops therefore have the right and the duty in this struggle to use any means, without restriction, even against women and children, provided they are successful." Doenitz maintained that "at all times the [German] Navy remained within the confines of international law,"[114] while Frank, the Gauleiter of Poland, "stated that he had a feeling of 'terrible guilt' for the atrocities committed in the occupied territories."[115] It was not only the members of the supreme Nazi hierarchy who were aware that their activities

were contrary to the rules of law. Klein, one of the
medical officers hanged for his activities in the
concentration camps, stated at his trial: "Three days
before the British came,... I had a talk with Kramer
[commandant at Belsen] about the conditions....
I told him, had I been the English officer taking the
camp over, I would have taken the Commandant and the
doctor, put them against the wall and shot them."[116]
Even Eichmann recognized that the "Final Solution"
was contrary to law, although in his view legal responsibility should rest with his superiors. All he was
prepared to acknowledge was "menschlich schuldig"
(moral guilt).[117] When major criminals recognize
that their actions, or the actions of those associated
with them, are in breach of law, there is something to
be said in favour of accepting their statements as
evidence of the existence of the legal system in question.

There is no need to examine the various "sources"
or "creative processes" of international law listed
in article 38 of the Statute of the World Court as
the elements to be applied in deciding issues submitted
to it; namely, "international conventions... establishing rules expressly recognised by the contesting States;
international custom, as evidence of a general practice
accepted as law; and the general principles of law
recognised by civilised nations."[118] It is enough to
point out that states do have relations with each other
and do regard themselves as being bound by certain rules
of conduct, so much so that when a new entity is
recognized as a state it is understood, in accordance
with the traditional rules, that it is bound by the
rules which are accepted as binding by already existing
states whose ranks it wishes to join,[119] although this
rule is now being increasingly challenged by the states
which have been created since 1945.[120]

On the other hand, it must be recognized that

... the official thinking of a State may not keep pace
with the changes in the international life; it may be
slow to apprehend the disintegrating effect of some of
them upon what is assumed to be the law. It may
misconceive the significance of persistent and oft-
recurring breaches, regarding them as merely perverse
instances of lawlessness, rather than as grim tokens
of resolute effort never to heed certain restrictions
which the law once appeared to exact of all. Accordingly, it is constantly necessary to observe with care
how far repeated and widespread breaches of the law by
numerous States are such tokens of gradual modification.
To that end, it is imperative to endeavor to ascertain
how States generally are expected to react when confronted
with particular rules, and in the course of that
endeavor to accept no guidance that is heedless of
obvious propensities, or shuns what experience has made
the basis of reasonable expectations. The predictable
conduct of States in many situations has become so
obvious, that to ignore it betrays mental inertia or
unconcern as to what the future may bring.[121] ... To
distinguish between what the several members of the
family of nations may be fairly deemed to have
accepted or acquiesced in as the law governing their
mutual relations, and what does not in fact appear to
have received such acceptance is a never-ending
task. The most delicate and elusive phase of the study
of international law is that which exacts of the
investigator a rigid examination of, and a judicial
conclusion with respect to, the actual condition of
the law at any given time. He may note the processes
by which changes are wrought, the causes of evolution,
current demands for particular modifications, and the
probable influence of thought focused on the solution of
defined problems; he may also never cease to be aware
of the fact that international law is bound to respond
to the changing needs of international society,[122]
and he may prophesy the nature of some responses that
the future may bring. Nevertheless, his primary task
is to see things as they are, and if he attempts to
mirror the law, to let no play of imagination or vision
of the future mar the accuracy of the portrayal. The
form of his utterance is relatively unimportant, so
long as he remains a realist and grimly reflects the
image that he sees. It may be that the very truthful-
ness of his pen and the very grotesqueness of what it
records may serve in small measure to hasten the day
when the law of nations presents a lovelier aspect.[123]

This comment by Hyde emphasizes that the significance
or reality of any system of law does not depend upon
its satisfying any preconceived formal requirements.
It lies rather in its satisfying the needs of the group
or society whose actions it purports to regulate.
"Law [is] a social institution to satisfy social
wants - the claims and demands and expectations involved
in the existence of civilized society - by giving effect
to as much as we may with the least sacrifice, so far
as such wants may be satisfied or such claims given
effect by an ordering of human conduct through politically organized society."[124] Broadly speaking, law -
any kind of law - is intended to facilitate the living
together of individuals within a group in such a way
as to reduce the frictions and tensions existing among
them, and to establish, in so far as it may, peace and
good order among them.

With this as a premise, it is clear that the validity
of law in no way depends upon one universal definition
or on the identity of any particular pundit. What is
important is to define concepts in such a way as to
enable them to regulate the situations that it is
desired that they should control. If they satisfy
the purpose that they are called upon to serve,
regardless of whether there is a sovereign, a legislature, a command, a threat, a court, or a law-enforcing
agency, they constitute law. From this point of view,
there is little doubt that, in order to facilitate
their relations inter se, states have accepted a code
of conduct which they regard as binding upon themselves,
which they consider ought to be obeyed, and in respect
of breaches of which they are prepared to tender
apologies, make reparation, or go to court, as the
case may be. It matters little, therefore, whether the
system which states are prepared to observe does not

satisfy the positivists or is regarded by "ordinary" lawyers as not amounting to law, or whether it is, as is so often the case, described as 'primitive' law:

The legal nature of international law can only be vindicated by putting it within the frame of the general conception of law based on the legal experience of the modern states which constitute the membership of the international community, and by the admission that it is a weak law in a stage of transition to a developed law as it exists within the State. This and no other is the place of international law in jurisprudence. This and no other is the relation of jurisprudence to international law. The future development of international law is conditioned by its incorporation into the body of general principles and into the conception of law as evolved by civilized communities without regard to the 'state of nature' existing among States. The more international law approaches the standards of internal law, the more it approximates to those standards of morals and order which are the ultimate foundation of all law. It is more scientific to regard international law as incomplete and in a state of transition to a true society of States under the organized and binding rule of law, as generally recognized and practiced by civilized communities within their borders,[125] than that, as the result of the well-meant desire to raise its authority as law, it should be treated as a species of wider conception of law so diluted and deprived of its imperative essence that it is not law at all. It is unscientific to let primitive law, if we can call it law, overshadow developed law as the decisive factor in determining the conception of law. We flout both science and progress if in order to give authority and permanence to the authority of international law we create ad hoc a conception of law so wide as to be meaningless.[126]

For this reason, discounting any need for philosophical background, international law may be defined as that system of laws and regulations which those who operate on the international scene recognize as being necessary for their orderly conduct, and which they recognize as being binding upon themselves in order to achieve that orderly conduct.

* Based on a paper published in 14 Univ. of Toronto Law J. (1962) 176.

[1] International Law, vol. 1 (1905), s.89 (italics added).

[2] Vol. 3 (1956), 800-4.

[3] Vol. 2 (1906), s. 253.

[4] Cmd. 1422 (1921), 45; 2 Annual Digest 1923-24, 436; G. Schwarzenberger, International Law and Totalitarian Lawlessness (1943), 128.

[5] See G. Schwarzenberger, International Law, vol. 2 (1968), ch.39.

[6] Axtell's Case (1661), Kelyng 13.

[7] (1865) U.S. Exec. Docs., House of Reps., 40th Cong., 2nd Sess., 1867-8, vol.8.

[8] (1900) 17 Cape Reports 561 (S.C.).

[9] Vol. 2, s. 253.

[10] Nowhere is it hinted that the fifth and sixth revised editions were prepared by the same editor. It is perhaps relevant here to draw attention to the latest German approach to the problem of superior orders. In December, 1961, Vice-Admiral Heye, Bundestag Commissioner for the Bundeswehr, announced that an official study would shortly be initiated into the question of how far an individual soldier may go in disobeying orders to which he objects on grounds of conscience. "The type of German soldier for whom others act and think must belong to the past." Such a survey is of added importance in view of the decision of the High Court of Karlsruhe against a Bremen man who had twice been court-martialled during the war for refusing to carry out his military duties because of his opposition to the Nazi regime. The High Court ruled that such resistance could be justified only when "the aims and chances of success make the endeavour appear a serious attempt to overthrow an unjust regime." Since the accused was acting on his own account and not for this higher political purpose, his plea was rejected. The Times (London), Dec. 12, 1961. See also, on the refusal of superior orders, (1961) 105 Solicitors' Journal 1113. For a fuller discussion, see Green, 'Superior Orders and the Reasonable Man,' 8 Canadian Y.B. Int'l Law (1970) 61.

11 International Law, Chiefly as Interpreted and Applied by the United States (1947), vol. 1, p.vii.

12 McDougal, 'Law and Power,' 46 Am. J. Int'l Law (1952), 102, 110.

13 Lauterpacht, 1 Collected Papers (1970), 9, 193, 16.

14 On the nature of society and community law, see Schwarzenberger, The Frontiers of International Law (1962), ch. 1.

15 Kozhevnikov, ed., International Law (196?), 7,11.

16 Pravda, 25 Sept. 1968 (tr., Bozeman, The Future of Law in a Multicultural World (1971) 187).

17 'Positive Law and International Law', 51 Am. J. Int'l L. (1957), 691, 727-8.

18 Vattel, Le Droit des Gens (1758), Lib. 1, Prelim., 3 (Carnegie tr. (1916), vol. 3, s.1).

19 Vol. 1 (1963), 1.

20 Phleger, 'Some Recent Developments in International Law of Interest to the United States', 30 Dept. of State, Bulletin (1954), 196 (italics added).

21 For the meaning of 'civilized', see III above.

22 Bogotà, 1448, 119 U.N.T.S. 3.

23 See, however, VI below.

24 See, e.g., Joint Dissenting Opinion by Basdevant, Winiarski, McNair and Read on Admission of a State to Membership in the U.N., [1948] I.C.J. 57,85.

25 See, e.g., Garciá-Mora, International Law and Asylum as a Human Right (1956); cp., however, VIII below.

26 (1950) 217 P.2d 481, 218 P.595 (italics added); see Green, 'Human Rights and Colour Discrimination', 3 Int'l Law Q. (1950), 422.

27 (1952) 242 P.2d 617; 19 Int. Law Rep. 312,316.

28 Williams, 'International Law and the Controversy Concerning the Word "Law"', 22 Brit.Y.B.Int'l Law (1945), 146, 148.

29 'The Legal Nature of International Law', 1 Am. J. Int'l Law (1907), 831, 837, 839, 851.

30 Cp. Jenks, The Common Law of Mankind (1958) - "the law of an organized world community", 58.

31 Locksley Hall, lines 127-30.

32 Reparation for Injuries Suffered in the Service of the U.N. [1949] I.C.J. 174, 179.

33 [1971] I.C.J. 16, 51-2, 54, 52, 54.

34 Ibid., 56.

35 U.N., Y.B. Int'l Law Comm. 1949, 232.

36 Ibid., 1961, 258.

37 Op.cit., n.15, 321, 13.

38 Erickson, International Law and the Revolutionary State (1972) 37.

39 Competence of Assembly regarding Admission to the U.N. [1950] I.C.J. 4, 10.

40 See, e.g., Judge Lauterpacht's Separate Opinion on South-West Africa - Voting Procedure [1955] I.C.J. 90, 115; Judges van Wyk, Tanaka, Jessup, Padilla Nervo in South-West Africa Cases (Second Phase) [1966] I.C.J. 6, 171-2, 291-3, 432-41, 455-7, 464-70; also, Sloan, 'The Binding Force of a "Recommend-ation" of the General Assembly of the United Nations', 22 Brit.Y.B. Int'l Law (1948)1; Kelsen, The Law of the United Nations (1951) 40, 63, 99, 195-6, 459; Johnson, 'The Effect of Resolutions of the General Assembly of the United Nations', 32 Brit.Y.B. Int'l Law (1955-6) 97, 111; Fitzmaurice, 'The Law and Procedure of the International Court of Justice, 1951-4; Questions of Jurisdiction, Competence and Procedure', 34 ibid. (1958) 1,3; Cheng, 'United Nations Resolutions on Outer Space: "Instant" International Customary Law' 5 Indian J. Int'l Law (1965) 23; Asamoah, The Legal Significance of the Declarations of the General Assembly of the United Nations (1966); Bleicher, 'The Legal Significance of Re-Citation of General Assembly Resolutions', 63 Am.J.Int'l Law (1969) 444.

41 [1948] I.C.J. 15.

42 At 32; see also Dissenting Opinion of Daxner,

Judge ad hoc 33-5.

43
See Mosul Case (1925) P.C.I.J. Ser. B No. 12, 27.

44
See n. 40 above; also Bleicher, ibid., 452, 465.

45
In the Namibia advisory opinion, Judge Padilla Nervo
said that G. A. Resolutions "propose or evolve
additional subsidiary means which the Court should
apply for determination of rules of law", loc.cit.,
111.

46
Ibid., 334.

47
Op.cit., n.40 above, 40.

48
U.S. Dept. of State, 19 Bulletin (1948), 751.

49
18 Jan. 1949. H.C. Deb., vol. 460, cols.16, 18.

50
(1951) 18 Int. Law Rep. 144, 157.

51
Y.B. Int'l Law Comm. 1951, Vol. 2, 123, 141.

52
Ibid., 1956, vol. 2, 253, 256.

53
[1969] I.C.J. 3.

54
Cmnd. 584 (1958).

55
Report of the 47th Conference (1956), 88.

56
Lord McNair, Law of Treaties (1961), 316. Cf.,
however, his "Treaties Producing Effects 'Erga
Omnes'" in Scritti Perassi (1957), 23 (op.cit., 255).

57
(1923) P.C.I.J. Ser. B, No.5; The apparent finding
to the opposite effect in the Bernadotte Case, l.c.,
n.32 above, is to be explained by the nature of the
question presented to the Court in that case.

58
G. Clark and L. B. Sohn, World Peace through World
Law (1966), 35.

59
See Schwarzenberger, 'The Impact of the East-West
Rift on International Law' (1950) 36 Grotius
Transactions 226; Higgins, Conflict of Interests
(1965); and V. below.

60
The Cristina [1938] A.C. 485, 502.

61
Le Droit des Gens (1758), Preface, s.18 (Carnegie
tr.7) (italics added).

62 11 U.N.C.I.O. Documents, 493.

63 My Name is Tom Connally (1954), 282 (italics in original).

64 Animal Farm (1945), ch. 10 (1949 ed., 10).

65 Green, 'Gentlemen's Agreements and the Security Council', (1960) 13 Current Legal Problems 255; 'Representation in the Security Council', (1962) 11 Indian Y.B. Int'l Aff. 48.

66 Green, 'The Security Council in Retreat', (1954) 8 Y.B. World Aff. 95, 107.

67 Tractatus de Iure Suprematus (1677 - c.Jones, 'Leibnitz as International Lawyer', (1945) 22 Brit. Y.B. Int'l Law 1, 4.

68 See Williams ed., Salmond on Jurisprudence (1957) 518.

69 See Fawcett, The Inter Se Doctrine of Commonwealth Relations (1958).

70 Cheng, The Law of International Air Transport (1962); Lowenfeld, Aviation Law (1972), ch.II.

71 See, e.g., R. v. Brailsford [1905] 2 K.B. 730; Joyce v. D.P.P. [1946] A.C. 347.

72 W. Harvey Moore, Int. Law Assoc. Edinburgh Conf., Report of the 46th Conference 1954, 36.

73 4 Collected Papers of John Bassett Moore (1944) 133.

74 Op.cit., n. 13 above, 21.

75 Loc.cit., n. 55 above, 62, referring to n. 72 above, 21.

76 Art. 65.

77 Part III, The Law of War on Land (1958), ss.113 and 107, n.1(b).

78 The Law of Land Warfare, FM 27-10 (1956), s.35.

79 Nuclear Tests [1973] I.C.J. (Australia) 99, (New Zealand) 135.

80 Rosenne, The International Court of Justice (1957),

2,3,4: "[I]nternational adjudication is a function
which is performed within the general framework of
the political organization of the international
society, and ... the Court has a political task
to perform, that is, a task related to the pacific
settlement of international disputes and hence to
the maintenance of international peace. That
international adjudication is a political operation
does not cease to have political consequences
when the States concerned agree to have recourse
to the Court. The political factor continues
influencing the litigating States in their handling
of the case,... and emerges again to the fore
after judgment has been given, and the litigating
States are faced with the problem of complying with
what has been decided. Litigation is but a phase
in the unfolding of a political drama. ... All
international litigation presupposes a dispute ...
and is therefore concerned with finding a solution
to the conflicting and contradictory aspirations
of two or more political, norm-creating, groups, in
this case the States.... The essential difference
between diplomatic and judicial settlement is the
extent to which co-ordinated sovereignties agree
to forego their right to insist upon the direct
settlement of the dispute."

81
[1957] I.C.J. 9.

82
S.C. Official Records, 988th Meeting, 18 Dec. 1961;
see also V below.

83
Press Conf., 18 Apr. 1970, 9 Int'l Legal Materials
(1970) 600, 602-4.

84
See, e.g., statement in G.A. 6th Committee, 2 Oct.
1974, Canadian Press Release No. 10.

85
(1923) P.C.I.J. Ser. A, No. 1, 32 (italics added).

86
(1930-9) 9 U.N., Rep. Int. Arb. Awards 84.

87
[1948] I.C.J. 15; [1949] I.C.J. 4, 244.

88
Israel v. Bulgaria, [1959] I.C.J. 127.

89
Fisheries Jurisdiction [1973] (U.K.-Iceland) 3,
[1974] 3; (Germany-Iceland) [1973] 49 , [1974] 175.

90
See n. 79 above.

91
1928, 94 L.N.T.S. 57.

92 See, e.g., Bebr, Judicial Control of the European
    Communities (1962); Brinkhorst and Schermers,
    Judicial Remedies in the European Communities
    (1969, 1972); Elles, Community Law through the Cases
    (1973); see also, Van duyn v. Home Office [1974]
    C.M.L.R. 347; H.P. Bulmer Ltd. and Showerings Ltd.
    v. J. Bollinger SA and Champagne Lanson Perè et Fils
    [1974] 2 All E.R. 1226; Application des Gaz SA v.
    Falks Veritas [1974] 3 All E.R. 88.

93 See Green, 'Legal Aspects of the Schuman Plan',
    (1952) 5 Current Legal Problems, 274, 291; Green,
    Political Integration by Jurisprudence (1969);
    Mann, Function of Judicial Decision in European
    Economic Integration (1972).

94 See, e.g., Bassiouni and Nanda, A Treatise on
    International Criminal Law (1973).

95 International Law (1894) 263-4.

96 (1854) 14 C.B. 487.

97 [1951] 2 K.B. 1003.

98 1956 (3 vols.).

99 1887 (3 vols.).

100 1906 (8 vols.).

101 1940-4 (8 vols.).

102 1963-73 (14 vols.).

103 British Digest (1967-).

104 British Practice in International Law (1963-).

105 1962-9 (6 vols.).

106 1970- .

107 See, e.g., Bissonnette, La Satisfaction comme mode
     de réparation en droit international (1952).

108 [1905] 2 K.B. 391, 401 (italics added).

109 S. S. Lotus (1927) P.C.I.J., Ser.A., No.10, 18.

110 [1950] I.C.J. 266, 276-7; see also U. S. Nationals
     in Morocco [1952] I.C.J. 176, 200.

111 (1843) 10 Cl. & Fin. 200.

112 Cmd. 6964 (1946) 48, 91.

113 The Times (London) 21 Dec. 1961.

114 Loc. cit., n. 112 above, 108.

115 Ibid., 98.

116 The Belsen Trial, ed. Phillips (1949), 717.

117 The Times, 8 Jul. 1961 (the minutes of the trial
translate this as 'For the human point of view',
Minutes of Session 88, 7/7/61, S1); see also
Green, loc.cit., n.10 above, 94.

118 On the general principles, see Cheng, The General
Principles of Law as Applied by International
Courts and Tribunals (1953); Fitzmaurice, 'The
Law and Procedure of the International Court of
Justice, 1951-4: General Principles and Sources
of Law', (1953) 30 Brit. Y.B. Int'l Law 1, and
'1954-9', (1958) 35 Ibid. 183. Schwarzenberger,
Frontiers of International Law, (1962) ch. 4;
McNair, 'The General Principles of Law Recognized
by Civilized Nations', (1957) 35 Brit. Y.B. Int'l
Law 1; Lauterpacht, The Development of Inter-
national Law by the International Court (1958),
158; Verzijl, 1 International Law in Historical
Perspective (1968), 47; Herczegh, General
Principles of Law and the International Legal
Order (1969); and VII below. On sources generally,
see bibliography in Schwarzenberger, 1 International
Law (1957), ch. 2.

119 See O'Connell, 'Independence and Problems of State
Succession', in O'Brien, The New Nations in
International Law and Diplomacy (1965) 12.

120 See V below.

121 Cp. Pound,: 'Law must be stable and yet it cannot
stand still. Hence all thinking about law has
struggled to reconcile the conflicting demands of
the need of stability and the need of change'
(Interpretations of Legal History (1923)1); and
Holmes: 'The prophecies of what the courts will
do in fact and nothing more are what I mean by
law' ('The Path of the Law' (1897) 10 Harv. Law
Rev. 457, 461).

122 See, e.g., n. 82 above.

123 Hyde, op.cit., n.11 above, vii, viii-ix.

124 Pound, An Introduction to the Philosophy of Law (Yale Paperback, 1959) 47.

125 See III above.

126 Lauterpacht, op.cit., n. 13 above, 200.

V

THE IMPACT OF THE NEW STATES ON INTERNATIONAL LAW*

A new state is born into a world of law.
It is a state ... only because of a law
that lays down the conditions for and
attributes of statehood.

O'Connell, 'Independence and Problems
of State Succession', in O'Brien,
The New Nations in International Law
and Diplomacy (1965) 12.

There has been a growing tendency since the establishment of the United Nations in 1945 to differentiate
general international law from the law of international
organization. If one were to accept this bifurcation
it would be necessary to deal with the impact of new
States under two distinct rubrics.[1] For the purpose of
this paper it is more convenient to make no such
distinction, but to deal with the effects of the creation
of some eighty new States since the end of the Second
World War on international legal relations at large.

Although

the Government of the United States has on various
occasions announced the principle that international law
as a system is binding upon nations not merely as something to which they may be tacitly assumed to have agreed,
but as a fundamental condition of their admission to
full participation in the intercourse of civilized
States[2],

it nevertheless remains one of the paradoxes of international law that its binding authority rests to a
great extent upon the consent of those it purports to

bind. This consensual basis of international law finds
expression in the judgment of the World Court in the
S. S. Lotus:[3]

The rules of law binding upon States emanate from their
own free will as expressed in conventions or by usages
generally accepted as expressing principles of law and
established in order to regulate the relations between
these co-existing independent communities or with a
view to the achievement of common aims.

This is only a judicial version of what Lord Russell
of Killowen said to the American Bar Association at
Saratoga in 1896:[4]

What, then, is international law? I know no better
definition of it than that it is the sum of the rules
or usages which civilized States have agreed shall be
binding upon them in their dealings with one another.

This consensual characteristic of international law
is embodied also in the Statute of the International
Court of Justice, article 38, which deals with the
"sources" of international law and refers to conventions "establishing rules expressly recognized by the
contesting States". It also speaks of custom "as
evidence of a general practice accepted as law", and
this concept has been explained by the World Court in
the Asylum case:[5]

The Party which relies on a custom ... must prove that
this custom is established in such a manner that it
becomes binding on the other party. [It] must prove
that the rule invoked by it is in accordance with a
constant and uniform usage practised by the States in
question, and that this usage is the expression of a
right appertaining to the [one] State ... and a duty
incumbent on the [other] State.

Other provisions of article 38 of the Court's Statute
are perhaps even more explicit in their acknowledgement
of the significance of consent. First, there are the
general principles of law recognized by civilized

nations, although there is no hint as to what these principles are,[6] what constitutes the standard of civilization[7] or how general must be the recognition that they are accorded. It would appear that in international practice this concept is merely a paraphrase for those principles of law which are or ought to be generally recognized by those nations which seek to be considered as civilized by "us" - and it must be remembered that the "us" here referred to relates to states having European traditions. As Verzijl has remarked:[8]

Now there is one truth that is not open to denial or even to doubt, namely that the actual body of international law, as it stands today, not only is the product of the conscious activity of the European mind, but has also drawn its vital essence from a common source of European beliefs, and in both of these aspects it is merely of Western European origin, a point that was made very clear by India at the time of the Goa crisis in 1961.[9]

Article 38 goes even further in its declaration of the importance of consent, stating that the normal rules of international law may be supplemented by principles ex aequo et bono if the parties agree thereto. The dispute between the United Kingdom and Guatemala concerning Belize/British Honduras illustrates this. The United Kingdom accepted the jurisdiction of the World Court in 1930, renewed the declaration of acceptance in 1940, and in February 1946 expressly declared that this acceptance applied equally "to all legal disputes concerning the interpretation, application or validity of any treaty relating to the boundaries of British Honduras".[10] A year later Guatemala responded, accepting the Court's jurisdiction "in all legal disputes. [But] this declaration does not cover the dispute between England and Guatemala concerning the restoration of the territory of Belize, which the Government of Guatemala would, as it has proposed, agree to submit to the judgment of the Court, if the case were decided <u>ex aequo et bono</u>".[11] Both States are apparently equally desirous of having their dispute settled judicially, but since the United Kingdom will only agree that this be done in accordance with law, a proposal that Guatamala expressly rejects, the case has never come before the Court. In fact, neither of these declarations now appears in the Court's <u>Yearbook</u>, and Guatemala no longer accepts the "compulsory" jurisdiction of the Court at all.

The assertion of a consensual basis to international law would mean, if carried to its logical conclusion, that a State is bound only by so much of the law as it clearly accepts. In so far as treaty law is concerned, this would be relatively easy to determine. The Nuremberg Judgment has raised the possibility that treaties regulating the use of force and resort to war and to which the larger proportion of the States are parties create a type of universal law binding upon all. A problem does arise, however, when international society consists of more newly created States than there were in existence either at the time the treaties were signed or when they were interpreted by the Tribunal, or even than there were in the General Assembly when that body adopted its Resolution[12] affirming the Principles of International Law Recognized by the Charter and the Judgment of the Nuremberg Tribunal. In so far as this Resolution is concerned, it may well be argued that States which have been admitted to the United Nations since its adoption have become members in the knowledge of its existence and may be construed to have accepted the law of the United Nations as it has developed between the adoption of the Charter and their entry into the Organization. Of more importance from the point of view of the United Nations is

article 2 (6) of the Charter, which purports to bind
non-members, although the only enforcement process
would be by way of the members, who are bound to
carry out a decision of the Security Council directed
against a non-member under Chapter VII.[13]

Although the decision in the Lotus case appears to be
a clear assertion by the Court of its acceptance of
consent as the basis of obligation in international
law,[14] its attitude has in fact been somewhat equivocal.
The Court refused, in its advisory opinion on the
Status of Eastern Carelia,[15] to recognize the imposition
of any obligation arising from the League Covenant
upon the Soviet Union while a non-member. On the other
hand, in the Bernadotte case[16] the Court, completely
ignoring the Eastern Carelia opinion, went to the other
extreme and held that

fifty States, representing the vast majority of the
members of the international community [- there are now
more than 130 members -], had the power, in conformity
with international law, to bring into being an entity
possessing objective international personality, and
not merely personality recognized by them alone,
together with capacity to bring international claims.

The judgment on the preliminary objection in the
Monetary Gold case[17] shows a return to the more traditional view. On this occasion, it pointed out that
when

the vital issue to be settled concerns the international
responsibility of a third State, the Court cannot,
without the consent of that third State, give a decision
on that issue binding upon any State, either the third
State, or any of the parties before it.

Since the Court completely ignored the Bernadotte
opinion in the Monetary Gold judgment, there is no point
in trying to reconcile these conflicting views,
especially as in the Namibia opinion the Court considered

the General Assembly's rejection of South Africa's sovereignty over Southwest Africa as effective erga omnes.[18]

To allow the principle of consent to remain completely supreme would mean that there would be no international law. Each State would announce, and not necessarily in advance - for the history of codification conferences suggests that States frequently only become aware of the rules they do not like when those rules are actually enunciated - which rules it was prepared to accept indicating that any other rules would only be commented upon when they became relevant, either because the State in question wished to rely upon them or because some other State sought to assert them against that State. Reference might usefully be made to the statements issued by some of the newly-independent States as regards their willingness to continue to recognize treaties which had been entered into by their imperial rulers and which, in accordance with the traditional rules of international law,[19] they might have been expected to continue to observe. In 1963, Uganda informed the Secretary-General of the United Nations[20] that, in so far as treaties entered into on its behalf by the United Kingdom were concerned, it would

continue on a basis of reciprocity to apply the term of such treaties from the time of its independence, that is to say October 9, 1962, until December 31, 1963, unless such treaties are abrogated, or modified by agreement with the other high contracting parties before December 31, 1963. At the expiry of this period,... the Government of Uganda will regard such treaties, unless regarded as otherwise surviving, as having terminated.

The statement issued by Malawi in 1964[21] indicated a somewhat more selective intent:

The Government of Malawi proposes to review each of [the bilateral and multilateral treaties in question]

individually, and to indicate to the depositary in each
case what steps it wishes to take in relation to each
such instrument - whether by way of confirmation of
termination, confirmation of succession or accession.
During such interim period of review, any party to a
multilateral treaty which has, prior to independence,
been applied or extended to the former Nyasaland
Government, may, on a basis of reciprocity, rely as
against Malawi on the terms of such treaty.

A statement which showed its government's awareness of
the normal position was sent to the Secretary-General
by Zambia in 1965,[22] and subsequently formed the model
for Guyana, Barbados, Mauritius, Bahamas and Fiji:[23]

The Government of Zambia, conscious of the desirability
of maintaining existing legal relationships, and
conscious of its obligations under international law
to honour its treaty commitments, acknowledges that
many treaty rights and obligations of the Government
of the United Kingdom in relation to Northern Rhodesia
were succeeded to by Zambia upon independence by virtue
of customary international law.

Since, however, it is likely that in virtue of customary
international law, certain treaties may have lapsed
at the independence of Zambia, it seems essential that
each treaty should be subjected to legal examination.
It is proposed, after the examination has been completed
to indicate which, if any, of the treaties which may
have lapsed by customary international law the Government of Zambia wishes to treat as having lapsed. ...

It is desired that it be presumed that each treaty has
been legally succeeded to by Zambia and that action be
based on this presumption until a decision is reached
that it should be regarded as having lapsed. Should
the Government of Zambia be of the opinion that it has
legally succeeded to a treaty and wishes to terminate
the operation of the treaty, it will in due course
give notice of termination in the terms thereof.

Since the clearest evidence of the reality of international lies in the actual doings of States,[24] whether
this be shown in treaties or by their practice, it is
obvious that the international law with regard to
succession must today be ascertained in the light of
the practice of the states created since 1945, and this

is reflected in the draft convention on succession to
treaties drawn up by the International Law Commission.
In the light of the above quotations, however, it is
somewhat strange to find the Commission adopting the
view that according to customary law no succession
occurred:[25]

It is in the nature of things that more recent practice
must be accorded a certain priority as evidence of the
opinio juris of today, especially when, as in the
case of succession of States in respect to treaties,
the very frequency and extensiveness of the modern
practice tends to submerge the earlier precedents. ...
The Commission has borne in mind that new factors have
come into play that affect the context within which
State practice in regard to succession takes place
today. Particularly important is the much greater
interdependence of States, which has affected the policy
of successor states in some measure in regard to
continuing the treaty relations of the territory to
which they have succeeded, and the fact that modern
precedents reflect the practice of States conducting
their relations under the principles of the Charter of
the United Nations .... In modern international law,
having regard to the maintenance of the system of
multilateral treaties and of the stability of treaty
relationships, as a general rule the principle of de jure
continuity should apply. On the other hand, the
'traditional' principle that a 'new State' begins its
treaty relations with a clean slate was more consistent
with the principle of self-determination as it is
applicable in the case of newly independent States.
The clean slate principle was well-designed to meet the
situation of newly independent States, namely, those
which emerge from former dependent territories. ...
[T]he main implication of the principle of self-
determination in the law concerning succession in respect
of treaties was precisely to confirm the traditional
clean slate principle as the underlying norm for cases
of newly independent States or for cases that may be
assimilated to them. The 'clean slate' metaphor ...
is merely a convenient and succinct way of referring to
the newly independent State's general freedom of
obligation of its predecessor's treaties. In the first
place, ... modern treaty practice recognizes that a
newly independent State has the right ... to establish
itself as a 'party' or as a 'contracting State' to
any multilateral treaty, except one of a restricted
character, in regard to which its predecessor State
was either a 'party' or a 'contracting State' at the

date of the succession of States. In other words the fact that prior to independence the predecessor State had established its consent to be bound by a multilateral treaty and its act of consent related to the territory now under the sovereignty of the newly independent State creates a legal nexus between the territory and the treaty in virtue of which the newly independent State has the right, if it wishes, to participate in the treaty on its own behalf as a separate party or contracting State. In the case of multilateral treaties of a restricted character and bilateral treaties, the newly independent State may invoke a similar legal nexus between its territory and the treaty as a basis for achieving the continuance in force of the treaty with the consent of the other State or States concerned. Accordingly the so-called clean slate principle, as it operates in the modern law of succession of States, is very far from normally bringing about a total rupture in the treaty relations of a territory which emerges as a newly independent State. The modern law while leaving the newly independent State free under the clean slate principle to determine its own treaty relations, holds out to it the means of achieving the maximum continuity in those relations consistent with the interests of itself and of other States parties to its predecessor's treaties. In addition, the clean slate principle does not, in any event, relieve a newly independent State of the obligation to respect a boundary settlement and certain other situations of a territorial character established by treaty

even though these are clearly relics of colonialism.

The Commission's commentary then proceeds to cast

doubt on the value of its own proposed Convention:

Since a succession of States in most cases bring into being a new State, a convention on the law of succession in respect of treaties would ex hypothesi not be binding on the successor State unless and until it took steps to become a party to that convention; and even then the convention would not be binding upon it in respect of any act or fact which took place before the date on which it became a party. Nor would other States be bound by the convention in relation to the new State until the latter had become a party.

It would appear, therefore, that the Commission envisages

a situation in which Xland would be bound by a treaty

while it remained a dependency, but that upon independence

that treaty would lapse, only to be revived when Xland
as an independent State formally announced its succession to the treaty, provided that the other parties
were now willing to continue recognizing that treaty
as valid for Xland. It would seem that the Commission
sees no difficulty in connection with such a hiatus.

It must not be thought that it is only the newly
created States that seek to pick and choose among the
rules of international law. Thus, at the time that
Canada introduced her water pollution legislation and
amended her acceptance of the jurisdiction of the
World Court,[26] Prime Minister Trudeau explained that
Canada would not accept judicial decision in this
field because no law existed.[27] However, only some six
months earlier he had expressly stated:[28]

Membership in a community imposes ... certain limitations
on the activities of all members. For this reason,
while not lowering our guard or abandoning our proper
interests, Canada must not appear to live by double
standards. We cannot, at the same time that we are
urging other countries to adhere to regimes designed
for the orderly conduct of international activities,
pursue policies inconsistent with that order simply
because to do so in a given instance appears to be to
our brief advantage. Law, be it municipal or international, is composed of restraints. If wisely
construed they contribute to the freedom and the well-
being of individuals and of states. Neither states
nor individuals should feel free to pick and choose, to
accept or reject, the laws that may for the moment be
attractive to them.

But this appears to be exactly what Canada was doing.

If every State were to base its attitude towards the
obligations of international law on this type of
eclecticism, and thus run the risk of having others
retaliate in kind with 'self-cancelling consequences'[29]
it would mean that rather than use the increasing number
of works being published on international law as

interpreted and applied by individual States[30] to ascertain the extent of agreement among States,[31] such examination would be directed at ascertaining the extent of disagreement and how limited the commitment to what were formerly regarded as generally accepted rules.

With the increase in the number of newly independent States and their natural sense of pride in having overthrown foreign imperialist rulers, it is perhaps understandable that there is a growing tendency for States to assert their right to assume the claims made by others in maintaining that international law is based on consent for them as well as for their "older brothers". Such an attitude undoubtedly contributes to the aggrandizement of a particular State's self-importance, and evidence of this may be found in a statement made as early as 1947 by the Philippine member of the International Military Tribunal for the Far East. He felt that the Tokyo tribunal would accomplish more than Nuremberg, for "eleven nations, representing a wider variety of legal tradition, form the Tokyo tribunal, whereas judges from only four nations formed the court at Nuremberg"[32] - it is perhaps of interest that at the first election of judges for the World Court by the Security Council the Philippine nominee received only one vote,[33] that no Philippine judge was elected to that Court until after the South West African Fiasco[34], in 1966, and that Dean Santos of the College of Law in the University of the Philippines, in compiling his <u>Cases and Other Materials on International Law</u>, included Nuremberg rather than Tokyo, even though "it has been possible to include a substantial amount of Philippine materials."[35] In addition to this type of national self-aggrandizement, it would become impossible to ascertain at any particular time what the rules of international law were. Instead of it being possible

to establish an international rule of law to produce
and control international order, there would be a
breakdown of rules and the reassertion of anarchy.[36]

It should not be thought that denial of the right
of the individual State to pick and choose the rules
by which it will be bound is to deny completely all
freedom of choice. When new States come into existence
and seek recognition from other members of international
society they do not make any express declaration as to
the rules of law that they accept, nor are they
expected to make any such declaration when recognition
is actually extended to them, although there have been
occasions when particular States have been required to
make express statements concerning specific obligations
either in return for or in advance of recognition.[37]
Today, it is becoming normal practice for a new State,
especially if it has come into being under the auspices
of the United Nations, to affirm its acceptance of
and willingness to abide by the Purposes and Principles
of the Charter, for the cachet of statehood today
appears to be admission to the United Nations, so much
so that we have even seen entities which are about to
achieve their independences, as, for example, Guinea-
Bissau, formally accepted before independence has in
fact been granted, and it is a condition of membership
that members accept the obligations of the Charter.
It is also not uncommon for a group of States, whether
old or new, to declare that they intend among themselves
to be governed by certain rules of international law,
even though such rules may be deviations from those
normally regarded as universal international law.
Article 38 of the Court's Statute recognizes this
possibility in so far as treaties are concerned, but
this type of regional law may also be the result of
custom.[38]

For some time it has been suggested that there was a
difference so far as international law was concerned
between the common law countries and the Continent,[39]
but by the 'thirties the emphasis had changed so as
to distinguish between American international law and
that of the rest of the world. The reason for this
shift has largely been the activities of the Pan-American
Union and its successor, the Organization of American
States, especially as expressed in such codification
exercises as that of Havana in 1928.[40] What is
perhaps the best exposition of American international
law is to be found in the dissenting opinion of Judge
Alvarez in the Asylum case:[41]

... As far as international law is concerned, the States
of America have, since their independence, wished to
modify the law so as to bring it into harmony with the
interests and aspirations of their continent ....
This expression 'American international law'... does
not mean, as may appear at first sight as many would
have believed, an international law which is peculiar
to the New World and entirely distinct from universal
international law,[42] but rather the complex of principles,
conventions, customs, practices, institutions and
doctrines which are peculiar to the Republics of the
New World .... I have referred to the 'Republics'
of the New World because Canada, which is a British
Dominion, and the European colonies in America, did
not participate in Pan-Americanism or in the establishment of American international law. If certain percepts,
which are held to be universal, are not accepted by
the countries of the American continent, it is obvious
that they no longer have that character; and if
American precepts are not recognized by the countries
of other continents, they must be applied only in the
New World.

A principle, custom, doctrine, etc., need not be adopted
by all the States of the New World in order to be
considered as part of American international law. The
same situation obtains in this case as in the case of
universal international law.

American international law is binding upon all the States
of the New World; it is also binding upon the States of
other continents in matters affecting America, such as
immigration, the security zone of the continent in time

of war, etc.

American international law has its sub-divisions, such
as, for instance, Latin-American international law or
the law of the Latin Republics of the New World, which
is not binding upon the United States.

American international law has exercised a considerable
influence over universal international law and has
given it its peculiar character; many concepts or
doctrines of American origin have achieved or tend to
achieve universal acceptance and many concepts of a
universal nature have, or tend to have, a special application in the New World. The influence of that law has
increased since the last world war. The number and
especially the quality of the institutions and principles
which have lately appeared in America and which tend
to be incorporated in new international law is truly
impressive ....

It has been maintained...that American international law
... must be subordinated to universal international
law .... Such a statement is not accurate .... Such
systems of law are not subordinate (sic) to universal
international law, but correlated (sic) to it....

The view that there is a special American law is
fairly generally held among Latin American writers. Its
origin, it has been suggested,[43] may possibly be part
of "a by-product of the circumstances surrounding the
independence movement in Latin America which induced
a desire for a greater break with Europe than eventually
transpired." Thus, as long ago as 1884, Rafael
Fernando Seijas wrote that

the origin of the public and private law of the
Hispano-American republics ought to be looked for in
the source of the international differences with
foreign powers which have produced inequality in the
treatment of the nations of the ... hemispheres,
obliging us to establish a special   law   which answers
to the satisfaction of our aspirations' and to the
necessities of our general interests.44

In their State practice, the countries of Latin
America have not hesitated to assert their own views
of international law. Some of these are what might be

expected from newly independent States, but others are conditioned by geographic considerations. Of the former, perhaps the best known are the Calvo and Drago doctrines, both of which may be regarded as reactions against unequal treatment.

It is perhaps not surprising that new States are usually economically underdeveloped. However altruistic the imperial power may have been, it is almost a sine qua non of human nature that economic interests will have tended to exploit the overseas territory. As a result, even a "conservative" government of a new State is likely to be attracted by protectionist policies, even though it may be compelled, in a desire to improve its own economic potential, to grant concessions to foreign exploiters[45] and investors. At the same time, the foreign economic interest will seek to protect its interests by way of diplomatic protection when necessary, while the government of the investor concerned will be inclined to use its greatest military and economic power on behalf of its nationals abroad.[46]

A tendency grew up in the Latin American States to compel foreign investors and contracting parties to agree that they receive treatment similar to that enjoyed by - or meted out to - local nationals and renounce their right to call for diplomatic inter-vention by their own States on their behalf. The basis of the doctrine is to be found in Calvo's Le droit international théorique et pratique[47] and may be expressed as follows:

America as well as Europe are inhabited today by free and independent nations, whose sovereign existence has the right to the same respect, and whose internal public law does not admit of intervention of any sort on the part of foreign peoples, whoever they may be....

According to strict international law, the recovery
of debts and the pursuit of private claims[48] does not
justify de plano the armed intervention of governments, and, since European states invariably follow
this rule in their reciprocal relations, there is no
reason why they should not also impose it upon themselves
in their relations with nations of the new world....

It is certain that aliens who establish themselves in
a country have the same right to protection as
nationals, but they ought not to lay claim to a
protection more extended. If they suffer any wrong,
they ought to count on the government of the country
prosecuting the delinquents, and not claim from the
state to which the authors of the violence belong any
pecuniary indemnity....

The rule that in more than one case it has been attempted
to impose on American states is that foreigners merit
more regard and privileges more marked and extended
than those accorded even to the nationals of the
country where they reside.

This principle is intrinsically contrary to the law
of equality of nations....

To admit in the present case governmental responsibility,
that is the principle of an indemnity, is to create
an exorbitant and fatal privilege, essentially favourable to the powerful states and injurious to the
weaker nations, establishing an unjustifiable inequality between nationals and foreigners. From another
standpoint, in sanctioning the doctrine that we are
combating, one would deal, although indirectly, a
strong blow to one of the constituent elements of the
independence of nations, that of territorial jurisdiction; here is, in effect, the real extent, the true
significance of such frequent recourse to diplomatic
channels to resolve the questions which from their
nature and the circumstances in the middle of which
they arise come under the exclusive domain of the
ordinary tribunals....

The responsibility of governments toward foreigners
cannot be greater than that which these governments
have toward their own citizens.

Despite these assertions by Calvo, the embodiment
of clauses giving effect to such principles in
national constitutions,[49] or express stipulations to
this effect in commercial contracts, the nations to

which the alien contractors belonged were not willing
to recognize the validity of the doctrine. This
refusal was supported by international tribunals which
tended to interpret the doctrine as having meaning
only to the extent that there had been no denial of
justice or exhaustion of local remedies.[50] This has
led one commentator to suggest that

> if it is true that the exhaustion of local remedies
> is always required by international law before a claim
> for State responsibility in respect of breaches of
> contract or denial of justice can be brought, the
> insertion of a Calvo Clause in a contract is super-
> fluous. If the exhaustion of local remedies is not
> always a necessary prerequisite according to internation-
> al law, no contractual Calvo Clause can make it such.
> Thus there is some substance in the statement of those
> tribunals which have held that the Calvo Clause is
> altogether ineffective in international law.[51]

As Calvo had pointed out, creditor States had not
hesitated to resort to armed intervention in order to
compel the new States in Latin America to meet their
contractual obligations which resulted in the imposition of the Maximilian regime in Mexico in 1861, and
led to the armed intervention by European powers in
Venezuela in 1902.[52] This caused Drago, Foreign
Minister of the Argentine, to contend that:[53]

> while a capitalist who lends his money to a foreign
> state always takes into account 'the resources of the
> country and the probability, greater or less', of
> repayment, it is also true that 'it is an inherent
> qualification of all sovereignty that no proceedings
> for the execution of a judgment may be instituted
> or carried out against it'; that, while it was not
> intended to defend 'bad faith, disorder, and deliberate
> and voluntary insolvency', yet the state should not
> 'be deprived of the right to choose the manner and the
> time of payment';... that, as the collection of loans
> by military means implied 'territorial occupation to
> make them effective,' a situation would be created
> at variance with [the Monroe Doctrine] ...; that it
> was not pretended, however, that South American nations
> were 'exempt from the responsibilities of all sorts'

which 'violations of international law impose on civilized peoples', or that European powers had not the right to protect their subjects as fully there as elsewhere against 'the persecutions and injustices' of which they might be victims; that the principles which the Argentine Republic wishes to see set forth, with the authority and prestige of the United States, was ... the principle 'that the public debt can not occasion armed intervention nor even the actual occupation of the territory of American nations by a European power'....

This Note received the support of the United States and led to the adoption at the Hague Conference of 1907 of the Porter Convention respecting the limitation of the employment of force for the recovery of contract debts.[54] By this,

the contracting Powers agree not to have recourse to armed force for the recovery of contract debts claimed from the Government of one country by the Government of another country as being due to its nationals. This undertaking is, however, not applicable when the debtor State refuses or neglects to reply to an offer of arbitration, or, after accepting the offer, prevents any compromis from being agreed on, or, after the arbitration, fails to submit to the award.

Because of this limitation, only six Latin American States ratified the Convention, and, at Chapultepec, Mexico called for its abrogation. It has been suggested, in fact, that any gaps in the Convention have now been supplemented by the inhibitions on the use of force in the Charter of the United Nations.[55] In so far as the Latin American States are concerned, at the Buenos Aires Conference of 1910 a Convention was adopted obliging the Contracting Parties to submit all claims relating to pecuniary debts to arbitration, and this was ratified by eleven of the Republics,[56] while at the Buenos Aires Conference of 1936 a Declaration of Principles of Inter-American Solidarity and Co-operation was adopted declaring that the "forcible collection of pecuniary debts is illegal."[57]

This affirmation, however, is, subject to any obligations stemming from the Charter of the United Nations, only valid for the parties thereto. It must be remembered, however, that the United Nations has adopted a Declaration on Permanent Sovereignty over Natural Resources proclaiming "the inalienable right of all States freely to dispose of their natural wealth and resources in accordance with their national interests", and recognizing an obligation to pay 'appropriate compensation' in the event of expropriation, although Dr. Bedjaoui the Algerian member of the International Law Commission in his Report on succession in respect of matters other than treaties condemned compensation as a 'repurchase of freedom' and "almost tantamount to repurchasing the whole country."[58]

In addition to these economic considerations, the Latin American countries have developed their own approach to international law in relation to the concept of asylum, and this too reflects their disturbed histories since the date of their establishment. As the International Court showed, however, non-American international lawyers find it very hard to understand the background of this institution or to concede that there is a special American law relating to it.[59] There are other fields, partly dictated by the geography of the area, in which the Latin American States attempt to assert their own view of international law. While these contentions have been put forward since the end of the Second World War, it is still possible to view them as arguments by new States, for it is really only in the last twenty years or so that the world has been prepared to concede that the views of the Latin Americans need to be taken into consideration - sufficiently to guarantee them, at least before the balance was altered by the influx of new members consequent upon the 'winds of change' that swept through the colonial empires in the fifties and after, disproportionate representation in various United Nations bodies.[60] One of the most glaring examples of an assertion of a special type of international law operating on behalf of at least some of the Latin American States was the claim put forward by many of them to sovereignty over a two-hundred mile territorial sea, a claim which most other States refused to concede and which was tacitly rejected at the 1958 Geneva Conference on the Law of the Sea, when the Convention on the Territorial Sea impliedly limited such a belt to twelve miles.[61] More blatant, however, and reminiscent of the Philippine attitude to the Tokyo Tribunal, were the official statements coming from Peru at the time of the bombing of the Onassis whaling fleet in 1954.[62] Her Foreign Minister declared that "the world must accept the fact that America is elaborating its own code of rights based on its social needs which are at variance with the freedom of the seas",[63] and when the fine imposed by the Peruvian courts had been paid in order to avoid confiscation of the fleet, even though Britain as the country of the insurers which had put up the money had reserved all the legal rights involved, the Chief of Naval Headquarters at Lima proclaimed that "payment of the fine implies recognition of the Peruvian claim to sovereignty over a 200-mile sea-strip."[64] As already indicated, the 1958 Conference on the Law of the Sea did not agree, although by the time of the Caracas Conference of 1974 it looked as if a majority of states, and not only those in Latin America, were in favour of a two - hundred mile economic zone.

Even in a field described by Alvarez as one in which a specific law exists, that relating to a continental security zone, non-American States have shown their objection to recognizing such a system as being valid against themselves if the American "rules" deviate from their rights under what would otherwise be generally accepted international law. Perhaps the best evidence of this is the Battle of the River Plate and the scuttling of the Graf Spee.[65]

Much of what has been said about Latin American law may also be adequately described as evidence of regional international law. It must be borne in mind, however, that deviations introduced by a single new State on its own are not likely to receive any sympathy from the remaining States of the world. It is only when innovations or rejections are put forward by a group of States that they are likely to be of any validity, and it is obvious that convenience and self-interest will be best served when the group affected comes from a particular geographic region. In the case of the Latin American Countries - and for that matter of the Afro-Asian States - a group of new States has in fact come into existence in the same region. Use of a regional title does not obviate the need to examine with some care the exact group of States that is regarded as falling within the group. Thus, in his dissenting judgment in the Asylum Case[66] Judge Read, a Canadian and not Latin American, commented that

...[R]eferences to 'American international law'[67] ... use the word 'American' in a special sense - as relating to a regional group of States, the twenty Latin-American Republics. The region covers the greater part of South and Central America, and extends to parts of North America south of the Rio Grande, including two of the Caribbean Islands. It does not, however, include the whole of either North, South, or Central America, and, in that sense, the use of the word 'American' is misleading....

With regard to 'American international law', it is unnecessary to do more than confirm its existence - a body of conventional and customary law, complementary

to universal international law, and governing inter-
State relations in the Pan American world.

Here we find an implied acknowledgement of the fact
that regional international law can apply only within a
region and for and among the members of that region -
a matter which already appeared from the reaction of the
world towards Latin American maritime claims. Even
within the region, regional international law cannot
operate so as to detract from the rights of non-regional
States unless the latter are prepared to recognize such
detractions. In fact, this was already conceded by
Alvarez when distinguishing between American and Latin
American law, the latter being "the law of the Latin
Republics of the New World, which is not binding upon
the United States." Just as this law does not apply
as against the United States, so it has no application
against any other State refusing to acknowledge its
authority, and the position is not affected in any way
by the assertions of politicians within the region to
the contrary.

The arguments put forward with regard to the Latin
American countries would apply with equal validity to
any other regions or groups of States which might evolve
their own system of law, for, as Alvarez pointed out in
the same case,

since the last social upheaval, there exist not only an
American international law, but also a European international law, and an Asian international law is in the
process of formation. And apart from these important
continental systems of law, another important international system of law is emerging - Soviet Law. 68

For our purposes the reference to Soviet Law may be
ignored, for none of the States within this group
constitute new States, even though they may have
adopted an economic system which demands a different

approach to international problems, particularly those concerning the protection of foreign investments. Alvarez' reference to "Asian" law, which is inherently connected with a particular continent, is really too narrow. By 1945 Accioly was referring to the idea of an "African" international law[69] although we ought properly to speak of an Afro-Asian or Asian-African law,[70] for the new movement in international law is spearheaded by the newly independent States of Africa and Asia, representing "a by-product of the independence movement ... [indicating] a desire for a greater break with Europe,"[71] and with all things that have an aura of the establishment or vested interest attached to them. Thus Dr. Engo, Minister Plenipotentiary of the Foreign Service of the Republic of Cameroon, has said:[72]

Customary law ... has developed in the so-called existing international law from an intercourse between a limited but vocal number of states. The credibility and record of some of these states, in their dealings with Africa, can only politely be referred to as objectionable. This explains the consistent rejection of the so-called 'existing rules of customary international law' by delegations from Africa to United Nations Conferences and elsewhere. The aim is not to spurn 'custom' as a rational source of effective law, but to deny the 'existing rules' the status that their upholders seek to accord them....

It may be argued that since some African states have followed some rules of existing (European) custom in this field, they have by implication adopted or accepted them. This is debatable.... This is not enough to lead to the conclusion that the practice has become accepted as a rule. In any case, the adoption of one practice in a body of rules does not necessarily mean the acceptance of the whole.

A similar view, but in far more sweeping and condemnatory language was expressed by the Indian delegate when justifying India's seizure of Goa before the Security Council.[73] The attitude is, however, perhaps

best expressed in the words of 'a senior African
diplomat' explaining the attitude of the new states at
the 1974 Caracas law of the sea conference:[74]

The existing law of the sea was laid down by the
developed nations. We did not participate in its
formulation, and we do not necessarily accept it.
This conference has been our first big opportunity to
challenge. We are here to reach agreement on a
completely new law of the sea. But some of the
advanced countries are still talking in terms of
merely amending the old. They hear what we say, but
they are not really listening.

Delegates from the older countries apparently considered
that the new states were 'often more concerned with
taking up the "correct" political attitude than with
making realistic proposals.' That this is probably
true is indicated by the statement of the Uganda
delegate to the 1974 Montreal conference of ICAO at
which the executive committee voted to allow 'national
liberation movements' to enjoy observer status at
future conferences:[75]

... We have been preparing this resolution for the past
six years, ever since the formation of the Organization
for (sic) African Unity. On most political issues,
we more or less receive our orders from the various
leaders of state in Africa and we have been trying to
extend the policy of African unity here.

A similar attitude is to be seen in the regularity with
which the General Assembly, subject as it is to an
almost automatic Asian-African majority - even an
Asian scholar has said they "have come to acquire an
unusual and disproportionate weight in influencing the
course of history"[76] - has refused to accept the
credentials of South Africa's delegation, culminating
in the 1974 call to the Security Council to expel that
member from the United Nations.[77]

It matters little whether one is examining the

municipal or international sphere; in both, law is a product of the era in which it is produced and the society which it is intended to serve. While there is a tendency to assume that international law was created by those "fathers" whose writings have found their way into the Carnegie collection of Classics, it must be remembered that even they, and particularly writers like Gentili, Grotius and Zouche, often reflected State interests. Moreover, many of the principles which were accepted as generally recognized rules of international law until 1945 were to a great extent products of the nineteenth century and reflect the interests of laissez-faire liberalism and the imperialism which it produced. In that period colonial territories were regarded as belonging to the "motherland", and their inhabitants, regardless of their own desires, were considered to have acquired the imperial power's nationality. At that time, too, it was considered that States were completely free to treat their nationals, regardless of race or religion, as they wished and there was no restriction on the sovereign's power to convey part of his territory to another power without any consultation with the inhabitants. At the same time, reflecting economic power, overseas investment was regarded as sacrosanct and immune from local regulation or expropriation, other than by what might be described as due process of law in the Anglo-American sense of that term.

Perhaps one of the first traditional rights to come under pressure, and that even before the new States came onto the scene, was that relating to treatment of nationals. Reflecting the revulsion of the peoples of the victorious States at the disclosures of the horrors of the Nazi concentration camps, the Preamble to the Charter of the United Nations reaffirms "faith in

fundamental human rights, in the dignity and worth of
the human person, in the equal rights of men and women
and of nations large and small", and this affirmation
is reiterated in various articles of the Charter. In
addition, article 1 (2) describes one of the Purposes
of the Organization as being the development of
"friendly relations among nations based on respect
for the principle of equal rights and self-determination
of peoples," a purpose which is repeated in article 55,
while, in so far as non-self-governing peoples are
concerned, chapters XI and XII recognize self-government
or independence as ultimate aims of development. The
extent to which any of these provisions of the Charter
constitute actual binding legal obligations is somewhat
controversial, while there is great doubt how far
resolutions of the General Assembly, the Economic and
Social Council and the Trusteeship Council, the bodies
concerned with these matters, are anything more than
exhortatory statements. The situation is further compl-
icated by the limitation imposed by article 2 (7) upon
the power of the Organization to "intervene" in matters
within the domestic jurisdiction of a State. This is
not the place to examine or assess these contentions.[78]
Here it will suffice to draw attention to the impact of
the new States upon the concepts of human rights and
self-determination.

As early as 1948 the United Nations adopted the
Universal Declaration of Human Rights[79] which reflected
their Judaeo-Christian heritage and was predicated
upon an acceptance of the basic worth of man as an
individual. This Declaration makes no reference to the
idea of self-determination, but it does preclude any
discrimination on the grounds of race, colour, sex,
language, religion, national or social origin, and the
like, and provides in article 21 that

everyone has the right to take part in the government
of his country, directly or through freely chosen
representatives [,] ... [and] the will of the people
shall be the basis of the authority of government;
this will shall be expressed in periodic and genuine
elections which shall be by universal and equal
suffrage and shall be held by secret vote or by equivalent free voting procedures.

In the period of the "cold war" the Declaration was
used largely for ideological purposes, as exemplified
by the "Russian wives" case in 1949.[80] To a great
extent it only served its true purpose on behalf of
human rights as such in connection with apartheid in
South Africa,[81] originally raised in the General
Assembly by 13 members from Africa and Asia. It did
not take long before it became clear that much of the
controversy concerning South Africa stemmed from
inequality with regard to political life and the denial
of "self-determination" to the majority of that country's
inhabitants. Gradually, the emphasis changed and the
new members of the United Nations showed that they were
not so concerned with how a State treated its own
nationals, provided they were of the same colour as
the governing group, as they were with the denial of
political and governmental rights to a majority population of a different pigmentation from the minority
government - at least, if the governing group was
"white" and the majority "coloured", for a somewhat
different standard of assessment has been applied when,
for example, criticism has been made of such things as
Indonesian rule in West Irian, the treatment of one
African tribal group by another, or the expulsion of
Asians from African countries. To some extent, this
change in emphasis was perhaps to be expected. The
new States are ex-colonial territories which secured
their independence from colonial powers whose "racial"
origin, colour and religious and ethical traditions were

different from those of the majority of the inhabitants
of the territories concerned. While it may be true
that there is need for "an intellectual revolution ...
which will give us a legal system with sufficiently
broad and deep foundations to command the allegiance of
a world community with a fundamentally changed
composition and distribution of influence,"[82] there has
developed among the new States and between them and
their'brothers'in countries still governed by racial
minorities a strong sense of solidarity. In their view,
therefore, the continuance of a colonial or neo-colonial
régime - whatever these terms may now mean - whereby
the majority do not enjoy equal economic, cultural or
political rights with their imperialist rulers, or of
a system of government in what is generally recognized
as an independent sovereign State, like South Africa,
where a minority group exercises authority over a
majority of a different race and denies to that majority
equality with itself, constitutes a denial of the
United Nations "commitments" on human rights, and may
even amount to a threat to the peace of so grave a
nature that the reservation of domestic jurisdiction
cannot apply. It might be relevant here to cite the
comments of two Asian writers. One[83] has described
colonialism as permanent agression, effected

in contravention of international law, and the duration
of a few centuries could not legalise the illegality
of the European rule.... [P]rescription is not applicable in the case of colonialism.

The other[84] has said that

a strange irony of fate now compels those very members
of the community of nations on the ebb tide of their
imperial power to hold up principles of morality as
shields against the liquidation of interests acquired
and held by an abuse of international intercourse....
To the extent to which the law ... favours such rights
and interests, it protects an unqualified status quo...

[and] makes itself a handmaid of power in the preservation of spoils.

Similar views have been expressed in Latin America too, and the United States position in Panama has been condemned as not conforming "to the principles, precepts and norms of international law, justice and international morality".[85] Even an 'old' State like Spain has used similar language in condemning the continuance of British colonial rule in Gibraltar,[86] despite the fact that the local population has gone on record as being in favour of its continuance.

The new States have been assisted in their endeavours to achieve a changed attitude towards human rights and the implications of article 2 (7) of the Charter by the number of votes they are able to control. The United Nations has fifty-one foundation members, together with some 180 new members who played no part in the drafting of the Charter and most of whom were admitted after the adoption of the Universal Declaration of Human Rights. According to the Charter, recommendations of the General Assembly are carried on important matters by a two-thirds majority, and until the late 'fifties it was fairly easy for the "western" alliance to muster the necessary voting strength. It is far more difficult to be sure of gathering some 120 votes, especially as there are no fewer than 75 drawn from Africa and Asia, even excluding such countries as China, Japan, Israel and Turkey, with a further 6 new States from the Carribbean. This means that if the older States are not prepared to make any concessions towards the newcomers it will be impossible for the General Assembly ever to adopt a recommendation if the Afro-Asians refuse to cooperate. Further, given the fact that on many issues which affect their interests the Afro-Asian States will receive sympathy from some of the Latin

Americans, and that the "eastern" bloc can sometimes be relied upon to support them in order to oppose their ideological cold-war antagonists, it is clear that the balance of power in the United Nations has shifted drastically. In almost every case, if the new States back a recommendation and are firm in their unity - as they tend to be on issues that appeal to their national-ism or newly won sovereignty - it is fairly certain that such a resolution will be carried,[87] regardless of any reservations that some of the older delegations may have as to the competence of the United Nations in a particular field or concerning limitations as to the legal effect of such resolutions. Moreover, the complexities of the cold war have meant that when this group of new States puts forward a proposition which may be considered as reflecting their ideological ethic, the major protagonists of the East-West confrontation find themselves on the horns of a dilemma, almost vying with each other to support their potential "allies".

This situation has resulted in the adoption by over-whelming majorities of resolutions framed in the form of declarations on such matters as the granting of Independence to Colonial Countries and Peoples,[88] although in practice it would appear that this only applies when the colonial people is "coloured" and seeking to secure its independence from a "white" administration and has no application when both rulers and ruled are "coloured", as has been made clear by the situation in African countries like Nigeria at the time of the civil war in the Eastern Region (Biafra), or the attitude of Indonesia to its obligations concerning a plebiscite in West Irian. Likewise, the interpret-ation of "self-determination" is somewhat one-sided. It may in certain circumstances achieve a meaning which appears to be directly contrary to the dictionary

meaning of the term. This has been made clear in the
discussions concerning Gibraltar. The Assembly has
appeared to reject the local acceptance of Britain's
offer of increased internal self-government, but far
from calling for independence for the territory it
seems to consider that self-determination is satisfied
by transferring the territory from Britain's social
democratic imperialism to Spanish fascist imperialism.[89]
A similar attitude has been expressed towards the
Elimination of All Forms of Racial Discrimination.[90]
The Afro-Asian States tend to deny that there can ever
be racial discrimination in the new countries, even
though tribal warfare breaks out; preferential clauses
are embodied in Constitutions, as is the case in
Malaysia; or a policy of Africanization adopted in
Uganda, leading to the denial of employment opportunities to or physical expulsion of Asians, and resulting
in the enactment of restrictive immigration legislation
in Britain, which enables all the hatred of racial
discrimination to be levelled at that country - which
may well deserve it. However, silence is preserved
at the African policies which created the situation or
the Indian refusal to admit to India 'British' Indians
from Africa - even though in 1946 India raised in the
United Nations the whole issue of South African
treatment of people of Indian origin in that State,
maintaining that

the Indian government felt that it has a moral and
political obligation towards them, because it was
responsible for the departure of the first Indian
immigrants to South Africa.[91]

As with the Latin American States before them, the
new States of Asia and Africa have been concerned with
the activities of foreign capital. While nationalization and expropriation programmes by their forbears

in the western hemisphere tended to receive strong
reaction from the older States,[92] the new members of
the United Nations have managed to secure the passage
of a resolution by the Assembly in the form of a
Declaration on Permanent Sovereignty over Natural
Wealth and Resources.[93] This Declaration reflects the
same shift from the rights of man to the rights of
people in organized groups, proclaiming that "the right
of peoples and nations to permanent sovereignty over
their natural wealth and resources must be exercised
in the interest of their national development and of the
well-being of the people of the State concerned."
That this statement was not understood in the same way
in the older developed countries as it was in the new
States is clear from the debates on nationalization
held at the Conferences of the International Law
Association after 1958.[94] Nevertheless, the new voting
distribution in the United Nations makes it possible
for the new States to ensure that their view prevails
and they are able to contend that these Declarations
carry the force of law,[95] and some of the judges of the
World Court tend to agree.[96]

Their impact is to be seen in the opening clauses of
the two Covenants on Human Rights.[97] The first article
of both that on economic, social and cultural rights,
as well as that on civil and political rights, are in
identical terms and reflect the nouvelle vague in
international law:

1. All peoples have the right of self-determination.
By virtue of that right they freely determine their
political status and freely pursue their economic,
social and cultural development.

2. All peoples may, for their own ends, freely dispose
of their natural wealth and resources without prejudice
to any obligation arising out of international economic
co-operation, based upon the principle of mutual benefit,
and international law. In no case may a people be

deprived of its own means of subsistence.

3. The States Parties to the present Covenant, including those having responsibility for the administration
of Non-Self-Governing and Trust Territories, shall
promote the realization of the right of self-determination,
and shall respect that right, in conformity with the
provisions of the Charter of the United Nations.

Before leaving this aspect of the subject, it is
perhaps apt to refer to the more generally accepted
view of the so-called right of self-determination.
As recently as 1965 Dr. Whiteman, Assistant Legal
Adviser to the Department of State, made it clear in her
Digest of International Law that she adopts the view of
those who consider that self-determination is a
political right and not a right under international
law.[98]

It is not only in the field of general international
law or of the United Nations that the new States have
exercised their influence. Their impact is also being
felt on a regional basis. At Addis Ababa in 1963
there was established the Organization of African Unity,[99]
a number of the constitutional rules of which substantially alter or retreat from those which were formerly
accepted. The purposes of the new Organization generally speaking are similar to those of the United Nations,
but the constituent Charter includes express reference
to the Universal Declaration of Human Rights and
reflects certain aspects of Africa's colonial past.
Among other things, it exists to eradicate all forms of
colonialism from Africa and, therefore, has as one of
its principles "absolute dedication to the total emancipation of the African territories which are still
dependent". There is also "unreserved condemnation,
in all its forms, of political assassination as well
as subversive activities on the part of neighbouring
States or any other State ... [and] affirmation of a

policy of non-alignment with regard to all blocs." The
Parties declare in the Preamble that they are "persuaded
that the Charter of the United Nations and the Universal
Declaration of Human Rights, to the principles of which
we reaffirm our adherence, provide a solid foundation
for peaceful and positive co-operation among States."
On this basis, one of the Principles of the Organization
is the promotion of "international co-operation, having
due regard to the Charter of the United Nations and
the Universal Declaration of Human Rights."

Although the Preamble acknowledges the significance
of the Charter of the United Nations, there is no
express reference to that document or the obligations
arising under it in the substantive portions of the
African Charter, other than an acknowledgement of the
necessity of registering the document with the United
Nations Secretariat in accordance with article 102 of
the Charter. Another omission from the 1963 document
is reference to judicial interpretation. Instead,
disputes of this kind are to be settled by a decision
reached by two-thirds of the Assembly of Heads of State
and Government of the Organization. It might be asked
whether this process is also to apply if a member of
the Organization of African Unity were to suggest that
an interpretation so given was incompatible with membership of the United Nations, an institution of which
all the signatories of the later document are members.
While Article 103 of the Charter of the United Nations
provides that obligations arising under it are supreme
and that inconsistent duties cannot prevail, it is
clear that the African States are more inclined to pay
attention to the obligations they have created for
themselves under the Addis Ababa Charter than to those
arising from a Conference in which they did not
participate; at which the "imperialists" had a completely

free hand in organizing the legal protection of their vested interests; and to which they, the new African States, have to accede without being able to express their own views as to the true meaning or relevance of the obligations postulated therein. Moreover, at the meetings of the United Nations Committee which was responsible for preparing the Declaration on Principles of International Law concerning Friendly Relations[100] "many of the African representatives ... stressed the fact that conformity of obligations with the provisions of the Charter should be construed in the broadest sense."[101]

At least of equal significance as the potential disregard of Charter obligations are the aims of the new Organization which involve disregard of actual duties of the members of the United Nations or of established rules of law, for "in the areas of international relations and international law ... Africa's contribution has been minimal.... To Africa, classical international law has been merely a projection of colonialism - protectorates, concessions, capitulations - designed in part to legalize European acquisitions and privileges. Now there is an opportunity to make a fresh start, to enact and put into practice a system of law for settling inter-State conflicts and regulating relations among African States."[102] Every independent sovereign African State is entitled to join the Organization, all that is required being notification of adherence or accession. For the accession to become effective a simple majority of the members must acquiesce. This is important in view of the fact that the African States do not mean by independence and sovereignty what has previously been meant by these words. It might be thought that "absolute dedication to the total emancip-ation of the African territories which are still

dependent" refers to the remaining European colonies
on the African continent, but this is not the case.
While these are included, the ideological basis of the
Organization finds expression in anti-imperialism,
the conviction of the parties "that it is the inalienable right of all people to control their own destiny",
and the conviction that "freedom, equality, justice
and dignity are essential objectives for the achievement
of the legitimate aspirations of the African peoples",
all make it clear that South Africa is not considered as
a State eligible for membership, for its belief in
government by minority - the white population - is
regarded as a complete denial of self-determination
which has been elevated into the fundamental principle
of international law[103] and led to the attempt in
October 1974 to have South Africa expelled from the
United Nations, which was only prevented by the exercise
of their veto by France, the United Kingdom and the
United States.

The attitude of the African States, as well as of
most of the other new States, may be seen from the
Resolution adopted by the Conference of Heads of State
or Government of Non-Aligned Countries which assembled
at Cairo in 1964[104] and was attended by representatives
of the Afro-Asian States, including the members of the
Arab League, as well as Yugoslavia;

The Heads of State or Government of the Non-Aligned
Countries declare that lasting world peace cannot be
realized so long as unjust conditions prevail and
peoples under foreign domination continue to be deprived
of their fundamental right to freedom, independence
and self-determination.

Imperialism, colonialism and neo-colonialism constitute
a source of international tension because they endanger
world peace and security. The participants in the
Conference ... call for the unconditional, complete and
final abolition of colonialism now ....

218

The process of liberation is irresistible and irreversible. Colonised peoples may legitimately resort to arms to secure the full exercise of their right to self-determination and independence if the colonial powers persist in opposing their natural aspirations.

The participants in the Conference undertake to work unremittingly to eradicate all vestiges of colonialism and to combine all their efforts to render all necessary aid and support, whether moral, political or material, to the peoples struggling against colonialism and neo-colonialism.

Presumably, all the States taking part in the Cairo Conference, as loyal members of the United Nations, subscribe to the General Assembly's Resolution on the Nuremberg Principles[105] with its acceptance of the view that aggressive war is a crime. Nevertheless, when the Special Committee of the General Assembly set up for the purpose published its Draft Definition of Aggression,[106] it was seen that the new states had ensured that though

The sending by or on behalf of a State or armed bands, groups, irregulars or mercenaries, which carry out acts of armed force against another State ...

constitutes aggression,

Nothing in this definition,... could in any way prejudice the right to self-determination, freedom and independence, as derived from the Charter, of peoples forcibly deprived of that right referred to in the Declaration on Principles of Friendly Relations and Cooperation among States in accordance with the Charter of the United Nations,107 particularly peoples under colonial and racist régimes or other forms of alien domination; nor the right of these people to struggle to'that end and to seek and receive support, in accordance with the principles of the Charter and in conformity with the abovementioned Declaration.

Moreover, when the Assembly adopted its Convention on the Prevention and Punishment of Crimes against Internationally Protected Persons,[108] these states were

successful in writing into the Resolution to which the
Convention was annexed a provision that the Convention

could not in any way prejudice the exercise of the
legitimate right to self-determination and independence,
in accordance with the purposes and principles of the
Charter of the United Nations and the Declaration on
Principles of International Law concerning Friendly
Relations and Cooperation among States in accordance
with the Charter of the United Nations, by peoples
struggling against colonialism, alien domination,
foreign occupation, racial discrimination and apartheid.

and this statement is always to be published together
with the text of the Convention.

The same ideological assertions are to be seen in
the Resolution on Measures to Prevent International
Terrorism adopted in 1972,[109] which

reaffirms the inalienable right to self-determination
and independence of all people under colonial and racist
régimes and other forms of alien domination and upholds
the legitimacy of their struggle, in particular the
struggle of national liberation movements... [and]
condemns the continuation of repressive and terrorist
acts by colonial, racist and alien régimes in denying
peoples their legitimate right to self-determination
and independence and other human rights and fundamental
freedoms.

It is clear, therefore, that the new states have
succeeded in elevating their concept of self-determination into the highest principle of current international
law - even though it does not extend to their own
minorities - prevailing over any ban on aggression or
terrorism, or such traditional customary rights as the
protection of diplomats.

Making use of their majority in the Assembly, the
new states have been more successful than were their
Latin American predecessors in securing general
support for many of their views on international law -

220

for who dare oppose support for self-determination
or international friendly relations? Determined to
secure support from outside their own ranks, they took
over the Communist concept of 'peaceful coexistence'[110],
renamed it the Principles of Friendly Relations and
Cooperation among States, and secured a Resolution[111]
confirming

that the faithful observance of [these] ... principles
of international law ... is of paramount importance
for the maintenance of international peace and security
and the improvement of the international situation.

These Principles had already been postulated in a
Resolution of 1962[112] which affirmed

the paramoung importance, in the progressive development
of international law and in the promotion of the rule
of law among nations, of the principles of international
law concerning friendly relations among states and
the duties deriving therefrom embodied in the Charter
of the United Nations which is the fundamental statement of these principles

- namely, the obligation to refrain from the threat or
use of force, the requirement to settle disputes
peacefully, non-intervention in matters of domestic
jurisdiction, the duty to cooperate in accordance with
the Charter, recognition of equal rights and self-
determination of peoples, sovereign equality of states,
and fulfilment in good faith of the obligations of the
Charter. As we have seen, these principles were
subsequently embodied into a Declaration with the
principle of self-determination elevated into a new
law of the Medes and Persians overriding all else.
So much is this so, that after the Palestine Liberation
Organization was recognized by the Arab powers at their
Rabat Conference in October 1974 as the official
spokesman for the Palestinians, they asserted in their
first published statement that Israel was to be

liquidated as the General Assembly resolutions creating that state were illegal, since they were in contravention of the principle of self-determination.

In view of the above, it is perhaps not surprising that one Indian writer has said:[113]

The end of colonialism and racialism has become a matter of faith with them which takes precedence over other obligations of International Law, including the prohibitions relating to the use of force.... They refuse to concede that the Charter gives precedence to peace over justice

while proclaiming that the end of colonialism is prescribed by the Charter. Even more striking is the Separate Opinion of Judge Ammoun of the Lebanon in the Barcelona Traction case:[114]

What the Third World wishes to substitute for certain legal norms now in force are other norms profoundly involved with the sense of national justice, morality and humane deeds. It is, in short, a matter of change of course towards natural law as at present understood, which is nothing other than the natural sense of justice; a change of course towards a high ideal which sometimes is not clearly to be discerned in positive law, peculiarly preoccupied as it is with stability.

Judge Ammoun drew attention to the 1969 Vienna Treaties Convention[115] which was not yet in force. Article 64 provides that "if a new peremptory norm of general international law emerges, any existing treaty which is in conflict with that norm becomes void and terminates," and in his view self-determination is such a norm, for after all the 1964 Conference of Non-Aligned Countries which first stressed this principle comprised the majority of the members of the United Nations.

As long ago as 1946, E. H. Carr foresaw some of the problems that the new world was likely to confront, pointing out[116] that

respect for international law and for its sanctity
of treaties will not be increased by the sermons of
those who, having most to gain from the maintenance
of the existing order, insist most firmly on the
morally binding character of the law,

and some fifteen years later an Indian judge was
reminding the world that international law was no
longer "the prerogative of countries bearing the
cultural heritage of the West but the common task of
all the members of the international community."[117]
Nevertheless, not all western commentators were prepared to see or acknowledge future portents. As
recently as 1964 one American international lawyer
was writing in the American Journal of International
Law[118] of

... the upheaval in international society which has
occurred since the second world war. Too little weight
has been given to the devastating inroads which the
myth of universality has chiseled into the very
foundations of traditional international law ....
[Any] complete evaluation must impeach the practice
of admitting into the Society of Nations primeval
entities which have no real claim to international
status or the capacity to meet international obligations, and whose contribution consists in replacing
norms serving the common interests of mankind by
others releasing them from inhibitions upon irresponsible conduct. A further consequence has been to impair
respect for that rule of law whose primacy is essential
to a minimum world order of human decency. To an
impartial observer - rarely encountered though he
might be - it should be apparent that the development
of international law as a code of responsible action
in the advancement of human values has hardly been
expedited by abandonment of prior standards. An
undignified compulsion to admit these entities as
full-blown members of the international society upon
achieving independence has impeded, not advanced, the
emergence of a mature code of conduct.

One can perhaps understand the irritations of a
representative of the older states when he sees traditional concepts being treated in the cavalier fashion
in which the Indonesian member of the General Assembly's

223

Committee on Peaceful Uses of the Seabed dismissed the three-mile rule:[119]

The three-mile limit ... had never been a rule of international law since a general international convention providing for it had never been accepted by all States and since it had never been practiced by all States.

A more reasoned and more reasonable approach - and one that was more in keeping with the historic development of the law of the sea - was adopted by Singapore's delegate to the same committee.[120] In his view the new law of the sea "should be development oriented and aimed at improving the economics of the developing countries". He was therefore of opinion that if the developed states were to establish economic zones they should contribute a percentage of the revenue to an international authority for the benefit of the disadvantaged states. Similar views have been expressed by Judge Ammoun:[121]

Policy does of course crop up under the veil of resolutions or declarations in the United Nations Assembly.... Policy, the policy of the great powers and the colonialist powers, dominated classic traditional law: it cannot be dissociated from law today any more than yesterday; but it is a new policy, one which does not escape the influence of the great principles which are destined to govern the relationships of modern nations. The 1969 Vienna Convention [on treaties] took this consideration fully into account when it adopted numerous solutions to meet the suggestions included in individual opinions and proposals by new members of the international community.... The diplomatic protection of shareholders injured by a third state does not constitute an international custom that is unequivocally and unambiguosly demonstrated by the web of precedents which form the material element, and definitively established by the conjunction of that element with the psychological element of opinio juris.[122] This conclusion is reinforced by the opinion ... held by a multitude of States - new States and other, very numerous, developing States - with regard to the application of diplomatic protection, the rules of which are acceptable by them

to the extent that they take account of their state of
under-development, economic subordination and social
and cultural stagnation, in which the colonial powers
left them and in which they are in danger of remaining
for a long time, in the face of Powers strong in
industry, knowledge and culture.

The debates which took place while the principles of
international law concerning friendly relations and
cooperation among states in accordance with the Charter
of the United Nations were being drafted and finally
adopted, together with the use to which these principles
have since been put, illustrate the attitude of the
new states towards some of what were previously
regarded as basic principles of international law with
sufficient clarity to enable differences on particular
rules to be dismissed almost peremptorily. As to these,
differences arise whenever a new State has relations
with an old one, particularly if the rules in question
concern rights which the latter is asserting against the
former, and especially if they arise under a treaty
signed before the new State achieved its independence,
or if they seem to be opposed to what are coming to be
considered as twentieth-century principles of democratic international life. The increasing practice of
the new States to nationalize foreign economic investments in their territory - now blessed by General
Assembly resolution[123] - and their hesitancy in
recognizing the old concept of the right to compensation[124] tend to emphasize this. It is also manifested
in the somewhat peculiar approach adopted by these
States to the idea of political asylum, as exemplified
by the attitude envisaged by the Organization of
African Unity , although both Botswana and Lesotho
have warned such asylees that they would not be
permitted to use the territory of either State as a
base for operations against South Africa,[125] while the
subjective character of the approach of the new States

is perhaps best illustrated by the treatment meted
out to M. Tshombe by Algeria in 1967.[126]

The most recent example of the somewhat cavalier
approach to international law and vested rights on the
part of the new States is illustrated by the Stockholm
Protocol Regarding Developing Countries attached to
the Berne Copyright Convention, whereby the new States
have secured the right to produce foreign material without royalty or consent if the work concerned is
considered to be of educational value.[127]

The extent to which some of the new States are
prepared to subscribe to the principles of friendly
relations and co-operation, solely to the extent that
is necessary to enable them to preserve an ideological
stance of morality and right conduct, is brought out
by the attitude of, for example, the Arab States in
their conflict with Israel. All the parties involved
are members of the United Nations and, as such, bound
by the normal commitments of the Charter in so far as
respect for each other's sovereign rights are concerned,
as well as the obligation to maintain friendly relations
and to abide by the terms of the Charter. In addition
to this, the Arab States have willingly accepted the
principles - in the drafting of which they played a
large part - regarding abstinence from the threat of
the use of force, peaceful settlement of their disputes,
the duty to do-operate and the fulfilment in good faith
of the obligations of the Charter. Moreover, they all
participated in the Cairo Conference of 1964 and
subscribed to the statement that "the policy of peaceful
coexistence is an indivisible whole. It cannot be
applied partially, in accordance with special interests
and criteria."[128] Further, while they do not hesitate
to assert the validity and authority of the General

Assembly Resolutions which lay down "new" international law regarding such matters as neo-colonialism,
self-determination and sovereignty over natural resources,
even against countries which have not accepted them,
these States are not prepared to give equal authority
to the resolutions of either the Security Council or
the General Assembly which do not totally accept their
view of the rights and wrongs in the Middle East crisis.
This has meant that, despite the validity of the
Armistice Agreement of 1949,[129] the cease-fire of 1956,
and Security Council resolutions regarding navigation
through the Suez Canal,[130] a Prize Court in Cairo was
happily condemning Israeli and neutral shipping in
1960.[131] They were also able to prevent any condemnation
of themselves consequent upon their initiation of
hostilities at the time of the Yom Kippur War in 1973,
while securing further resolutions condemning Israel
and demanding her evacuation of 'occupied' territories.
At the same time, the Arab States have introduced a
new conception of the law of war and the existence of
belligerent rights. While they reject any obligation
to regard Israel as an equal, since only equals can be
members of the United Nations, or to treat with her on
a basis of the law of peace, they demand that the world
body condemn Israel for resorting to warlike measures
against States which regard themselves as the enemies
of Israel pledged to her destruction. In fact, as we
have seen, the first official statement issued by the
Palestine Liberation Organization after its recognition
by the Arab states as representative of the Palestinians
was a call for the liquidation of Israel, on the
specious ground that the resolutions of the United
Nations establishing that state were contrary to the
fundamental principle of international law known as
self-determination.

In behaving in this way, the Middle Eastern States are merely aping their older sisters in international society, for the application of a double standard in international life goes back to the days of Machiavelli and the just war, as well as operating in the middle of the twentieth century.[132]

There can be no quarrel with the African or the "uncommitted" States if they restrict their new views of international law to their relations inter se, and they are obviously able to operate them as between themselves[133] and such other States as may be willing to have such relations so regulated. In practice, it may transpire that the new régime is so advantageous that, as happened with some elements of Latin American law, it becomes a model for wider and more general adoption. But the innovators must remember that there are always two parties to any issue. If one party rejects what it chooses to, it cannot protest if the other party discards rules which are acceptable to the former but disliked by the latter. The potential result of a universalization of this type of relationship could result in international anarchy par excellence. Moreover, as with individuals so with States: patience has its limits, and the older States may eventually refuse any longer to acknowledge the established rules under which the new ones claim their right to exist.

There is, however, much truth in the 1966 Report of the Special Committee concerned with the Friendly Relations Declaration:[134]

Several ... States feared that they would be subject to customary rules of international law which they did not recognize and which they had played no part in framing. Others added that the codification and progressive development of international law would facilitate the elimination of out-dated and unjust treaties by which the colonial Powers were guaranteed positions and economic, political and military privileges and would thus strengthen the confidence of the new States in international law and in the legal settlement of disputes .... [T] he codification and progressive development of international law would help to dispel the misgivings of States, particularly the new developing countries, about the compulsory jurisdiction of the International Court of Justice.[135] By participating in the formulation of contemporary international law through the process of codification and progressive development, the new States would be able to play a part in bridging the gap which sometimes existed between the present-day international legal order - which was the product of an era when their interests had not been considered - and justice. By way of example, it was mentioned that with regard to responsibility of States and to foreign investments many of the rules of traditional law conflicting with the interests of the new economically weak States.[136]

Some of the most respected jurists among the older States are fully cognizant of the importance of this problem. Henri Rolin, then President of the Institute of International Law, drew attention[137] in 1962 to

the danger resulting for the unity and universality of international law from the sudden appearance of new States whose representatives are often without any legal knowledge at all and who, when confronted with principles derived from customary law, are inclined[138] to reject them en bloc as being inventions of imperialistic, capitalistic or colonial countries and, at the same time, to decline the jurisdiction of the International Court of Justice. We must all of us try to help these new countries to overcome that suspicion and to get them to understand that the greater part of international law is based on general practice, accepted as legally binding because the experience of many centuries has proved it to be necessary. The Institute of International Law decided at its last session to increase the number of its Associates and to reserve every year a proportion of the new seats for jurists of the new countries, who are professionally in charge of the international relations of their countries, even if they could not be recommended for election on the basis of their scientific production.

In accordance with this realism, both States and writers must recognize the fears, aspirations and

suspicions of the new States. They must concede to
them the same hearing that they demand for their own
views, and read the expositions of international law
coming from the scholars of the developing countries
with the same respect and understanding that they
afford to Oppenheim and other authorities of the
established order. If the scholars of the new States
expect to be treated seriously they must be prepared
to adapt their exposition of what they contend to be
the law so that it appears in an objective form, free
of emotionalism and what often seems to be the legacy
of anti-imperialist hatred. Their Foreign Offices, too,
must recognize that stability is sometimes more useful
than the contention that is put forward out of pique
or convenience. They must accept the fact that the
old States are as sincere and honest as they are, and
have interests to which they are attached with equal
tenacity. There must be an abandonment of the present
tendency to apply a double standard, and it must be
acknowledged that if international law is to have any
meaning at all its rules must apply with equal validity
to old and ndw alike. The new States must also
recognize that a time may come when some of the
principles that they now put forward against the old
States, contending that they form part of modern
international law, cannot be used in quite the same
way. It is not beyond the realm of possibility, for
example, that the next two or three years will see the
end of colonialism in the old sense - that is to say
that all dependent territories will have become independent, and it may even be possible that a new order will
prevail in South Africa and Rhodesia. What then will
happen to the glorious principle of self-determination?
Will it still remain "an open question whether the
right can be extended to other subordinate groups within
the existing state system if they claim to be without

control over their own destiny,"[139] or will such
arguments be reserved for "coloured" minorities seeking
to exercise "black power" in States with "white"
majorities like the United States?

If the traditionalists and the innovators - the old
and the new States - fail to come to terms in this way
there can be no prospect of a rule of law. If they
accommodate themselves to the new situation, while the
international law which develops may have little in
common with Grotius, Wheaton, Lorimer, Oppenheim,
Hackworth or Whiteman, it will in fact be a law which
is suited to the needs of the modern world, enabling
those to whom it is directed to regulate their
relations in peace and good order for the greater
benefit of man and the vindication of the rule of law
by which it is sought to govern him.

* Based on a paper published in 4 Israel Law Rev.
(1969) 27.

1 See, e.g., El-Ayouty and Brooks, Africa and International Organization (1974).

2 Moore, 2 Collected Papers of John Bassett Moore
(1944) 280.

3 (1927) P.C.I.J. Ser.A, No.10, 8.

4 'International Law' (1896) 12 Law Quarterly Rev.311.

5 [1950] I.C.J. 266, 276.

6 See Cheng, General Principles of Law as Applied by
International Courts and Tribunals (1953).

7 See Schwarzenberger, Frontiers of International Law
(1962) ch.4; IV above, n.118; and VII below.

8 1 International Law in Historical Perspective (1968)
435-6.

9 See IV above, n. 82.

10   13 Feb. 1946, I.C.J.Y.B. 19 46-7, 217.

11   27 Jan. 1947, ibid., 219.

12   Res. 95 (I).

13   See IV above,n.34 et seqq.

14   See Brierly, The Basis of Obligation in Inter-
     national Law (1955), ch. 1, 9.

15   (1923) P.C.I.J., Ser. B, No. 5, 27-8.

16   Reparation for Injuries Suffered in the Service
     of the U.N. [1949] I.C.J. 174, 185.

17   [1954] I.C.J. 19, 33.

18   [1971] I.C.J. 16, 56.

19   See, e.g., O'Connell, State Succession in Municipal
     Law and International Law (1967), vol. 2; Marcoff,
     Accession à l'indépendence et succession d'états
     aux traités internationaux (1969); Udokang,
     Succession of New States to International Treaties
     (1972).

20   Int. Law Ass'n, The Effect of Independence on
     Treaties (1965) 118.

21   Ibid., 388. For Nigeria's attitude to a treaty
     conferring 'perpetual' rights on France, see Elias,
     The Modern Law of Treaties (1974), 62-4.

22   Report of the Int'l Law Comm'n for 1974, Doc. A/9610,
     82.

23   Ibid., 83.

24   See, e.g., I.C.J. Statute, Art. 38; IV above,
     nn. 11, 98 et seqq.

25   Loc. cit., n. 23, 20, 24-5, 27.

26   I.C.J.Y.B. 1968-69, 46; Green, 'Canada and Arctic
     Sovereignty' (1970) 48 Can. Bar Rev. 740, 761;
     'Int.Law and Canada's Oil Pollution Legislation'
     (1971) 50 Oregon Law Rev. 462, 484.

27   Press Conf., 8 Apr. 1970, 9 Int'l Legal Materials
     600; see IV above, n. 83.

28   24 Oct. 1969, Canada, Commons Debates, vol 114, 38-9.

29 O'Connell, 'Independence and Problems of State Succession', in O'Brien, The New Nations and International Law and Diplomacy (1965) 12.

30 See, in addition to works cited IV above, nn. 98 et seqq., Hyde, International Law Chiefly as Applied and Interpreted by the United States (1947); Castel, International Law Chiefly as Applied and Interpreted in Canada (1965); O'Connell, International Law in Australia (1966); Chaudhuri, International Law - Indian Courts and Legislature (1965); Khadduri, The Islamic Law of Nations (1966); Institute of Law, Soviet Academy of Sciences, International Law (196?); Macdonald and Others, Canadian Perspectives on International Law and Organization (1974).

31 U.N., Ways and Means of Making the Evidence of Customary Law More Readily Available (1949) Doc.A/CN. 4/6.

32 U.S.I.S. (London, U.K.), Daily Wireless Bulletin. No. 298, 25 Jan. 1947.

33 Journal of the Security Council. 1st Year, No. 9. p. 145.

34 See, 'The United Nations, South West Africa and the World Court' (1967) 7 Indian J. Int'l Law, 491, 521.

35 1966.

36 Lowes Dickinson, The International Anarchy (1926). See also, Wortley, Jurisprudence (1967) ch. 8.

37 Lauterpacht, Recognition in International Law (1947) s. 107; Chen, The International Law of Recognition (1951) ch. 17 ("Conditional Recognition").

38 See, e.g., Asylum Case [1950] I.C.J. 266; Green, 'New States, Regionalism and International Law', (1967) 5 Can. Y.B. Int'l Law 118.

39 Lauterpacht, 'The So-called Anglo-American and Continental Schools of Thought in International Law', (1931) 12 Brit. Y.B. Int'l Law 31.

40 4 Hudson, International Legislation, 2279 et seqq. See also, 1 Accioly, Tratado de Derecho Internacional (1945), 76 et seqq.

41 Loc.cit., n. 38, 293-4 (italics added).

[42] Cp.Engo, 'Peaceful Co-Existence and Friendly Relations among States: The African Contribution to Progressive Development of Principles of International Law', in El-Ayouty and Brooks, Africa and International Organization (1974), 31, 34.

[43] Jacobini, A Study of the Philosophy of International Law as Seen in Works of Latin American Writers (1954) 122.

[44] El derecho internacional hispano-americano, vol. 1, 511 (ibid. 124, italics added).

[45] This term is here used solely in its economic and non-polemic sense.

[46] See, e.g., Friedmann and Pugh, Legal Aspects of Foreign Investment (1959); Schwarzenberger, Foreign Investments and International Law (1969).

[47] 5th ed. (Paris, 1896), vols. I, 350-51, VI, 231, III, 140, 142, 138 (translation by Shea, The Calvo Clause (1955) 17-19).

[48] In another place Calvo makes it clear that his remarks apply to any form of intervention: "The form in which intervention takes place does not alter its character. Intervention by way of diplomatic process is still intervention. It is an act of interference, sometimes direct, sometimes disguised, but often nothing but the precursor of armed intervention" (Vol. I, 267 - my translation).

[49] E.g., Mexican Constitution (1917/1966), art. 27 (I), 4 Peaslee, Constitutions of Nations 900.

[50] See, e.g., North American Dredging Co. Claim (1926, U.S./Mexico), 4 U.N. Reports Int'l Arb. Awards, 26; Mexican Union Railway Ltd. Claim (1936, U.K./Mexico), 5 ibid., 115.

[51] Lipstein, 'The Place of the Calvo Clause in International Law' (1945) 22 Brit. Y.B. Int'l Law 131, 141.

[52] See Venezuelan Preferential Claims (1904), P.C.A. No. 11 (1 Scott, Hague Court Reports, 56).

[53] Note to Argentine Minister in Washington, 29 Dec. 1902 (6 Moore, Digest of Int'l Law, (1906), 592-93).

[54] Convention II, art. 1 (Scott, Reports to the Hague Conferences of 1899 and 1907 (1917) 489).

55 Jessup, A Modern Law of Nations (1948) 114.

56 See Accioly, op.cit., n. 40 above, vol. 1, s. 384, 293-94.

57 6 Hackworth, Digest of Int'l Law 16.

58 G. A. Res. 1803 (XVII) (1962); see also, Res. 2158 (XXI) (1966); 2 Y.B. Int'l Law Comm., 1969, 94, 69.

59 Loc.cit., n. 38 above.

60 See Green, 'Gentlemen's Agreements and the Security Council', (1960) 12 Current Legal Problems 255, 275; 'Representation in the Security Council', (1967) 6 Indian Y. B. Int'l Law 48, 49, 58, 73.

61 Art. 24 (2), 516 U.N.T.S. 205.

62 'Territorial Waters and the Onassis Case', (1955) 11 The World Today 1.

63 The Times (London), 4 Dec. 1954. See also Trudeau statement IV above, n.83; and for similar attitude of African and Asian States, n. 71 et seqq. below.

64 Ibid., 14 Dec. 1954.

65 Uruguayan Blue Book (1940); 7 Hackworth, op.cit., 450, 509.

66 Loc. cit. n. 38 above, 316.

67 Cp. the Organization of African Unity which denies that South Africa is an "African" state.

68 At 294.

69 Op.cit., n.40 above, s. 7, p. 3.

70 See the Reports of the Asian African Consultative Legal Committee.

71 See text to n. 43 above.

72 Loc.cit., n. 42 above, 34.

73 See IV above, text to n. 82.

74 The Times (London), 30 Aug. 1974 - cp. comments by Prime Minister Trudeau in defence of Canada's antipollution legislation, IV above, text to n.83.

75 Globe & Mail (Toronto), 5 Oct. 1974.

76 Anand, 'Attitude of the Asian-African States toward Certain Problems of International Law', (1966) 15 Int'l & Comp. Law Q. 55.

77 The Times, 2 Oct. 1974.

78 See, e.g., Sloan, 'The Binding Force of a "Recommendation" of the General Assembly of the United Nations' (1948) 25 Brit. Y.B. of Int'l Law 1; Johnson, 'The Effect of Resolutions of the General Assembly of the United Nations' (1955-56) 32 ibid. 97; Virally, 'La Valeur juridique des recommendations des organes internationales' (1956) 2 Annuaire Français de Droit International 66; Rajan, United Nations and Domestic Jurisdiction (1961); Higgins, The Development of International Law through the Political Organs of the United Nations (1963) Part II; Asamoah, The Legal Significance of the Declarations of the General Assembly of the United Nations (1966); see IV above, text to n. 40.

79 G. A. Res. 217 (III) A.

80 See Green, 'Human Rights and the Colour Problem' (1950) 3 Current Legal Problems 238, 245-6; Rajan, op.cit., 287-9.

81 Rajan, 271 et seqq.

82 Jenks, Common Law of Mankind (1958) 87.

83 Anand, loc.cit., n. 76, 65.

84 Roy, 'Is the Law of Responsibility of States for Injuries to Aliens a Part of Universal International Law?' (1961) 55 Am. J. Int'l Law 863, 866.

85 Castaneda, 'The Underdeveloped Nations and the Development of International Law' (1961) 16 Int'l Org. 39.

86 The Times (London), 4 Oct. 1974.

87 See text to n. 75 above for Asian criticism of this situation.

88 Res. 1514 (XV) 1960.

89 See The Times, 2, 6, 17 Oct. 1964, 11 Apr. 1965; Sp. Committee, Doc. A/AC.109/SR284, A/AC.109/PV284; GA Res. 2231 (XXI), 1966, and statement by the

Minister of State for Commonwealth Relations (1967)
(6 Int. Legal Materials, 830); in 1973 the General
Assembly reached a consensus calling on Great
Britain and Spain to work together for a solution
consonant with the principles of the Charter.

90 Res. 1904 (XVIII) 1963.

91 Indian Council of World Affairs, India and the
United Nations (1957) 107-13, 207-8, 112; Rajan,
op.cit., 228-55; GA Res. 44 (I), 1946.

92 See 1 Hyde, International Law (1947), 710 et seq.

93 Res. 1803 (XVII), 1962. See also Report by Dept.
of State to Senate Committee on Foreign Relations,
'Major Instances of Expropriation [of U.S. nationals]
since World War II', 7 May 1962 (1 Int'l Legal
Materials 76).

94 See, in particular, Hamburg, 1960, and Brussels,
1962 (Report, pp. 175, 101, resp.).

95 See Asamoah, op. cit., passim; and Brownlie,
Principles of Public International Law (1973), 14-15.

96 See IV above, nn. 33,40.

97 Res. 2200 (XXI), 1966.

98 Vol. 5, 38. See also, Green, 'Self-Determination
and Settlement of the Arab-Israeli Conflict', (1971)
65 Am. J. Int'l Law, Proceedings, 40, 48, Cp.,
however, Nawaz, 'The Meaning and Range of the
Principle of Self-Determination': "... self-
determination constitutes one of the modern principles of international law", (1965) Duke Law J.
82, 99; Dinstein, 'Terrorism and Wars of Liberation
applied to the Arab-Israeli Conflict: An Israeli
Perspective', (1973) 3 Israel Y.B. on Human Rights,
78, 79.

99 (1963) 2 Int'l Legal Materials 766. See Boutros-
Ghali, The Addis Ababa Charter, (1964) 564 Int'l
Conciliation; El-Ayouty and Brooks, op.cit., n.42
above.

100 Res. 2625 (XXV) 1970.

101 Engo, loc. cit., n. 42, 39.

102 Boutros-Ghali, op.cit., 5. See, also Anand, New
States and International Law (1972) III; Separate

Opinion of Judge Ammoun in <u>Barcelona Traction Case</u>
[1970] I.C.J. 3, 310.

103 Anand, <u>op.cit.</u>, 53-4.

104 Press Release, Consulate-General of U.A.R.,
Singapore, 11 Oct. 1964 (italics added).

105 Res. 95 (I) 1946.

106 Doc. A/AC.134/L.46, 1974 (13 Int'l Legal Materials
710).

107 Res. 2625 (XXV) 1970, annex.

108 Res. 3166 (XXVIII) 1973, annex.

109 Res. 3034 (XXVII) 1972.

110 Institute of Law, Soviet Academy of Sciences,
<u>International Law</u> (196?), 16: 'The new, present-
day <u>International</u> Law is the law of peaceful
co-existence.'

111 Res. 2181 (XXI) 1966.

112 Res. 1815 (XVII) 1962.

113 Anand, <u>op.cit.</u>, n. 102, 53, 54.

114 [1970] I.C.J. 3, 310, 311-2; see also VII below.

115 8 Int'l Legal Materials (1969) 679.

116 <u>The Twenty Years' Crisis</u> (1946) 191-2.

117 Pal, 'Future Role of the International Law
Commission', (Sept. 1962) 9 UN Rev. 31.

118 Freeman, 'Professor McDougal's "Law and Minimum
World Public Order"', (1964) 58 Am. J. Int'l Law,
711, 712.

119 Doc. A/AC. 138/SC.II/SR.31 (1973) 13. See, however,
Swarztrauber, <u>The Three-Mile Limit of Territorial
Seas</u> (1972).

120 Doc.A/AC.138/SC.II/SR.67 (1973) 15; see also
Prime Minister Trudeau, text to IV above, n.83.

121 <u>Loc.cit.</u>, n. 114, 303-4, 329.

122 See, e.g., Garcia Amador and Others, <u>Recent</u>

Codifications of the Law of State Responsibility for Injuries to Aliens (1974).

123 Declaration on Sovereignty over Natural Resources, Res. 626 (VII) 1952; Declaration on Permanent Sovereignty over Natural Resources, Res. 1803 (XVII) 1962.

124 See text to n. 94 above.

125 The Times (London), 28 Oct. 1966, 30 Mar. 1967.

126 Ibid., 3, 4, 20, 24 Jul. 1967; see also British attitude to Lt. Col. Amekrane who sought asylum in Gibraltar after the failure of an assassination attempt against King Hassan of Morocco, ibid., 13 Aug. 1974.

127 Ibid., 8, 13, 14, 15, 18, 19, 21, 28 Apr., 3, 5, 9 May, 20 Jul, 10 Nov. 1967, 20 Jan. 1968; The Times Literary Supplement, 29 Jun., 16 Jul. 1967 (vol. 66, pp. 579, 606).

128 Loc. cit. n. 104 above (italics added).

129 42 U.N.T.S., p. 251.

130 e.g., Res. of Sept. 1, 1951, S.C., Official Records, 6th Yr. 558th Meeting, p. 7. See Stone, Legal Controls of International Conflict (1954) 641-42.

131 The Inge Toft, 31 Int'l Law Reports, 251.

132 See Green, 'The Double Standard of the United Nations' (1957) 11 Y.B. World Aff. 104.

133 See Green, 'New States, Regionalism and International Law', (1967) 5 Can. Y.B. Int'l Law 118.

134 Doc.A/AC.125/1.38/Add.2 (2 Apr. 1966), 28, 37-8 (italics added).

135 It is doubtful, to say the least, whether this is correct since the 1966 South West Africa decision - see Report of 52nd I.L.A. Conference, Helsinki (1964) 298-9. The new Indian Declaration accepting the Court's jurisdiction in accordance with Art. 36 of the Statute is so encumbered by reservations as virtually to deny any role to the Court, Letter by Indian Minister to External Affairs to Se.Gen., U.N., 15 Sept. 1974.

136 See Friedmann, The Changing Structure of

International Law (1964) 206 et seqq. See, also,
Judge Ammoun, text to n. 121 above.

137
Fraternal greetings at 50th I.L.A. Conference,
Brussels, Report, 12-3. Cp., However, statement
by Freeman, text to n. 118 above.

138
Anand, however, points out that "despite all
their anti-colonial outcry, which is sometimes
emotional, impassioned and aggressive on account
of their past history, the new States do not in
practice dispense with the international legal
principles ... [Their] differences with the
Western Powers ... should not be understood as
rejection of the present system. They only
indicate conflicts of interest ...", op. cit.,
n. 102, 62-3. See, also, Engo, text to n. 72
above.

139
Johnson, Self-Determination within the Community
of Nations (1967) 204.

VI

THE INDIVIDUAL IN INTERNATIONAL LAW*

I only mean that when one thinks coldly I see
no reason for attributing to man a significance
different in kind from that which belongs to
a baboon or to a grain of sand

(Oliver Wendell Holmes, 2 Holmes-Pollock Letters
(1941) 252.)

Humanists have long been concerned with seeking and
asserting the fundamental rights of man. Since the
doctrinaire writings of the eighteenth century, and
particularly since the French and American Revolutions,
constitutional lawyers have sought to give such rights
a legal basis. A similar concern has been shown by
international lawyers who, since the days of the
classical writers on the subject, have discussed the
position of the individual in international law,
although the result of such deliberation has often
been to deny him any position, despite the fact that
it is accepted that the individual is the basic unit
to which any legal system is directed, and it is he
who has to comply with what the law demands.

In classical international law, the individual was
regarded as an object; that is to say, he enjoys no
rights and was burdened by no duties. By and large, it
may be said that international law worked itself out
upon the individual, using his home State for the
purpose. Thus, there was nothing to stop a ruler, who
was regarded as the owner of the territory over which

he exercised his authority, from alienating that territory without any reference to the views of its inhabitants. In such a case, the inhabitants of the territory concerned would find that their former nationality had ceased to exist, and that they had been endowed, whether it was to their liking or not, with the nationality of their new sovereign. The so-called right of option, or the alleged human right of freedom of choice and self-determination, had no existence outside of treaties, although this may no longer be true in view of the way in which the new States have, by reason of their automatic majority in the United Nations, elevated self-determination into the supreme principle of modern international law.[1] In the same way, in more modern times, with the annulment of the Nuremberg Laws and other Nazi racial legislation stateless persons, Jew and Gentile alike, frequently found that, without being consulted in any way, they were once again endowed with German nationality, regardless of the fact that many of them had strong emotional reasons for not wanting to have anything further to do with Germany and things German.[2]

During the seventeenth and eighteenth centuries, with the expansion of the commercial activities of the inhabitants of western Europe, European States sometimes found it necessary to make specific provision in their treaties for the protection of particular groups of nationals. Both the United Kingdom[3] and the United States[4] entered into treaties with the Sherif of Morocco whereby the latter agreed to treat all nationals of these two western States alike, whether they were Christian or not. Sometimes, express mention is made of the rights of, for example, Jews coming from the United Kingdom or the United States, while at others, efforts are made to preserve, for example, the British

status of an Englishman becoming a Moslem.[5] Despite the
fact that Christian States claimed the right to intervene in the affairs of others when Christians were
persecuted, the so-called international right of
humanitarian intervention tends to be nothing but an
ideological excuse to enable a more powerful State to
interfere in the affairs of a weaker State.[6] It was
easier to deal with Turkey as 'the sick man of Europe'
than it was to do anything effective against Czarist
Russia or Nazi Germany. By the twentieth century,
little was heard of this right of humanitarian intervention. Something similar to it was, however, resorted
to on behalf of Europeans in the Congo in 1960.

Even though occasional actions or diplomatic démarches
were resorted to in the past on behalf of individuals
not nationals of the protesting State, the general
tendency was to arrange by way of bilateral treaty or
the use of safe-conducts for one's own nationals to
receive what might be termed civilised treatment when
abroad. The convenience of this practice eventually
led to the evolution of what is generally described as
treatment in accordance with the minimum standard of
international law for the treatment of aliens.[7] This
merely means that an alien is entitled to receive from
the country in which he is residing, or which he happens
to be visiting, the bare modicum of civilised rights.
By and large, those rights are tantamount to what
western European civilisation regards as the minimum
conditions of the rule of law:[8] the right to a trial,
the right to receive a fair hearing and to be heard in
one's own defence, being defended by counsel of one's
own choice, within the limits laid down by the local
authority regulating the conditions under which persons
are allowed to appear before the courts.[9]

The minimum standard of international law in respect
of the treatment of aliens does not operate to give
the alien any rights which he can exercise himself.
Any infringement of this minimum standard will remain
uncorrected unless the State of which the injured
alien is a national decides to take the matter up with
the offending State. If the alien happens to be
stateless, there is, in the absence of any treaty
giving the parties to the treaty the right to protest
against the ill-treatment of stateless persons, no
State to whom the injured individual can turn for
protection, or able in law to act on his behalf on its
own initiative.[10]

An interesting case illustrating this type of situation
arose in connection with the transport of illegal
immigrants to Palestine. It has long been recognised
that the high seas are open to the traffic of all men,
and, many of the early safe-conducts on behalf of
aliens concerned their freedom of movement on these
waters.[11] In March 1946, the _Asya_ was seized in the
Mediterranean by a British destroyer and was found to
be carrying over 700 persons, none of whom carried
passports or travel papers authorizing entry into
Palestine. The ship had no papers and flew no national
flag to which she was entitled. An action for her
condemnation in accordance with the Palestine Immigration
Ordinance, 1941, as amended by the Defence Regulations,
was brought before the Palestine courts. On behalf of
the _Asya_ it was contended that the high seas were open
to all and that the ship was therefore immune from
seizure thereon. The court pointed out that the
freedom of the seas, like any other right or freedom
under international law, belongs to States and not to
individuals, and the vessel was condemned. This
decision was upheld by the Judicial Committee of the

Privy Council.[12] The 1958 Geneva Convention on the
High Seas[13] gives treaty effect to this principle, which
has much in common with judgments in various jurisdictions which have held that a person kidnapped abroad
and brought before a local court, was, rightly, under
that court's jurisdiction. Only the country from which
he had been kidnapped enjoyed a right of protest.[14]

It is not only stateless persons who lack any protection under international customary law. Normally
speaking, a State will not intervene on behalf of aliens
coming from a third State, although inroads into this
principle of the nationality of claims have been made
on behalf of 'United Nations' nationals under the 1947
Peace Treaties with the Axis 'satellites'[15] and by the
European Convention on Human Rights.[16] Individuals who
are oppressed by their home State are also, in the
absence of specific treaties, at the complete mercy of
their oppressors. International customary law imposes
no restrictions on a State to respect the life, liberty,
or happiness of its nationals, and does not authorise
any other State to protest or intervene on their behalf.
It is true that in the nineteenth century Sir Moses
Montefiore conducted a one-man lobby which resulted in
British protests to Russia against anti-Jewish excesses.
But Russia at that time was weak and was in no position
to defy England. Today, however, it is possible for
matters of this kind to be taken up in the United
Nations, while no nationality link is required under
the European Convention.

After 1933 it became clear that States had become
somewhat unwilling to make such protests, and when
made they tended to be ignored. The British Government,
for example, invariably replied to suggestions that it
protest to Hitler Germany about the ill-treatment of
German nationals under the Nazi régime that there was

insufficient evidence that atrocities were being committed, and that, even if they were, it would be contrary to international law for one sovereign State to protest about the treatment being meted out to the nationals of another sovereign State by the government of that State. This 'ostrich' attitude led Professor H. A. Smith to declare in 1938: 'In practice we no longer insist that States shall conform to any common standards of justice, religious toleration and internal government. Whatever atrocities may be committed in foreign countries, we now say that they are no concern of ours. Conduct which in the nineteenth century would have placed a government outside the pale of civilised society is now deemed to be no obstacle to diplomatic friendship. This means, in effect, that we have now abandoned the old distinction between civilised and uncivilised States.'[17]

The attitude of some Commonwealth members towards South Africa on account of that country's treatment of its black and coloured population leading to its withdrawal from the Commonwealth, and later the reaction of the United Nations leading to its suspension from that body in 1974, suggest that Smith's condemnation may be a little too general. It is of interest to note, therefore, why Britain's attitude towards Nazi Germany provoked his comments. The Second World War commenced for Great Britain on September 3, 1939, and almost immediately the Stationery Office published a White Paper on 'The Treatment of German Nationals in Germany'.[18] Apparently, it was no longer contrary to international law for the United Kingdom to comment adversely on Germany's treatment of Germans in Germany. It must be remembered, however, that the Nuremberg Tribunal in its judgment on the Major Nazi War Criminals[19] expressed itself in a form that was fully consistent with the traditional view of international law, rather than in conformity with the emotional view then current. The Tribunal expressly declared that "to constitute crimes against humanity, the acts relied on before the outbreak of war must have been in execution of, or in connection with, any crime within the jurisdiction of the Tribunal."[20] While the judgment gives a very full account of the abominable manner in which the German Government treated - or ill-treated - large numbers of its nationals, none of the accused was found guilty of ill-treating Germans, unless it could be shown that such ill-treatment was part and parcel of one of the war crimes, such as the waging of aggressive war, over which the Tribunal had jurisdiction. Even in cases in which United States Military Tribunals condemned those accused of offences against German citizens committed independently of the waging of aggressive war,[21] they did so by virtue of the unconditional surrender of Germany and the operation of Control Council Law No.10,[22] whereby the Tribunals were to all intents and purposes German municipal tribunals, giving effect to the municipal law of Germany postulated by the effective sovereign of Germany.

As the details of Germany's treatment of her own nationals, as well as of the non-German inhabitants of occupied territories, became public knowledge, the pressure in favour of the international protection of human rights gathered pace. At the same time, what must have been the most potent one-man[23] pressure group known to history went into action with the word · 'genocide' as the device upon its banner, the climax of whose efforts is to be seen in the adoption by the General Assembly of the Genocide Convention in 1948.[24] Before analysing the extent to which these two concepts have affected the position of the individual in international law, it is as well to pause a moment to consider some of the evidence occasionally invoked to prove the subjectivity of the individual in that legal system.

Pirates and war criminals, perhaps the two most blatant hostes humani generis, are invariably cited as proof of the fact that international law does recognise the subjective character of the individual. If it were not regarded as unkind, one's natural reaction would be that a case must be weak that seeks its support among the dregs of the criminal world. In ordinary circumstances, a State possesses jurisdiction only over its nationals, aliens within its territory, aliens committing offences against its nationals and subsequently falling into its hands, and such other persons as are placed within its jurisdiction by treaty. In the case of pirates, however, both customary and conventional international law authorise every State to try such individuals for offences committed, without the authority of a State, upon the high seas.[25] It is essential however, that the offenders should in fact be pirates, and not merely rebels[26] or persons seeking political asylum.[27] War criminals are in a category by themselves. The law of war permits the punishment of breaches of that law by whatever State finds the offender within its power. Normally, such trials are conducted by belligerents against their own forces - although usually the national military law is sufficiently wide to obviate any need to try them for war crimes as distinct from the ordinary municipal criminal law - or against enemy personnel for offences against their own forces, the forces of allies, the civilian population of the prosecuting State or its allies, or for offences committed within the territory of this group of States.

It would appear from this that pirates and war criminals

are in an exceptional position. Far from international
law giving them any rights - unless it be the right to
trial, and a drum-head court martial would suffice - it
authorises a State which would not normally be able to
exercise jurisdiction over the accused to try for the
alleged offences. Not only does international law not
grant the accused any subjective rights, it reduces
the right he would normally have not to be tried by
those seeking to judge him. It is because of this
problem of the grounding of jurisdiction that some of
the criticism has been levelled against Israel in its
determination to try the alien Eichmann for offences
committed outside Israel, against individuals who were
not Israelis, and who, for the main part, having died
before Israel came into existence, could not become
naturalised Israelis ex post.[28] The fact that the
indictment refers to crimes against humanity and war
crimes against non-Jews as well, makes the situation,
if anything, even more complex.

Those who support the view that the individual possesses personality in international law frequently support
their view by reference to the practice of the Mixed
Arbitral Tribunals established after the First World
War, or to the international protection of minorities,
or to the sphere of activity of the International
Labour Organization. What they tend to overlook is
that, in each of these cases, any rights that may be
said to belong to the individual have been created by
treaty; that, normally speaking, such individual rights
can only be invoked by a State which is a party to the
treaty in question - as may be illustrated by the
decision of the Permanent Court of International Justice
in the Danzig Railway Officials case;[29] and that what
has apparently been granted to the individual under a
treaty may just as easily be taken away from him by

virtue of another treaty between the same parties, or
by the parties allowing the treaties to fall into
desuetude - as in the case of the Minorities Treaties.[30]

It is sufficient here to treat only the Minorities
Treaties,[31] for they, to a great extent, have formed
the basis for the present attitude towards human rights.

The territorial settlements following the First
World War resulted in a number of national groups
finding themselves as minorities in an alien environment. Often, these minorities belonged ethnically to
the former territorial sovereign and, to protect them
against unfair discrimination, the new sovereign was
required to enter into treaty commitments to afford
them equal treatment with the majority among whom they
lived.

Problems concerning the treatment of these national
minorities, especially the German minority in Poland,
frequently came for consideration before the Permanent
Court of International Justice. In the case concerning
the German Settlers in Poland[32] the Court had occasion
to define what it meant by 'equality' emphasising that
this term was used in the Minorities Treaties to
indicate 'real' and not merely 'formal' equality. This
may mean that if a minority is to receive true equality,
it may well have to be afforded preferential treatment
as compared with the majority among whom it is living.

Such a situation arose in connection with the Greek
Minority Schools in Albania.[33] There was no Treaty
by which Albania was obliged to afford protective
treatment to the Greek minority within its borders.
However, when Albania was admitted to the League of
Nations it undertook to afford to this minority
treatment in accordance with the minorities régime.

When, at a later date, the Albanian Government decided
to amend the constitution to forbid private schools,
the Greek Government persuaded the League to apply to
the Court for an Advisory Opinion as to whether the
decision to close Greek schools under this legislation
was compatible with Albanian undertakings. Despite
the absence of a treaty, the Court reached the conclusion
that enough common standards were to be found in the
existing Minorities Treaties for it to be possible to
speak of a definite minorities régime. In the view of
the Court, equality of treatment between the minority
and the majority was a basic condition of this régime.
Since the Greek community could only preserve its
national characteristics if its children were educated
in their own language, culture, religion and traditions,
undue discrimination would be exercised against the
community if it were not allowed to preserve its own
schools. The majority, on the other hand, would not
suffer in the same way by being required to attend
State schools.

This Advisory Opinion is only relevant where the
State whose conduct is impugned is under a clear
obligation, either by way of treaty or by unilateral
undertaking, to treat a particular portion of its
population in a special way. Even then, it is not the
members of the minority who are afforded rights. It
is third States to which their sovereign has undertaken
the obligation. The rights of the individuals are only
protected to the extent that these States are prepared
to take up the cudgels on their behalf. If no State
is so prepared, then, regardless of any paper undertakings that the sovereign may have pretended to
assume, such a minority is completely at the mercy of
its ruler. In such a case the minority is in the same
position as it would be if no treaty existed. Such is

the situation when, for example, a sovereign State
decides to take over assisted denominational schools
and training colleges, as happened in Ceylon, or in
South Africa with regard to Native schools. These are
issues, which, in the terms of Article 2, paragraph 7,
of the Charter of the United Nations, are essentially
within the domestic jurisdiction of the State
concerned, even though where South Africa is concerned
the General Assembly has persistently ignored the
relevance of this Charter provision.

It sometimes happens that, in its municipal legislation, a State does afford protective treatment to
minorities. Care must, however, be taken to remember
that such treatment is afforded under municipal legislation or practice. It does not in any way reflect
or indicate that the State concerned regards the
individual as being entitled to protection because
international law so prescribes. This is true, however
close may be the similarity between the municipal and
the international position. Thus, in the case of
Missouri, ex rel. Gaines v. Canada,[34] the Supreme
Court of the United States upheld the right of the
states to segregate white from non-white students, so
long as the treatment afforded to each group was
'separate but equal' - nobody has even been able to
explain how one Negro student plays baseball with himself.
It was not until the Brown case[35] that the Supreme
Court, under the leadership of Chief Justice Warren,
recognised that 'separate but equal' was the negation of
true equality. It may be said that the atmosphere
engendered by the United Nations contributed to this
decision, but the Court based itself firmly on a liberal
and up-to-date interpretation of the Constitution of
the United States. In fact, when, earlier, an attempt
had been made in Sei Fujii v. California[36] to assert

that an individual alien had acquired personal rights
under the Charter protecting him against legislative
discrimination, the Court of Appeals upheld his right
on the basis of the Fourteenth Amendment to the
Constitution, completely ignoring the text of the
Charter, even though this document had, to a great
extent, formed the basis of the decision in the lower
court.

Too often, when talking of individual and minority
rights, one tends to forget the rights of the majority.
An interesting case from this point of view concerned
the Bombay schools.[37] Under the Indian Constitution,[38]
minorities are entitled to send their children to
vernacular schools. The state of Bombay introduced
legislation by which only Europeans, Anglo-Indians,
Christians and other foreigners were to be allowed to
send their children to schools in which the language
of instruction was English. A case was brought
against the state by two parents whose children were
precluded by this legislation from attending an English
school. They contended that this legislation infringed
the constitutional right of the children to receive
equal treatment in all respects. The Supreme Court of
India invalidated the legislation, holding that to
grant rights to a minority did not in any way mean that
rights were thereby taken away from the majority.[39]

On the international level minority language rights
were considered by the European Court of Human Rights
in the Belgian Linguistics Case.[40] This arose from
the requirement that children living in Flemish areas
of Belgium were required to attend Flemish-speaking
schools. The Court held that

the legislature in adopting the system in issue, has
pursued an objective concerned with the public interest:

253

to favour linguistic unity within the unilingual
regions and, in particular, to promote among pupils
a knowledge in depth of the usual language of the
region. This objective concerned with the public
interest does not, in itself, involve any element of
discrimination

so long as the means employed are proportionate to the
justification for discrimination.

Those who believe in the subjective personality of
the individual under international law frequently
refer to the work of the League of Nations in connection
with minorities and in the connected field of stateless
refugees. They tend to overlook, however, that the
success of endeavours in these matters was directly
proportionate to the political interests of the major
Powers.[41] Thus, as France's political interests came
to depend more and more on the goodwill of the Little
Entente, so the Minorities Commission found it more
difficult to deal adequately with the problems raised
by minorities resident in the territory of France's
allies. Similarly, the protection afforded by treaty
to stateless persons only had meaning to the extent that
any party was prepared to carry out the obligations
of the treaty, or to recognise the travel papers
carried by such a person.

This is still largely the case today. The Minorities
Treaties, however, were a casualty of the Second World
War. After 1945 no real attempt was made to protect
minorities in Europe. The Peace Treaties of 1947[42]
with the defeated minor Axis Powers did, however,
forbid these Powers from introducing legislation that
would deny rights to their political minorities -
provided, of course, that these minorities were not
fascist,[43] a term sufficiently vague to enable these
States to do very much what they liked, secure in the
knowledge that the Soviet Union would protect its

satellites against criticism by other signatories to these Treaties. The uselessness of these clauses was well demonstrated by the snook that was cocked by Bulgaria, Hungary and Rumania at the Western Powers, the United Nations and the International Court of Justice, after the latter had rendered its Opinion on the Interpretation of the Peace Treaties.[44]

In rare circumstances, true minorities treaties have been effected since 1945. One such treaty exists between India and Pakistan,[45] while the Special Statute appended to the Memorandum of Understanding on the Free Territory of Trieste relates to the Trieste border region between Italy and Jugoslavia.[46] The success of such treaties depends, however, on the goodwill of the parties. This fact has received emphasis in the dispute between Austria and Italy concerning the Austrian minority in the Tyrol, which led to bitter debates in the United Nations and, in 1961, produced rioting in Italy.[47]

More has been done on behalf of stateless persons by way of the Convention relating to the Status of Stateless Persons of 1954 and that on the Reduction of Statelessness of 1961, although the latter is not yet in force.[48]. In so far as refugees in general are concerned, to some extent they are protected by the work of the International Refugee Organization[49] and the Convention and Protocol relating to their status.[50] Here, too, achievement is measured by the extent of co-operation shown by the parties to the relevant Conventions. Examples of this may be found in the difficulties experienced in the latter part of 1960 by 'Indian' immigrants arriving in the United Kingdom without any papers to show that they were really Indians and, as such, British nationals. A more tragic case concerned a

stowaway from Ceylon. When the vessel returned him
to Colombo, the local authorities declined to re-admit
him as he had no papers to prove his Ceylonese nationality. The fact that he was claimed by relatives on
shore was of no evidential validity. The United Kingdom allowed him in, only after he had sailed round the
world two or three times without being admitted by any
member of the United Nations, all of which of course,
accepting the Preamble of the Charter, have faith in
the fundamental rights of man, as well as in the dignity
and worth of the human personality.[51] If there were
a recurrence today, the wanderer would not be so
fortunate. As a result of the expulsion of Asian minorities from Uganda and other African countries, which
action was not condemned by the United Nations, the
United Kingdom enacted legislation[52] as a result of
which holders of British passports, and therefore of
British nationality, were denied entrance to the United
Kingdom, even though they were unable to immigrate
elsewhere. Perhaps even more tragic is the case of
Anthony Lewis, born in France to an American father
and his English wife. An American marrying a foreigner
must live in the United States for ten consecutive
years for his children to be American citizens.
Sergeant Lewis was born in Germany and had spent only
eight years in the United States, although he maintained
that his family had lived there since 1725. The child
was not French since its birth in France had not been
registered immediately upon birth, as is required for
the children of foreign parents. He would become
American if his mother became naturalized before his
sixteenth birthday. She declined to surrender her
British passport, and the child was thus stateless.[53]

People concerned with the position of the individual
in international law, and especially those who maintain

that he has now achieved a standing of his own, base
themselves primarily on the contention that there are
certain basic human rights which inhere to all mankind,
and which all states are or ought to be bound to
recognize and protect. This development stems largely
from the revulsion that was felt at the Nazi atrocities
in Europe which provided the impetus to a movement in
favour of the international recognition of the rights
of man. Many believed that peace in the future depended
not only upon the abolition of war, but also upon the
limitation of State sovereignty, accompanied by recognition of the indivual as a subject of international
law. One of the most ardent advocates of this idea
was the late Sir Hersch Lauterpacht, who published
his International Bill for the Rights of Man[54] in 1945
while the Second World War was still being fought.
To a great extent he regarded the human rights clauses
in the Charter of the United Nations as the culmination
and fruition of his campaign.[55]

It is interesting to recall that all the States
gathered at San Francisco found it possible to accept
the Charter in its entirety, and that one of the chief
draftsmen of the Preamble with its lofty references
to human dignity and equality for all, without
distinction as to race, sex, language or religion, was
Smuts. These facts alone should have put the partisans
of human rights upon their guard. They should have been
warned that no great step forward could have been
effected in this field if it were acceptable to, for
example, the Soviet Union, the Union of South Africa,
and the United States at one and the same time. They
also tended to ignore the fact that, although it makes
frequent reference to the promotion and encouragement
of human rights and fundamental freedoms, the Charter
nowhere defines what is means by those words - and it

is difficult to contradict South African statesmen and others who assert that apartheid - or as it is now described by South Africa 'separate development' - enables the various races to develop fully and freely to their maximum potential without risk of contamination one by another. It is irrelevant that apartheid, as practiced in South Africa,[56] runs counter to everything for which human dignity stands, and is clearly contrary to the spirit of the Charter. Even the General Assembly's condemnation of apartheid as a crime against humanity,[57] and its suspension of South Africa from its membership in 1974, make little difference, for the actions are so clearly one-sided since the Assembly totally ignores situations like that concerning Asians in Uganda which equally amount to apartheid. As to the legality of South Africa's treatment of its black and coloured populations and the creation of independent Bantustans, one must bear in mind that there is a tendency in international law, particularly when considering treaty limitations upon the freedom of action of States, to interpret words in their strict and narrow meanings, for, as was pointed out by the Permanent Court of International Justice, "restrictions upon the independence of States cannot be presumed.[58] ... If the wording of a treaty is not clear, in choosing between several admissible interpretations, the one which involves the minimum of obligations for the Parties should be adopted."[59]

It must also be remembered that the Charter nowhere lists any human rights, nor imposes any direct legal obligation upon the members of the United Nations to recognise these rights. Of equal significance, it fails at any time to grant any right to the individual which he can maintain against an oppressor. What is more, in the Statute of the International Court of

Justice, which is an integral part of the Charter, it is expressly provided that only States may be parties to actions before the Court. Since the decision to go to Court is a political decision to accept legal settlement of what is a political dispute,[60] there is little likelihood of any member of the United Nations being prepared to take another to the Court on account of the latter's non-recognition of the human rights of its own nationals. Where nationals of the complainant State are concerned, the Charter adds nothing to the existing rules of customary international law. There, individuals are already sufficiently protected by the minimum standard regarding the treatment of aliens.

It is true that the United Nations has adopted a variety of Resolutions and Conventions on human rights covering such matters as servitude and forced labour, freedom of information and association, employment policy, the rights of women, marriage and the family, childhood and youth, and the right to enjoy culture,[61] it has also drawn up two International Covenants on Human Rights, the one on Economic, Social and Cultural Rights, and the other on Civil and Political Rights, both of which were adopted in 1966[62] but, since they require 35 ratifications, neither had come into force by the end of 1974. In no case, however, has the individual who may suffer from a breach of any particular right any positive channel of recourse, although there is appended to the two Covenants an Optional Protocol for the establishment of a Human Rights Committee to which aggrieved individuals would have a right of protest. Of more practical significance is the European Convention on Human Rights[63] which has established both a Commission for receiving individual complaints and a Court to which the Commission or a signatory state may, in certain circumstances, refer an

alleged breach of the Convention. While the objective
of all these agreements is the individual and his
rights, it cannot really be argued that any of them
have in the fullest sense conferred true legal personality upon the individual. The only way in which a
tribunal can become seised of a case involving a
breach of human rights is through the medium of some
other agency enjoying international legal personality.[64]
In so far as the European Community is concerned, the
situation is a little different for individuals have
access on certain economic matters to the Court of
Justice of the European Communities which has recently
held[65] that

fundamental human rights were part of the general
principles of law of which the court was the custodian.

In protecting such rights the court considers the
constitutional traditions common to member states.
It could not, therefore, uphold measures which were
found to be incompatible with fundamental rights
recognized and guaranteed by the constitutions of
these member states. Similarly international treaties
and agreements to which member states had adhered in
order to protect human rights were of a nature to supply
guidelines which should be considered within the
framework of Community law ....

However, the protection afforded to private property
by the constitutional instruments of all member states
and the guarantee likewise afforded the free exercise
of trade, work, or other professional occupations, far
from being absolute perogatives, must be viewed in the
light of the social function of private and individual
rights. Rights of this order were therefore granted
within the limits set by public interest.

It was legitimate to hold that in the field of Community
law, such rights were limited by the objectives of
general interests pursued by the Community, always
granted that the substance of such rights was left
unspoiled.

In particular, as regards the guarantees specifically
granted to economic undertakings, such guarantees
could not extend to the protection of commercial
interests from the risks ensuing therefrom, which were

part of the very essence of economic activity.[66]

In point of fact, the disadvantages [suffered] by the
applicant ... were the consequence of evolution of the
economy. In the face of economic change resulting from
the recession in the field of coal production it was
for the applicant firm itself to assess the new situation
and to proceed to make the necessary adjustments....

That the parties to the San Francisco Conference did
not intend to profilerate the number of international
judicial issues, particularly where human rights are
concerned, is made clear both in the proceedings of
the United Nations Conference on International Organisation and the Charter itself. Article 2, paragraph
7, of the latter precludes the United Nations from
intervening in any matter which is essentially within
the domestic jurisdiction of any State, unless the
application of enforcement measures is called for in
connection with threats to the peace, breaches of the
peace, and acts of aggression. It was only when the
Afro-Asian majority in the United Nations decided to
move against South Africa that any suggestion was made
that a State's denial of human rights constituted a
threat to the peace,[67] and even then the Security Council,
because of the vetos exercised by France, Great Britain
and the United States, refused to take any step to
support this view. It is not really surprising that
member states have been hesitant in asserting that the
denial of human rights amounts to a threat to the peace,
for such a threat really comes not so much from the
country denying the human rights, as from the State
which protests at the situation in that country,
contending that if that situation continues the
complaining country will be so outraged that it will
have no option but to take action to bring the situation
at an end. By a process of convoluted reasoning this
can of course be construed as proof that the State

whose conduct is objected to is in fact threatening a breach of the peace or indulging in action likely to result in such a breach.

As regards the question of domestic jurisdiction, it must be pointed out that, in the Charter as drafted, this provision appeared in the Chapter relating to the pacific settlement of disputes. It was during the San Francisco Conference that it was decided to transfer it to Chapter II, where it is elevated to one of the Principles in accordance with which the Organisation is to act. This means that the exception embodied in this paragraph now operates over the whole field in which the United Nations has jurisdiction and, strictly speaking, enables a State to evade those obligations of the Charter which impinge upon its domestic jurisdiction. What is more, the measuring rod of international law which appeared in the similar provision of the Covenant of the League of Nations[68] has been removed. Many international lawyers argued that this made no difference and that the test would still be that of international law as interpreted by the Court.[69] Unfortunately, however, a number of States when accepting the compulsory jurisdiction of the Court have done so while excepting matters which fall essentially within their domestic jurisdiction as determined by themselves.[70] It is generally recognised that courts decide issues of their own jurisdiction, and Article 36 of the Statute of the World Court expressly provides that any dispute as to the jurisdiction of the Court shall be so decided. Nevertheless the Court, which has shown what some may regard as an unfortunate willingness to deny itself jurisdiction, has upheld the validity of such exception clauses.[71] This practice makes it exceedingly easy for any State to preclude judicial assessment of its treatment of its own nationals.

Another problem relating to domestic jurisdiction concerns the nature of intervention. International lawyers recognise this as a technical term signifying unwarranted, and therefore, illegal, interference, generally by force, in another State's affairs. They contend, therefore, that so long as the United Nations merely discusses a matter within a State's domestic jurisdiction it is not infringing the prohibition of Article 2, paragraph 7. This ignores the fact that the Charter was drawn up and adopted by politicians, with the aid of advisers whose advice was accepted only so long as it was politically agreeable, for political purposes. They used terms in their ordinary rather than technical meaning, and it is perfectly clear from the debates at San Francisco[72] that, as used in the Charter, intervention is synonymous with interference. It is clearly interference for one State to discuss or criticise the internal affairs of another with which it is at peace, a point already made before 1939 by Great Britain in so far as her relations with Nazi Germany were concerned.

The fact that the General Assembly does discuss matters concerning the rights of man and proceeds to pass resolutions in this field, does not mean that it has a right so to do, although constant reiterations to this effect, especially when they receive complete or near unanimous support, may have the effect of a de facto revision of the Charter in which the members of the United Nations have acquiesced. Like other organs of the United Nations, the Assembly is a political body comprising politicians, who decide political questions for political reasons. It is not a court, nor are its members competent to interpret a complex legal document like the Charter. The General Assembly never asked the Court for an interpretation of its

rights in the light of Article 2, paragraph 7, and
declined the challenge thrown to it by South Africa
to obtain an Advisory Opinion as to whether it could
discuss such matters as apartheid within the Union.
This is the more surprising in that the General
Assembly has demonstrated that it will not regard an
Advisory Opinion as binding when it considers political
or other reasons to demand otherwise.[73] This is not
an unreasonable attitude ofr a political body to adopt,
and the political nature of the United Nations is
perhaps best brought out in the words of the Joint
Dissenting Opinion appended to the World Court's view
on Admission of a State to Membership in the United
Nations: Recommendations of the General Assembly, as
well as decisions of the Security Council, "emanate
from political organs .... The main function of a
political organ is to examine questions in their
political aspect, which means examining them from every
point of view. It follows that the Members of such an
organ who are responsible for forming its decisions
must consider questions from every aspect, and, in
consequence, are legally entitled to base their
arguments and their vote upon political considerations."[74]

Should a similar challenge be thrown to the United
Nations today, while there is little doubt that the
Assembly would follow its own precedents and assert
its right to discuss any issue affecting human rights,
it is possible that the members might be more willing
to refer the matter to the Court, since recent decisions,
and especially the separate opinions of concurring
and dissenting judges, show a tendency to regard the
protection of human rights as having become part and
parcel of modern international law. In its 1966
judgment on South West Africa[75] the Court refused to
adopt this approach:

throughout this case it has been suggested, directly or indirectly, that humanitarian considerations are sufficient in themselves to generate legal rights and obligations, and that the Court can and should proceed accordingly. The Court does not think so. It is a court of law, and can take account of moral principles only in so far as these are given a sufficient expression in legal form. Law exists, it is said, to serve a social need;[76] but precisely for that reason it can do so only through and within the limits of its own discipline. Otherwise, it is not a legal service that would be rendered.

Humanitarian considerations may constitute the inspirational basis for rules of law, just as, for instance, the preambular parts of the United Nations Charter constitute the moral and political basis for the specific legal provisions thereafter set out. Such considerations do not, however, in themselves amount to law. ...

Since the decision was only reached through the casting vote of the Court's President, we may perhaps pay more attention to the views of the dissenting judges than might otherwise be permissible. Thus Judge Jessup considered[77]

The 'general philosophical views prevalent in the world' certainly include the content of Articles 1, 55 and 73 of the Charter of the United Nations and the worldwide condemnation of apartheid....

The accumulation of expressions of condemnation of apartheid as reproduced in the pleadings of Applicants in this case, especially as recorded in the resolutions of the General Assembly of the United Nations, are proof of the contemporary international standard.

Judge Tanaka is to the same effect:[78]

The repeated references in the Charter to the fundamental rights and freedoms ... presents itself as one of its differences from the Covenant of the League of Nations, in which the existence of the intimate relationships between peace and respect for human rights were not so keenly felt as in the Charter of the United Nations. However, the Charter did not go so far as to give the definition of fundamental rights and freedoms, nor to provide the machinery of implementation for the protection and guarantee of these rights and freedoms.

The Universal Declaration of Human Rights and Fundamental Freedoms of 1948 which wanted to formulate each right and freedom and give them concrete content, is no more than a declaration adopted by the General Assembly and not a treaty binding on the member States...

... It seems difficult to recognize that the Charter expressly imposes on member States any legal obligations with respect to the fundamental human rights and freedoms. On the other hand, we cannot ignore the enormous importance which the Charter attaches to the realization of fundamental human rights and freedoms .... Those who pledge themselves (Article 56) to take action in cooperation with the United Nations in respect of the promotion of universal respect for, and observance of, human rights and fundamental freedoms, cannot violate, without contradiction, these rights and freedoms. How can one, on the one hand, preach respect for human rights to others and, on the other hand, disclaim for oneself the obligation to respect them? From the provisions of the Charter referring to the human rights and fundamental freedoms it can be inferred that the legal obligation to respect human rights and fundamental freedoms is imposed on member States ....

... There is little doubt of the existence of human rights and fundamental freedoms; if not, respect for these is logically inconceivable; the Charter presupposes the existence of human rights and fundamental freedoms which shall be respected; the existence of such rights and freedom is unthinkable without corresponding obligations of persons concerned and a legal norm underlying them. Furthermore, there is no doubt that these obligations are not only moral ones, and that they also have a legal character by the very nature of the subject-matter.

Therefore, the legislative imperfections in the definition of human rights and fundamental freedoms and the lack of mechanism for implementation do not constitute a reason for denying their existence and the need for their legal protection....

The accumulation of authoritative pronouncements such as resolutions, decisions, etc., concerning the interpretation of the Charter by the competent organs of the international community can be characterized as evidence of international custom referred to in Article 38 (1)(b) [of the Court's Statute and which the Court is instructed to apply], ... We consider that the norm of non-discrimination or non-separation on the basis of race has become a rule of customary international law.

Judge Padilla Nervo delivered himself in like manner:[79]

A new order based on the proposition that 'all men are
by nature equally free and independent', has conquered
solemn recognition in the basic law of many nations and
is today ... norm and standard in the constitutional
practice of States ....

The statesmen, the jurists, legislators, and the courts
of justice, they all have to recognize the realities
of today, for the sake of freedom, justice and peace.

The Court is well aware of such realities and shall
consider, in its interpretation of the relevant
international instruments and obligations, the prevailing ideas of today regarding human rights and fundamental freedoms ...

The Court ... is not limited by the strict enumeration
of Article 38 [of its Statute] , whose prescriptions
it is free to interpret in accordance with the constant
evolution of the concepts of justice, principles of
law and teachings of publicists.

Racial discrimination as a matter of official government policy is a violation of a norm or rule or standard
of the international community.

By the time the General Assembly decided to recognize
Namibia as the proper term by which to describe South
West Africa, the personnel of the International Court
had changed, and with it the attitude towards human
rights. In the Advisory Opinion on Namibia[80] the
majority appear to have accepted the views expressed
by individual judges a mere five years earlier in 1966.
The Court accepted that the Security Council in its
attitude towards this territory had been acting in
accordance with Article 24 of the Charter which related
to matters affecting international peace and security,
and was of opinion that its resolutions were binding on
those voting against as well as non-members of the
Security Council, and further regarded non-members of
the United Nations as being equally bound.[81] Thus:[82]

... Under the Charter of the United Nations, the former
Mandatory has pledged itself to observe and respect,
in a territory having an international status, human
rights and fundamental freedoms for all without distinction as to race. To establish instead, and to enforce,
distinctions, exclusions, restrictions and limitations
exclusively based on grounds of race, colour, descent
or national or ethnic origin which constitute a denial
of fundamental human rights is a flagrant violation of
the purposes and principles of the Charter.

The Court was aware, of course, that the attitude to

human rights in the seventies was different from what

it had been after the first world war, but[83]

the Court is bound to take into account the fact that
the concepts embodied in Article 22 of the League
Covenant - 'the strenuous conditions of the modern
world' and 'the well-being and development' of the
people concerned - were not static, but were by definition
evolutionary, as also, therefore, was the concept of
the 'sacred trust'. The parties to the Covenant must
consequently be deemed to have accepted them as such.
That is why, viewing the institutions of 1919, the
Court must take into consideration changes which have
occurred in the supervening half-century, and its
interpretation cannot remain unaffected by the subsequent development of law, through the Charter of the
United Nations and by way of customary law. Moreover,
an international instrument has to be interpreted and
applied within the framework of the entire legal
system prevailing at the time of the interpretation....
In this domain, ... corpus juris gentium has been
considerably enriched, and this the Court, if it is
faithfully to discharge its functions, may not ignore.

While it may be true that the Charter, despite the

way in which the Court and its members have interpreted

it, does not of itself improve the lot of the individual,

it must not be forgotten that it opened the way for

further developments. To assert an obligation to

encourage and promote respect for fundamental freedoms

and human rights automatically creates the realization

that something more is needed to give flesh and

substance to this wraith. In order to achieve this

the United Nations established its Commission on Human

Rights which drafted the document which was accepted - not unanimously as is often stated, but nemine contradicente - in 1948 as the Universal Declaration of Human Rights.[84] As its name indicates, this document was no tablet of the law, but a mere exhortation as to what the law should be and the enunciation of a standard of behaviour which,hopefully, the members of the United Nations might eventually carry into effect. Perhaps its basic fault lies in its attempt to achieve universality, for any statement of rights which might be acceptable to, for example, Canada, France, the United Kingdom, the United States - both north and south of the Mason-Dixon Line - South Africa, the Soviet Union, and all the other members of the United Nations, is merely to postulate the highest common factor, or perhaps the lowest common multiple, which means leaving the situation as it is. The draftsmen of the Declaration were fully aware that, like other General Assembly Resolutions, it was not a binding document but a mere guide to practice.[85] Moreover, the Declaration recognized its own shortcomings. Having condemned persecution it nevertheless provided that individuals possessed the right to seek asylum when they were persecuted, which act would of course be in breach of the Declaration. The draftsmen, however, failed to make any provision for the individual to receive the asylum he might need to seek.

Eventually, in 1966 the General Assembly of the United Nations was able to adopt a Convention on the Elimination of all Forms of Racial Discrimination,[86] which came into force in 1969, and two Covenants on Economic, Social and Cultural Rights and on Civil and Political Rights,[87] neither of which is yet in force. The two Covenants indicate in their very first article, which is common to both and was approved by the drafting

committee long before any of the more substantive
articles, the change of emphasis in the attitude of
the United Nations towards human rights, especially
as they affect the individual. Above all else it
appears are the right of self-determination and of
exploitation of natural resources - hardly rights which
affect the individual or may strictly be called
'human'. It is true that Article 2 of the Civil
Rights Covenant provides

Each State party to the present Covenant undertakes
to respect and to ensure to all individuals within its
territory and subject to its jurisdiction the rights
recognized in the present Covenant, without distinction
of any kind, such as race, colour, sex, language,
religion, political or other opinion, national or
social origin, property, birth, or other status.

But there is no way, other than in the case of those
states which accept the Optional Protocol recognizing
the right of individual protest to the Human Rights
Committee which, however, enjoys no effective remedial
powers, whereby an aggrieved individual can secure
redress. It is even doubtful whether a co-signatory
would have the right to bring an action for breach of
treaty against the offender before the International
Court. In its 1966 Judgment in the <u>South West Africa</u>
<u>Cases</u>[88] the Court held that the individual parties to
a mandate treaty did not

possess any separate self-contained right which they
could assert ... to require the due performance of the
Mandate in discharge of the 'sacred trust'.... Any
divergences of view concerning the conduct of a mandate
were regarded as matters that had their place in the
political field, the settlement of which lay between
the mandatory and the competent organs of the League.

It is true that, with the present composition of the
Court and its current view of the law concerning human
rights and fundamental freedoms, in a future case the

Court might be far more in line with the views of
Lauterpacht who considered[89] that signatories to
minorities or mandates treaties could

> juridically enforce the rights of the Minority in
> question.... A foreign State is thus placed in the
> position of being able to protect rights of persons
> other than its own subjects; it need not prove any
> interest other than its general interest in the
> maintenance of ... the provisions in question; it
> need not prove any other interest than its general
> interest in the protection and enforcement of rights
> of the individuals protected by these Treaties.

The nearest that the individual has reached so far in
being able to secure respect for his rights or
condemnation of their breach is through the medium of
the European Convention on Human Rights,[90] which
provides for a Commission to which an aggrieved
individual may protest or to which another party to
the Convention may lodge its complaint. Moreover, both
the Commission and parties may,in the event of inability
to settle a complaint satisfactorily, refer the issue
to the European Court on Human Rights, although the
aggrieved individual possesses no such right. In some
cases the Court has been effective in securing a
change in national legislation,[91] while on other
occasions the state complained against has avoided
judicial proceedings by way of an ex gratia payment
to the individual affected.[92] An interesting problem
may arise in the near future, for, as we have seen,[93]
the Court of the European Communities also has the
competence to deal with individual claims in particular
circumstances. After the United Kingdom refused to
allow entry into Britain of Asians holding British
passports and possessing British nationality who had
been expelled from Africa, this issue was referred to
the European Commission and may finish before the
Court. It may well be that this will produce an

incompatibility in judicial approaches to this problem. In 1974 the Court of the European Communities decided in van Duyn and Home Office[94] that since

it is a principle of international law, which the EEC treaty [in providing for freedom of movement] cannot be presumed to disregard in the relations between member states, that a state is precluded from refusing its own nationals the right of entry or residence, it follows that a member state, for reasons of policy, can, where it deems necessary, refuse a national of another member state the benefit of the principle of freedom of movement for workers in a case where such a national proposes to take up a particular offer of appointment even though the member state does not place similar restrictions upon its own nationals.

It is perhaps interesting to note in this connection that, despite the treaty of association between Kenya, Uganda and Tanzania, with its provision for freedom of movement and the right of establishment, in December 1974 Kenya decided to expel all Tanzanians holding jobs which might be filled by Kenyans and to refuse employment to any alien if the post in question could be filled by a Kenyan.

Probably the aspect of protection of the individual that has aroused most emotive reaction and a sense of real recognition of him as an indivual flows from the Genocide Convention,[95] for this purports to make criminal acts directed against particular groups with a view to the destruction of their group character and their existence as groups. This Convention was produced from the sense of horror generated by Nazi Germany's persecution and physical extermination of minorities. However, the concept of genocide, as the Convention makes clear, is highly technical and while it may cover such situations as arose in Biafra, Bangladesh or Cyprus, care must be taken not to use the term as an emotional outlet for condemning such happenings as, for example, the United States bombings

in Vietnam, which may well have constituted war crimes
in accordance with the ordinary law of war. On paper,
the Genocide Convention appears to provide for the
trial of those accused of genocide. It envisages the
ultimate creation of an international court with criminal
competence, but until its creation genocide is
punishable by the courts of the country in which it has
been committed. This is but poor comfort to those
believing in the rule of law. Save in a case like that
of Bangladesh where the offender may be a captured
alien, the possibility of a trial is unlikely to say
the least. Genocide is hardly likely to be committed
by a private individual exercising his own initiative.
It is far more likely that it will be committed on the
orders or with the tolerance of the state of which the
offender is a national. It is somewhat difficult to
envisage a situation in which the Attorney-General of,
let us say, Ruritania would institute proceedings for
genocide before the Ruritanian Supreme Court against
the Commander-in-Chief of the Ruritanian Army for
actions perpetrated by him against a Ruritanian minority
group in execution of a policy dictated by the
Ruritanian Government. Even in the case of Bangladesh,
political desires for a resumption of relations
between that country and Pakistan and between the latter
and India led to an abandonment of genocide trials.

It may be of interest to mention that the International
Court has considered the legitimacy of Reservations to
the Genocide Convention[96] and decided, somewhat
surprisingly, that reservations are valid if they are
'compatible with the object and purpose of the
Convention'. It may well prove difficult to define
whether a particular reservation in fact satisfies
this requirement.

In its hesitancy to recognize the direct right of an
individual under a treaty, international law is merely
confirming municipal decisions like that in <u>Civilian
War Claimants Association</u> v. <u>The King</u>[97] in which the
House of Lords pointed out that while the reparation
clauses of the Treaty of Versailles recognized that it
was individuals who had suffered injury who should be
compensated, it was the Crown which was given the right
of recovery and which would decide, solely within its
own discretion, whether moneys received should be used
for the purposes implied by the Treaty. It is only by
virtue of a municipal law to this effect that private
claimants become entitled to any compensation obtained
by their government.[98] While this view has been confirmed
by the International or World Court,[99] Commissioner
Parker of the United States - German Mixed Claims
Commission said[100]

where a demand is made on behalf of a designated national,
and an award and payment is made on that specific
demand, the fund so paid is not a national fund in the
sense that title vests in the nation receiving it
entirely free from any obligation to account to the
private claimant on whose behalf the claim was asserted
and paid and who is the real owner thereof.

Nevertheless, he himself referred to two nineteenth
century decisions of the Supreme Court of the United
States,[101] prior to legislation to the contrary,[102]
to show that

even if payment is made to the espousing nation in
pursuance of an award, it has complete control over the
fund so paid and held by it and may ... return the
fund to the nation paying it or otherwise dispose of
it.

The traditional view has been emphasised since the
second world war, as may be seen in the reparations
agreement signed between the Federal Republic of Germany

and Israel.[103] On the surface this appears to recognize the rights of Jews who suffered under the Nazi regime. However, it was not by virtue of any obligation imposed by international law in respect of these individuals that Germany entered into this agreement, but solely out of a desire to acknowledge some responsibility for its predecessor's acts and thus rehabilitate itself morally. The agreement gives no more status to the individual who is supposed to benefit by it, than does the Peace Treaty with Japan,[104] which recognized a Japanese liability to compensate prisoners of war, such compensation to be paid to the International Committee of the Red Cross to be distributed to the appropriate national agencies for disbursement in accordance with their own arrangements.

It is true that international law since 1945 has made some faltering steps towards recognizing the rights of the individual, and even more haltingly towards protecting them. The difficulty lies in the fact that such recognition encroaches seriously upon the traditional concepts of sovereignty and the rights flowing therefrom. Moreover, proper international protecting of human rights depends upon the ordinary man accepting a sense of responsibility for his fellows and a feeling of personal loss when the latter is injured. Too often, however, his attitude approaches that of the Irish delegate at the drafting conference of the European Convention when it was suggested that periodic elections should be counted among man's human rights. He commented that while he was prepared to die for his own right to participate in elections, he was in no way ready to fight for someone else's similar right.[105] It will only be when people anywhere are prepared to assert that people everywhere are entitled to equal rights and equal treatment from all States and are prepared to

support their own States in ensuring that such rights
are in fact realised that we can approach a situation
in which the individual can ever enjoy any status in
international law.

* This paper is based on the Barou Memorial Lecture
delivered at University College London, 8 Nov. 1960.

1 See V above.

2 Lauterpacht, 'The Nationality of Denationalised
Persons', Jewish Y.B. Int'l Law (1948) 164. See
Lowenthal v. A.G. [1948] I All E.R. 295, Re Mangold's
Patent (1951) 68 R.P.C. 1; see also Loss of National-
ity (Germany) Case (1965) 45 Int'l Law Rep. 353.

3 1856, Art. 16 (X Hertslet's Commercial Treaties 903).

4 Cf. Adler and Margalith, With Firmness in the Right:
American Diplomatic Action Affecting Jews 1840-1945
(1946), Part I, Near East and Morocco.

5 See, e.g., 2 McNair, International Law Opinions (1956)
28.

6 Green, 'Human Rights in Public International Law',
in Singhvi, Horizons of Freedom (1969) 58, 74.
See also VII below.

7 See Roth, The Minimum Standard of International Law
Applied to Aliens (1949).

8 See, however, Garcia-Amador, Sohn and Baxter, Recent
Codification of the Law of State Responsibility for
Injuries to Aliens (1974); see, also, IV above, n.20
et seqq.

9 See, e.g., Re D. N. Pritt, Q.C., 20 Malayan Law J.
1954, xxiii.

10 Some measure of protection is, however, given to
stateless persons by the Convention relating to the
Status of Stateless Persons, 1960, 360 U.N.T.S. 117.

11 See Colbert, Retaliation in International Law (1948),
40; Schwarzenberger, 'International Law in Early
English Practice', 25 Brit. Y.B. Int'l Law (1948)
52, 86.

12 Molvan v. Att. Gen., Palestine (The Asya) [1948] A.C. 351.

13 450 U.N.T.S. 11, Art. 6 (2).

14 E.g., Kerr v. Illinois (1886) 119 U.S. 436; Ex p. Elliott 1949 1 All E.R. 373; Eichmann v. Att.Gen., Israel (1961/2) 36 Int'l Law Rep. 18. 117. See, however, U.S. v. Toscanino (1974) 500 Fed. 2d 267.

15 See, e.g., U.S., ex rel. Menkes v. Italian Republic (1953) 14 U.N. Rep. Int'l Arb. Awards 137, and Mergé Claim (1955) ibid., 236.

16 Y. B. Human Rights [1950] 420.

17 19 The Listener (1938) 183. See, also, Schwarzen-berger, Frontiers of International Law (1962) ch.4; II above, VII below. On humanitarian intervention generally, see Stowell, Intervention in International Law (1921) 51-277, and Lillich (ed.), Humanitarian Intervention and the United Nations (1973).

18 H.M.S.O., Cmd. 6120 (1939).

19 41 Am. J. Int'l Law (1947) 172.

20 Ibid., 249.

21 See, e.g., Re Brandt (Doctors' Trial) (1947), and Re Milch (1947), 1 U.S., Trials of War Criminals 3, 2 ibid., 355, resp.

22 Control Council Official Gazette, No. 3, 1 Jan. 1946; Schwarzenberger, 1 International Law (1957) 297-8, 2 ibid. (1968) 467.

23 Rafael Lemkin - see his Axis Rule in Occupied Europe (1944) Ch. IX, and 'Genocide as a Crime under International Law', 41 Am. J. Int'l Law (1947) 145.

24 78 U.N.T.S. 277.

25 Geneva Convention on the High Seas, 1958, Art. 15 (n. 13 above).

26 Cp. The Magellan Pirates (1853) 1 Spinks 81 with the treatment accorded to the Santa Maria in Feb. 1961, see Green, 'The Santa Maria: Rebels or Pirates' (1961) 37 Brit. Y.B. Int'l Law 496.

27 See R. v. Governor, Brixton Prison, Ex p. Kolczynski [1955] 1 Q.B. 540.

[28] See Green, 'The Maxim Nullum Crimen Sine Lege and the Eichmann Trial' (1962) 38 Brit. Y.B. Int'l Law 458.

[29] (1928) B/15.

[30] See, e.g., Robinson, Were the Minorities Treaties a Failure? (1943); Azcarate, The League of Nations and National Minorities (1945); Green, 'Protection of Minorities in the League of Nations and the United Nations', in Gotlieb, Human Rights, Federalism and Minorities (1970) 179.

[31] See n. 30 above.

[32] (1923) B/6, 25.

[33] (1935) A/B 64.

[34] (1938) 305 U.S. 337.

[35] Brown v. Board of Education (1954) 347 U.S. 483, (1955) 349 U.S.294.

[36] (1950) 217 Pac. (2d) 481 (1952) 242 Pac. (2d) 617; see also Green, 'Human Rights and Colour Discrimination', (1950) 3 Int'l Law Q. 422.

[37] State of Bombay v. Bombay Education Society A.I.R. 1954 S.C. 561. All these education cases are discussed in Green, 'The Right to Learn' (1954) 3 Indian Y.B. Int'l Aff. 268; see also Hartman, 'The United States Supreme Court and Desegregation', (1960) 23 Modern Law Rev. 353.

[38] Art. 29 (2).

[39] On the nature of 'equality' as a 'reality' and a 'formality', with particular reference to its relevance for Canada's Indians, see Green, 'Tribal Rights and Equal Rights', (1974) 22 Chitty's Law J. 97.

[40] (1968) 45 Int'l Law Rep. 114, 216.

[41] See n. 30 and Weis, Nationality and Statelessness in International Law (1956) 165.

[42] Italy, Art. 15; Bulgaria, Art. 2; Hungary, Art. 2; Romania, Art. 3 (49 U.N.T.S. 126; 41 ibid., 21,135; 42 ibid. 3, resp.).

[43] Arts. 17, 3, 3, 4, resp.

44   [1950] I.C.J. 65, 221.

45   18 Apr. 1950 (2 Indian Y.B. Int'l Aff. (1953) 302).

46   3 Whiteman, Digest of International Law (1964) 98-109.

47   Ibid., 38-50.

48   360 U.N.T.S. 117; Doc.A/CONF.9/15, resp. See also Weis, op.cit.

49   Constitution 1946, 18 U.N.T.S. 3.

50   1951, 189 U.N.T.S. 137; 1967, 606 ibid. 267, resp.

51   See Re Hanna (1957) 8 D.L.R. (2d) 566, for a somewhat similar case in Canada.

52   See, e.g., Immigration Act, 1971, c. 77. See, also, the Report on Passports - Going Abroad, published by Justice (1974), paragraphs 12-17.

53   The Times (London), 20 Aug. 1957.

54   It is perhaps of interest to mention that this was published under the imprint of the American Jewish Committee.

55   See his International Law and Human Rights (1950) vii, 145. See, however, Svarlien, 'International Law and the Individual', 4 J. of Public Law (1955), 138-145. See, also, McLaurin, The United Nations and Power Politics (1951) 34-40; Ganji, International Protection of Human Rights (1962); Halasz, Socialist Concept of Human Rights (1966); Sohn & Burgenthal, International Protection of Human Rights (1973).

56   See, e.g., Green, 'Human Rights and the Colour Problem', 3 Current Legal Problems (1950), 236; Roskam, Apartheid and Discrimination (1960); Strydom, Black and White Africans (1967); Laurence, The Seeds of Disaster (1968). For statements suggesting possible disavowal of discrimination, see The Times, 28 Oct. 1974.

57   E.g. Res. 3068 (XXVIII) for draft International Convention of Suppression and Punishment of Crime of Apartheid; and Res. 2074 (XX).

58   The Lotus (1927), A/10, 18-

59   Mosul Case (1925) B/12, 25.

60
Rosenne, The Law and Practice of the International
Court (1965), 2-6.

61
See, e.g., U.N., Human Rights: A Compilation of
International Instruments of the United Nations
(1968/1973).

62
Res. 2200 (XXI), Annex.

63
(1950) Y.B. H. R. 1950, 420.

64
For a general survey of this problem, see Gormley,
Procedural Status of the Individual before Inter-
national and Supranational Tribunals (1966).

65
J. Nold, Kohlen und Bastoffgrosshandleng, Darmstadt
v. Commission of the European Communities (1974)
The Times 17 May 1974.

66
Cp. Oscar Chinn case (1934) P.C.I.J. A/B 63.

67
See, e.g., Report of the U.N. Committee on Apartheid
to 1974 Session of General Assembly, Doc. A/9022
(1974).

68
Art. 15 (8): "If the dispute between the parties is
alleged by one of them, and is found by the Council,
to arise out of a matter which by international law
is solely within the domestic jurisdiction of that
party, the Council shall so report, and shall make
no recommendation as to its settlement."

69
See, e.g., Lauterpacht, op. cit., n. 55 above, 175.
See, also, Rajan, United Nations and Domestic
Jurisdiction (1961).

70
U.S.A., Pakistan, etc., see I.C.J.Y.B. (current
issue).

71
Norwegian Loans [1957] I.C.J. 9.

72
See, e.g., Canada, Report on the United Nations
Conference on International Organisation (1945) 18:
'The Conference was generally agreed that the
Organization must not interfere in the internal
affairs of its Members, and with this view the
Canadian delegation was fully in accord' (italics
added). 'Interfere' is also used in the U.S.
Report to the President (1945) 44. See, also,
Kelsen, The Law of the United Nations (1951) 772.

73
See General Assembly reaction to the Advisory
Opinion on Effect of Awards of Compensation made by

the U.N. Administrative Tribunal [1954] I.C.J. 47,
culminating in Res. 957 (IX).

74 [1948] I.C.J. 57, 85, per Basdevant, Vice President,
and Judges McNair, Winiarski and Read.

75 South West Africa Cases [1966] I.C.J. 6, 34.

76 See I, IV above.

77 At 439, 441.

78 At 288-90, 293.

79 At 457, 464.

80 [1971] I.C.J. 16.

81 At 51-4

82 At 57; see Sep. Op. by Judge Ammoun, 76, 78-9.

83 At 31-2.

84 U.N. Y.B. Human Rights [1948] 466.

85 See, e.g., Green, 'The Universal Declaration of
Human Rights', (1951) 24 Adult Education 44, 47.

86 660 U.N.T.S. 195.

87 Res. 2200 (XXI), Annex.

88 [1966] I.C.J. 6, 29, 51, 45.

89 1 Collected Papers (1970) 299.

90 Y.B. Human Rights [1950] 420. See Robertson,
Human Rights in Europe (1963); Fawcett, The Application of the European Convention on Human Rights
(1969).

91 See, e.g. De Becker Case (1962 - against Belgium),
33 Int'l Law Rep. 205.

92 See, e.g., Amekrane v. U.K. (1974) Council of
Europe, Report of the Commission, 19 Jul. 1974;
The Times 13 Aug. 1974.

93 See n. 65 above.

94 The Times 5 Dec. 1974 (for the English decision referring issue to the European Court, see [1974] 3 All
E.R. 178).

95 (1948) 78 U.N.T.S. 277.

96 [1961] I.C.J. 15, 29.

97 [1932] A.C. 14.

98 See, e.g., U.S. Act of 26 Feb. 1896, 29 U.S. Statutes at Large, 28, 32.

99 See, e.g., Mavrommatis Palestine Concessions (1924) A/2, 13; Serbian Loans (1929) A/20, 17; Peter Pazmany University (1933) AB/61, 221.

100 Administrative Decision No. V (1924) 7 U.N. Rep. Int'l Arb. Awards 119, 152.

101 Frelinghuysen v. U.S., ex rel. Key (1884) 110 U.S. 63; U.S., ex rel Baynton v. Blaine (1891) 139 U.S. 306.

102 See n. 98 above.

103 10 Sept. 1952, Jerusalem, Documents [1953] or Germany, Bundesgesetz-Blatt [1953] II, 37.

104 (1951) Art. 16, 136 U.N.T.S. 45.

105 Irish Press, 20 Aug. 1949.

VII

HUMAN RIGHTS AND THE GENERAL PRINCIPLES OF LAW*

L'homme est né libre, et partout il est dans
les fers - Man is born free and everywhere he
is in chains (Rousseau: Du Contrat Social
1762, ch.1)

In his De Jure Belli ac Pacis Grotius declares

that Kings, and those who are invested with a Power
equal to that of Kings, have a Right to exact Punishments, not only for Injuries committed against themselves, or their Subjects, but likewise, for those
which do not particularly concern them, but which are,
in any Persons whatsoever, grievous Violations of the
Law of Nature or Nations. For the Liberty of consult-
ing the Benefit of human Society by Punishments, ...
[means] that War is lawful against those who offend
against Nature.[1]

He goes on to warn, however that

'here some Precautions are to be observed; the first
of which is, that Civil Customs, tho' received among
many Nations, not without good Reason, be not mistaken
for the Law of Nature .... The second is, that among
Things forbidden by Nature, we do not inconsiderately
reckon those, of which we have not sufficient Evidence
that they are such, but that are rather repugnant to
some positive Law of God.[2]

This comment of Grotius, which refers to the right

of protecting all men regardless of nationality or of

residence, is far wider than the concept of the

minimum standards of international law, which 'approx-

imate to the minimum requirements of the rule of law

in the Anglo-American sense of the term or of the

Rechtsstaat, as understood in Continental law'.[3]

The doctrine of State sovereignty, however, implies
that, with the exception of any duty arising from
treaty obligations, there is, prima facie, the right
to treat one's own nationals as one pleases. This is
a matter of domestic jurisdiction, a principle which
reaches its climax in Article 2, paragraph 7, of the
Charter of the United Nations and in the reservations
to their declarations made under the 'Optional Clause'
of the Statute of the World Court by Liberia, Malawi,
Mexico, Philippines, Sudan and the United States, who
all claim the right of auto-determination, while
India and Israel make a similar reservation but without
indicating how this is to be assessed.[4] But as Judge
Huber pointed out in the Island of Palmas Arbitration,[5]

this right [sovereignty] has as corollary a duty: the
obligation to protect within the territory the rights
of other States.... together with the rights which
each State may claim for its nationals in foreign
territory.

The treatment afforded such aliens must be in accordance
with at least the minimum standards of international
law,[6] which today reflect such general principles of
law recognised by civilised nations - or perhaps more
correctly such principles of law as are generally
recognised by civilised nations - as have become
embodied in Western concepts of the rule of law. One
of the consequences of the increase in the number of
new economically underdeveloped states has been to
question the validity of these Western concepts, at
least in the economic and property field.[7]

In the past there was a religious basis, often framed
in the form of natural law, for such claims. Thus, in
his De Indis Noviter Inventis, 1952, Vitoria, calling in
aid 'the law of nations which either is natural law or
derived from natural law', maintained that the Spaniards
had the right to reside in the Indies 'provided they do

no harm to the natives, and the natives may not prevent them'. This right was claimed, however, nor merely against non-Catholic aborigines, for

it would not be lawful for the French to prevent the Spanish from travelling or even from living in France, or vice versa, provided this in no way enured to their hurt and the visitors did no injury.

He also postulated the inalienable right of the Spaniards to carry on trade with the Indians, and

if the Spaniards kept off the French from trade with the Spaniards, and this not for the good of Spain, but in order to prevent the French from sharing in some advantage, that practice would offend against righteousness and charity.

Righteousness and charity are religious concepts and if the Indians offended against them by denying such rights to the Spaniards they would have committed a wrong authorising the Spaniards to resort to a just war against them.[8] What is significant in Vitoria's view of natural law, however, is not only his assertion of the right of peaceful penetration, but his recognition of the Indians as being within the international system even though they were 'barbarians'. The rights which belonged to Spaniards also belonged to Indians, and he conceded that even they could reply to the Spanish just war by themselves waging a just war, 'seeing that on one side there is right and on the other side there is invincible ignorance'.[9] Apart from any title that the Spaniards might have had to enjoy such rights on the basis of natural law, Vitoria did not fail to point out that 'another possible title is by way of propagation of Christianity, [for] Christians have a right to preach and declare the Gospel in barbarian lands'.[10]

The religious nature of claims to protect one's own nationals at times spread into the field of protection of aliens. Although international law prescribed that foreign States could only intervene to secure fair treatment for their own nationals, there have been treaties concluded at various times embodying principles guaranteeing the observance of some of the rights of man, and in particular the right of religious toleration. Thus, although the Treaty of Augsburg, 1555,[11] was directed to ensuring the equality of Catholic and Protestant Princes and postulated the principle cujus regio, ejus religio, it provided that in the Free Cities of the Holy Roman Empire where either Protestants or Catholics were often in only a small majority the two confessions were to live 'quietly and peacefully together'.[12] Within one hundred years this principle was so well recognised that by the Treaty of Westphalia, 1648,[13]

"subjects who in 1627 had been debarred from the exercise of their religion, other than that of their ruler, were ... granted the right of conducting private worship, and of educating their children, at home or abroad, in conformity with their own faith; they were not to suffer in any civil capacity nor to be denied religious burial, but were to be at liberty to emigrate, selling their estates or leaving them to be managed by others."...
The principle of religious equality was placed as part of the peace under an international guarantee.[14]

With the expansion of the known world and the development of economic and political rationalism, a situation developed which, in the nineteenth century especially, was generally favourable to the protection of human rights.[15] This is perhaps most manifest in the series of treaties between Vienna, 1815,[16] and Brussels, 1890,[17] dealing with slavery and the slave trade. In the Le Louis,[18] Sir William Scott pointed out that the 1815 Treaty was both declaratory of fact and promisory of future measures:

the contracting parties mutually inform each other of

the fact that they <u>have</u> in their respective dominions
abolished the slave trade, without stating at all the
mode in which the abolition has taken place. It next
engages to take future measures for the universal
abolition. That with regard to both the declaratory
and promisory parts Great Britain has acted with the
<u>optima fides</u> is known to the whole world, which has
witnessed its domestic laws as well as its foreign
negotiations .

Although France was a party to the Treaty and the
British Government acted with

perfect propriety in accepting the assurance that the
French Government had actually abolished the slave
trade, as a sufficient proof of the fact,

Sir William accepted as final the statement that the
slave trade had not yet been made illegal by French
legislation. By 1822 the slave trade had been rejected
by the United States and the whole of Europe with the
exception of France and Portugal, and in <u>La Jeune</u>
<u>Eugénie</u>,,[19] Story, J., was called upon to consider
the compatibility of slavery and the slave trade with
the natural rights of man. He admitted that

under some circumstances slavery may have a lawful
existence, and the practice may be justified by the
conditions, or wants, of society, ... [but the traffic]
necessarily carried with it a breach of all the moral
duties, of all the norms of justice, mercy and humanity,
and of the admitted rights, which independent Christian
nations now hold sacred in their intercourse with
each other.

A similar point was made by the Umpire in <u>The Enterprise</u>
(1855). He pointed out that although not contrary to
international law, slavery was 'contrary to the principles of justice and humanity'.[20]

By the twentieth century this type of treaty developed
still further and eventually gave birth to the minorities régime of the League of Nations era,[21] based on
the assumption of true equality between nationals and

minority groups alike.[22] Since the Second World War
there seems to have been a retreat from the practice
of protecting national minorities and minorities
treaties are now practically unknown. It is only in
such circumstances as arose from the division of India
into India and Pakistan with large minorities in each,
that minority rights have been protected by treaty.[23]
When, however, the United Nations has been responsible
for creating a situation in which minority problems may
arise, attempts have been made to ensure protection.
This has been done by conferring legal force upon the
Universal Declaration of Human Rights, as was the case
with Libya[24] and Italian Somaliland.[25] The nearest
the United Nations has got to protecting the rights of
minorities as such is the International Convention on the
Elimination of all Forms of Racial Discrimination[26]
which came into force in 1969, is in general terms,
applying to everyone, and does not use the word
'minority' as such. In addition, the Covenant on Civil
and Political Rights[27] recognizes the right to worship
in groups and, in Article 27, states

in those States in which ethnic, religious or linguistic
minorities exist, persons belonging to such minorities
shall not be denied the right, in community with the
other members of their group, to enjoy their own culture,
to profess and practice their own religion, or to use
their own language.[28]

As a result of the ideological conflicts with
which the world has been confronted
since 1945 and the increase in number of one-party
States, the type of minority that requires protection
today is often political rather than religious and
ethnic, a situation that was recognised by the Court of
Queen's Bench when it redefined the concept of 'political
offender' in connection with extradition treaties,[29]
although it was not long before there was a retreat from

this more liberal approach.[30] This change of emphasis
was already fully recognized in the Peace Treaties
between the United Nations and the Axis satellites.[31]
Each defeated State expressly undertook to

take all measures necessary to secure to all persons
under [its] jurisdiction, without distinction as to race,
sex, language or religion, the enjoyment of human rights
and the fundamental freedoms, including freedom of
expression, of press and publication, of religious worship,
of political opinion and public meeting.[32]

When a dispute arose as to the observance of these
obligations, it was not the matter of substance but
a question concerning the machinery for interpreting
the Treaties that was referred to the World Court. The
Court considered[33] that the Treaties could not be
interpreted without the co-operation of the parties
alleged to have broken them, allegations which were of
course denied.

Even in the absence of treaties some States have
claimed the right to intervene in the affairs of other
States. This type of intervention had already been
approved by Vitoria, at least when undertaken on
religious grounds. He considered that

if any of the native converts to Christianity be
subjected to force or fear by their princes in order
to make them return to idolatry, this would justify
the Spaniards ... in making war and in compelling the
barbarians by force to stop such misconduct, ... and
in deposing rulers as in other just wars.... Suppose
a large part of the Indians were converted to Christianity,
and this whether it were done lawfully or unlawfully,
... so long as they really were Christians, the Pope
might for a reasonable cause, either with or without
a request from them, give them a Christian sovereign
and depose their other unbelieving rulers.[34]

In these words of Vitoria is to be found the ideological basis for many of the interventions conducted
by some Powers into the affairs of others. Thus it has

been said that

to save the faith of England we made demonstrations
in the Netherlands, and, when it appeared that the
Catholic League, or the Austrian Hapsburgs, would carry
all before them in Germany, it seemed to Protestants
that, in answer to their petitions, the Lord God aroused
himself and brought down the Danish and the Swedish
armies from the north. By faith, or rather for the
faith, Oliver Cromwell made his effort on behalf of
the Duke of Savoy's Vaudois .... [Similarly] although
religious intervention practically ceased in Western
Europe after the Treaty of Westphalia, in Eastern
Europe where the writ of Westphalia never ran and
religion remained a more important criterion than
State allegiance, it was destined to endure as a very
real factor. The Tsaritsa Catherine's first intervention in Poland was, ostensibly at least, produced by
concern for those Polish subjects who were Orthodox in
faith. Her Turkish policy was largely affected by her
claim to exercise a guardianship over the Greek Orthodox subjects of the Sultan.[35]

The attitude adopted by England and Russia in these
cases may well have been an ideological cover for
political ends, but this was certainly not always so.
In 1844 Lord Aberdeen condemned the Porte for its
'barbarous practice' of executing Mahomedan subjects
who had adopted Christianity. He referred to the
British practice in India and, in words reminiscent of
Vitoria, maintained that for the British Government,

as a Christian Government, the protection of those who
profess a common belief with themselves, from persecution and oppression, on that account alone, by their
Mahomedan rulers, is a paramount duty with them, and one
from which they cannot recede.[36]

It was not only on behalf of Christians with whom
they shared common belief, nor solely against non-
Christian States, that the Western Christian States
were prepared to intervene. In 1840 the United States
Secretary of State sent a despatch to the American
Consul at Alexandria in connection with atrocities
committed against the Jews of Damascus:

The President has witnessed, with the most lively
satisfaction, the effort of several of the Christian
Governments of Europe, to suppress or mitigate these
horrors, and he has learned with no common gratific-
ation, their partial success. He is, moreover, anxious
that the active sympathy and generous interposition of
the Government of the United States should not be
withheld from so benevolent an object, and he has
accordingly directed me to instruct you to employ,
should the occasion arise, all those good offices and
efforts which are compatible with discretion and your
official character, to the end that justice and humanity
may be extended to these persecuted people.[37]

Again, in 1872, a Consul's Note was delivered in

Bucharest by the consuls of Germany, Austria, Hungary,

France, Great Britain, Greece, Italy and the United

States, who

deem it their duty to address to the government of the
Prince, collectively, and in the most formal manner,
the verbal observations which most of them have been
ordered by their governments to present to it in
relation to the Israelitish question.... The governments
of the undersigned will judge whether the impunity which
has been enjoyed by the assailants of the Jews is not
of a nature to encourage a repetition of scenes of
violence quite unworthy of a civilised country, which,
as such, ought to ensure freedom and security to all
religious denominations.[38]

These documents indicate that intervention on behalf

of those persecuted for religious belief was frequently

motivated not merely by narrow concepts of religious

sympathy, but by a secularisation of the fundamentals

of religious belief. It reflects what may be described

as a community of spirit in the countries of the Western

world, based on a common belief in the worth and dignity

of man and of his right to enjoy his life free from

persecution and in the same freedom as those among whom

he lives. In these messages there is an assertion of

a right to intervene, at least by way of protest,

when the treatment of nationals fell below those minimum

standards which might be described as general principles

of conduct recognised by civilised Christian nations,
and which within those nations frequently amounted to
broad principals of law.

It was not only in the field of religion that intervention took place, and in the nineteenth century
there grew up the concept of humanitarian intervention.
This is perhaps not surprising in view of the fact that
Christian States expected State conduct to conform to
the basic principles of Christian civilisation although
it was often recognised that the legal ground for such
intervention was tenuous to say the least. In 1827
Great Britain, France and Russia intervened in the
Greco-Turkish troubles to stop Turkish atrocities. In
1848 Britain suggested Franco-British mediation in the
Civil War in the Two Sicilies to end the cruelties of
that war, while British representatives were encouraged
to maintain contacts with revolutionary forces and
remind them of the rules of warfare in civilised countries, and there were frequent occasions when British
embassies afforded

shelter to men marked down by their political opponents.
Justification for these acts is not primarily to be
sought on narrow legal grounds but on the grounds of
common humanity and decency and in a healthy British
reaction to the departure by others from such standards.[39]

Similarly, in 1867 the United States Secretary of
State communicated with the American Minister in Mexico
about atrocities committed by the Republican armies, for

such severities would be injurious to the national
cause of Mexico and to the Republican system throughout
the world. You will communicate to President Juarez
promptly, and by effectual means, the desire of this
Government, that in case of capture the prince
[Maximilian] and his supporters may receive the humane
treatment accorded by civilised nations to prisoners
of war.[40]

That the United States was aware of the possible
weakness of its legal right to intervene in such
circumstances was made clear when Russian pogroms
resulted in an influx of Russian Jews into the United
States:

The Government of the United States does not assume to
dictate the internal policy of other nations, or to
make suggestions as to what their municipal laws should
be or as to the manner in which they should be administered. Nevertheless, the mutual duties of nations
require that each should use its power with a due regard
for the other and for the results which its exercise
produces on the rest of the world. It is in this respect
that the condition of the Jews in Russia is now brought
to the attention of the United States, upon whose
shores are cast daily evidences of the suffering and
destitution wrought by the enforcement of the edicts
against this unhappy people. I am persuaded that His
Imperial Majesty the Emperor of Russia and his council-
lors can feel no sympathy with measures which are forced
upon other nations by such deplorable consequences.
(You will read this instruction to the minister of
foreign affairs).[41]

The record of the nineteenth century shows that
humanitarian intervention as a policy was only of value
when resorted to by a stronger Power against a weaker
one. Sir William Harcourt's comments on the British
intervention in Greece indicate the political character
of such acts:

it was the natural and almost inevitable consequence
of a forcible intervention to prevent the Turkish
Government from reducing its subjects to submission.
The emancipation of Greece, effected by Europe , was
a high act of policy above and beyond the domain of
law. As an act of policy, it may have been, and probably
was, justifiable; but it was not the less a hostile act,
which, had she dared, Turkey might properly have
resented by war .... Intervention is a question rather
of policy than of law. It is above and beyond the
domain of law, and when wisely and equitably handled by
those who have the power to give effect to it, may be
the highest policy of justice and humanity.[42]

A similar view of intervention, although in an

entirely different context, was taken by the World Court in the Corfu Channel Case:

The Court can only regard the alleged right of intervention as the manifestation of a policy of force,
such as has, in the past, given rise to most serious
abuses and such as cannot, whatever be the present
defects in international organisation, find a place
in international law.... From the nature of things,
it would be reserved for the most powerful States, and
might easily lead to perverting the administration of
international justice itself.[43]

Before the nineteenth century intervention was based on Christian beliefs and the religious concept of the worth of man. By the time of the French Revolution, however, new libertarian political teachings were current and inherent in them was the concept of the equality of man as a fundamental right. The teachings, however, were rationalist rather than religious, and the interventions of the period may to a great extent have been motivated by the declarations of rights embodied in the constitutions of the democratic intervening States. Thus, it has been suggested that

in the nineteenth and twentieth centuries the recognition of the fundamental rights of man in the constitutions of States has become, in a paraphrase of Article
38 of the Statute of the Permanent Court of International
Justice, a general principle of the constitutional law
of civilised States.[44]

Since, however, constitutions are not irrevocable,

the rights of man cannot, in the long run, be effectively
secured except by the twin operation of the latent
forces of the law of nature and of the compelling force
of the law of nations.[45]

Unfortunately, however, the concept of natural law, particularly in this connection, is often relegated to purely ideological purposes. This prospect was clearly seen by the United States-Mexican Claims Commission in the North American Dredging Company Claim:

The law of nature may have been helpful, some three
centuries ago, to build up a new law of nations, and the
conception of inalienable rights of men and nations
may have exercised a salutary influence, some one hundred and fifty years ago, on the development of modern
democracy on both sides of the ocean; but they have
failed as a durable foundation of either municipal or
international law and cannot be used in the present
day as substitutes for positive municipal law, on the
one hand, and for positive international law, as
recognised by nations and governments through their acts
and statements, on the other hand. Inalienable rights
have been the cornerstones of policies like those of
the Holy Alliance and of Lord Palmerston; instead of
bringing the world the benefit of mutual understanding,
they are to weak or less fortunate nations an unrestrained
menace.[46]

By the twentieth century there was evident in State

practice a backsliding from the former willingness

to intervene on humanitarian grounds, and even on

religious grounds, and there seemed to be no desire

to tie respect for human rights to either the law of

nature or of nations.[46a] In 1938, the United States,

which some fifty years before had been willing to inter-

vene against religious persecution abroad, declined

to intervene in the religious situation in Mexico.

While expressing American policy as being directed to

the actual grant of religious liberty in every country
of the world,... it should be borne in mind that ...
it is not appropriate or proper that we should seek to
determine or influence the circumstances of domestic
problems in a foreign country by taking any official
action with relation thereto, however peaceable, friendly
or well intentioned.... There are certain limits binding
every government in its proper relations to other
governments, to exceed which would defeat the very
purposes sought.... Within these limits the President
has championed, and will continue to champion, the
principles of the freedom of worship and education for
all nationals in every country of the world.[47]

A similar unwillingness to intervene was shown by the

Powers in relation to Hitler's excesses in Germany, and this led Professor H. A. Smith to declare that 'we have now abandoned the old distinction between civilised and uncivilised States'.[48]

Some fifteen or twenty years after the end of the second world war, there seems to have been a modified return to higher standards, at least on the level of criticism. Firstly, the Council of Europe with its commitment to the European Convention on Human Rights[49] was not prepared to have (Franco) Spain as a member, and later, during the period of the 'Colonels' régime' in Greece that country found itself the recipient of criticisms and complaints by fellow members to the Commission.[49a] Moreover, it was largely because of criticism of its <u>apartheid</u> policy by its fellow members that South Africa withdrew from the Commonwealth, while this policy was responsible for its suspension from the General Assembly in 1974 and the attempt to invoke sanctions against it. In the same year, the United States Congress sought to attach a proviso to a trade agreement with the Soviet Union whereby the latter, if it hoped to enjoy its rights under the agreement, would have to modify its policy with regard to emigration, particularly by Jews seeking to leave for Israel.

Despite their unwillingness to intervene on behalf of foreigners denied treatment equivalent to the minimum demanded for their own nationals abroad, States do not refrain from appealing to general principles of law or human rights on behalf of aliens for ideological reasons.[50] Too often,

the usual vindication of freedom, democracy, and culture can be described as ideological because the discussion generally terminates in showing that freedom in itself is better than regimentation, self-determination better than dictatorship, and spontaneous culture better than

censorship of self-expression. No reasonable man will
deny this so long as the question arises in abstract
form .... [But] these problems cannot be solved as long
as freedom and democracy are regarded merely as ideological postulates, or abstract principles of universal
application. We really begin to grapple with them only
when we are in a position to analyse them sociologically.
... The relevance of principles of political organisation can only be discovered by empirical means, that
is by recognising the social processes which either
allow a mechanism to function in a society or else
annihilate it.[51]

While States have been willing to defend their own

nationals abroad and even protest about the treatment

afforded to other aliens, even by their own governments,

they have been unwilling to accept similar criticisms

directed at themselves. This led Lauterpacht to

question[52] whether it is not an

incongruous situation [for] a State [to assert] internationally as its own, rights which it denies and condemns
within its borders with regard to the same individuals

and he went on to suggest that

the proper view ... is that international law grants
these rights to the individual as such - be he an alien,
a national, or a stateless person: With regard to
aliens these rights are in theory enforceable by their
own State; this it the reason why they have become firmly
established in international law. There is no agency -
national or international - to enforce or protect
these rights in the case of stateless persons[53] or in
the case of nationals with regard to their own State.[54]
But this important procedural difference clearly cannot
have an effect on these rights as such; these are
fundamental rights of the individual in the international
sphere,irrespective of nationality, although some of
them may for the time being exist as imperfect rights
because of the absence of legal machinery to enforce
them. It is pathetic to see writers elaborating in
detail the fundamental rights of the individual in his
capacity as an alien while remaining oblivious to these
rights when that individual happens to be within his
own State. It is only by the assumption that the
difference is one between a perfect and an imperfect
right that we can escape the somewhat absurd phenomenon

of the individual suffering a _capitis diminutio_, from
the point of view of the protection of the fundamental
rights of his personality, as soon as he ceases to be an
alien residing in a foreign State and assumes residence
in his home State.

Lauterpacht was among those who campaigned during the
second world war for recognition of human rights and
sought to secure their protection by international law,
contending that they were fundamental rights inherent
in man by reason of his very existence and thus constituting general principles of law recognised by all
civilized nations.[55] In due course the partisans of
this view secured in the Preamble of the Charter of the
United Nations a reaffirmation of 'faith in fundamental
human rights, in the dignity and worth of the human
person, [and] in the equal rights of men and women'.
In the Charter this declaration of faith is repeated,[56]
but is so expressed as to amount to no more than a pledge
that the United Nations shall seek to 'encourage and
promote' respect for human rights and fundamental
freedoms for all without distinction as to race, sex,
language or religion. No attempt is made to define the
content or nature of these rights, although some
preliminary efforts in this direction had already been
made in the Declaration by United Nations, 1942,[57]
when the parties declared their conviction

that complete victory over their enemies is essential
to defend life, liberty, independence and religious
freedom, and to preserve human rights and justice in
their own lands as well as in other lands, and that they
are now engaged in a common struggle against savage
and brutal forces seeking to subjugate the world.

Some of the participants in the 1945 Conference
sought to include a list of human rights in the Charter,[58]
but the majority disagreed, apparently assuming that
everybody knew what human rights and fundamental freedoms were. If it could be assumed that the statement

in the Declaration by United Nations was what the
participants had in mind, it would appear that the
human rights referred to in the Charter are in fact
the principles of law which are generally recognised
by civilised nations, even though they may not amount
to general principles of law recognised by civilised
nations in the sense of Article 38 of the Statute of
the World Court.[59] That this is probably the case is
further indicated by the rights which are embodied in
the Universal Declaration of Human Rights.[60] It must
be remembered, however, that this Declaration is nothing
more than a statement of aims and hopes which is not, and
was not when adopted intended to be, binding on anybody.
Nevertheless, when political necessity has demanded,
members of the United Nations have not hesitated to
allege that other members have disregarded the rights
embodied in the Declaration. Perhaps one of the most
glaring examples of this was the debate on the 'Russian
Wives' in 1949, when the General Assembly condemned the
Soviet Union for its breach of human rights. The
Resolution obtained support from many States whose
record on miscegenation and the freedom of spouses to
reside where they liked left almost as much to be
desired as did the Soviet practice.[61] While, from a
strictly formalistic and juridical point of view, the
legal status of the Declaration has remained that of any
other General Assembly resolution and so merely
hortatory or recommendatory, one cannot overlook the
fact that the Declaration has formed the basis of an
entire series of United Nations resolutions and
conventions relating to human rights[62] and numerous
members of the International Court of Justice have
maintained that it is not only the forerunner of a
series of legally binding documents, but has itself
hardened into law.[63] Moreover, in its judgment in the
Barcelona Traction case the Court said[64]

obligations [erga omnes binding upon all] derive, for
example, in contemporary international law, from the
outlawry of acts of aggression, and of genocide, as
also from the principles and rules concerning the basic
rights of the human person, including protection from
slavery and racial discrimination. Some of the
corresponding rights of protection have entered into the
body of general international law; others are conferred
by international instruments of a universal or quasi-
universal character.

The essentially Western-oriented character of these
rights as originally formulated is illustrated by
President Eisenhower's Proclamation setting aside
December 10, 1954, as Human Rights Day. He described
the basic rights, for which

men and women in many countries have striven and died,
... and still others strive and die in defence of human
dignity against the claims of totalitarian governments,
 as freedom of speech and of the press; freedom to
worship in accord with the dictates of conscience;
fair trial and freedom from arbitrary arrest; the right
to own property and to profit by the fruits of our
labours.[65]

In other words, he sought to generalise those standards
the observation of which Western nations, reflecting
their Christian traditions and their libertarian
political beliefs, demand for their nationals abroad,
and which they regard as inherent in any civilised
system of law, but many of which do not command the same
respect from either the socialist or developing
countries.[66] The general principles of law recognised
by civilised nations, which have been described as 'in
some ways a modern version of the law of nature',[67]
constitute, by Article 38(1)(c) of the Statute of the
World Court, one of the sources of international law to
be applied by international tribunals when necessary.
It is clear from the Article that the general principles
to be applied are not those of international law, for
they constitute a source of international law and

indicate one of the fields in which rules of international law are to be found. Further, the principles of law recognised by nations are, in the normal course of things, the principles embodied in the municipal laws of the nations in question. What Article 38 envisages, therefore, is the application of those basic principles of municipal law which are recognised as valid by civilised States, and it is this generality of recognition that elevates the principles from the level of municipal to that of international law. But the warning of Grotius must not be forgotten, so

that Civil Customs, tho' received among many Nations, ... be not mistaken for the Law of Nature,

especially as

the answer to the question: Must principles be universal to be 'general'? is emphatically No; for any other view renders the Article unworkable. There are general principles of law - general in the sense of being applied by the principal systems of the world. But they are extremely rare[68] and must be applied with caution, for what may be a general principle found equally in civil and common law may well be subject to different interpretations in those systems.[68a]

It is not only here that differences in interpretation arise. It repays study to note how South Africa and the majority of the other members of the United Nations differ in their understanding of the words 'to encourage and promote respect for human rights and fundamental freedoms' in the Charter. Thus, the United Nations has condemned apartheid as a threat to the peace and a crime against humanity[69] while South Africa describes it as a policy of 'separate development', conducive to the 'building up of each race in its own area'[70], and has therefore instituted a system of compulsory 'ghettoiastion' for the Blacks, asserting that these will eventually become separate States which might or might not remain in some special relationship with the

Republic. Moreover, in an apparent attempt to modify the criticism which led to South Africa's suspension from the United Nations, her chief delegate stated in the Security Council

I want to state here today very clearly and very categorically, my government does not condone discrimination purely on the grounds of race or colour. Discrimination based solely on the colour of a man's skin cannot be defended. And we shall do everything in our power to move away from discrimination based on race or colour. I would mislead you if I imply that this will happen overnight. There are schools of thought, tradition and practices which cannot be changed overnight. But we are moving in that direction. We shall continue to do so.[71]

The majority of the members of the Security Council had a different interpretation of the situation, and it was only by virtue of the veto exercised by the Western great powers that South Africa was not expelled from the United Nations because of her apartheid policy.

Determination of the general principles of law recognised by civilised nations requires examination of municipal systems of law and the application to international law, by analogy, of the principles common to them, but it must be remembered that there may be a danger in

the analogous application of rules of private law to the relations of States [because of] the existence of the doctrine of State sovereignty.[72]

There can be no doubt that

the recourse, in the domain of public international law, to private law sources ... is fraught with danger. Some of them lie in its abuse, frequent and deliberate, for the purposes of special pleading. Whenever international tribunals have recourse to "general principles of law" they apply, as a rule, a general principle of private law, i.e., a principle not belonging to the system of law prevalent in one country, but representing a rule of uniform application in all or in the main systems of private jurisprudence.[73]

In seeking such general principles of law, however, care
must be taken to avoid falling into the trap, already
warned against by Grotius, of assuming that because a
particular principle of law is basic to one's own
municipal system it is therefore a general principle
of law which is entitled to observance by all civilised
nations.[74] To some extent this warning pervades the
dissenting opinion of Judge Tanaka in the South West
Africa Cases:[75]

What international law can with advantage borrow from
these sources must be from the viewpoint of underlying
or guiding 'principles'. These principles, therefore,
must not be limited to statutory provisions and institutions of national laws: they must be extended to the
fundamental concepts of each branch of law as well as
to law in general so far as these can be considered as
'recognised by civilized nations'.

Accordingly, the general principles of law in the sense
of Article 38 [of the Court's Statute], are not limited
to certain basic principles of law such as the limitation of State sovereignty, third-party judgment,
limitation of the right of self-defence, pacta sunt
servanda, respect for acquired rights, liability for
unlawful harm to one's neighbour, the principle of good
faith, etc. The word 'general' may be understood to
possess the same meaning as in the case of the 'general
theory of law', 'théorie générale de droit', 'die
Allgemeine Rechtslehre', namely common to all branches
of law. But the principles themselves are very extensive and can be interpreted to include not only the
general theory of law, but the general theories of each
branch of municipal law, so far as recognized by
civilized nations. They may be conceived, furthermore,
as including not only legal principles but the fundamental legal concepts of which the legal norms are
composed, such as person, right, duty, property, juris-
tic act, tort, succession, etc. ... The recognition of
[a] norm by civilized nations can be ascertained. If
the condition of 'general principles' is fulfilled,
namely if we can say that the general principles include
the [particular] norm ... by adopting the wide interpretation of Article 38(1)(c), the norm will find its
place among the sources of international law.

... Originally, general principles are considered to be
certain private law principles found by the comparative

law method[76] and applicable by way of analogy to matters of an international character. These principles are of a nature common to all nations, that is of the character of *jus gentium*. ...

... The recognition of a principle by civilized nations ... does not mean recognition by all civilized nations, nor does it mean recognition by an official act such as a legislative act; therefore the recognition is of a very elastic nature. ...

The manifestation of the recognition... may include the attitude of delegations of member States in cases of participation in resolutions, declarations, etc., ... adopted by the organs of the League of Nations, the United Nations and other organizations which ... constitute an important element in the generation of customary international law. ...

When applying rules of municipal law to international law by analogy it is, however, essential to bear in mind that the system of international law differs from that of municipal law. The social conditions which each regulates differ and the function of law likewise varies. Broadly speaking, the State, in which municipal law operates, may be described as a community,[77] while the international field in which international law functions may be described as a society.[78]

This sociological distinction between national and international society is important when examining attempts to transfer the realities of the municipal sphere to the international level. In international society, the functions of law are primarily those of the laws of power and reciprocity, rather than those of a community law of co-ordination[79]. Even when lip-service is paid to principles of co-ordination, it is more often than not power interests that are being served, with the element of co-ordination serving as an ideology. Particularly is this so in the field of human rights.

Human rights may be classified into those which are

enjoyed by the individual in isolation, such as freedom
of conscience, personal freedom and private property;
those which are enjoyed by the individual in conjunction
with other individuals, such as freedom of speech,
discussion, writing and publication; and those which
the individual enjoys as a citizen, such as equality
before the law, of franchise and in access to public
office.[80] The idea of human rights, therefore,

presents a combination of liberal and individualistic
guarantees of the sphere of personal freedom and the
democratic and political rights of the individual
citizen.[81]

The assertion and successful achievement of such rights
depend on a measure of cohesion and agreement which
tends to be lacking on the international level. To a
great extent the rights which are recognised in
municipal life have been secured

by overwhelming pressure or on the point of the threat
of rebellion or revolution[82]

and frequently as a result of libertarian trends
consequent upon religious upheavals in the seventeenth
and eighteenth centuries. Modern international society
may be considered as, at present, just passing through
this stage of upheaval:

We have antagonisms now as deep as those of the
Reformation and its reactions which led to the Thirty
Years' War. But now they are spread over the whole
world instead of only over a small part of Europe. We
have, to some extent, the geographical division of the
Mongol invasion in the thirteenth century, only more
ruthless and more thorough.[83]

In such a division it is easy to make use of lofty
conceptions of human rights as a standard of criticism
of the conduct of others, but it is rare for the same
standards to be used for self-examination. This was

noticeable in the debates that led to the promulgation of the Universal Declaration of Human Rights. It has been equally obvious in the cold war relations between East and West,[84] in the discussions in the Council of Europe prior to the adoption of the European Convention on Human Rights,[85] and the conflicts between the older western and new members of the United Nations concerning such matters as friendly relations, self-determination and the like, culminating in the confrontations of the 1974 session of the General Assembly.[86]

When statesmen look at the position of individuals not their own nationals abroad, their attitude is conditioned by the realities of the political situation. In the abstract, they tend to regard the treatment meted out by their own countries as the standard by which all should live and to describe States which do not satisfy that standard as if they fell short of civilised behaviour. They are unwilling, however, to take any concrete steps which would result in their being able to treat such States as having broken international law and liable to make reparation. It has been aptly said that

in the relations between Western nations, which have largely forgotten their spiritual heritage, and Eastern nations, which have either jettisoned it or never shared it, the efforts to agree on any joint definition and protection of human rights have degenerated, of necessity, into aimless and venomous battles of words between the champions of East and West. Discrimination against negroes in the United States[87] and forced labour camps in the Soviet Union existed before, during and after the Second World War.[88] Like the concentration camps of the Third Reich, such black spots are conveniently forgotten and remembered, as the expediencies of world politics dictate.[89]

The ideological function of concepts of human rights at the present day suggests the need for caution when examining the extent to which such alleged rights amount to general principles of law recognised by civilised

nations. This is particularly so as this concept
itself, in an international society ruled by power
politics, often amounts to no more than a means of
asserting that one's own conduct is civilised and in
accordance with international law, while that of one's
political enemy is not. Further, as has been indicated,
the conditions of social life in municipal society
differ from those in international society, and in
the former it is far easier for principles of a true
community law based on co-ordination to develop.

A convenient way to indicate one of the reasons why
human rights, even though they amount to principles
of law generally recognised by civilised nations, do
not normally amount to general principles recognised
by civilised nations and, as such, part of international
law is to outline the manner in which one or two of
these rights have developed. A historical analysis shows
that what have become described as inalienable rights
are the product of a particular need in a particular
social grouping at a particular time. What is necessary
for one group may not be equally necessary in another
group, even though the same surrounding circumstances
be present, for local traditions also have a part to
play.[90]

It would appear that in western society many of the
rights on which much store is now set, and which are
often described as if they were as old as man himself
and enjoyed by him as his birthright, are in fact often
products of economic thought in the 16th and 17th
centuries. Thus, it is contended that the right of
religious toleration and, consequent thereon, the right
of political liberty are inextricably interwoven with
the duty of charity and the right of property.

It was in the seventeenth century that the phrase was

coined: "In essentials unity, in non-essentials liberty, in all things charity",[91] and the Church started from the premise that it was incumbent upon those who possessed worldly goods to extend charity to those who were not so fortunate, and especially to the Church which could do charitable work at large. When the Church itself became a large landowner in this way the emphasis changed from the duty of charity to the right of property. This concept of the right of property had become so firmly founded by the middle of the eighteenth century that Samuel Adams could write in 1774 that the claim to no taxation without representation was man's "indisputable privilege - it was founded on the eternal law of equity. It is an original right of nature. No man in a state of nature can justly take another's property without his consent. The Rights of Nature are happily interwoven in the British Constitution. It is its glory that it is copied from nature. It is an essential part of it that the supreme power cannot take from any man any part of his property without his consent."[92]

Even as late as 1906 Winslow, J., in Nunemacher v. State,[93] rejected as unconstitutional a Wisconsin statute which imposed an inheritance tax, even though the Constitution of Wisconsin did not guarantee property rights:

The statute violated natural rights of property and inheritance "existing in the people prior to the making of any of our constitutions.... The right to take property by inheritance or will has existed in some form among civilised nations from the time when the memory of man runneth not to the contrary".

It has likewise been pointed out that

a society of peasants could be homogeneous in its religion, as it was already homogeneous in the simple uniformity of its economic arrangements. A many-sided business community could escape constant friction and obstruction, only if it were free to absorb elements drawn from a multitude of different sources, and if each of those elements were free to pursue its own way of life, and - in that age the same thing - to practice its own religion.... English economic organisation had long been elastic enough to swallow Flemish weavers flying from Alva, and Huguenots driven from France. But the traditional ecclesiastical system was not

equally accommodating. It found not only the alien
refugee, but its homebred sectaries, indigestible.
Laud, reversing the policy of Elizabethan Privy Councils,
which characteristically thought diversity of trades
more important than unity of religion, had harassed
the settlement of foreign artisans,... and the problem
recurred in every attempt to enforce conformity down
to 1689.... When the collision between economic
interests and the policy of compulsory conformity was
so flagrant, it is not surprising that the economists
of that age should have enunciated the healing principle that persecution was incompatible with prosperity,
since it was on the pioneers of economic progress that
persecution principally fell. "Every law of this
nature"... is not only "expressly against the very
principles and rules of the Gospel of Christ", but is
also "destructive to the trade and well-being of our
nation by oppressing and driving away the most industrious working hands, and depopulating, and thereby
impoverishing our country!"[94]

It was frequently contended that one of the reasons

for the commercial success of the Netherlands was its

religious toleration and that the wealthiest towns of

England were those in which there was most nonconform-

ity, while India and the Ottoman Empire were cited to

prove that

economic progress is compatible with any religion, [for]
the class which is its vehicle will always consist of
the heterodox minority, who "profess opinions different
from what are publicly established."[95]

In the light of what has been said it is not surpris-

ing that what is enjoyed and protected on the municipal

level is normally speaking neither fully enjoyed nor

protected in the international sphere. There is not

sufficient in common among the nations of the world, nor

in their historical development, to allow human rights,

even though they may be generally recognised in the

various systems of law, to be considered as general

principles of law recognised by civilised nations and,

as such, rules of international law. It must not be

forgotten, however, that individual judges of the

International Court have argued otherwise and maintained
that human rights and fundamental freedoms are in fact
part of modern international law, since they are general
principles of law recognised by civilized nations. It
is perhaps enough to cite but two or three of these.
In the dissenting judgment already referred to, Judge
Tanaka said[96]

In the case of the international protection of human
rights... what is involved is not the application by
analogy of a principle or a norm of private law to a
matter of international character, but the recognition
of the juridical validity of a similar legal fact
without any distinction as between the municipal and
the international legal sphere.

In short, human rights which require protection are
the same; they are not the product of a particular
juridical system in the hierarchy of the legal order,
but the same human rights must be recognised, respected
and protected everywhere man goes. The uniformity of
national laws on the protection of human rights is not
derived... from considerations of expediency by the
legislative organs or from the custom of a community,
but it already exists in spite of its more-or-less
vague form. This is of nature jus naturale in roman
law.

The unified national laws of the character of jus gentium
and of the law of human rights, which is of the character of jus naturale in roman law, both constituting
a part of the law of the world community which may be
designated as world Law,[97] Common Law of Mankind,[98]
Transnational Law,[99] etc., at the same time constitute
a part of international law through the medium of
Article 38(1)(c). But there is a difference between
these two cases. In the former, the general principles
are presented as common elements among diverse national
laws; in the latter, only one and the same law exists
and this is valid through all kinds of human societies
in relationships of hierarchy and co-ordination....
The international protection of human rights... must
not be regarded as a case of analogy. In reality, there
is only one human right which is valid in the international sphere as well as in the domestic sphere.

The question here is not of an 'international', that is
to say, inter-State nature, but it is concerned with the
question of the international validity of human rights,
that is to say, the question whether a State is obliged

to protect human rights in the international sphere
as it is obliged in the domestic sphere.

The principle of the protection of human rights is
derived from the concept of man as a person and his
relationship with society which cannot be separated from
universal human nature. The existence of human rights
does not depend on the will of a State; neither inter-
nally on its law or any other legislative measure, nor
internationally on treaty or custom, in which the express
or tacit will of a State constitutes the essential
element.

A State or States are not capable of creating human
rights by law or by convention; they can only confirm
their existence and give them protection. The role of
the State is no more than declaratory....
Human rights have always existed with the human being.
They existed independently of, and before, the State.
... There must be no legal vacuum in the protection
of human rights. Who can believe, as a reasonable man,
that the existence of human rights depends upon the
internal or international legislative measures, etc.,
of the State and that accordingly they can be validly
abolished or modified by the will of the State?

If a law exists independently of the will of the States
and, accordingly, cannot be abolished or modified even
by its constitution, because it is deeply rooted in the
conscience of mankind and of any reasonable man, it may
be called 'natural law' in contrast to 'positive law'.

Provisions of the constitutions of some countries
characterize fundamental human rights and freedoms as
'inalienable','sacred', 'eternal', 'inviolate', etc.
Therefore, the guarantee of fundamental human rights and
freedoms possesses a super-constitutional significance.

If we can introduce in the international field a category
of law, namely jus cogens,... a kind of imperative law
which constitutes the contrast to the jus dispositivum,
capable of being changed by way of agreement between
States, surely the law concerning the protection of
human rights may be considered to belong to the jus
cogens.

As an interpretation of Article 38(1)(c), we consider
that the concept of human rights and of their protection is included in the general principles mentioned
in that Article.

... From this kind of source international law could
have the foundation of its validity extended beyond
the will of States, that is to say, into the sphere of

natural law[100] and assume an aspect of its supranational and supra-positive character....

... [As to] whether the alleged norm of non-discrimination and non-separation as a kind of protection of
human rights can be considered as recognized by civilized nations and included in the general principles
of law ... the alleged norm ... being based on the
United Nations Charter, ... and on numerous resolutions
and declarations of the General Assembly and other
organs of the United Nations, and owing to its nature as
a general principle, can be regarded as a source of
international law according to the provisions of
Article 38(1)(a-c). In this case three kinds of sources
are cumulatively functioning to defend the above-
mentioned norm: (1) international convention, (2) international custom and (3) the general principles of law...

To somewhat similar effect, but in not quite so sweep-

ing terms, are the comments of Judges Morrelli,

concurring, and Riphagen, dissenting, in the Barcelona

Traction case:[101]

The ... rules of international law concerning the
protection of human rights ... are concerned not with
the protection of such rights as may already have been
conferred by the internal legal system but with the
actual predication, binding upon States, of rights
within the municipal order. While it is true that ...
it is to human 'rights' that reference is made as
being the subject of the protection sought by the rule
of international law, the term is here employed in the
sense of natural rights.... International law envisages
the protection of certain individual interests and not
of rights already resulting from any positive legal
order....

... Customary international law recognizes ... respect
for fundamental human freedoms as an interest of the
international community.... Here, ... it is not a
matter of creating a common legal order determining the
legal relationships between the public authorities and
private persons or between private persons inter se,
but of 'checking' the application of the municipal
legal order in order to sanction the unlawful use of
force, arbitrary discrimination and usurpation of
jurisdiction which violate a human being's 'right to
existence'. Here,... the different methods adopted
by the municipal law of different countries are
irrelevant to the attainment of the objectives of the
rules of customary international law.

In the course of its judgments, the International
Court as such has been hesitant to base itself on the
general principles of law recognized by civilized
nations. It has, however, in such cases as the Namibia
opinion[102] come very near to recognizing the condemnation of discrimination as such a principle, while in
the Barcelona Traction case, as we have seen,[103] the
Court included 'the basic rights of the human person'
among the obligations of international law which it
regarded as being binding erga omnes.

Despite these judicial comments, it is perhaps still
true that it is only in an organization like the
Council of Europe where there is commonality of outlook
and acceptance by all of a similar concept of the rule
of law, or even more strongly perhaps in a federation,
that there is really to be found anything approaching
that community spirit which is essential to make
people as interested in ensuring that strangers enjoy
the same rights as they do themselves and guaranteeing
them by constitutional means. Care must be taken,
however, not to mistake words for deeds for what may
appear to be a federal State may really be like the
Soviet Union, a pseudo-federal State, and

if absolute rulers choose to pervert the meaning of
words, no subject of any of these totalitarian systems
can prevent them from transforming truth into falsehood.
With modern techniques of mass control, the ruling
minority can even pervert their robots in a short spell
of time into believing that they live in a democracy
and enjoy all the benefits of basic human rights and
of fundamental freedoms.[104]

Even on the truly federal level, the history of political and legal development in the United States shows
the difficulties that exist,[105] and even today there
are disputes as to the treatment of Negroes, and the
Supreme Court decision in the Segregation Cases, 1954,[106]

left unsolved as much as it solved, as the issues of
school integration and busing show.

One must not ignore the comment by Field, J., in
Butcher's Union Co. v. Crescent City Co.,[107] that

as in our intercourse with our fellow men certain
principles of morality are assumed to exist without
which society would be impossible, so certain inherent
rights lie at the foundation of all action, and upon
a recognition of them alone can free institutions be
maintained.

In this field, however, it is equally important to
recall the words of Bentham:

Right ... is the child of law: from real laws come real
rights; but from imaginary laws, from laws of nature,
fancied and invented by poets, rhetoricians, and
dealers in moral and intellectual poisons, come
imaginary rights, a bastard brood of monsters....
Natural rights is simple nonsense: natural and
imprescriptible rights, rhetorical nonsense - nonsense
upon stilts. But this rhetorical nonsense ends in
the old strain of mischievous nonsense: for immediately
a list of the pretended natural rights is given, and
those are so expressed as to present to view legal
rights.[107]

[*] Based on a lecture delivered in the 1955 Current
     Legal Problems series at University College London.

[1] (1625) Lib. II, Cap. 20, s. 40, 1,4 (Eng. tr. (1738)
     436-7, 438; Carnegie tr. (1925) 504, 506).

[2] Ibid., ss.41, 42 (439, 507, resp.).

[3] Schwarzenberger, International Law, vol. 1 (1957)
     201.

[4] I.C.J.Y.B. [1972-3] 66, 68, 71, 75, 77, 81, 62, 63.

[5] (1928) 2 U.N. Rep. Int. Arb. Awards 829, 939.

[6] See Roth, The Minimum Standards of International
     Law Applied to Aliens (1949); Garcia-Amador and
     others, Recent Codification of the Law of State
     Responsibility for Injury to Aliens (1974) .

[7] See IV above, n. 20 et seqq.

[8] S.3, paras. 386-93 (Scott, The Spanish Origin of International law, Part I, Francisco de Vitoria and his Law of Nations (1934), App.A, XXXVI-XXXIX).

[9] S.3, para. 394 (XI).

[10] S.3, para. 396 (XLI).

[11] 4 Dumont, Corps Universel Diplomatique du Droit des Gens (1726), Part 3, 88-93.

[12] Schwarzenberger, Power Politics (1951), 614.

[13] 1 Parry, Consolidated Treaty Series, 1 and 119.

[14] Gross, 'The Peace of Westphalia, 1648-1948', (1948) 42 Am.J.Int'l Law 20, 22 (citing Ward, 'The Peace of Westphalia' (1934) 4 Cambridge Modern History 412).

[15] de Visscher, Théories et Réalités en Droit International Public (1970), 191.

[16] Declaration of the 8 Powers, relative to the Universal Abolition of the Slave Trade, 8 Parry, op.cit., 473.

[17] General Act Relative to the African Slave Trade (82 B.F.S.P. 55).

[18] (1817) 2 Dods. 210, 260-1; see, also, The Antelope (1825) 10 Wheat. 66.

[19] (1822) 2 Mason 409, 445-6.

[20] 4 Moore, International Arbitrations 4934; see, also, 2 McNair, International Law Opinions (1956) 79 et seqq.

[21] See, e.g., Robinson, Were the Minorities Treaties a Failure? (1943); Green, 'Protection of Minorities in the League of Nations and the United Nations', in Gotlieb, Human Rights, Federalism and Minorities (1970) 179.

[22] See German Settlers in Poland (1923 - P.C.I.J.) B/6 24, and Minority Schools in Albania (1935 - P.C.I.J.) AB/64, 19-20.

[23] Indo-Pakistan Minorities Agreement, 1950 (1953) 2 Indian Y.B. Int'l Aff. 302; also Special Statute on

Trieste, 1954 (Cmd. 9288, Annex 2), and Italo-Yugoslav Memo. of Understanding, U.N.Y.B. [1954] 398.

24 Res. of Committee of 21, 1950, Y.B. Human Rights [1951] 225; also Report of U.N. Commissioner to Gen. Ass., Y.B.U.N. [1951] 269.

25 Annex to trust agreement, Declaration of Constitutional Principles, Art. 10, Y.B. U. N. [1950] 806.

26 660 U.N.T.S. 195.

27 G.A. Res. 2200 (XXI) Annex (adopted 1966 - not yet in force).

28 The Belgian Linguistics Case (1968 - 45 Int. Law Rep. 114) and the Quebec law (Bill 22, 1974) on language in the schools illustrate the difficulties of both Belgium and Canada in this connection.

29 R. v. Governor, Brixton Prison, Ex p. Kolczynski [1955] 1 Q.B. 540.

30 Schtraks v. Govt. of Israel [1964] A.C. 556; see, also, Cheng v. Governor, Pentonville Prison [1973] 2 All E.R. 204; see, also VII below.

31 (1948) 41 U.N.T.S. 21, 135,42 ibid. 3.

32 Bulgaria, Art. 3; Hungary, Art. 2; Romania, Art. 3.

33 Interpretation of Peace Treaties [1950] I.C.J. 65,221.

34 Op.cit., para. 401 (XLIII).

35 Butler and Maccoby, The Development of International Law (1928), 69; de Visscher, op.cit., 153.

36 32 B.F.S.P. 915-6; see, also, Schwarzenberger, Frontiers of International Law (1962) ch. 6, n. 14.

37 Forsyth to Gliddon, 14 Aug. 1840 (c. Adler & Margalith, With Firmness in the Right: American Diplomatic Action affecting Jews 1840-1945 (1946)4).

38 18 Apr. 1872, ibid. 106.

39 Schwarzenberger, op.cit., n. 36, 144; see, also, Butler & Maccoby, op.cit., 69-73.

40 Seward to Campbell, 6 Apr. 1867, c. 1 Wharton, International Law Digest (1887) 238.

41 Blaine to Smith, 18 Feb. 1891, op.cit., n.37, 220-1.

42 Historicus on International Law (1863) 6, 14.

43 [1949] I.C.J. 4, 35.

44 Lauterpacht, International Law and Human Rights (1950) 89.

45 Ibid., 93.

46 (1926) 4 U.N. Rep. Int. Arb. Awards 26, 29-30.

46a See, e.g., Halasz, Socialist Concept of Human Rights (1966) 267.

47 Welles to King, 28 Apr. 1938, 2 Hackworth, Digest of International Law 152.

48 (1938) 19 The Listener 183. See, also, Schwarzenberger, op.cit., 36, ch.4; also VI above, n.19.

49 Y.B. Human Rights [1950] 420.

49a See, e.g., Coleman, 'Greece and the Council of Europe', (1972) 2 Israel Y.B. H. R.

50 For political purposes, an ideology may be defined as 'a political creed embodying ideal good or bad, the realization of which its devotees are taught to believe is essential for the salvation of mankind', Wellesley, Diplomacy in Fetters (1944) 43.

51 Mannheim, Man and Society in an Age of Reconstruction (1940) 9.

52 1 International Law: Collected Papers (1970), 297-8.

53 See, however, e.g., Convention relating to the Status of Stateless Persons (1954), 360 U.N.T.S. 117; Weis, Nationality and Statelessness in International Law (1956); 1 Grahl-Madsen, Refugees in International Law (1966) 76-8, 85-101, 315-7, 2 ibid. (1972) 299-300.

54 See, however, European Convention on Human Rights, loc.cit., n.49 above.

55 See op.cit., n. 44 above, and IV above, n.54 et seqq.

56 Arts. 1, 13, 55, 62, 68, 76.

57 Cmd. 6388 (1942).

58 6 U.N.C.I.O. Documents 296.

59 See Cheng, The General Principles of Law as Applied by International Courts and Tribunals (1953).

60 (1948) G. A. Res. 217A (III).

61 G.A. Res. 285(III). See Green,'Human Rights and the Colour Problem',(1950) 3 Curr. Legal Prob. 236,245-9; McLaurin, The United Nations and Power Politics (1951) 34-40.

62 See, e.g., U.N., Human Rights - A compilation of International Instruments of the U.N. (1973-ST/HR/1), issued to mark the 25th anniversary of the Declaration.

63 See VI above, n.75 et seqq. See, also, South West Africa Cases 1966 I.C.J.6, Diss.Op. of Judge Tanaka, 294-300; Barcelona Traction Case 1970 I.C.J.3, Sep. Op. of Judge Morelli, 232, and Diss. Op. of Judge Riphagen, 337-8.

64 1970 I.C.J.3, 32

65 6 Dec. 1954, 31 Dept. of State Bull. 963.

66 See, e.g., V above.

67 Lauterpacht, op.cit., n.44 above, 115; see, also, Judge Tanaka, loc.cit., 298, and Judge Morelli, 232.

68 See, however, Cheng, op.cit., App.2.

68a Gutteridge,'Meaning and Scope of Article 38' (1952) 38 Grotius Transactions 125, 127.

69 See, e.g.,Res.2074(XX), 3068(XXVIII); see VI above, nn. 56-7.

70 Der Transvaler, 18 Jan. 1955 (The Times (London) 19 Jan. 1955).

71 The Times, 28 Oct. 1974.

72 McNair, 'So-called State Servitudes', Selected Papers (1974), 17, 28.

73 Lauterpacht, Private Law Sources and Analogies of International Law (1927), 84, 69.

74 See Dicey, The Law of the Constitution (1952),192-3, 194, 201-2.

75 1966 I.C.J. 6, 295-6, 299-300.

[76] See, e.g., Green, 'Comparative Law as a "Source" of International Law' (1967), 42 Tulane Law Rev. 52.

[77] For a judicial definition of 'community', see Adv. Op. on Greco-Bulgarian Communities (1930 - P.C.I.J.) B/17, 21.

[78] See Schwarzenberger, op.cit., n.36, ch.1, at 10-11; Lauterpacht, The Function of Law in the International Community (1933), ch. 20.

[79] See Schwarzenberger, ibid., ch. 2.

[80] See the Covenants on Economic, Social and Cultural Rights and on Civil and Political Rights, Res. 2200A (XXI), and op.cit., n. 62 above.

[81] Op.cit., n. 12 (1st ed. 1941), 382.

[82] Ibid. (2nd ed. 1951), 644.

[83] Churchill, House of Commons, 1 Mar. 1955, 537 Hansard, col. 1897.

[84] See Schwarzenberger, op.cit., n.36, ch.7; Lissitzyn, 'International Law in a Divided World' (1963) 542 Int'l Conciliation; Higgins, Conflict of Interests (1965).

[85] See Green, 'The European Convention on Human Rights', (1951) 5 World Aff. 432.

[86] See V above, and the debates in the 29th (1974) session of the G.A., esp. speech by U.S. delegate Scali, New York Times 7 Dec. 1974.

[87] See, e.g., Green, loc.cit., n.61 above; 'Human Rights and Colour Discrimination' (1950) 3 Int'l Law Q. 422; 'The Legality of Jim Crow Regulations', ibid., 590; Greenberg, Race Relations and the Law (1959); Miller, Petitioners: The Negro and the Supreme Court (1966).

[88] See Dallin and Nicolaevsky, Forced Labour in Soviet Russia (1947); Report of U.N. Ad Hoc Committee on Forced Labour, Doc. E/wrel (1953); Solzhenitsyn, The Gulag Archipelago 1918-1956 (1973).

[89] Schwarzenberger, op.cit., n.12 (2nd ed.), 712.

[90] See Clark, 'Early Modern Period', in 2 Barker, The European Inheritance (1954) 119-20.

91 Ibid., 120; see, also, Tawney, Religion and the Rise of Capitalism (Pelican ed. 1938) 140-1.

92 1 Works, 46, 53 (c. Stone, Human Law and Human Justice (1965) 97).

93 108 N.W. 351 (c. ibid., 97-8).

94 Tawney, op.cit., 186-7 - citing A Letter from a Gentleman in the City to a Gentleman in the Country about the Odiousness of Persecution (1677), 29.

95 Ibid., 187 - citing Petty, Political Arithmetic (1690), 23; see, also, Laski, 'Economics in the Light of the Past', 1 Encyclopaedia of Modern Knowledge (n.d.), 361, 363-4.

96 Loc.cit., n.75, 296, 297-8, 299-300.

97 Clark and Sohn, World Peace Through World Law (1966).

98 Jenks (1958).

99 Jessup (1956).

100 For a socialist interpretation of this natural law idea, see Halasz, op.cit., n. 44a, 119.

101 [1970] I.C.J. 3, 232, 337-8, resp.

102 [1971] I.C.J. 16, see VI above, nn.81-83.

103 See n. 64 above.

104 Schwarzenberger, op.cit., n.12 (2nd ed.), 646.

105 See, e.g., Emerson & Haber, Political and Civil Rights in the United States (1967); Dorsin, Discrimination and Civil Rights (1969).

106 Brown v. Board of Education (1954) 347 U.S. 483,497. See Green, 'The Right to Learn', (1954) 3 Indian Y.B. Int'l Aff. 268.

107 (1883) 111 U.S. 746, 756-7.

108 Anarchical Fallacies (1824), 2 Collected Works (Bowering ed. 1843), 523, 501.

VIII

THE RIGHT OF ASYLUM IN INTERNATIONAL LAW*

To see no difference between political
and other offences is the sure mark of
an excited or stupid head (Cockburn, I
An Examination of the Trials for
Sedition in Scotland (1888) 63).

As one of his Epigrams of Treason John Harrington
wrote in 1618

Treason doth never prosper; what's the reason?
Why, if it prosper, none dare call it treason

while in his Persian Letters[1] Montesquieu, one hundred
years later, told of a king who,

having defeated and imprisoned a prince who disputed
the crown with him, began to reproach him for infidelity
and treachery. "It was decided only a moment ago",
said the unfortunate prince, "which of us was the
traitor."

A somewhat more liberal view of treason was taken by
Secretary of State Jefferson in 1792[2]:

Most codes extend their definition of treason to acts
not really against one's country. They do not distinguish between acts against the government and acts
against the oppressions of the government. The latter
are virtues, yet have furnished more victims to the
executioner than the former.... The unsuccessful strug-
glers against tyranny have been the chief martyrs of
treason laws in all countries.... Treasons, often,
taking the simulated with the real, are sufficiently
punished by exile.

In the 180 years since then, governments have tended

to become less rather than more liberal. They have
sought therefore to punish those guilty of 'simulated'
or 'real' treason and, far from sending them into
exile, have endeavoured to prevent them from going into
voluntary exile, and to recover them from the country
concerned when they have succeeded in so doing. The
increase in the number of dictatorial States governed
by a monolithic party denying all political rights to
its opponents, has led to a desire to temper tyranny
with mercy, at least where the enemies of one's
political opponents are concerned.

This 'humanitarian' sentiment find perhaps its
loftiest expression in Article 14, paragraph 1, of the
Universal Declaration of Human Rights:[3] "Everyone has
the right to seek and to enjoy in other countries asylum
from persecution", but nowhere in this Declaration does
there appear any obligation upon any State to grant
asylum to the refuge seeker, and it is therefore our
purpose to examine how far international law recognizes
or imposes any duty upon the States which are its
subjects to grant such asylum.

International law may be defined as that system of
laws and regulations which those who operate on the
international scene recognize as being necessary for
their orderly conduct, and which they regard as being
binding upon themselves in order to achieve that
orderly conduct.[4] It would certainly not be conducive
to orderly conduct if a State's law enforcing officers
could, at their pleasure, invade the territorial
limits of another State to bring back for trial or
punishment one who was seeking 'asylum from persecution',
but 'persecution' must not be confused with 'prosecution'.
The second paragraph of Article 14 clearly states
that "this right [of asylum] may not be invoked in the
case of prosecutions genuinely arising from non-political

crimes or from acts contrary to the Purposes and
Principles of the United Nations". This proviso is
intended to enable a State to recover by proper process,
or another to deny hospitality as an 'undesirable' to
a fugitive who is nothing but a common criminal. Such
individuals are dealt with in accordance with the
ordinary law of extradition, which itself, generally
speaking, recognises the immunity of the political
offender.[5]

Although the Universal Declaration of Human Rights
recognizes asylum 'in other countries', there are in
fact two forms of asylum, the one within the country
seeking the fugitive and the other outside its territorial limits.

The former is described as diplomatic asylum and the
latter as territorial, and it is only when territorial
asylum is involved that questions of extradition arise.
The difference between the two forms of asylum has been
well brought out by the International Court of Justice
in its first judgment in the Asylum Case between
Colombia and Peru:[6]

In the case of extradition, the refugee is within the
territory of the State of refuge. A decision with regard
to extradition implies only the normal exercise of the
territorial sovereignty. The refugee is outside the
territory of the State where the offence was committed,
and a decision to grant him asylum in no way derogates
from the sovereignty of the State. In the case of
diplomatic asylum, [that is to say asylum within the
buildings of an embassy,] the refugee is within the
territory of the State where the offence was committed.
A decision to grant diplomatic asylum derogates from
the sovereignty of that State. It withdraws the offender
from the jurisdiction of the territorial State and
constitutes an intervention in matters which are
essentially within the competence of that State. Such
a derogation from territorial sovereignty cannot be
recognized unless its legal basis is established in
each particular case.

As regards political fugitives, a distinction must be drawn between the offence and the offender. Reference to the leading books on international law indicates that political offences are, normally, regarded as non-extraditable. The concept of political offences which appears to have gained popular acceptance is that propounded by Denman J. in 1891.[7] The learned judge expressly rejected the view of John Stuart Mill[8] that a political offence was "<u>any</u> offence committed in the course of or furthering of civil war, insurrection, or political commotion." Instead, he propounded the view that

to exclude extradition for such an act as murder, which is one of the extradition offences, it must at least be shown that the act is done in furtherance of, done with the intention of assistance, as a sort of overt act in the course of acting in a political matter, a political rising, or a dispute between two parties in the State as to which is to have the government in its hands.... The question really is, whether, upon the facts, it is clear that the man was acting as one of a number of persons engaged in acts of violence of a political character with a political object, and as part of the political movement and rising in which he was taking part.

Just under twenty years later in the <u>Rudewitz</u> case Secretary of State Root used similar language in refusing an extradition request by the Russian Ambassador.[9] The fugitive was a member of the Social Democratic Labour Party who had taken part in a meeting which had decided upon certain acts of murder and arson as 'revolutionary acts and measures'. Root wrote:

The aim, purpose, and work of this Social Democratic Labour Party was revolutionary and the death of [these] persons was ordered by one of the organizations of that party.

The Department ... finds ... that the offence of killing and burning with which the accused is charged are clearly political in their nature, and that the robbery committed on the same occasion was a natural incident to executing the resolutions of the revolutionary groups and cannot be treated as a separate offense.... Therefore none of these offenses is such as will afford a proper and sufficient ground for the extradition of the accused to Russia....

The Government of the United States finds itself impelled to these conclusions by the generally accepted rules of international law which forbid the surrender of political fugitives, by the principles of international jurisprudence, which proclaimed and acted upon by the courts of this and other countries, declare that "a person acting as one of a number of persons engaged in acts of violence of a political character, with a political object, and as part of the political movement and rising in which he is taking part" is a political offender and is entitled to an asylum in this country; and by the long and consistent course of rulings in which the executive branch of Government has expressly adopted and carried out such laws and principles, but also by the express provisions of Article 3 of the Extradition Treaty between this Government and Russia [1893], which, in precise terms, prohibits the surrender of political offenders.

But not all those whose crimes might be described as political were covered by the _Castioni_ definition, which clearly reflects the era of general liberal democracy, based on rival organised political parties, in which it was enunciated. So much was this so that in 1894[10] Cave J. refused to concede that a terroristic act by an anarchist could ever be a political offence, for

there are not two parties in the State, each seeking to impose the Government of their own choice on the other for the party with whom the accused is identified, namely, the party of anarchy, is the enemy of all Governments.

The tendency to regard anarchists as something apart from other political offenders has sometimes been expressly embodied in national legislation[11] and is by no means uncommon in treaty practice, particularly among Latin-American countries,[12] while the 1902 Pan-American Treaty for the Extradition of Criminals and for Protection against Anarchism[13] provides

there shall not be considered as political offences
acts which may be classified as pertaining to anarchism

by the legislation of both countries involved, and a
similar provision appears in the 1934 Central American
Convention on Extradition.[14] The view of anarchists
as opposed to all forms of organized government has,
in some jurisdictions, been interpreted widely enough
to embrace communists.[15] However, in a world in which
anarchism, other than in the form of such emanations
as the Spanish anarcho-syndicalists or the Weathermen
in the United States and similar groups elsewhere, has
virtually disappeared as a political creed, and in which
there is an increasing number of one-party states where
it is impossible for there to be any organized political
movement capable of indulging in acts directed against
the government, it becomes increasingly common for the
fugitive offender to act on his own or together with a
small group of other 'non-party' individuals, or to
commit his offence while outside the national territory
and directly against the national property or interests.
For this reason, it may well be considered that the
classical view, tied as it is to the character of the
offence, has outlived its usefulness. It is now time
to revise the definition and to apply the test not to
the act committed, but to the individual committing it.
While such an approach might not solve much, it would
result in shifting the burden of proof from the fugitive,
who now has to prove that his offence was political,
to the demanding State which would have to prove that
he was not a political offender but a common criminal.

Such a functional approach was in fact adopted by
Lord Goddard C.J.[16] In 1955 he was faced with a group
of Polish sailors who had mutinied and sought asylum
in the United Kingdom. There was no suggestion that
these seamen were part of an organised political

movement seeking to overthrow the established Polish
government. Instead, they feared that they would be
subjected to political persecution when the ship
reached Poland and they sought to evade this fate.
The evidence showed that

a political officer was ... recording their conversations
and keeping observation upon them for the purpose of
preparing a case against them on account of their
political opinions, presumably in order that they might
be punished for holding or at least expressing them.
A resultant prosecution would thus have been a political
prosecution. A revolt of the crew was to prevent themselves being prosecuted for a political offence and...
therefore the offence had a political character.

Lord Goddard explained his deviation from the classical
view by pointing out that in Castioni's case the Court
had emphasised

that they were not giving an exhaustive definition of
the words 'of a political character'.

In view of this Lord Goddard found no difficulty in
holding that:

the evidence about the law prevalent in the Republic
of Poland today shows that it is necessary, if only
for reasons of humanity, to give a wider and more
generous meaning to the words we are now construing,
which we can do without in any way encouraging the
idea that ordinary crimes which have no political
significance will be thereby excused.

Prima facie, the learned Lord Chief Justice preserved
the fiction that it was the nature of the offence that
qualified the fugitive for political asylum - or, more
correctly, for non-extradition. In this case, however,
the offence was mutiny aimed at preventing the possibility of a charge for a political offence. Further,
the fugitives had acted as individuals protecting their
own liberty, and not as members of an organised political
movement seeking to take over the reins of government.

327

While preserving the appearance of continuity with
earlier practice, Kolczynski's case opens the door to
granting asylum to an individual qua individual, rather
than as an offender who has committed a particular type
of offence.

A clear instance of this is to be found in the decision
of the High Court of Dublin in Re Shields,[17] when it was
held that the charge against the defendant relating to
the possession of explosives in England in connection
with Irish Republican Army activities; was 'if not a
political offence, certainly connected with a political
offence.'

In a written answer to a parliamentary question the Home
Secretary implied that British practice with regards to
the grant of asylum accorded with this view, explaining[18]
that applications for political asylum are

dealt with on their merits.... If it is reasonable to
assume that the result of refusing admission... would be
his return to a country in which, on grounds of political
opinion, race or religion, he would face danger to life
or liberty, or persecution of such a kind and extent as to
render life insupportable, he would normally be admitted
unless there were positive grounds for considering him
undesirable.

This statement is only expressive of executive policy.
It may not be taken to indicate the line likely to be
followed by a court when confronted with a request for
extradition in accordance with a treaty, and, in fact,
later British cases show a return to the more traditional
point of view. Thus, in Re Schtraks[19] Viscount Radcliffe
recognized that

if... the idea of 'political offence' is not altogether
remote from that of 'political asylum', it is easy to
regard as a political offence, an offence committed by
someone in furtherance of his design to escape from a
political regime which he found intolerable. I have no
criticism to make of the decision in ... Kolczynski,
but the grounds on which it was decided are expressed
too generally to offer much guidance for other cases in
the future.... The idea that lies behind the phrase

'offence of a political character' is that the fugitive
is at odds with the State that applies for his extradition on some issue connected with the political control
or government of the country.

Lord Hodson also reverted to the guiding principle of
Castioni,[20] for

there must be either in existence or in comtemplation
a struggle between the State and the fugitive criminal.
... It may be that cases will arise as in [Kolczynski],
where special circumstances have to be taken into
account. In some modern States politics and justice
may be inextricably mixed, and it is not always easy,
for example, to say what amounts to a revolt against
the Government. No special feature exists in this case,
and I find no substance in the contention that extradition should be refused because of the political character of the offence charged.

As recently as 1973, the House of Lords again applied [21]
the more restricted conception of 'political' in connection
with an offence committed in the United States but not

directed against the United States.... The object ...
was wholly directed to the overthrow of Chiang Kai-Shek's
regime and to establish a free and democratic Republic
of Taiwan: The objective was not hostile to the United
States although the movement sought to persuade the
American government to change its policy towards Taiwan.
... [Applying Schtraks] political character ...
connotes the notion of opposition to the requesting
State.

Despite the intimate relationship between the United
States and the Nationalist authorities in Taiwan, the
British Home Secretary refused to extend asylum to the
fugitive,[22] perhaps suggesting that political friend-
ships and animosities play some part in deciding who will
and who will not receive asylum.

Courts in both the United States and Canada have also
continued to follow the more traditional Castioni
approach. Karadzole v. Artukovic[23] occurred shortly
after Kolczynski and well before Schtraks, and while

the United States Court of Appeals stated, citing
Kolczynski expressly, that Castioni had

recently been reconsidered in English courts ...
American courts have more or less adopted language
used in Castioni.

One of the Canadian cases[24] arose from a riot by
members of a Puerto Rican independence movement, while
the other arose from a charge of murder and arson
during campus rioting against the Vietnam war.[25] In
both, Castioni and Schtraks were applied and it was
held that neither constituted a political offence.

In contrast to these, the German Federal Constitutional
Court in Bonn has adopted the more humanitarian
approach.[26] In February 1959, when a Yugoslav citizen
maintained that the charges lodged against him by
Yugoslavia were false and claimed asylum as a political
refugee in accordance with Article 16 of the Federal
Constitution,[27] the Court pointed out that the legislative history of this clause indicated that political
asylum was

"a right granted to a foreigner who cannot continue
living in his own country because he is deprived of
liberty, life or property by the political system
prevailing there." The concept of political persecution must not be narrowly interpreted. It is character-
ised by deep-seated socio-political and ideological
contrasts between States which have developed basically
different internal structures. There are a number of
States in which, for the purpose of enforcing and
securing political and social revolutions, the power
of the State is exercised in a manner contradictory to
the principles of a liberal democracy. Hence the
concept of political persecution must not be limited to
so-called political offenders, ... but must be extended
to persons prosecuted for non-political offences
"where such persons, if extradited, would be liable
in their home country to suffer measures of persecution
involving danger to life and limb or restrictions of
personal liberty for political reasons."

As has already been mentioned, it is sometimes alleged
that asylum may be granted within diplomatic premises
on the ground that embassy buildings are exterritorial,
representing a small piece of the sending State within
the territory of the receiving State - when Khrushchev
welcomed Kennedy to the Soviet Embassy in Vienna he
invited him to enter Russian territory. Today, however,
this theory is outworn and it is generally accepted that
the immunity of an embassy depends on a waiver of
jurisdiction by the receiving State. While it has been
confirmed by the International Court of Justice

that asylum may be granted on humanitarian grounds in
order to protect political offenders against the violent
and disorderly action of irresponsible sections of the
people,

or even to preserve a fugitive from the operation of
justice if,

in the guise of justice, arbitrary action is substituted
for the rule of law,[28]

it is by no means established that an ambassador may,
let alone must, offer the hospitality of his hotel to
one who may be described as a political offender. In
fact, the latest edition of Satow[29] specifically states
that "it is now an established doctrine in Europe that
no right to give asylum to political refugees in the
house of a diplomatic agent exists". This was also the
view of the United States in the latter part of last
century. An American missionary had given asylum in
his residence to a Persian Jew who had become a Christian
and refused to wear a patch on his garments. The American
Secretary of State was explicit in his comments:

This Government does not claim that its agents have the
right to afford asylum.... The domiciliary rights of
citizens of the United States in Persia may not be
expanded to embrace the protection by them of Persian

subjects, when such protection is expressly disclaimed
by the Government of the United States, and when its
assertion by their diplomatic and consular representatives is positively inhibited

by the 1856 Treaty between the two countries.[30]

It has not, however, always been true that the subjects
of international law have denied the existence of a right
to grant diplomatic asylum. Perhaps as a reflection of
his own experience of asylum as a political refugee in
France, Grotius stated that

a fixed Abode ought not to be refused to Strangers, who
being expelled from their own country, seek a Retreat
elsewhere.

In his view , asylum should be available

only for the Benefit of them who suffer undeservedly, and
not for such whose malicious Practices have been injurious to any particular Men or to human Society in
general[31].

This view was commented upon, but by no means accepted
by Pufendorf, who introduced limitations and reservations
that one might expect to find coming from a twentieth
century statesman defending an illiberal policy in the
field of political asylum:

Humanity, it is true, engages us to receive a small
number of Men, expelled their Home, not for their own
Demerit and Crime, especially if they are eminent for
Wealth or Industry, and not likely to disturb our Religion, or our Constitution.... But no one will be fond
of asserting, that we ought in the same manner to receive
and incorporate a great Multitude, ... since it is scarce
possible, but that their Admission should highly endanger
the Natives. Therefore every State may be more free or
more cautious in granting these Indulgences, as it shall
judge proper for its Interest and Safety. In order to
which Judgment, it will be prudent to consider, whether
a great increase in the Number of Inhabitants will turn
to Advantage; whether the Country be fertile enough to
feed so many Mouths; whether upon Admission of this new
body, we shall be strained for room; whether the Men are

industrious, or idle; whether they may be conveniently placed and disposed, as to render them incapable of giving any Jealousy to the Government. If on the whole, it appears that the Persons deserve our Favour and Pity, and that no Restraint lies on us from good Reasons of State, it will be an Act of Humanity to confer such a Benefit on them, as we shall neither feel very Burthen-some at present, nor are likely to repent of hereafter. If the Case be otherwise, we ought to so temper our Pity with Prudence, as not to put ourselves in the ready way of becoming Objects of Pity we may justly reckon as a Matter of free Bounty in us, hence it follows, they are not presently to lay hands on what they please, nor to fix themselves as it were by some Right, in any Spot of Waste-ground they find among us, but that they ought to rest satisfied with the Station and Privileges we assign them.[32]

It would thus seem that while Grotius, the refugee diplomat, considered that persecutees had a right to receive asylum, Pufendorf, secure in the ivory castle of his academic chair, recognized the desirability of this, but was highly conscious of the significance of raison d'état and almost foretold the attitude of such countries as Great Britain and Canada when faced with expellees and refugees from Africa, Chile or Haiti.

One of the classicists who seemed anxious to combine the humanism of Grotius with the practical approach of Pufendorf was Wolff. He preached compassion towards the exile,

driven out of the city or land where he has a domicile [and who] by nature [has] the right ... to dwell any-where in the world, [but] since it depends altogether on the will of the people, or on the will of the one who has the right of the people, whether or not he desires to receive an outsider into his state, ... if admittance is refused, that must be endured.... Since nations are free, the decision concerning these matters must be left to the nations themselves, and that decision must be respected. The right belongs to an exile to dwell anywhere in the world, but no absolute right to settle in any lands belongs to him ... Consequently no nation can be compelled to receive exiles. [33]

Here Wolff is revealed as the direct ancestor of the

asylum clause in the Universal Declaration, but unlike
that document he specifically states that asylum is a
right only in the widest and most popular sense of the
term, pointing out that there is no duty upon any State
to afford the asylum to which the refugee imagines he
has a right. It is also interesting to note that Wolff
rejects the thesis that an ambassador's immunity rests
on exterritoriality and, with it, any idea of a "right
of asylum in the house where the ambassador resides."[34]

Of the remaining putative 'fathers' of international
law, it is only necessary to refer to Vattel, a diplomat
philosopher. In accordance with natural law, exile does

not take away from a man his human personality, nor
consequently his right to live somewhere or other. ...
But if in the abstract this right is a necessary and
perfect one, it must be observed that it is only an
imperfect one relative to each individual country; for
... every Nation has the right to refuse to admit an
alien into its territory when to do so would expose it to
evident danger or cause it serious trouble .... Hence
an exile has no absolute right to choose a country at
will and settle himself there as he pleases; he must ask
permission of the sovereign of that country, and if it
be refused, he is bound to submit. Nevertheless,...
no Nation may, without good reason, refuse even a perpetual residence to a man who has been driven from his
country. But if for definite and just reasons a State
is prevented from offering him an asylum, the man has
no further right to demand it.

Having thus reduced the right to asylum to a completely
discretionary power on the part of a State to admit or
bar one who has asked for protection, Vattel remembers
that he has earlier stated that the exile "holds this
right from nature", and therefore, in exercising its
discretion, the State should "[never lose] sight of the
charity and sympathy which are due to the unfortunate".[35]

It has been suggested[36] that these views of the 'found-
ing fathers' recognize the sanctity of the individual and
are in direct linear ascendancy of current attempts to

secure international respect for the natural rights of
man. It is submitted, however, that the conscious
juxtaposition of right and discretion tends, if anything,
to prove the veracity of Benthan's comment:

Right ... is the child of law: from real laws come real
rights; but from imaginary laws, from laws of nature,
fancied and invented by poets, rhetoricians, and dealers
in moral and intellectual poisons, come imaginary rights,
a bastard brood of monsters ... Natural rights is simple
nonsense: natural and imprescriptible rights, rhetorical
nonsense - nonsense upon stilts.[37]

With these words in mind, it is time to examine State
practice in this matter.

Asylum in its earliest forms is related to the right of
sanctuary enjoyed in holy places at home or abroad. As
the idea of religious sanctuary fell into desuetude it
was replaced by that of territorial asylum, for

hospitality and protection had come to be regarded as
the fugitive's right, and in the end each separate
country became a place of refuge for offenders against
the laws of other nations.[38]

This view accords with that of the Emperor Charles V,
Charles I of Spain, who recognized diplomatic asylum in
embassies. He considered that the houses of ambassadors
must serve as "inviolable asylums, as did once the
temples of the gods".[39] Nevertheless, this right to
asylum, together with the State's right to grant it, was,
like so many 'rights' under international law to the
present day, only valid so long as the State of refuge
was strong enough to resist the demands made upon it
by the State of flight, and it is perhaps not surprising
that in the days of absolute monarchs attempts were made
to deny asylum to their political opponents. Thus, in
1506 when Philip of Castile became, by stress of weather,
an involuntary guest of Henry VII, the latter demanded

as the price of his hospitality the surrender of Edward
de la Pole, Earl of Suffolk, who was enjoying asylum in
Castile. At first Philip refused, but later agreed
having secured a promise from Henry that Suffolk's life
would be spared. The duress upon Philip is clear when
it is borne in mind that he was not allowed to leave
England until Suffolk was safely in the Tower. Henry's
son did not regard his father's promise as binding, and
Suffolk was executed in 1513.[40] Similarly, Charles II
made treaties with Denmark in 1661 and with the States-
General in 1662, whereby these States undertook to
surrender the regicides seeking asylum within their
territories.[41]

From the reaction of the King of Castile and the awareness of Charles II that a treaty was necessary it may
be argued, a contrario, that in the sixteenth and
seventeenth centuries the right of asylum was recognized
in international law. In fact there is evidence to show
that it was still recognized in the eighteenth century
in so far as both State ships and diplomatic premises
were concerned. As regards the former, it was not until
1939 that the doctrine of exterritoriality - expressed
in the terms 'a floating portion of the flag-State'[42] -
was finally rejected.[43]

Perhaps the most famous instances of ships providing
asylum relate to escaping slaves. In these cases,
although slavery could not exist on a British ship,[44]
asylum could not be extended to a slave so as to grant
freedom so long as the ship remained in the territorial
sea of the State from which he was escaping, in fact if
the ship "returns within the limits of the country from
which he has escaped, he will be liable to be surrendered".[45] Where criminals were concerned the British view
was that, while they could not be forcibly removed from
a public ship, they ought to be surrendered,[46] for there

was

no such right of protection belonging to the British
flag, and ... such a pretension is unfounded in point
of principle, is injurious to the rights of other
countries, and is inconsistent with those of our own.[47]

It is not only the United Kingdom that denies any
right of asylum on board public ships. The United States,
too, declines to regard its State vessels as places of
hospitality for refugees, political or otherwise, for

the right of asylum ... has no foundation in international
law ... [Ships'] officers should refuse all applications
for asylum except when required by the interests of
humanity in extreme or exceptional cases, such as the
pursuit of a refugee by a mob.[48]

This ruling is the culmination of a long practice. Thus,
in 1831 the Vice-President of Peru was afforded asylum,
with the concurrence of the Government of Peru, only for
so long as was necessary to protect him from mob violence.
The problem frequently arose with regard to Latin
American refugees during the nineteenth century and
United States diplomats were constantly reminded that
asylum, as an act of grace, might only be afforded when
the dictates of humanity made it inevitable.[49] It would
appear that French practice is identical with that of the
United Kingdom and the United States. In fact, the
leading French textbooks, while affirming the rule of
humanity, cite the practice of these two States as
evidence of the position in international law.[50]

What is true of the situation with regard to public
ships is of course even more true in the case of
merchant ships, for no fiction of exterritoriality can
be found to give them this type of sanctity.

Territorial and diplomatic asylum have also presented
problems to the legal advisers of foreign offices. As

in the case of ships, the problem has frequently
concerned asylum, that is to say, freedom, for slaves.
In the early eighteenth century the Law Officers of the
Crown did not think that a slave's arrival in Great
Britain or Ireland gave him freedom - not even if he
were baptised.[51] By one hundred years later a different
view was in vogue. In 1842 Lord Ashburton pointed out
to Secretary of State Webster that England and every
part of the United States not recognising slavery
recognised a right of asylum for slaves finding themselves within the local jurisdiction.[52] The situation
was, however, controversial if the slaves were on a ship
within British jurisdiction not by the voluntary act of
the master alone. Between 1831 and 1841 four American
slave ships were driven by stress of weather into
British ports, while a fifth was brought in by the slaves
who had mutinied and murdered a passenger. In all cases
the slaves were freed, in the case of the fifth ship
after the mutineers had been tried for piracy and acquitted. Acting on the advice of the Law Officers, the
British Government rejected American requests for the
return of any of the slaves.[53] The United States Legal
Adviser rested his argument on the contention that, while
a merchant ship might not be exclusively within the
jurisdiction of its flag State when in foreign territorial waters,

if a vessel be driven by weather into the ports of
another nation, it would hardly be alleged by anyone,
that, by the mere force of such arrival within the
waters of the state, the law of that state would so
attach to the vessel as to affect existing rights of
property between persons on board.[54]

The disputes concerning these ships were referred to
an individual umpire who sustained the American point
of view.[55] The decisions and the American stand have
been criticised by contemporary American authorities

like Dana.[56] Today, the problem is covered by the fact
that slavery and the slave-trade are contrary to both
customary and conventional international law.

In so far as refugees other than slaves are concerned
the practice of States, certainly until the end of the
eighteenth century, has been more or less in accord
with the views of the classical writers. Fugitives
would find that foreign States would decide in their
discretion whether to give them hospitality or not.
Customary international law imposed no obligations upon
any State to expel or return a wanted fugitive. By the
end of the nineteenth century it was possible to say that

France, Russia, England, and the United States of North
America, have constantly, either by diplomatic acts or
decisions of their tribunals, expressed their opinions,
that upon principles of International Law ... the
surrender of a foreign criminal cannot be demanded.[57]

On the other hand, there was nothing to stop a State
from surrendering the fugitive, for, although there is
no right to demand, the surrender of criminals is a
matter of comity,[58] and in 1864, for example, the
United States surrendered a Cuban fugitive from justice
to the Spanish Government at the latter's request.[59]

Since the grant of asylum to fugitives from abroad
may easily result in criminals evading justice, States
have sought to avoid this possibility by imposing treaty
obligations of a kind to deny asylum and to grant
surrender. This has been done through the medium of,
for the most part, bilateral treaties which have become
so common as to comprise today a veritable network
reproducing rules in common, so that it is almost possible
to refer now to the customary law of extradition treaties.
These treaties date from the eighteenth century,[60] and
have become so fundamental a part of the law that it is
generally recognised today that there is no right to

demand extradition in the absence of treaty. There is,
however, in the absence of any restrictions imposed by
municipal law, no obligation upon a State not to
surrender a fugitive in the absence of a treaty. Even
when municipal law tends to prevent such surrenders,
as does the English Extradition Act,[61] the same result
may be achieved by declaring the fugitive an undesirable
alien and deporting him. Although great inroads into
the institution of asylum have been made by extradition
treaties, such treaties generally preserve the right in
so far as political offences are concerned.

It is far easier for a fugitive to seek asylum in a
local embassy than it is for him to escape abroad, and
during the eighteenth century States were inclined to
recognize their embassies as places of asylum, while
the territorial State was just as inclined to deny this.
In 1726 the Duke of Ripperda had been given asylum in
the British Embassy in Madrid from where he was forcibly
removed by the Spanish authorities. The British Government demanded reparation which the King of Spain denied.
The controversy was interrupted by the outbreak of war
between the two States, and liquidated by the Treaty of
Seville, 1729, which provided for "an oblivion of all
that is past". Similarly, in 1747 the British Minister
in Stockholm afforded asylum to Springer accused of
high treason against the King of Sweden. The latter
demanded his surrender under threats and this was
complied with. In its protest the British Government
asserted that there was no doubt that the residence of
a minister should enjoy the right of asylum. Sweden did
have doubts and the two ambassadors were withdrawn.[62]

The Spanish authorities were not always successful in
denying to foreign ambassadors the right to afford
asylum to fugitives. Of those incidents which occurred
in the 'forties, when "the houses of the foreign ministers

[in Madrid] were filled with refugees", it is sufficient
to refer solely to those in which, in 1841 and 1843, the
Chevalier d'Alborgo, Danish chargé d'affaires, gave
refuge to various opponents of the Spanish Government.
When the refugees came into power d'Alborgo received a
Spanish title as Baron de Asilo.[63]

The European Powers during the nineteenth century were
prepared to extend asylum to non-Christians in Christian
countries and to Christians in non-Christian countries.
Thus, in 1876 when Jews were being persecuted in Moldavia,
Wallachia and Serbia, the British Consul at Galatz let
it be known that persecutees would be able to find refuge
in the British consulate[64] - this, despite the fact that
British practice, in the absence of direct consent by
the country concerned, does not recognize its own or
foreign consulates as constituting places of asylum.[65]
In so far as Christians are concerned, there is a long
record of asylum being afforded to Christians, regardless
of nationality, in the Barbary States, Turkey and
Morocco,[66] and it is this right to protect such individuals which formed the basis of the régime of capitulations
which, in so far as Morocco was concerned, was examined
by the World Court in its judgment on the Rights of
United States Nationals in Morocco.[67]

The issue of asylum for religious refugees has again
become of topical interest because of the evidence in
the Eichmann trial that various members of the diplomatic
corps offered asylum to Jews in order to save them from
the Nazi "Final Solution".

Outside Europe and outside the field of asylum for
religious persecutees, the problem has been of importance in Latin America. In that area, revolutions are
endemic and it may well be said that today's president
is yesterday's revolutionary leader and tomorrow's

political refugee. In view of this it is perhaps not
surprising that questions involving diplomatic asylum
have been most frequent in that part of the world. The
refusal of the United States to recognize diplomatic
asylum was made clear as early as 1794[68] and was well
expressed by Black in 1857. In his view, such asylum
would mean an embassy becoming the

place of refuge for any discontented wife [or] rebellious
child. ... If this were the law of nations, there is no
government in the world that would not be compelled, in
self-defence, to refuse all other governments permission
to be represented by ministers within its territory.[69]

Nevertheless, United States ambassadors in South American
countries did occasionally afford asylum to political
refugees in times of unrest. Thus, in 1898 the American
Minister in Bolivia took the initiative in drawing up
with his French and Brazilian colleagues a code governing
the asylum which might be granted, primarily on account
of threats by the mob against the refugee's life, during
the current insurrection.[70] Other cases occurred and,
for example, Secretary of State Webster wrote to the
United States Minister in Chile that

the propriety of your granting an asylum to Colonel
Arteaga will depend upon circumstances which are at
present unknown to the Department. If there should
be any precedent showing that the Chilean Government
had previously acquiesced in such a proceeding on the
part of the diplomatic representative of any foreign
nation at Santiago, it could not justly complain of
our course, unless formal notice should have previously
been given that it would not in future tolerate the
exercise of the right.[71]

Even as recently as 1931 humanitarian asylum was granted
to the former President of Ecuador, although a year
later it was denied to the family of the Present of
Chile who were threatened with violence as a means of
compelling the President to resign.[72]

Despite this tendency to allow United States diplomats to grant asylum on humanitarian grounds - sometimes defined more narrowly than at others - the Department of State informed its representatives in Latin American countries that

the affording of asylum is not within the purposes of a diplomatic mission. ... It is but a permissive local custom practiced in a limited number of states where unstable political and social conditions are recurrent,

and this view was reiterated in the 1939 Foreign Service Regulations of the United States which, having expressly denied any right of diplomatic asylum, went on to permit it on humanitarian grounds to

afford refuge to uninvited fugitives whose lives are in imminent danger from mob violence but only during the period active danger continues. [Nevertheless,] refuge must be refused to persons fleeing the pursuit of the legitimate agents of the local government.[73]

It would seem from the duration of Cardinal Mindszenty's sojourn in the American embassy in Budapest that the United States interprets 'imminent danger from mob violence' with some elasticity.

Perhaps we might mention here that when the Allende regime was overthrown in Chile in 1973 a number of embassies afforded asylum for varying lengths of time to supporters of that regime whose lives were threatened by its successor.

In so far as the countries of Latin America themselves are concerned, their practice inter se in this field has led to the general assumption

that the law of diplomatic asylum is an accepted part of general international law governing the Latin American Nations.[74]

This view has been encouraged by such actions as the

assertion of a right to grant asylum in the Latin American embassies in Madrid during the Spanish Civil War. However, it was only after the despatch of an Argentine warship to Spain that the Spanish Government conceded the right.[75]

In view of the possibilities of abuse in an unrestricted right of asylum, the Latin American States have attempted to control its exercise by treaties. The Convention on Asylum adopted by the 1928 Havana Conference of American States explained that these States

being desirous of fixing the rules they must observe for the granting of asylum, in their mutual relations have agreed to establish them in a Convention.[76]

This Preamble implies that asylum is well-known in the area, but that its extent needs definition. This Convention was followed by the Montevideo Convention on Political Asylum, 1933, which was intended "to define the terms of the one signed at Havana".[77] While asylum is not to be granted to common criminals,

political asylum, as an institution of humanitarian character, is not subject to reciprocity. Any man may resort to its protection, whatever his nationality, without prejudice to the obligations accepted by the State to which he belongs; however, the States that do not recognize political asylum, except with limitations and peculiarities, can exercise it in foreign countries only in the manner and within the limits recognized by such countries.

These sentiments are, broadly speaking, reiterated in the 1939 Montevideo Convention on Political Asylum and Refuge,[78] the Preamble of which stated that

the principles governing asylum ... require amplification in order that they may ... serve to confirm the doctrines already sanctioned in America. [It is provided, however, that] the State which grants asylum does not thereby incur an obligation to admit the refugees into its territory, except in cases where they are not given admission by other States.

344

The fact that reciprocity was not considered necessary, that asylum extends to all regardless of nationality, including non-Latin Americans, the acknowledgment that it may be recognized subject to limitations, and the assertion that the 1939 Treaty is to "confirm the doctrines already sanctioned in America", all tend to suggest that asylum is a right recognized in the area, regardless of any Conventions. This implies that Argentina, which has not ratified these Conventions, purported to be exercising its rights under Latin American international law by extending asylum to Eichmann.[79] This ignores, however, that regional international law will not operate against a non-member of the region unless the latter recognizes it.[80] It also disregards any obligations that may bind Argentina to surrender war criminals.[81]

Latin American practice on asylum was considered at some length by the International Court of Justice in the Asylum Case between Colombia and Peru.[82] The Court pointed out that Peru had not ratified the Montevideo Conventions and so it was primarily concerned with examining whether asylum, and the right unilaterally to qualify it as political, existed under "American international law in general". In the first place, the Court considered that the small number of States which had ratified the 1933 Convention indicated that they did not regard this Convention as a declaratory codification of existing law. However, it can equally be argued that States did not ratify because they were satisfied with the existing law and, as is so often the case, feared that by enacting a treaty they were opening the door to a narrow and rigid approach to the problem. The view of the Court serves to deny reality to asylum, for it is unlikely that both the ambassador granting refuge and the State against which it is sought will agree that the fugitive is a political offender rather than a common

criminal. The Court went even further towards destroying the idea that asylum is a part of Latin American
customary or conventional international law.[83]

The Court cannot admit that the States signatory to the
Havana Convention intended to substitute for the practice
of the Latin-American republics, in which considerations
of courtesy, good-neighbourliness and political expediency
have always held a prominent place, a legal system which
would guarantee to their own nationals accused of
political offences the privilege of evading national
jurisdiction. Such a conception, moreover, would come
into conflict with one of the most firmly established
traditions of Latin America, namely non-intervention.[84]

It is perhaps not uninteresting to mention that the
Judges from Brazil, Chile and Colombia dissented from
this judgment. The Inter-American Convention on Diplomatic Asylum signed at Caracas in 1954 redresses the
situation.[85] In Article 4, the Convention, which was
not signed by Peru, declares that

it shall rest with the State granting asylum to determine
the nature of the offence or the motive for the
prosecution. [However, while Article 2 recognizes that]
every State has the right to grant asylum, it is not
obligated to do so or to state its reasons for refusing
it.

Before turning to developments that have taken place
under the auspices of the United Nations, it might be
as well to mention two statements made by Canada with
regard to diplomatic asylum, for even though they confirm
the traditional view already mentioned, they are somewhat
more recent than the statements referred to earlier. In
1961 the Under-Secretary for External Affairs said:[86]

... on February 15, 1961, following the death of Patrice
Lumumba, the Belgian Embassy in Cairo was set on fire
and one or more staff members sought and was granted
refuge for a number of hours in the neighbouring Canadian
Embassy. The position that Canada takes is that our
consulates and diplomatic missions abroad may not grant
asylum on the premises of a post except in extraordinary

circumstances. The sort of circumstances we have in mind is where temporary asylum would be granted on humanitarian grounds to a person whether a Canadian citizen or not, if he is in imminent personal danger to his life during political disturbances or riots, with care being taken to ensure that the humanitarian character of the mission's intervention should not be misinterpreted.... The Government of Canada has not signed or ratified any international convention establishing a right of asylum, Canada's position concerning asylum being based upon general principles of international law which recognize that the right of asylum may be exercised under very exceptional circumstances.

Some five years later this position was reiterated:[87]

... no general right of asylum on diplomatic premises is recognized in contemporary international law. However ... in exceptional cases, temporary asylum may be granted for humanitarian reasons where not only the life, liberty or person of an individual seeking asylum is threatened by violence, but when the life of such a person is actually in imminent danger. Such incidents, in which Canada's representatives abroad have granted asylum, are ... extremely rare. As far as concerns the right of a foreign mission to grant asylum in Canada, we are not aware of any instances in which this has occurred. It is, however, not likely that Canada would recognize such a right, in view of the principle cited, if such occasion were to arise.

These views should be compared with the Soviet conception of asylum which has consistently reflected the ideological approach of that country's legal philosophy, while emphasising how easily an institution like asylum can be used for purely partisan political ends.[88] As early as the Fundamental Law of the Russian Socialist Federal Soviet Republic of 10 July 1918,[89] the R.S.F.S.R.

grants the right of asylum to all foreigners persecuted for political and religious offences

and this principle appears in Article 129 of the 1936 Soviet Constitution, whereby

the U.S.S.R. affords the right of asylum to foreign citizens persecuted for defending the interests of the working people, or for scientific activities, or for struggling for national liberation.

A similar approach is to be found in the textbook on international law published under the auspices of the Soviet Academy of Sciences:[90]

The right of asylum means the granting of entry for the purpose of settlement to persons persecuted in their own country for their political or scientific activity or for their support of the national-liberation movement. The granting of asylum to any person presupposes that he shall not be extradited. The granting of asylum and refusal to extradite is a sovereign right.... The right of asylum was proclaimed a principle of bourgeois democratic law by the French bourgeois revolution of 1789, and recognized by other bourgeois States....

During its struggle for power the bourgeoisie utilized the right of asylum to assist the opponents of feudalism.

Having defeated feudalism, the bourgeoisie imposed a series of limitations upon the right of asylum in respect to those active in the labour movement. The bourgeoisie uses the institution of asylum in its own class inter- ests.... The institution of asylum has acquired a genuinely democratic, progressive character in the legislation and international legal practice of the Soviet Union and other socialist countries....

While in the Soviet Union and the People's Democracies the right of asylum has received genuinely democratic and progressive expression and application, in many capitalist countries it is used in a manner contrary to its real purpose. Capitalist States now refuse asylum to progressives....

The cruelties of the Nazi régime and the hunt for war criminals after 1945 attracted new attention to the problem and strengthened the case of those who demanded recognition of the right of asylum. In the first place it was necessary to make it clear that asylum was not to be granted to those whose crimes placed them beyond the pale of civilisation and this was done by wartime agree- ments and General Assembly resolutions.[91] This part of the problem, however, is not today of pressing importance. The countries of refuge have adopted the line that many

of the "criminals" are wanted for trial not so much as
war criminals, but as political opponents of the demanding State which is using the war crimes allegation purely
for ideological purposes. In addition, the countries
of refuge have in many cases applied the test that their
courts would apply in matters of extradition[92] and
asserted that the period since the war constitutes
unconscionable delay rendering it unjust and repressive
to return the wanted man,[93] even though the United Nations
has adopted a Convention on the Non-Applicability of
Statutory Limitations to War Crimes and Crimes against
Humanity.[94] In any case, the passage of the years of
necessity renders this aspect of the matter somewhat
transient in significance.

What is far more important is for the United Nations
to protect those who have fled because the post-war
condition of the home State is such as to cause them to
seek asylum elsewhere. As has already been indicated,
in the Universal Declaration of Human Rights the right
to seek asylum is included among the fundamental human
rights, although no effort is made to give this "right"
any sort of legal recognition, and no concomitant duty
is placed on any State to afford to the asylum seeker
the hospitality which it is stated he has a right to
seek. In any case, it must be remembered that, despite
the fanfares that are sounded in certain countries to
mark the anniversary of "Human Rights Day", the Declaration is not a treaty but a mere statement of pious hope
as to the standards of conduct that might one day be
achieved. However, if the other rights mentioned in the
Declaration did become real, it may be thought that there
would no longer be any need to seek asylum from persecution. An attempt was made to give effect and substance
to these rights in the International Covenants adopted
in 1966[95], although these had not yet come into force by

the end of 1974, and the Covenant on Civil and Political
Rights makes no reference to the right of asylum.

Even before the second world war, the League of Nations
had been concerned with the problem of refugees and their
number was radically increased as a result of the Nazi
régime in Germany and the political changes in Europe
after 1945. By 1951 the United Nations had adopted its
Convention on the Status of Refugees, as amended by the
Protocol of 1967[96], while an Office of the United Nations
High Commissioner for Refugees was established in 1950
and an International Refugee Organization in 1946.[97]
While no right of asylum is conferred by the Convention,
the Preamble recognizes that "the grant of asylum may
place unduly heavy burdens on certain countries", and
therefore calls for international cooperation. A refugee
is defined as any person who

owing to well-founded fear of being persecuted for reasons
of race, religion, nationality, membership of a particular
social group or political opinion, is outside the country
of his nationality and is unable, or owing to such fear,
is unwilling to avail himself of the protection of that
country; or who, not having a nationality and being
outside the country of his former habitual residence is
unable or, owing to such fear, is unwilling to return
to it.

The Convention affirms the refugee's duty to obey the
law and provides that the state of refuge is to take no
punitive action against refugees entering illegally so
long as they present themselves to the authorities without delay and show good cause for their illegal entry.
Moreover, refugees are to be treated as are other aliens
and may only be expelled "on grounds of national security
or public order."

Perhaps the most important provision in the Convention
from the point of view of the right of asylum is Article
33, which forbids refoulement - expulsion or return

350

to the frontiers of territories where his life or freedom would be threatened on account of his race, religion, nationality, membership of a particular social group or political opinion.

However, this protection against refoulement does not extend to a refugee when there are reasonable grounds for regarding him as a danger to the security of the inhabitants of the country in which he seeks refuge.

In fine, it may be said of the Convention that while it does not attempt to place any obligation upon the parties to grant asylum, it does stipulate the treatment to be enjoyed by refugees once asylum has been granted.

The Refugees Convention only deals with a particular aspect of the problem of asylum and was really concerned with members of groups, reflecting the historical interest of the League in this problem. There still remained the question of the ordinary individual who might be in need of asylum and by 1960 the Human Rights Commission of the United Nations was able to draw up a draft Declaration. In its drafting, however, a cleavage appeared[98] and

the members of the Commission were divided into two groups: the first (consisting mainly of representatives of Afro-Asian countries) pleaded for the maintenance of the State's sovereignty and implicite its right to be free in granting or refusing asylum for reasons of its own security and welfare, while the other (mostly European States) stressed the humanitarian duties of the States which should oblige them to deviate only in exceptional cases from the principle of non-refoulement.

A compromise was eventually evolved and in 1967 the General Assembly adopted a Declaration on Territorial Asylum.[99] This Declaration stems from the Universal Declaration affirmation of the right and refers also to that Declaration's statement that

everyone has the right to leave any country, including

351

his own, and to return to his country

even though some members of the United Nations, for
example, the Soviet Union, place obstacles in the way of
such departures or treat those seeking to leave as if
they were criminals. Another important preambular
statement recognizes that

the grant of asylum ... is a peaceful and humanitarian
act and ... as such ... cannot be regarded as unfriendly
by any other State.

While the Declaration does not impose any duty upon the
members of the United Nations to grant asylum it does
confirm that some persons - undefined - may be entitled
to invoke asylum under the Universal Declaration of Human
Rights, and goes on, reflecting the compromise, to include
within this group'persons struggling against colonialism',
but such asylum cannot be claimed by anyone

with respect to whom there are serious reasons for considering that he has committed a crime against peace, a
war crime or a crime against humanity.

Presumably, since the General Assembly has decided that
apartheid is a crime against humanity, no South African
who may be regarded as having participated in apartheid
policies would be entitled to 'seek and enjoy' asylum,
and

it shall rest with the State granting asylum to evaluate
the grounds for the grant of asylum.

As if conscious of the views of the classical writers on
the subject of asylum, the Declaration confirms that
asylum is of concern to the international community and,
therefore,

where a State finds difficulty in granting or continuing
to grant asylum, States individually or jointly or through
the United Nations shall consider, in a spirit of

international solidarity, appropriate measures to lighten
the burden of that State.

The Declaration is also committed to the principle of
non-refoulement, banning

expulsion or compulsory return to any State where [the
asylum seeker] may be subjected to persecution [and]
exception may be made ... only for overriding reasons
of national security or in order to safeguard the population, as in the case of a mass influx of persons,

although even in such cases the State of potential refuge
should consider the possibility of granting an opportunity, even by way of temporary asylum, to go to some State
willing to grant asylum.

The Declaration is, of course, merely a General Assembly
resolution and in no way binding. Moreover, it only
deals with the problem of territorial and completely
ignores diplomatic asylum. Even the Vienna Convention
on Diplomatic Relations[100] is silent on this issue.
However, various humanitarian bodies and learned
societies devoted their attention to drafting model
conventions that might prove acceptable as a basis for
binding treaties regarding both territorial and diplomatic asylum. Of these, perhaps the most comprehensive
is the Declaration of Buenos Aires[101] adopted in its
original by the International Law Association at its
1968 Conference. This Declaration embodies drafts in
both fields and seeks to impose an obligation upon States
to grant the asylum that is sought, but at New York, when
finally adopted, States were again given the option.
The debate that preceded the adoption of the Declaration
fully represents the divergences in opinion that are
likely to be confronted if and when a proper diplomatic
conference on this matter should take place. So far, the
developments that have taken place on the state level
have been primarily regional. Thus, the European

Convention on Extradition[102] provides for non-extradition
in the event of a political offence or if it is reasonably
believed that the request is really intended to prosecute
or punish the fugitive on account of his race, religion,
nationality or political opinion. In 1969 the Latin
American States adopted the American Convention on Human
Rights[103] which expressly states that

every person has the right to seek and be granted asylum
in a foreign territory, in accordance with the legislation
of the state and international conventions, in the event
he is being pursued for political offences or related
common crimes.

The Convention, thus, as such imposes no obligation upon
a party to grant asylum, but it does provide for non-
refoulement.

In so far as the United Nations is concerned, the 1974
session of the General Assembly had before it a Draft
Convention on Territorial Asylum which had been prepared
by the High Commissioner for Refugees.[104] While this
document does not impose an absolute obligation upon
States to grant asylum, it calls upon them to act

in an international and humanitarian spirit [and use their]
best endeavours to grant asylum in [their] territory,
which ... includes permission to remain in that territory,
to any person who, owing to well-founded fear of
(a) persecution for reasons of race, religion, nationality,
membership of a particular social group, or political
opinion, or for reasons of struggle against apartheid
or colonialism; or
(b) prosecution or severe punishment for acts arising out
of any of the [above]
is unable or unwilling to return to the country of his
nationality, or if he has no nationality, the country of
his former habitual residence.

Asylum is not, however, to be granted in the case of those
suspected of crimes against peace, war crimes or crimes
against humanity, of serious common crimes, acts contrary
to the purposes and principles of the United Nations or

to those seeking asylum for purely economic reasons.
The draft extends the non-refoulement principle, for
it makes no provision for exceptions of the type included
in the Declaration on Asylum, and also forbids extradition
to any territory in which a similar type of persecution
or fear thereof may exist. The comments of governments
upon these provisions reflect every type of political
and national divergence and it will be interesting to
see what eventually emerges from the Committee of Experts
to which the 1974 Assembly referred the text.[105]

While the United Nations seems at least interested in
establishing a right of territorial asylum as between
the member states, it is perhaps interesting to note its
attitude towards itself as an asylum granter, especially
as this may give some guide to what its attitude may be
to diplomatic asylum as such. In accordance with the
Headquarters Agreement of 1946[106] the buildings and
Headquarters area are granted immunity and United States
officials may not enter without the consent of the
Secretary General. However, without attempting to
distinguish between political and other offenders, the
Agreement provides that

the United Nations shall prevent the headquarters
district from becoming a refuge either for persons who
are avoiding arrest under the federal, state or local
law of the United States or are required by the United
States for extradition to another country, or for persons
who are endeavouring to avoid service of legal process.

As yet, despite the debates and the drafts, there is
no recognized right of asylum, either territorial or
diplomatic, in any universally accepted convention, and,
as the Asylum case has shown, even within a region where
it has generally been granted it is not possible to
regard it as being obligatory upon all. However, the
law of extradition has demonstrated[107] that most countries
will grant asylum to political offenders, even though

355

the scope of the political offence may vary from State
to State. In addition, a number of constitutions, as
varying as those of the Soviet Union and of the Federal
Republic of Germany[108], guarantee this right, while the
United Nations and various of its organs have all
reiterated a belief in the right of the individual to
seek and enjoy asylum. This raises the interesting
question of what would happen if a problem relating to
asylum were to come before the World Court as at present
constituted, in view of the way in which that body and
individual judges have proclaimed that protection of
human rights, including self-determination and
non-discrimination, have hardened into general principles
of law recognized by civilized nations and as such part
of the corpus of international law.[109]

* Based on an inaugural lecture delivered from the Chair
of International Law in the University of Singapore,
1961.

1 (1721) tr. Healy (1964) 174.

2 4 Moore, Digest of International Law 332.

3 1948 - G.A. Res. 217 A (III).

4 See IV above.

5 See, e.g., Green, 'Recent Practice in the Law of
Extradition' (1953). 6 Curr. Legal Prob. 274, 281;
Shearer, Extradition in International Law (1971)
ch.7; Sinha, Asylum and International Law (1971)
ch.8; 5 Verzijl, International law in Historical
Perspective (1972) ch.7; 6 Whiteman, Digest of International Law, 799-857.

6 [1950] I.C.J. 263, 274-5.

7 In re Castioni [1891] 1 Q.B. 149, 157, 159. See
also Re Ezeta (1894) 62 F. 972, 998-9, and Re
Giovanni Gatti (1947) 14 Ann. Dig. 145.

8 House of Commons, 6 Aug. 1884, 184 Hansard Col. 2115.

9 26 Jan. 1909, 4 Hackworth, Digest of International Law

49. See also Re Federenko (No.1) (1910) 17 C.C.C.268.

10 In re Meunier [1894] 2 Q.B. 415, 419.

11 E.g. El Salvador Constitution, Art.20, Y.B. Human
     Rights [1954] 254.

12 E.g., Bolivia/Brazil, 1938, Colombia/Peru, 1927
     (Garcia-Mora, International Law and Asylum as a
     Human Right (1956) 86-7.

13 Art. 2, 29 Am.J.Int'l Law, Supp. (1935) Part I,
     Extradition, 30.

14 Art. 3, 6 Hudson, International Legislation, 835.

15 See, e.g., Swiss case of Malatesta (1891 - c.
     Papadatos, Le Délit Politique (1954) 84), and Evans,
     'Reflections upon the Political Offense in Inter-
     national Practise' (1963) 57 Am. J. Int'l Law 1, 13.

16 Ex parte Kolczynski [1955] 1 Q.B. 540, 550, 551.

17 The Times (London), 5 Dec. 1973.

18 House of Commons, 6 Mar. 1958, 583 Hansard, Written
     Answers, col. 153.

19 [1964] A.C. 556, 584.

20 At 612.

21 Cheng v. Governor, Pentonville Prison [1973] 2 All
     E.R. 204, 206-7, per Lord Hodson, see also Lords
     Diplock and Salmon, 209, 223; cp., however, Lord
     Simon of Glaisdale (Wilberforce concurring) 215,
     220-1.

22 The Times, 4 Jun. 1973.

23 (1957) 247 F. 2d 198, 203.

24 Re Commonwealth of Puerto Rico and Hernandez (1972)
     30 D.L.R. (3d) 260, 268.

25 Re State of Wisconsin and Armstrong (1972) 28 D.L.R.
     (3d) 513, 520.

26 Summarized without a name, (1960) 54 Am. J. Int'l
     Law 416, 417; see also Swiss case, Re Kavic & others
     (1952) 19 Int. Law Rep. 371 (see IX below, n.20).

27 Para.2: '... The political persecuted shall enjoy
     the right of asylum.'

28 Loc. cit., n. 6 above, 282-3, 284.

29 Guide to Diplomatic Practice, (ed. Bland, 1957) 219.

30 18 Aug. 1894, cited in Adler and Margalith, With Firmness in the Right (1946) 13.

31 De Jure Belli ac Pacis (1625) Lib. II, Cap. II, s.16, Cap. XXI, Carnegie tr. (1925), 201, 530). 5(Eng. tr., (1738) 156, 460.

32 De Jure Naturae et Gentium (1688) Lib. III, Cap.III, s. 10 (Eng. tr. by Carew (1729) 246; Carnegie tr. (1934), 366).

33 Jus Gentium Methodo Scientifica Pertractatum (1764) ss. 145-150 (Carnegie tr. (1934) 79-81).

34 Ibid., ss. 1059, 1061 (tr., 534-5, 536).

35 Le Droit des Gens ou principes de la Loi Naturelle appliqués àla conduite et aux affaires des Nations et des Souverains, (1758) Liv. I, Chap. XIX, ss. 229-231 (Carnegie tr. (1916) 92).

36 Garcia-Mora, op.cit., n.12, 41.

37 Anarchical Fallacies, 1824, 2 Collected Works (Bowring ed. 1843) 523, 501.

38 1 Moore, A Treatise on Extradition (1891) 8.

39 Rousset, Le Cérémonial diplomatique du Droit des Gens, vol. 1, Supp. IV to Dumont, Corps universel diplomatique (cited Silving, "In Re Eichmann: A Dilemma of Law and Morality", (1961) 55 Am. J. Int'l Law, 307, 319). It is of interest to note that, as late as 1937, the mandatory régime in Palestine recognised the Mosque of Omar as a place of asylum for the Grand Mufti of Jerusalem (see entry on "Asylrecht" in Strupp-Schlochauer, Worterbuch des Volkerrechts (1960)). Cp., however, India's non-recognition of Sikh temples as places of asylum in 1955 and 1961, The Times, 16 Sept. 1961.

40 Hosack, The Rise and Growth of the Law of Nations (1882) 117-118 (in a footnote Hosack quotes from Bacon's history of Henry's reign the terms of the conversation between the two Kings).

41 Moore, op.cit., 10.

42 1 Oppenheim, International Law, 5th ed., (1937)

para. 450, 666; now see 8th ed., para. 450, 853.
See also Fauchille, Traité de Droit International
Public (1925) tome 1, 2me partie, s.619.

43 Chung Chi Cheung v. The King [1939] A.C. 160,174-5.

44 Forbes v. Cochrane (1824) 2 B. and C. 448.

45 Report of the Law Officers of the Crown, 14 Oct.
1875 (2 McNair, International Law Opinions (1956)93).

46 Report by Paul, 20 Sept. 1733 (ibid., 68).

47 Sir Wm. Scott, 18 Nov. 1820 (ibid., 71).

48 Art. 0621, U.S. Navy Regulations, 1948 (cited
Brittin and Watson, International Law for Seagoing
Officers, (1972) 160-1).

49 4 Moore, op. cit., n. 2 above, 849-55.

50 Fauchille, op.cit., 997-8; 1 Sibert, Traité de Droit
International Public, (1951) 950.

51 Report by Yorke and Talbot, c. 1729 (2 McNair, op.
cit., 79).

52 Ashburton to Webster, Aug. 6, 1842 (2 Moore, op.cit.,
n. 2 above, 355).

53 The relevant Reports are to be found in McNair,
op.cit., 79-88.

54 Webster to Ashburton, Aug. 1, 1842 (2 Moore, 354).

55 Ibid., 354-61.

56 See Wheaton, Elements of International Law (Dana ed.,
1866) s. 103, n. 62.

57 1 Phillimore, International Law, (1879) 519.

58 Ibid., 522. See also, 2 Wharton, International Law
Digest, (1866) s. 268.

59 Wharton, ibid., p. 746 et seq.

60 Moore, op.cit., n. 38 above, 10-11.

61 1870, 33 & 34 Vict. c. 52. See decision in Ex p.
Westerling (1950) 17 Int. Law Rep. 82. See R. v.
Governor of Brixton Prison, ex p. Soblen [1963]
2 Q.B.43, for a case in which a declaration of

undesirability and non-admission avoided consideration of the political plea in an extradition
arising under treaty.

62 Satow, op.cit., 219-20.

63 Moore, op.cit., n.2. 354-61. For the position during
the Spanish Civil War, see 2 Hackworth, op.cit.,
631-2.

64 62 B.F.S.P. 1009 et seq.

65 2 McNair, 74-6. See also, Adler and Margalith,
op.cit., passim.

66 1 Wharton, op.cit., 675 et seq.

67 [1952] I.C.J. 176 (see Index under 'Capitulations
(Régime of in Morocco)').

68 Att. Gen. Bradford, c. Deener, The United States
Attorneys General and International Law (1957)
271-2.

69 Att. Gen. Black in Hulseman's Case (1857) ibid.,272.

70 2 Moore, op.cit., n.2 above, 784.

71 (1851) ibid., 787.

72 2 Hackworth, op.cit., 620. Other instances of U.S.
practice in Ethiopia and Spain will be found ibid.,
630-632.

73 Ibid., 623.

74 Thomas and Thomas, Non-Intervention: The Law and its
Import in the Americas, (1956) 392.

75 Padelford, International Law and Diplomacy in the
Spanish Civil Strife (1939) 157.

76 4 Hudson, International Legislation, 2412.

77 6 Ibid., 608.

78 8 Ibid., 405.

79 See Green, 'The Eichmann Case' (1960) 23 Mod. Law
Rev. 507. For the judicial discussion of the juris-
dictional issues involved in the kidnapping, see
Rosenne, 6,000,000 Accusers: Israel's Case against
Eichmann (1961) 184-305; Baade, 'The Eichmann Trial'

[1961] Duke Law J. 400; Silving, 'In Re Eichmann: A Dilemma of Law and Morality' (1961) 55 Am. J. Int'l Law 307; Green, 'Legal Aspects of the Eichmann Trial', (1963) 37 Tulane Law Rev. 641, 641-9, and (1963) 9 Ann. Français de Dr. Int'l 150, 151-6; Hausner, Justice in Jerusalem (1966).

80 See Green, 'New States, Regionalism and International Law', (1967) 5 Can. Y.B. Int'l Law 118, 125.

81 See G. A. Res. 3(I), 170(II); see, also, Morgenstern, 'Asylum for War Criminals, Quislings and Traitors', (1948) 22 Brit. Y.B. Int'l Law 382; Green, 'Political Offences, War Crimes and Extradition' (1962) 11 Int'l & Comp. Law Q. 329.

82 [1950] I.C.J. 266.

83 At 285 (italics added).

84 Embodied, e.g., in declaration adopted at 1928 Havana Conference.

85 Y.B. Human Rights [1955] 330.

86 Castel, International Law Chiefly as Applied and Interpreted in Canada (1965), 541.

87 1 Apr. 1966 (1967) 5 Can. Y.B. Int'l Law 274 (italics added); see Green, 'Immigration, Extradition and Asylum in Canadian Law and Practice', in Macdonald and others, Canadian Perspectives in International Law and Organization (1974), 244, 270 et seqq.

88 On the ideological aspects of asylum, see de Visscher, Théories et Réalités en Droit International Public, (1970), 204.

89 Meisel and Kozera, Materials for the Study of the Soviet Union (1950), 81.

90 Kozhevnikov (ed.), International Law (1961), 164-6; see also Haraszti, 'The Right to Asylum' (1960 - Budapest) 2 Acta Juridica 359, and Gold, 'Non-extradition for Political Offenses: the Communist Perspective' (1970), 11 Harv. Int'l Law J. 191.

91 See n. 81 above.

92 R. v. Governor, Brixton Prison, ex p. Naranjan Singh [1961] 2 W.L.R. 980. See also Re Durcansky (1960) 29 Int. Law Rep. 11, for Argentine refusal to extradite to Czechoslovakia because of extinctive prescription under Art. 62 of Penal Code; and for

Canada, see statement of 16 Sept. 1966, (1967) 5 Can. Y.B. Int'l Law 270.

93 See Durcansky case, ibid.; British rejection of Soviet demand for surrender of Ain Erwin Mer, Daily Telegraph (London), 13 Mar. 1961 - as early as May 1949, the British Government stated that no further war criminals would be handed over for trial in the absence of a satisfactory explanation for the delay, 162 Hansard (Lords) col. 388; see also Chilean refusal to extradite Rauff, The Times, 29 Apr. 1963; cp. Romanian extradition of Mandousis to Greece, ibid., 19 May 1964.

94 1968, Res. 2391 (XXIII) (not ratified by any western State and only by Soviet Union among the Great Powers, but in force since 1970).

95 Res. 2200 (XXI) Annex.

96 1951, 189 U.N.T.S. 137; Protocol, 1967, 606 ibid. 267. On status of refugees generally, see Grahl-Madsen, The Status of Refugees in International Law (1967/72) - vol. 2 is particularly concerned with asylum).

97 Res. 428(V), 18 U.N.T.S. 3, resp.

98 11 Bull. of Int'l Comm. Jurists, Dec. 1960, 53.

99 Res. 2312 (XXII).

100 1961, 500 U.N.T.S. 95.

101 I.L.A., Report of 53rd (Buenos Aires) Conference 1968 (1969), 268-77, as amended 265-6, and see New York Report 199-207, 195.

102 (1957) 359 U.N.T.S. 273.

103 9 Int'l Legal Materials 673 (italics added).

104 G.A. (XXVIII) Off. Rec. Supp. 12B, and G.A. (XXIX) Doc.A/AC.96/508/Add.1 (italics added).

105 Res. 3272 (XXIX).

106 (1949) Y.B.U.N. [1946-47] 103.

107 See n.5 above, and Green,'The Nature of Political Offences', (1964) 3 Solicitor Q. 213.

108 Ibid., 216-20.

109 See, e.g., VI above, nn.75 et seqq., VII, nn.64,75 96 et seqq.

IX

HIJACKING, EXTRADITION AND ASYLUM*

Hijackers should be prosecuted in the name of
the peoples of the world, for the benefit of
all travelers and all pilots, irrespective
of their nationality, irrespective of their
political system
(U Thant, 14 Sept. 1970, U.N. Press
Release, SG/SM/1333, ANV/87)

The last few years have witnessed a spate of incidents
involving the diversion of aircraft in flight or seizures
at airports with the persons involved - hijackers -
using the aircraft, its crew and passengers as hostages
against demands they present to a variety of governments
for either political or private reasons. As a result,
writers, pilots' associations and States have all turned
their attention to the problem of the prevention and
punishment of aerial hijacking[1].

This issue has many facets, but perhaps one of those
which is of most interest to the lawyer is the institution
of judicial proceedings against those involved. In so
far as international hijackings are concerned, the offender
is always outside the territory of the country from or
to which the aircraft is flying, either because of the
diversion or because the hijacker had made his safe exit
a condition for the freeing of the aircraft or its
passengers and crew. Invariably, too, he is outside the
territory of the aircraft's state of registration. This
means that extradition becomes a major issue, with the
possibility of the hijacker seeking asylum in order to
avoid his return to any of the various countries that may

be seeking to place him on trial.

There are two categories of fugitive who may seek asylum. On the one hand there is the fugitive who maintains that he is fleeing from persecution and has been guilty of no crime, and who alleges that if he is denied hospitality and returned to the country of flight he is almost certainly going to be subjected to imprisonment or death without any legal basis for such action. On the other hand, there is the individual who is a fugitive from justice, but who maintains that his crime was really part and parcel of political activities and was incidental to these prime objectives, or that the charges against him are really nothing but a cover for political persecution.[2] In so far as hijacking is concerned, it is by no means unlikely that the act may have been perpetrated to enable the offender to escape from his country, or else it may have been committed with some political aim in view. What has to be considered is whether hijacking is the sort of offence that can ever be regarded as other than a common crime and whether the fact that an offence has some political colouration to it is sufficient to make it a political offence, as that concept is understood in the law concerning extradition.

In classical international law the individual was not regarded as having any rights of his own and it is only in recent years with acknowledgment of the need to recognize human rights that states have been prepared to consider giving individuals rights which might enjoy legal protection.[3] One of the more important indications of this trend is the Universal Declaration of Human Rights adopted by the General Assembly of the United Nations in 1948.[4] Although, like other resolutions of the General Assembly, this has no obligatory character, it has served as a guide and has even been responsible for the manner in which individual fundamental freedoms

have come to be expressed in some modern constitutions.[5]
Moreover, the Declaration has been of importance in the
subsequent history of the United Nations, either as a
measuring rod for criticizing the activities of some
states, or as a basis for further Declarations and,
ultimately, the two International Covenants on Human
Rights.[6] It is enough for our purpose to point out that
in Article 2 the Declaration states that

everyone is entitled to all the rights and freedoms set
forth in this Declaration, without distinction of any
kind, such as race, colour, sex, language, religion,
political or other opinion, national or social origin,
property, birth or other status,

and that Article 14 postulates that

everyone has the right to seek and to enjoy in other
countries asylum from persecution.

Apparently aware of the ease with which criminal fugitives
claim that they are in fact the victims of political
persecution, the drafters of the Declaration added a
second clause to Article 14, to the effect that the
right of asylum

may not be invoked in the case of prosecutions genuinely
arising from non-political crimes or from acts contrary
to the purposes and principles of the United Nations.

It has long been recognized in customary international
law that each country has absolute discretion in deciding
which aliens to admit, although limitations upon this
freedom may arise from treaties, both bilateral and
multilateral. Perhaps this is why the members of the
United Nations did not introduce into the Universal
Declaration any obligation upon states to grant the
asylum which the Declaration asserted was the right of
everyone. Even the General Assembly Resolution which is
known as the Declaration on Asylum[7] provides in its first
article that

it shall rest with the state granting asylum to evaluate the grounds for the grant of asylum... [which is] granted by a state in the exercise of its sovereignty.

The International Covenant on Civil and Political Rights,[8] which has not yet come into force, but which was adopted by the United Nations in 1966 and is the only universal document which purports to impose legal obligations, makes no reference to any right of asylum.

While there is no obligation in international law for any state to grant asylum, there is equally nothing to stop it from making such a grant if it so wills.[9] In fact, a number of states have embodied the right to asylum in their constitutions, and provisions to this effect may be found in the case of countries of varying political ideology. Among such constitutions are those of the Soviet Union, 1936, the German Federal Republic, 1949, the Chinese People's Republic, 1954, Venezuela, 1961, and the United Arab Republic, 1964.[10] The Soviet and Chinese provisions reflect the political philosophy of the state. Thus, the former

affords the right of asylum to foreign citizens persecuted for defending the interests of the working people, or for scientific activities, or for struggling for national liberation,

while the latter

grants the right of asylum to any foreign national persecuted for supporting a just cause, taking part in the peace movement or engaging in scientific activity.

The constitutions of the other People's Republics contain somewhat similar clauses, while those of non-Communist states tend to be phrased less specifically, and are apparently open to all seeking asylum. The German Constitution states _simpliciter_

Persons persecuted for political reasons shall enjoy the right of asylum.

366

Since, however, the decision as to whether a claimant is a political fugitive is to be made in the case of an offender by the courts, and in the case of an ordinary non-criminal refugee by the administration, it is often the case that only persons whose political allegiance tends to be sympathetic or to be approved by the state of refuge are the ones to receive asylum - unless, although politically opposed to the state of refuge, the fugitive is seeking asylum from a country which is the ideological antagonist of the state of flight and it is believed that the defection of the fugitive is likely to have some propaganda advantage.

By and large, states do not envisage being asked for asylum against countries or governments with which they are allied or politically sympathetic.[11] There is, however, no reason why states should not recognize that fugitives might be either political offenders or political refugees from a friendly government. Revolution is a common phenomenon in Latin America and is becoming increasingly so in Africa. Moreover, some recent acts of terrorism committed by partisans of the Palestine Liberation Organization seem to have been as much directed against some Arab countries or against rival segments of the Arab movement, as they are or are alleged to be against Israel. In some instances, attempts have been made to deal with the problem on a regional basis and in the case of Latin America there has been a number of conventions recognizing, as among those who have accepted the obligation, the right of asylum even in diplomatic premises and suggestions have even been made that this idea of diplomatic asylum is part of American international law.[12] However, despite the apparent desire of the Latin American states to secure recognition of a right to seek asylum and a concomitant duty to grant it when sought,[13] the American

Convention on Human Rights of 1969[14] does not really change the traditional situation. By Article 22 (7) it is provided that

every person has the right to seek and be granted asylum in a foreign territory, in accordance with the legislation of the state and international conventions, in the event he is being pursued for political offences or related common crimes.

Acknowledging that it imposes no obligation upon the state to grant such asylum, the Article goes on to provide that

in no case may an alien be deported or returned to a country, regardless of whether or not it is his country of origin, if in that country his right to life or personal freedom is in danger of being violated because of his race, nationality, religion, social status, or political opinions.

Other regional groups have not been prepared to concede any right of asylum, but have nevertheless accepted that those charged with political offences should not be liable to extradition, even inter se. This is the position under the European Convention on Extradition,[15] 1957, which grants exemption from extradition

if the offence in respect of which it is requested is regarded by the requested Party as a political offence or as an offence connected with a political offence. The same rule shall apply if the requested Party has substantial grounds for believing that a request for extradition for an ordinary criminal offence has been made for the purpose of prosecuting or punishing a person on account of his race, religion, nationality or political opinion, or that the person's position may be prejudiced for any of these reasons.

Most bilateral treaties contain similar reservations concerning the non-extradition of political offenders. Among the most recent of these is Article 4 (iii) of the 1971 Extradition Treaty between Canada and the United States[16] providing that extradition will not be granted

when the offense in respect of which extradition is
requested is of a political character: or the person whose
extradition is requested proves that the extradition
request has been made for the purpose of trying or punishing him for an offense of the above-mentioned character.
If any question arises as to whether a case comes within
the provisions of this subparagraph, the authorities of
the Government on which the requisition is made shall
decide.

National legislation, too, frequently provides protection
for political offenders, and s.27 of the Canadian Extradition Act[17] is as good an example as any:

no fugitive is liable to surrender... if it appears
(a) that the offence in respect of which the proceedings
are taken under this Act is one of a political character,
or (b) that such proceedings are being taken with a view
to punish him for an offence of a political character.

While this is the general practice, there does not seem
to be any rule of international law forbidding a state
from surrendering a person who is accused of a political
offence, subject of course to any provisions to the
contrary which may be embodied in its national legislation. This becomes clear from The State (Duggan) v.
Tapley[18] in which the Supreme Court of Eire stated:

The attempt to establish that the non-surrender of
political refugees is a generally recognized principle
of international law fails. The farthest that the
matter can be put is that international law permits and
favours the refusal of extradition of persons accused
or convicted of offences of a political character but
allows it to each State to exercise its own judgment as
to whether it will grant or refuse extradition in such
cases and also as to the limitations which it will
impose upon such provisions as exempt from extradition.

While, depending upon the provisions of its own
national law, there is no obligation upon a state to
grant extradition at the request of another, unless
there is a treaty between the two creating such an
obligation: there is equally no rule of international
law to prevent a state from exercising its discretion

so as to concede such a request even if there is no
treaty between itself and the requesting country. In
the absence of a treaty, however, the requesting state
can only rely upon the goodwill of the requisitioned
state but cannot assert that there is any duty upon that
state to comply with the request. There is no need to
trace the history of, or even to comment upon the whole
sequence of hijackings that have taken place, for they
are merely variations upon a theme. It is enough to
pay attention to some of the recent occurrences, since
in these cases the political aspects were most clear and
were given a somewhat new turn because of the role played
by the Palestine Liberation Organization. Thus, after
the Rome hijackings of 1974 it was reported that Italy
as the country most directly concerned - but there were
others, including the United States, Morocco and Germany,
who might equally wish to hold trials - sought the
extradition of the fugitive offenders from Kuwait where
they had eventually sought refuge. Ignoring the hijacking of the Lufthansa aircraft and paying attention solely
to the other crimes committed during the course of the
whole incident, there is no doubt that these crimes,
including murder, would have been listed in any extradition treaty to which Italy and other potentially requis-
itioning countries might have been parties. But there
is no extradition treaty between Italy and Kuwait and,
therefore, regardless of any question of the alleged
political character of the occurrence providing a ground
to claim exemption from extradition, Kuwait is under no
obligation to Italy to surrender the activists involved.
Moreover, so far as is known Kuwait has signed no
extradition treaty with any of the other countries
interested and so is no more obligated to them than it
is to Italy.

Kuwait made it clear that it did not intend extraditing

the fugitives to Italy or any of the other countries
involved and proceeded to indicate that it was of opinion
that the whole affair was political in character. However,
unlike the usual position with regard to political
offenders whereby the state of refuge refuses to surrender
them for trial, Kuwait announced that it intended surrendering these offenders to the Palestine Liberation
Organization to stand trial. Not even Kuwait has
recognized this Movement as the legitimate government
of a state, although it subscribes to the view of the
Rabat Conference of 1974 that this organization is the
proper representative of the Palestinian refugees and
in charge of all political activities undertaken on their
behalf. Whereas most countries which condemned the Rome
outrages were anxious to see the offenders brought to
trial in respect of these crimes, as well as for the
hijacking itself, Kuwait and the Arab spokesmen made it
clear that the surrender with which they were concerned
was aimed at bringing the men to trial for their crimes
against the Arab movement. The view was put forward that
the official spokesmen for the Arabs did not approve of
this particular outrage and regarded it as counter-
productive and thus an offence against Arab interests.
It may be true that trial on this ground might result
in a death sentence which might even be carried out,
whereas trial by Italy or one of the other countries
involved in respect of the crimes at Rome would almost
certainly result in a reprieve, perhaps even a pardon,
and almost certainly expulsion to some country of the
terrorists' own choice, as was the case with the terrorists sentenced to death in Greece in 1974 in respect of
the similar massacre at Athens airport. Nevertheless,
from the point of view of the rule of law and the
suppression and punishment of hijacking and terrorism,
it would be preferable that a trial should be held by
one of the countries really affected and the political

trimmings introduced by the Arab movement in this way ignored. Perhaps there will eventually be one country which will be prepared to stand up to the threats of blackmail being exercised against those who are the victims of hijackings; but until such time we might at least pretend that we are concerned with the judicial condemnation of common crimes rather than playing politics.

Towards the end of 1974, after the recognition of the Palestine Liberation Organization as the spokesman for the Palestinians and the acceptance of this fact by the General Assembly of the United Nations, Arab terrorists hijacked a British aircraft at Dubai and had it flown to Tunis. They demanded the release of convicted terrorists held in the Netherlands and in Egypt in return for the release of the aircraft and their hostages, one of whom, a German, they publicly murdered. They further demanded a guarantee that they would not be extradited or tried, or handed over to the Palestine Liberation Organization which had condemned their acts as treason against the Arab cause. At first it was believed that the Government of Tunis intended to disregard any undertakings it might have given, but it later declared that these commitments would be carried out as a matter of good faith - although it is difficult to appreciate what obligations are owed to those who have defied the rule of law and have secured the promises by way of blackmail involving the lives of innocent people. However, in December 1974 the terror-ists concerned were in fact handed over to the Palestine Liberation Organization, which announced its intention to bring them to trial. The way in which this was done looked as if subterfuges had been employed in order to save face, to serve political ideology and assuage world criticism. Tunis announced that the terrorists, together with their released comrades, had left the country "after

promising 'to put themselves at the disposal of the
P.L.O.'", which declared its intention to try them for
murder.[19] In view of the earlier announcement condemning
them as traitors to the Palestinian cause, it is not
clear whether this trial would be for murder qua murder,
or for murder as an instance of the betrayal of that
cause.

It has already been indicated that one of the questions
involved in considering acts of international hijacking
is whether such an offence can ever be treated as political. The general view is that when the alleged offence
involves both a political and a common law crime aspect,
the latter must be incidental to the former and in no
way overshadow it. If the crime is so outrageous that
its motive cannot be accepted as justifying what has
happened, many countries are unwilling to consider that
the criminal can claim that the political character of
his activities protects him from extradition. This has
probably been best expressed by the Swiss Federal
Tribunal in <u>Re Kavic, Bjelanovic and Arsenijevic</u>[20]
which resulted from the deviation of a Yugoslav passenger
aircraft to Switzerland. The deviation had been carried
out by three crew members in order to effect their flight
from Yugoslavia. In the court's view:

All the offences with which the accused are charged were
means to effectuate their escape abroad, and coincided
completely with that escape. The question must therefore
be examined whether that escape constituted a purely
political offence, [when extradition will not lie] ....
The purpose and motive of the acts with which the accused
are charged was to enable them to flee from a country
with whose regime they were not in agreement and where
they felt themselves to be watched and repressed....
That is not, however, enough to exclude the possibility
of extradition for these offences, it is also necessary
that their political character should outweigh their
common characteristics.... The Federal Tribunal [has
given] a restrictive interpretation to the concept of
relative political offences, and required, in particular,

that the act should be related to a general activity
directly aimed at the realization of political aims, and
should have been committed in the framework of a fight
for political power. This applies to the flight of a
political opponent from the country only if it is
intended to continue the fight for power from abroad....
That restrictive interpretation does not, however, bear
re-examination; it does not meet the intention of the
[Swiss Extradition] Law [of 1892], nor take account of
recent historical developments, such as the growth of
totalitarian States. In such States all political
opposition is suppressed and a fight for power is, if
not impossible from the start, at least practically
without any chance of success. Those who do not wish to
submit to the regime have no alternative but to escape
it by flight abroad.... This more passive attitude for
the purpose of escaping political constraint is no less
worthy of asylum than active participation in the fight
for political power used to be in what were earlier
considered to be normal circumstances. The spirit of
justice undoubtedly ascribes a political character to
such a flight abroad, and a liberalization of the practice of this Court, with a view to adjusting it to
recent developments, appears justified. In matters of
extradition in particular, the Court must not abandon that
spirit in favour of legalistic considerations, and must
take account of historical and political developments....
Recent practice has been too restrictive in making the
relative political character of an offence dependent
on its commission in the framework of a fight for
power. Such a character must also be attributed to
offences which were committed in order to escape the
constraint of a State which makes all opposition and,
therefore, the fight for power impossible. In this
connection there can also be applied the principle that
the relation between the purpose and the means adopted
for its achievement must be such that the ideals
connected with the purpose are sufficiently strong to
excuse, if not justify, the injury to private property,
and to make the offender appear worthy of asylum.
Freedom from constraint of a totalitarian State must
be regarded as an ideal in this sense. In the present
case the required relationship undoubtedly exists; for,
on the one hand, the offences against the other members
of the crew were not very serious, and, on the other,
political freedom and even existence of the accused
was at stake, and could only be achieved through the
commission of these offences.

Regardless of whether the sort of crime that was
committed at Rome and Dubai airports may be considered
as a political offence in the sense understood by the

Swiss Federal Tribunal, or whether it may be compared
with the desire to escape from a totalitarian regime to
freedom - as has been suggested, this offence was concerned with inter-Arab rivalries, even though the victims
were outsiders - it would appear beyond any doubt that
the large-scale character of the attack and the serious-
ness of the offences which were committed, as well as
the grave character of their consequences, would have
been sufficient to take this particular incident outside
the somewhat liberal interpretation of the Swiss court.
In view of the fact that even the hijacking of an empty
aircraft and embarking with it upon a non-scheduled
flight might, since it interferes with the expected
flight patterns, put other aircraft at risk, it might
well be arguable that hijacking even for the purpose of
flight in the sort of circumstances discussed by the
Swiss court is sufficient of a mixed crime to warrant
the trial of the hijacker, even though the punishment
might be mitigated because of its purpose. This attitude
can be seen in the decision of the Versailles Assize
Court in the Kay case[21]. Jean Kay was accused of
attempting to hijack a Pakistan airliner at Orly airport
in December 1971 in an attempt to fly medical supplies
to Bangladesh. The public prosecutor could not agree
that any hijacking, even with the highest motives,
could be condoned -

The taking of hostages leads only to the debasement of
man, which it turns into an object of bargain

but he recognized that the court could be charitable and
Kay received a five-year suspended sentence.

Of the more recent hijackings, especially those which
have been the most dramatic or which have allegedly
been concerned with the Middle East political situation,
many have placed large numbers of passengers at risk,
have resulted in the killing of hostages, and have on

occasion involved the needless destruction of the
aircraft. Invariably, the aircraft has not belonged
to the country from which the flight has been made,
while neither it nor the persons threatened or harmed
have been in any way involved with the country against
which the demonstration has purportedly been directed.
All these factors would suggest that international
hijackings are of so grave a character that the criminal
implications far outweigh any possibility of the act
being regarded as politically motivated.

A number of attempts have been made on both the
bilateral and the multilateral level to deal with hijacking and secure punishment of the hijackers. Nevertheless,
there seems to be a hesitancy in taking the steps
necessary to deny that hijackers might protect themselves
by alleging that their acts constituted political
offences and that, therefore, they were exempt from
extradition. By the Hague Convention for the Unlawful
Seizure of Aircraft[22] the contracting states undertook
to make hijacking punishable by severe penalties and
agreed that hijacking should be included as an extraditable offence in those treaties to which they were already
parties and in any such treaty signed in the future.
Since the Convention makes no mention of political
offences, it must be assumed that hijacking is to be
treated by the parties in the same way as every other
extraditable offence and so protected by any reference
in the treaty to the non-extraditability of political
offenders. On the other hand, Article 7 of the
Convention imposes an obligation on all parties ratifying
it,

without exception whatsoever and whether or not the
offence was committed in its territory, to submit
the case to its competent authorities for the purpose
of prosecution.

Presumably, therefore, even a political hijacker would

be liable to trial in the country in which he is, and that country would then be able to consider the political motivation as a ground for mitigation, even though the article stipulates that the decision shall be taken

in the same manner as in the case of an ordinary offence of a serious nature under the law of that State.

The Montreal Convention of 1971 to Discourage Acts of Violence against Civil Aircraft[23] sought to extend the possibility of criminal action against hijackers and the like, but it too has not dealt with the problem of political motivation, unless one argues that it does so by implication and, though silent, recognizes the possibility of the exemption. While Article 11 provides that the

Contracting States shall afford one another the greatest measure of assistance in connection with criminal proceedings brought in respect of the offences, the law of the State requested shall apply in all cases.

Even the most recent draft[24] proposed by the International Civil Aviation Organization and suggested as a new chapter to the 1944 Chicago Convention on International Civil Aviation deals with the situation in the same fashion, providing that while the obligation to extradite exists

extradition shall be subject to the other conditions provided by the law of the requested State,

and reiterates that while cooperation in the criminal field is to be afforded

the law of the State requested shall apply in all cases.

The difficulty with international agreements of the kind mentioned is that it invariably takes an undue length of time to secure the ratifications necessary to

377

bring any of them into force; that they tend to be
ratified by a very small group of states anyway; and
that some states are always willing to argue that certain
proposals must be approved because of special political
reasons, as for example the right of people involved
in so-called wars of national liberation to indulge in
virtually any activity they consider likely to advance
the cause. For this reason there are many who believe
that at present, and perhaps for the forseeable future,
action must be taken along bilateral lines. But even
in these cases one finds that the parties are unwilling
to make any departure from their established extradition
practices and to assert that hijackings cannot be
considered as political offences. Thus, the Canadian-
Cuban agreement of 1973[25] provides for the trial or
return of the offender "in conformity with its laws"
and the Cuban-United States Memorandum of Understanding
on the same issue is to the same effect.[26]

Even though the agreements referred to do not make any
reference to the fact that hijacking is a common crime
and the offender should be treated accordingly, and so
denied political asylum, they nevertheless do impose
an obligation upon the Parties that they shall treat
hijacking as a serious offence. In view of this there
is ground to consider that the approach of the Swiss
court should be remembered and the offence should be
measured by examining whether its criminal characteristics are more marked than its criminal.

But what is a political offence from the point of
view of the law of extradition? The case that has been
accepted for almost a century throughout the larger
part of the common law world - and has even had its
effect elsewhere - is <u>Re Castioni</u>[27]. Denman, J. laid
down that for an offence to be regarded as political
for the purpose of extradition proceedings,

378

it must at least be shown that the act is done in
furtherance of, done with the intention of assistance,
as a sort of overt act in the course of acting in a
political manner, a political rising, or a dispute
between two parties in the State as to which is to have
the government in its hands.... The question really
is, whether, upon the facts, it is clear that the man
was acting as one of a number of persons engaged in
acts of violence of a political character with a
political movement and rising in which he was taking
part.

Shortly after this decision was rendered, it was
held in Re Meunier[28] that an anarchist could not be a
political offender within the legal definition.
Cave, J. held that

to constitute an offence of a political character,
there must be two or more parties in the State, each
seeking to impose the Government of their own choice
on the other, and that, if the offence is committed by
one side or the other in pursuance of that object, it
is a political offence, otherwise not. In the present
case there are not two parties in the State, each seeking
to impose the Government of their own choice on the other;
for the party with whom the accused is identified...,
namely, the party of anarchy, is the enemy of all
Governments.

This decision is perhaps more topical than might have
been assumed some ten or twenty years ago. There is
increasing evidence that recent hijackings have been
the result of co-operative activities by terrorist
groups of varying nationalities, Japanese, Turkish,
American, Arab, and the like, who have come together
to give effect to each other's terroristic aims, almost
suggesting an attitude of 'terror for terror's sake'.[29]
There is also increasing evidence that, regardless of
the purpose for which political activists assert their
activism, the President of Lybia will support them in
his aim to embarrass and perhaps destroy the governments
of countries other than his own.[30] It sometimes seems
from the President's speeches that he is interested in
a social revolution and the redistribution of wealth

and will support any who profess to work to this end -
it has even been suggested that he is supporting both
Catholic and Protestant terrorist organizations in
Northern Ireland. This makes the decision in the
Malatesta case[31] of interest. The Swiss Federal Court
pointed out that the association with which the accused
was connected sought

the overthrow of the established political and social
order, and its replacement by another political and
economic system, namely anarchism. While it was true
that there was a clearly political end, the means by
which this was sought was not so much peaceful propaganda as by the use of violence, directed to overthrowing
the existing political system and redistributing the
economic wealth. Such an aim involves offences against
persons and property. Such an association is in reality
not a political organization, but a band of thieves and
brigands.

The attitude of Mathers, C.J. Manitoba was not so
different in Re Fedorenko (No.1).[32] The accused was a
member of the Russian Social Democratic Party who had
killed a watchman in a village under martial law. The
watchman had not known of the accused's party affilia-
tions but had investigated his identity as a stranger.
The Chief Justice inquired:

Was the crime of the accused committed in the furtherance of a political object? He belonged to the social
democratic party, whose object was, not only to alter
the form of government, but also to do away with private
ownership of property. A propaganda was carried on by
them throughout the country and numerous revolutionary
outrages were perpetrated by them.... [C]an it be said
that this killing was in furtherance of a political
object? I think not. Nor do I think the fact that the
crime of the accused would, in the demanding State, be
called a political crime and be tried by a special
tribunal make it a crime of a political character within
the meaning of the [Anglo-Russian Treaty, 1886]. The
crime of killing a policemen by a person in no way
identified with any political movement would in Russia
be so described, and would be tried by the same tribunal.

All these cases reflect the nineteenth century view

of democracy with political systems organized on the basis of reputable parties, with one in power and another seeking to overthrow it and take over the reins of government for itself. But it must not be thought that this view of political life is no longer acceptable by judicial tribunals, even though in many countries, as was made clear in the Swiss hijacking case, there is no longer any possibility of this type of political organization. In 1957, for example, the Chilean Supreme Court held in <u>Re Campara</u>[33] that

according to generally accepted principles, a political offence is one involving any attempt against the political organization of the State or the political rights of its citizens, that is, an attack upon the constitutional order of the country concerned. This definition also comprehends acts which have as their objective a change in the established political or social order of the country,

implying that the Chilean court might be more sympathetic to offenders like Meunier, Malatesta or Fedorenko than were the courts which tried them.

Perhaps the most comprehensive judicial statement in this field is to be found in the judgment of the Grenoble Appellate Tribunal in <u>Re Giovanni Gatti</u>:[34]

Political offences are those which are directed against the constitution of the Government and against sovereignty, which trouble the order established by the fundamental laws of the state and disturb the distribution of powers. Acts which aim at overthrowing or modifying the organization of the main organs of the state, or at destroying, weakening or bring into disrepute one of these authorities, or at exercising legitimate pressure on the play of their mechanism or on their general direction of the state, or which aim at changing the social conditions created for individuals by the constitution in one or all of its elements, are also political offences. In brief, what distinguishes the political crime from the common crime is the fact that the former only affects the political organizations of the state, the proper rights of the state, while the latter exclusively affects rights other than those of the state. The fact that the reasons of sentiment which prompted the offender to commit the offence belong to the realm of politics does not itself create a political offence. The offence does not derive its political character from the motive of the offender but from the nature of the rights it injures. The reasons on which non-extradition is based do not permit the taking into account of mere motives for the purpose of attributing to a common crime the character of a political offence.

An attempt to take into consideration the motives of the offender rather than the objective character of the offence was made by Goddard, L.C.J. in Re Kolczynski[35] arising from a mutiny on board a Polish ship, with the mutineers asserting that their action was politically motivated and that if they were returned to Poland they would be subjected to political persecution. The Lord Chief Justice said that

the revolt of the crew was to prevent themselves being persecuted for a political offence and... therefore the offence had a political character.

He pointed out that in the Polish Republic organized political movements were impossible, so that the seamen could not fall within the Castioni definition, but he was of opinion that the Castioni court was

not giving an exhaustive definition of the words of a political character ... [and he therefore felt free to hold that] the evidence about the law prevalent in the Republic of Poland today shows that it is necessary if only for reasons of humanity, to give wider and more generous meaning to the words we are now construing, which we can do without in any way encouraging the idea that ordinary crimes which have no political significance will be thereby excused.

The United States Circuit Court of Appeals in 1957 acknowledged that it was aware of this decision, but based its own findings on the Castioni definition pointing out that the language of that case had been adopted by American Courts.[36] Moreover, in a later hearing in the same matter,[37] the Commissioner used language which might have come straight from a nineteenth century judgment. Of the political offence, he said that

generally speaking it is an offense against the government itself or incident to political uprisings. It is
not a political offense because the crime was committed
by a politician. The crime must be incidental to and
from part of political disturbances. It must be in
furtherance of one side or another of a bona fide
struggle for political power.

This somewhat narrow acceptance of the Castioni definition does not accord with the attitude of the United States in 1950 when confronted with a hijacking from Czechoslovakia. On that occasion the government seemed to forecast the Kolczynski approach. Three Czech aircraft had been diverted while in flight and landed at an airfield in the United States Zone of Occupation in Germany. Czechoslovakia asked for the return of the aircraft and of the hijackers, accusing the latter of a variety of offences against the Czech Penal Code. For our purpose, the American comment that its extra-dition agreement with Czechoslovakia did not extend to the Occupation Zone may be ignored, but in its reply the United States declared:[38]

... it is clear that these individuals fled Czechoslovakia for political reasons by whatever means they could
find to escape. It has never been the practice of the
United States Government to take action which would
have the effect of subjecting political offenders to
criminal jurisdiction.... The United States Government
 pursuing a principle which has been followed since
1853 , therefore sees no reason to assist in the enforcement of Czechoslovak internal law by returning the
accused in this case. As a matter of comity, the United
States authorities endeavoured, of course, to return to
Czechoslovakia, as promptly as all necessary arrangements
could be completed, persons from the planes who expressed
a desire to return. The United States Government will
continue strictly to observe such standards of international conduct. Comity, on the other hand, could not
reasonably be construed to require the United States
authorities to arrange for the return of those who were

resolved to remain,[39]   In accordance with humanitarian
principles, the latter have been given the right of
political asylum.

The same approach was adopted soon after in the case of
a hijacked train.[40]

The liberal trend shown in Kolczynski was but short-
lived in England, and in 1962 there was a return to
the principle laid down in Castioni. Schtraks v. Government of Israel[41] arose from an Israeli request for the
return of an alleged child-kidnapper who contended that
the abduction was at the request of the child's grand-
father and related to the religious education of the
child, arguing that religious and educational issues
were political questions in Israel and that as a
political offender he should not be extradited. Lord
Reid referred to the political and philosophical views
prevailing at the time the English Extradition Acts
were enacted, and felt that in the instant case

there is nothing to indicate that the appellant
acted as he did in order to force or even promote a
change in government policy, or to achieve a political
objective of any kind.

Both Viscount Radcliffe and Lord Hodson referred to
Castioni, Meunier and Kolczynski, with the former
pointing out that the nineteenth century cases required
political motivation and contesting parties, and that
the matter had rested thus until the Polish Seamen's
case:

But the decision seems to me to show only that the
courts are unwilling to treat what was said in Re
Castioni as laying down any exhaustive definition of
'political offence'. Certainly it would have been
difficult to decide in favour of the fugitive in that
case if it were always necessary to find a 'disturbance'
in being reflecting an uprising, insurrection or other
struggle for State power. On the other hand, if...
the idea of 'political offence' is not altogether remote

from that of 'political asylum', it is easy to regard
as a political offence, an offence committed by someone
in furtherance of his design to escape from a political
regime which he found intolerable. I have no criticism
to make of the decision in ... Kolczynski, but the
grounds on which it was decided are expressed too
generally to offer much guidance for other cases in the
future.... The idea that lies behind the phrase
'offences of a political character' is that the fugitive
is at odds with the State that applies for his extradition on some issue connected with the political control
or government of the country. The analogy of 'political'
in this case is with 'political' in such phrases as
'political refugee', 'political asylum' or 'political
prisoner'. It does indicate... that the demanding
State is after him for reasons other than the enforcement of the criminal law in its ordinary,... its common
or international, aspect. It is this idea that the
judges were trying to express in ... Castioni and Meunier
when they connected the political offence with an
uprising, a disturbance, an insurrection, a civil war
or struggle for power: and... it is still necessary to
maintain the idea of that connection. It is not
departed from by taking a liberal view as to what is
meant by disturbance or those other words, provided
that the idea of political opposition as between
fugitive and requesting State is not lost sight of: but
it would be lost sight of ... if one were to say that
all offences were political offences, so long as they
could be shown to have been committed for a political
object with a political motive or for the furtherance
of some political cause or campaign. There may, for
instance, be all sorts of contending political organizations or forces in a country and members of them may
commit all sorts of infractions of the criminal law in
the belief that by so doing they will further their
political ends: but if the central government stands
apart and is concerned only to enforce the criminal law
that has been violated by these contestants, I see no
reason why fugitives should be protected by this country
from its jurisdiction on the ground that they are
political offenders. ... This case has evidently become
to some extent a political issue. But the evidence
does not suggest that the appellant's offences ... were
committed against, as a demonstration against any
policy of the government of Israel itself or that he
has been abetting those who oppose the Government...

Lord Hodson dealt with the issue somewhat peremptorily:

According to the Castioni test there must be either
in existence or in contemplation a struggle between the
State and the fugitive criminal. I prefer to adhere as

far as possible to the guidance which I find in the
Castioni case, judgment in which was delivered ...
not long after the passing of the first Extradition Act.
It may be that cases will arise as in the Polish Seamen's
case, where special considerations have to be taken into
account. In some modern States politics and justice
may be inextricably mixed, and it is not always easy,
for example, to say what amounts to a revolt against the
Government. No special feature exists in this case, and
I find no substance in the contention that extradition
should be refused because of the political character of
the offence charged....

Recently, Canadian courts have had occasion to deal

with extradition cases in which the offence charged

appeared to possess a 'political character', but in

which it was considered impossible to hold that the

offences concerned were of a political character in the

sense that the law requires for extradition to be denied.

Thus, in Re Commonwealth of Puerto Rico and Hernandez[42]

it was held, on the basis of Schtraks, that the killing

of a police officer during riots by members of a Puerto

Rican independence movement directed against the

activities of the R.O.T.C. on a university campus, as

distinct from the government as such, was not 'political':

The question in issue should be determined by looking
primarily at the events of the day and the actual circumstances of the murder. The actual political climate of
Puerto Rico at that time is of secondary interest. It
is important only if it is a predominant factor in the
circumstances of the murder. It is not relevant that
the act subsequently became a major political issue
if it was not of a predominantly political character
at the time of the act.... What took place ... was not
to overthrow the government but rather to force the
university authorities to divorce the R.O.T.C. from the
campus .... One cannot deny that political considerations were involved in the antagonism towards the
cadets, but I cannot feel persuaded that this could be
considered a political uprising against the government
or that the murder ... could be considered an act in
furtherance of a political uprising.

However, extradition was denied since the judge did not

consider there was sufficient evidence to identify the

accused as being involved. Moreover, in Re State of
Wisconsin and Armstrong,[43] concerning a charge of murder
and arson during campus rioting, it was held that the
burden of proof was upon the fugitive, and in the light
of Castioni, Fedorenko (No. 1) and Schtraks, this was
found not to be discharged:

The offences ... are not of a political character and
the proceedings are not taken with a view to prosecute
or punish the respondent for an offence of a political
character.

If one recalls the incidents that took place on certain
Canadian campuses, including the disturbance at the
University of British Columbia while the Prime Minister
of Singapore was there, and at Sir George Williams
University resulting in the destruction of computers
during a riot largely undertaken by West Indian students,
it is perhaps not surprising that the Canadian judges,
who like judges everywhere are affected by their environment, have taken the traditional view. This should be
compared with the somewhat more liberal attitude of the
German Federal Constitutional Court, when called upon to
interpret the constitutional right to enjoy asylum:[44]

The legislative history of Art. 16 shows that the right
of political asylum was understood as 'a right granted
to a foreigner who cannot continue living in his own
country because he is deprived of liberty, life or
property by the system prevailing there.' The concept
of political persecution must not be narrowly interpreted.
It is characterized by deep-seated socio-political and
ideological contrasts between states which have developed
basically different internal structures. There are a
number of states in which, for the purpose of enforcing
and securing political and social revolutions, the
power of the state is exercised in a manner contradictory
to the principles of a liberal democracy. Hence the
concept of political persecutee must not be limited to
so-called political offenders within the meaning of the
Extradition Law, i.e., to persons whose extradition is
demanded by reason of a criminal act as defined in that
law, but must be extended to persons prosecuted for
non-political offences 'where such persons, if extradited,

would be liable in their home country to suffer measures of persecution involving danger to life and limb or restrictions of personal liberty for political reasons.' A person can be a political persecutee even if he did not create the facts justifying fear of persecution prior to his coming to the Federal Republic. Such cases must, however, be scrutinized very carefully, for foreigners must not be encouraged to create subsequently the conditions for the right of asylum for the sole purposes of obtaining protection from punishment for an ordinary crime.

Even with this more extensive approach to the concept of a political offence, and even accepting the most liberal view of any adopted, including <u>Kolczynski</u>, it is clear that the courts of a variety of countries would not recognize acts of hijacking however highly motivated politically as constituting political offences of the kind that would warrant exemption from extradition. In every case, the offence has been construed as one that must be directed towards the overthrow of the governmental system of the country in which it has been committed, or else it must have been done as part of an attempt to escape from a territory in which political persecution of the fugitive was a reality or a justified fear. Invariably, the accused has been a national of the country seeking his return. In no case has it been possible for an offender to argue that the mere fact that there was a political purpose behind his offence, or that he was politically motivated in committing it, was sufficient to give the offence the necessary political <u>cachet</u>. However, in <u>Ex parte Shields</u>[45] the Dublin High Court refused to return an accused wanted in Northern Ireland for offences against the Firearms (Northern Ireland) Act. The offence was related to Irish Republican Army activities, and Butler J. held that it was, "if not a political offence, certainly connected with a political offence." While this might be considered a rational and functional approach to adopt, it did not appeal to the House of Lords which,

in Cheng v. Governor of Pentonville Prison[46] showed its
awareness of the proliferation of terroristic acts and
of the danger of treating as 'political', in the sense
required by extradition law, a politically motivated
crime committed in the territory of a state against which
that political motivation was not directed. A member
of a Taiwanese nationalist organization seeking to
overthrow Chiang Kai-Shek's regime in Taiwan had been
found guilty in the United States of complicity in an
attempt to murder Chiang's son who was his Vice-Premier.
The facts were reminiscent of those in Castioni, although
there was no intention to overthrow the government of
the United States, the country in which the crime had
been committed, but it was aimed at affecting and perhaps
changing that country's policy towards Taiwan. The
appellant had been denied asylum in Sweden and while
being escorted back to the United States became ill in
Britain, whence the United States sought his extradition.
Lord Simon of Glaisdale, with whom Lord Wilberforce
concurred, dissented from the judgment denying asylum.
In their view[47]

If [as appeared from Schtraks] ... the motive and purpose
of the offence is relevant and may be decisive, the
appellant's offence was certainly of a political
character.... It could hardly be gainsaid that the
crime ... was incidental to and formed part of a
political disturbance... and to some extent directed
against or involved with the policy of the United States.

A more traditional approach was adopted by the majority.
Lord Hodson held[48]

The contention that the offence was of a political
character can only be supported by giving the word
'political' a wider meaning than has hitherto been
given to it in this connection. The appellant was not
engaged in any political activity directed against the
United States. ... The object ... was wholly directed
to the overthrow of Chiang Kai-Shek's regime and to
establish a free and democratic Republic of Taiwan. The

objective was not hostile to the United States although
the movement sought to persuade the American Government
to change its policy towards Taiwan. There is no
authority which supports the argument of the appellant
that his political activity vis-à-vis the Taiwan regime
gives the crime committed in the United States which is
an offence against that state a political character
so as to prevent an extradition order being made....
[Applying Schtraks] political character ... connotes
the notion of opposition to the requesting state.

In the case of many of the aerial hijackings it has
been the effect upon innocent states or individuals,
involving the destruction of aircraft and the murder of
private individuals, that has most aroused international
interest. It is against such activities that endeavours
have been made to ensure international cooperation,
especially as these acts are only connected with political
activities from a propaganda point of view, being
intended to draw attention to the cause espoused by the
activists involved. While most of these have related
to the Arab-Israeli conflict, this has not always been
the case. Thus there have been two interesting cases
involving opponents of the 'colonels' regime' in Greece.
Olympic Airways v. Panichi and Giovine[49] arose from a
diversion of an Olympic Airways Boeing 707 by two Italians
as an operation against 'the fascist regime which rages
in Greece'. They were charged with violence, assault
and battery, illegal possession of arms and faced a
number of civil actions. Since they

let themselves be arrested without resistance... [and]
considering that after having first declared that they
belonged to an international resistance organization
which had as its objective provoking the fall of the
present Greek government, they later contended that they
had not acted under orders but had themselves taken the
decision to mount this operation of a non-violent
character [- they had used pistols merely to order the
pilot to return to Orly from which he had just taken
off -] to call the attention of public opinion to said
government

they were sentenced to almost nominal terms of imprisonment. The second case also concerned Olympic Airways,
on this occasion while on a domestic flight. Dr. Tsironis[50]
used a pistol threat to persuade the pilot 'in the name
of liberty and humanity' to fly to Albania, from where
he made his way to Sweden, which had been openly hostile
to Greece since the colonels' coup and which had invited
Andreas Papandreou to make Sweden his home. Tsironis
maintained that he, too, was a Greek patriot and should
receive similar treatment. In fact, the government
did give him a monthly allowance of about $2000, even
though under the Swedish Penal Code resident aliens
committing acts abroad could be tried in Sweden if the
act was an offence both abroad and in Sweden. After the
spate of hijackings in September 1970 proceedings were
instituted against Tsironis and two years after his
arrival in Sweden, where, as has been noted, he lived as
a government guest, he was tried and sent to jail for
3½ years, an extradition request from Greece having been
denied. Despite the incongruities of this particular
case it does illustrate what can be done even on a
unilateral basis and the Swedish practice is consistent
with that proposed in the various conventions that have
been drawn to deal with this problem.

In the light of the above arguments it should be clear
that even if it might be conceded that aerial hijackings
could be excluded from the scope of extradition because
they were more 'political' than 'criminal', it would
matter little in view of the fact that, as understood
today, the political motivation of the hijackings that
have been perpetrated in recent years cannot be considered
as 'political' in the sense in which that term is understood in State practice concerning extradition. In view
of the general horror that has been expressed, even
among Arab states, at some of the recent hijackings it

might be thought relatively easy to secure international
agreement on a convention outlawing hijackings and
providing for the trial and conviction of those concerned.
Even the I.C.A.O. conventions already agreed are deficient,
and any move to strengthen such measures is likely to be
met with the inevitable argument now being used by the
majority of the General Assembly of the United Nations
which has been effective in blocking, for example, any
practical measures against terrorism as such. Inevitably, the plea of self-determination[51] and the rights of
those involved to wage wars of national liberation will
be raised to ensure stalemate at best. Perhaps, hijacking
is one of those issues on which the like-minded will
eventually decide to go ahead despite the lack of
universality.

* Based on a paper first published in (1974) 22
Chitty's Law J. 135.

1 See, e.g., McWhinney (ed.), Aerial Piracy and
International Law (1971).

2 See VIII above.

3 See VI above.

4 Res. 217A (III).

5 See, e.g., Art. 2, Const. of Republic of Somalia
(1960), 1 Peaslee, Constitutions of Nations (1965)778.

6 See VII above.

7 Res. 2313 (XXII).

8 Res. 2200 (XXI) Annex.

9 See VIII above, and Report of Int. Law Assoc. Committee
on Legal Aspects of Asylum, Report of 51st (Tokyo)
Conference 1964, 246; Sinha, Asylum and International
Law (1971) 18,155; 8 Whiteman, Digest of International
Law, 681.

10 For details of some typical constitutional provisions
of this kind, see Green, 'The Nature of Political

Offences', (1964) 3 Solicitor Q. 213, 217-20; and for a fairly comprehensive list, Sinha, op.cit., 54, n.5.

11 For an interesting instance of avoidance of this, see the Eisler incident between the U.K. and the U.S.A. (1949), 9 Whiteman, op.cit., 129-39; Finch, The Eisler Extradition Case (1949) 43 Am. J. Int'l Law, 387; Green, 'Recent Practice in the Law of Extradition' (1953), 6 Curr. Legal Probl., 274, 284-7; see, also, R. v. Governor, Brixton Prison, ex p. Soblen [1963] 2 Q.B. 283 where a similar end was achieved by declaring the applicant an undesirable and denying him entry.

12 See Asylym Case [1950] I.C.J. 266.

13 See the debates of the Int'l Law Assoc. Conferences from Tokyo (1954) to The New York (1972).

14 9 Int'l Legal Materials 673 (italics added).

15 359 U.N.T.S. 273.

16 Dept. Ext. Aff., Canada, Communiqué No.92, 3 Dec.1971.

17 R.S.C. 1970, E-21.

18 [1952] I.R. 62, 18 Int. Law Rep. 336, 343.

19 The Times (London), 9 Dec. 1974; see, also, 253 The Economist (London, No.6849) 30 Nov. 1974, 13.

20 (1952) 19 Int. Law Rep. 371, 373-4.

21 The Times, 15 Oct. 1973. See, also, ibid., 15 Dec. 1973 for German conviction of Czech hijackers.

22 1970, 10 Int. Legal Materials 133, Arts. 2, 8.

23 Ibid., 1151.

24 1973, 12 ibid. 377, Arts. 87,89, not adopted at Nov. meeting, ibid. 1536.

25 Dept. Ext. Aff., Canada, Communiqé No.19, 15 Feb. 1973, Art. 1.

26 10 Feb. 1973, 12 Int. Legal Materials 370.

27 [1891] 1 Q.B. 156, 159.

28 [1894] 2 Q.B. 415, 419.

29   See, e.g., Green, The Nature and Control of International Terrorism (1974), Univ. Alta., Dept. Pol. Sci., Occasional Paper No. 1.

30   The Times, 17, 21 Jan. 1974.

31   (1891 - c. Papadatos, Le Délit Politique (1954) 84.

32   (1910) 17 C.C.C. 268.

33   24 Int. Law Rep. 518, 520.

34   (1947) 14 Ann. Dig. 145-6.

35   [1955] 1 Q.B. 540, 550, 551.

36   Karadzole v. Artukovic (1957) 257 F 2d 203.

37   U.S., ex rel. Karadzole v. Artukovic (1959) 170 F. Supp. 383, 392.

38   6 Whiteman, op.cit., 808-11.

39   This attitude should be compared with the law concerning prisoners of war, see Geneva Convention on Ps.W. (1949) 75 U.N.T.S. 135, Art. 18, as affected by Art.7; see, also, Baxter,'Asylum for Prisoners of War', (1950) 30 Brit.Y.B.Int'l Law 489; Mayda, The Korean Repatriation Problem and International Law' (1953), 47 Am.J.Int'l Law 414; de Visscher, Théories et Réalités en Droit International Public (1970), 207; Bethell, The Last Secret (1974).

40   Op.cit., n.38, 811-2.

41   [1964] A.C. 556, 584, 591-2, 612.

42   (1972) 30 D.L.R. (3d) 260,268 (per Honeywell, Co.Ct.J., Ontario), unaffected as to substance 30 D.L.R.(3d) 613 (Fed.C.A.).

43   (1972) 28 D.L.R.(3d) 513,520 (per Weisberg,Co.Ct.J., Ontario), unaffected as to substance, 32 D.L.R. (3d) 265 (Fed.C.A.).

44   4 Feb. 1959, summarized (1960) 54 Am.J.Int'l Law 416,417-8.

45   The Times, 5 Dec. 1973.

46   [1973] 2 All E.R. 204.

[47] At 215, 220, 221.

[48] At 206-7 (Lord Diplock and Salmon to same effect, 209, 223).

[49] (1969) Cour d'Appel, Paris - report in Lowenfeld, Aviation Law (1972) VII-36.

[50] (1971) City Court, Stockholm (ibid., VII-34).

[51] See V above.

X

AFTERMATH OF VIETNAM: WAR LAW AND THE SOLDIER*

I never expect a soldier to think
(Shaw: The Devil's Disciple, Act 3).

The Contracting Powers shall issue
instructions to their armed land forces
which shall be in conformity with the Regulations respecting the laws and customs of
war on land
(Hague Convention IV (1907) Respecting
the Laws and Customs of War on Land, Art.1(1)).

According to the criminal law of most countries the
ordinary citizen is presumed to know the law and
ignorance provides no excuse. To some extent, in the
Anglo-American system at least, a somewhat similar
approach is adopted even where the civil law is concerned, for so much of civil liability depends upon the
views of that imaginary - and perhaps imaginative -
person the ordinary reasonable man, the man on the
Clapham omnibus. This robot who serves as a standard
of behaviour has made his appearance in every country
to which the common law has been exported, although in
some areas local magistrates have realised how unreal
such a tertiis comparationis is.[1] To some extent it
would seem that a similar burden of knowledge is placed
upon the ordinary soldier in so far as the law of war
is concerned.[2]

The 1974 Caracas conference on the law of sea, together
with the failure of the two earlier Geneva Conferences
to decide upon the width of the territorial sea; the

endeavours of the International Law Commission to
codify a variety of rules of international law; the
impossibility of drawing up an effective convention on
the suppression of international terrorism and the
punishment of terrorists; the inability to settle upon
a really satisfactory definition of aggression; conflicts
as to the rules concerning state succession as well as
expropriation of private property and compensation
therefor ; the statement of the Prime Minister of
Canada when amending the Canadian declaration accepting
the compulsory jurisdiction of the World Court that the
law was unclear and insufficient;[3] controversies as to
the use of deleterious gases for controlling riots, even
when directed towards achieving national liberation, and
as to the meaning of wars of national liberation; and
incessant debates as to the true meaning of self-
determination, all indicate how complex international
law is and how difficult it would be today for anyone
dogmatically to state that he knows the law, or that
the ordinary man could be presumed to know it. In so
far as the law of war is concerned, the situation is
still not so very different from what it was in 1908
when Holland wrote[4]

The conduct of warfare is governed by certain rules,
commonly spoken of as 'the laws of war', which are
recognized as binding by all civilized nations. These
rules, which derive their origin partly from sentiments
of humanity, partly from the dictates of honourable
feeling, and partly from considerations of general
convenience, have grown up gradually, and are still
in process of development. They have existed, till
comparatively recent times, only as a body of custom,
preserved by military tradition and in the works of
international jurists. Their authority has been
derived from the unwritten consent of nations, as
evidenced by their practice.

On many points, the rules of international law which
relate to war on land have still to be gathered from
unwritten custom and tradition; but, within the last
forty years, attempts have been made to deal with the

topic in a more authoritative manner.

In the first place, many nations, following the example set by the United States in 1863, have issued instructions to their respective armies, in accordance with what have been supposed by the several Governments to be the rules in question. These instructions are, of course, author- itative only for the troops of the nation by which they are issued, and differ considerably one from another.

But something more was long felt to be desirable. In the second place, therefore, attempts were made, with varying success, to systematize the laws of war by international discussion, and to procure the general acceptance of a uniform code of those laws by internation- al agreement. Thus it has come to pass that the greater bulk of the rules applicable to this topic, as newly defined and amplified by conferences of delegates duly accredited by the various Powers, have now been expressed in diplomatic Acts, which have received the formal assent of so large a number of States recognized as members of the Family of Nations, as to constitute, beyond question, a body of written International Law, of general application, except on a few points, as against a few dissentient Powers.

Holland was much impressed by the achievements of the Hague Conferences of 1899 and 1907, especially by Hague Convention IV and the Regulations attached thereto, and one might assume that when he was writing, so soon after the Conference, there was some basis for his reliance upon the provisions for enforcement. Although Article 1 lays a duty upon the contracting parties to "issue instructions to their armed land forces which shall be in conformity with the Regulations respecting the laws and customs of war on land", the Convention does not impose any personal liability on the individual member of the armed forces. Instead, Article 3 stipulates that "a belligerent party which violates the provisions of the said Regulations shall, if the case demands, be liable to pay compensation. It shall be responsible for all acts committed by persons forming part of its armed forces." It would appear from this that it was for each belligerent to lay down the manner in which individual members of the forces infringing

the Regulations were to be punished as a matter of
military discipline or national criminal law. On
the other hand, it is provided in the Preamble that

Until a more complete code of the laws of war has been
issued, the High Contracting Parties deem it expedient
to declare that, in cases not included in the Regulations
adopted by them, the inhabitants and the belligerents
remain under the protection and the rule of the
principles of the law of nations, as they result from
the usages established among civilized peoples, from
the laws of humanity, and the dictates of the public
conscience.

This broad guiding principle seems to underlie the
attitude of military tribunals when faced with persons
accused of having committed war crimes by breaching the
rules of law, and international and national tribunals
alike have not hesitated to try such persons on the
basis of international law. Such an assumption of
jurisdiction is, of course, easy when the accused is a
member of the armed forces of the nation whose courts
are involved. Then it is possible to try him in
accordance with military law or the ordinary criminal
law, for most countries operate on the basis that while
their armed forces may be under special laws relating
to the armed forces, they nevertheless remain subject
to the ordinary criminal law as well, even though the
trial may be conducted by a special tribunal. As
regards those accused of war crimes who belong to
allied or enemy forces, the only basis of jurisdiction
in the absence of specific treaties is that stemming
from the general duty and interest to uphold the rule
of law, resulting "from the usages established among
civilized peoples, from the laws of humanity, and the
dictates of the public conscience."

It is one thing to make broad statements of this kind,
but they leave open complex issues as to the definition

of civilized peoples. This problem is not as futile as it may appear. After all, among the 'sources' of international law listed by Article 38 of the Statute of the World Court are the "general principles of law recognized by civilized nations." In the first place, while much has been written on the matter,[5] it would be difficult to decide what are general principles of law. Perhaps all that can really reasonably be said, allowing for varying environments, ideologies and ways of life, is that it is a general principle of law that culpable or unjustifiable homicide constitutes a criminal offence. It is even more difficult to define civilization and civilized conduct.[6] It is an accepted rule of the international law of war that poison is a forbidden weapon and that its use constitutes a war crime. Does this mean that the aborigine who uses a poison-tipped dart and blow-pipe, and who kills the enemy at whom he fires, is less civilized and more of a criminal than those who poison the atmosphere by releasing high explosives or nuclear bombs over a crowded city, when their only victims are likely to be civilians, for their enemies, at least the political leaders among them, are probably safe from harm in deep bomb-proof shelters? In this connection reference should be made to the United States Navy and Army Field Manuals. A note appended to Section 600 of the Naval Manual expressly states[7]

Unless restricted by customary or conventional inter-national law, belligerents legally are permitted to use any means of conducting hostilities. Article 22 of the Regulations annexed to Hague Convention No. IV (1907), Respecting the Laws and Customs of War on Land, states: "The right of belligerents to adopt means of injuring the enemy is not unlimited." This article, which refers to weapons and means of warfare, is merely an affirmation that rules of warfare are restricted by conventional (treaty) and customary international law. Although immediately directed to the conduct of land warfare, the principle embodied in Article 22 of the Hague Regulations is applicable equally to the conduct of naval warfare.

Commenting upon this, Tucker has said:[8]

... The guiding principle in a consideration of the rules governing the weapons and methods of warfare is that in the absence of restrictions imposed either by custom or by convention, belligerents are permitted in their mutual relations to use any means in the conduct of hostilities.... Historically, it is true that in the development of the means of waging hostilities it has been frequently asserted - both by governments and by writers on the law of war - that the introduction of a novel weapon or method must be regarded as unlawful until such time as expressly permitted by a specific rule of custom or convention. To the extent that such assertions have been based upon the alleged principle that what is not expressly permitted in war is thereby prohibited, they must be regarded as unfounded.

It is not uncommon, however, that claims as to the illegality of a novel weapon or method of war have been based upon the quite different premise that the method or weapon in question violates some general principle of the customary law of war; that although not expressly forbidden by a specific rule of custom or convention, the disputed means nevertheless falls within the purview of the prohibitions contained in one or more of these general principles. The validity of this latter claim has occasionally been obscured by its identification with the unwarranted assertion that what is not expressly permitted in war is thereby prohibited. In fact, what ought to be contended is that the lawfulness of the weapons and methods of war must be determined not only by the express prohibitions contained in specific rules of custom and convention but also by those prohibitions laid down in the general principles of the law of war....

... Recent experience has made it quite clear that the general principles of the law of war depend for their application upon standards which are themselves neither self-evident nor immutable. Hence, it is not merely the application of general principles to varying circumstances that is in question but the very meaning of the principles that are to be applied. It will be apparent, for example, that the scope of the immunity to be granted non-combatants must depend very largely upon the meaning given to the concept of military objective. But the concept of military objective will necessarily vary as the character of war varies.[9] And

even if it were possible today to enumerate with
precision those targets that could be regarded as
constituting legitimate military objectives there would
still remain the problem of determining the limits of
the 'incidental' or 'indirect' injury that admittedly
may be inflicted upon the civilian population in the
course of attacking military objectives. The answer
to the latter problem may largely depend, in turn, upon
the kinds of weapons that are used to attack military
objectives, including weapons whose legal status is
itself a matter for determination in accordance with
these same general principles.

This statement acquires fuller meaning in the light

of some of the provisions in the Army Field Manual on

the Law of Land Warfare, especially when compared with

the British counterpart:

35. Atomic Weapons.
The use of explosive 'atomic weapons', whether by air,
sea or land forces, cannot as such be regarded as
violative of international law in the absence of any
customary rule of international law or international
convention restricting their employment.

In contrast to this, the British Manual of Military

Law[10] says that the use of such weapons is governed by

'general principles', including "dictates of humanity,

morality, civilization and chivalry."

36. Weapons Employing Fire.
The use of weapons which employ fire, such as tracer
ammunition, flamethrowers, napalm, and other incendiary
agents, against targets requiring their use is not
violative of international law. They should not,
however, be employed in such a way as to cause unnecessary suffering to individuals.

The British Manual appears to be somewhat stricter,

stating that, in the light of the practice of the

belligerents in the Second World War,

the use of tracer and incendiary ammunition ... must
be considered to be lawful provided it is directed
solely against inanimate military targets (including
aircraft [-unmanned and on the ground only?]). The

use of such ammunition is illegal if directed solely
against combatant personnel.[11]

38. Gases, Chemicals, and Bacteriological Warfare
The United States is not a party to any treaty, now in
force, that prohibits or restricts the use in warfare
of toxic or nontoxic gases, of smoke or incendiary
materials, or of bacteriological warfare.... [While
t]he Geneva Protocol 'for the prohibition of the use in
war of asphyxiating, poisonous or other gases, and of
bacteriological methods of warfare'... has been ratified
or adhered to by and is now effective between a considerable number of States..., the United States Senate
has refrained from giving its advice and consent to the
ratification of the Protocol by the United States, and
it is accordingly not binding on this country.

While this was the United States view, the British
Manual implied[12] on the basis of the ban on poison, as
well as the Geneva Protocol, that such weapons are
illegal, and in addition considered them unlawful as
causing 'unnecessary suffering'. But the U.S. Manual
is important as illustrating the typical attitude of a
country which did not consider the Protocol to be
declaratory of customary law and is by no means unique.[13]
The American approach to poison is further illustrated
by the comment to paragraph 37 of the Manual concerning
the ban on poison in the Hague Regulations:

The foregoing rule does not prohibit measures being
taken to dry up springs, to divert rivers from their
courses, or to destroy, through chemical or bacterial
agents harmless to man, crops intended solely for
consumption by the armed forces (if that fact can be
determined).

In this connection it may be as well to mention the
position of the Department of Defense with regard to
the destruction of crops through chemical agents, as
reported to the Senate Committee on Foreign Relations[14]
when considering ratification of the Geneva Protocol in
1971, although ratification did not take place until
December 1974. According to the General Counsel of the
Department:

It is our opinion and that of the Judge Advocate Generals of the Army, Navy and Air Force that neither the Hague Regulations nor the rules of customary international law applicable to the conduct of war and to the weapons of war prohibit the use of antiplant chemicals for defoliation or the destruction of crops, provided that their use against crops does not cause such crops or food to be poisoned [- it would be interesting to know how this is to be avoided other than by complete destruction of the crop in question -] nor cause human beings to be poisoned by direct contact, and such use must not cause unnecessary destruction of enemy property.

The standard of lawfulness, with respect to the use of this agent either as a defoliant or as a means to destroy crops, under the laws of war, is the same standard which is applied to other conventional means of waging war.... Hence, in order to be unlawful, the use of a weapon in the conduct of war must either be prohibited by a specifically agreed-upon rule, or its use must be such as would offend the general principle of humanitarianism, that is to say, such as would cause unnecessary destruction of property or unnecessary human suffering [- many would now include long-term ecological damage.] ...

The discussion in paragraph 37 of the Manual [regarding the Hague Regulation ban on poison and poisoned weapons] is based on the standard set forth above to the effect that the prohibition against the use of one type of weapon, i.e., poison or poisoned weapons, does not affect any prohibition on the use of other weapons and, in particular, it does not prohibit the use of chemical herbicides for depriving the enemy of food and water. This discussion does not regard chemical herbicides harmless to man, as poison or poisoned weapons, for if they had been so considered, their use against crops intended solely for consumption by the enemy's armed forces would clearly have been prohibited by Article 23 (a) of the Hague Regulations [- in 1907?]. As the discussion points out, such a use does not fall within the prohibition [- and since we say it does not, _ergo_ it does not].

We therefore believe that the correct interpretation of paragraph 37 (b) is that the use of chemical herbicides, harmless to man, to destroy crops intended solely for consumption by the enemy's armed forces (if that fact can be determined) is not prohibited by Article 23(a) or any other rule of international law. It involves an attack by unprohibited means against legitimate military objectives. But an attack <u>by any means</u> [sic] against crops intended solely for consumption by noncombatants

not contributing to the enemy's war effort would be
unlawful for such would not be an attack upon a
legitimate military objective.

Before continuing to cite from this Opinion, it might
be as well to mention the view of Major General Cramer,
Judge Advocate General in 1945, in a memorandum on
destruction of crops by chemicals:[15]

... the use of chemical agents, whether in the form of
a spray, powder, dust or smoke, to destroy cultivations
or retard their growth, would not violate any rule of
international law prohibiting poison gas; upon condition,
however, that such chemicals do not produce poisonous
effects upon enemy personnel, either from direct
contact, or indirectly from ingestion of plants and
vegetables which have been exposed thereto.... The
proposed target of destruction, enemy crop cultivation,
is a legitimate one, inasmuch as a belligerent is
entitled to deprive the enemy of food and water, and to
destroy his sources of supply whether in depots, in
transit on land, or growing in his fields....

Such is my conclusion, reached after considerable
research, and I believe it to be sound. However, I
believe I should point out the possibility that the
Japanese may come to or pretend to come to an opposite
conclusion and invoke such use of these chemical agents
as an excuse for retaliatory measures.

To return to the 1971 Statement by the General Counsel:

Where it cannot be determined whether crops were
intended solely for consumption by the enemy's armed
forces, crop destruction would be lawful if a reasonable
inquiry indicated that the intended destruction is justified by military necessity under the principles of
Hague Regulation 23(g) [- the destruction must be
'imperatively demanded by the necessities of war'-],
and that the devastation occasioned is not disproportionate to the military advantages gained....

The Geneva Protocol of 1925 adds no prohibition relating
to either the use of chemical herbicides or to crop
destruction.... [A]ny attempt by the United States to
include such agents within the Protocol would be the
result of its own policy determination, amounting to a
self-denial of the use of such weapons. Such a determination is not compelled by the 1907 Hague Regulations, the
Geneva Protocol of 1925 or the rules of customary
international law.

It is universally recognized that the laws of war leave much to the discretion of the military commander. They reflect the principles discussed in this opinion. But in reflecting their application, the rules themselves have gained their content and origin in the practice of States engaged in war, and, in particular, have arisen out of their reciprocal tolerance of what conduct was considered legitimate and what was not.

The extracts quoted above clearly indicate how subjective some of the relevant decisions are and leave the way open for divergences among states, whether belligerent or not. In view of the comment that the rules of war 'have arisen out of their reciprocal tolerance' it raises the problem whether the potential divergences of behaviour by the United States indicate that that country is not civilized, assuming that the rest of the world adopts a different standpoint, or whether, since the United States is civilized, any rule regarding the use of poison or chemical destruction of crops is clearly not a general principle of law, for if it were it would be recognized by the United States as a civilized country. It would appear, therefore, that the most that can be said of general principles of law recognized by civilized nations is that this concept merely refers to those principles of law which are generally recognized by ourselves and those whom we regard as civilized. From the point of view of the member of the armed forces the situation is serious, for he may well find himself acting in a way, in the ordinary course of battle, whether on his own initiative or in compliance with an order, which is regarded by his own state as fully in accordance with the rules of international law concerning war. However, the same conduct may well be considered illegal by the enemy, and if he were to fall into the latter's hands he could easily face a trial for war crimes arising out of that conduct.

Since it is often alleged by those who criticise war

crimes trials as examples of vindictiveness and
"victors' justice" that the members of one's own armed
forces are never tried for war crimes, it is relevant
from our point of view to mention the position as
expressed by international and municipal war crimes
tribunals, as well as by courts trying members of their
own forces charged with offences under their own criminal law which if committed by the enemy would have been
treated as war crimes, for in such cases there is no
need to resort to international law as the basis for
jurisdiction. One of the problems that arises in
connection with the duty of a soldier to comply with
the law flows from the conflict between the demands of
the law and the obligation upon him to obey the orders
of his superiors. The position under the common law
is made clear by such cases as <u>Axtell</u>,[16] tried for his
part as one of the sentries on duty at the execution
of Charles I, He

> justified that all he did was as a soldier, by the command
> of his superior officer, whom he must obey or die. It
> was resolved that was no excuse, for his superior was
> a traitor, and all that joined with him in that act
> were traitors, and did by that approve the treason;
> and where the command is traiterous, there the obedience
> to that command is also traiterous

and must evidently be known as such by those to whom it
is addressed and who comply therewith. A somewhat
similar decision was rendered much more recently by the
Federal Supreme Court of the Federal Republic of
Germany, although direct knowledge was more in point
here. Despite its name, the <u>War Crimes (Preventive
Murder)(Germany) Case</u>[17] was a trial for murder under
German law, although questions of international law
were discussed and had the accused been an alien the
charge would have been for war crimes. The appellant
contended that the lower court

did not sufficiently ascertain the facts as to whether
the divisional commander knew he was giving an order to
commit a crime, and as to whether the accused was
aware of the mens rea of the divisional commander,
[but this argument] is irrelevant. ... Such ignorance
of the law as a military superior may be guilty of
does not free the person who received the order from
individual responsibility if he carries out an order
which he himself knows to be criminal. This applies
all the more where, as here, the divisional commander
was an engineer and the accused a lawyer.

On the other hand, one does not expect soldiers in
the field to carry a law library around with them, and
it is probably doubtful if units in action would even
have access to any basic textbook in international law,
and possibly not even to the Hague Regulations. However,
courts have a tendency to assume a certain amount of
knowledge as to what is right and what is wrong even
in these circumstances. Thus, in Chief Military
Prosecutor v. Melinki[18] the Israeli tribunal pointed
out that while a soldier can be held responsible for
any breach of the criminal law,

you cannot demand from a soldier to clarify for himself,
as soon as he gets a command from his commander and
just on receiving it, whether the command is legal from
all points of view.... The discipline of the army and
the supremacy of the law balance each other and also
complement one another. There is no contradiction
between them, and each has to be kept intact without
detracting from the other.

The subordinate soldier must seek

to interpret the feeling of law which is part of every
man's conscience because he is a human being, although
he is not familiar with a book of law.... Because of the
special circumstances in which a man, who should obey
the orders given to him by a superior authority, finds
himself, the lawgiver excuses him of not knowing the
command is illegal, only if the illegality does not
reach the state of 'manifestly illegal'.... An average
soldier could detect a clearly illegal order without
asking a legal advisor or without looking at a book of
law. These requirements of the law impose moral and

legal responsibility on every soldier regardless of rank.... It is the duty of each soldier to examine, according to his conscience, the legality of the commands given to him....

In order to deprive a defendant of the plea of 'justification', there is no need to prove that while obeying the order it was clear and obvious to the defendant that it was illegal, but the court has to be convinced that the order that was given was clearly and obviously illegal for every man of average common sense.... If the defendant believed that the order was clearly lawful, it will not help him if the order was not reasonable, which means justified from an objective point of view....

The legal issue is whether from the point of view of the defendant, which is entirely personal and different for each one, the illegality of the given order was clear and obvious, not from the point of view of a 'soldier of average common sense' in the position of the defendant....

The distinguishing mark of a 'manifestly unlawful order' should fly like a black flag above the order given, as a warning saying 'Prohibited'. Not formal unlawfulness, hidden or half-hidden, not unlawfulness discernible only by the eyes of legal experts, is important here, but a flagrant and manifest breach of the law, definite and unnecessary unlawfulness appearing on the face of the order itself, the clearly criminal character of the acts to be done, unlawfulness piercing the eye and revolting the heart, be the eye not blind nor the heart stony and corrupt - that is the measure of 'manifest unlawfulness' required to release a soldier from the duty of obedience upon him and make him criminally responsible for his acts.

This judgment and these comments were approved in the Eichmann case, and it is clear that the Israeli judges are convinced that certain acts are so clearly unlawful that the subordinate is obliged to disobey any order to commit them, and that he needs no law book to help him in deciding on the lawfulness of the order and presumably of the consequential actions.

American jurisprudence, too, presents instances illustrative of the issues under discussion, with most of the cases revolving around the legality of orders

410

received. As long ago as 1867 in McCall v. McDowell[19]
Deady D.J. pointed out that

The first duty of a soldier is obedience, and without
this there can be neither discipline nor efficiency in
an army. If every subordinate officer and soldier
were at liberty to question the legality of the order
of the commander, and obey them or not as they may
consider them valid or invalid, the camp would be turned
into a debating school, where the precious moment for
action would be wasted in wordy conflicts between the
advocates of conflicting opinions.... As a matter of
abstract law, it may be admitted that ultimately the
law will justify a refusal to obey an illegal order.
But this involves litigation and controversy alike
injurious to the best interests of the inferior, and
the efficiency of the public service.... True, cases
can be imagined, where the order is so palpably
atrocious as well as illegal, that one must instinctively
feel that it ought not to be obeyed, by whomever given....

There is no need to loiter over the series of United
States decisions which have been concerned with orders
which were manifestly unlawful,[20] but instead to consider
some of the decisions arising from United States military
operations in Korea and Vietnam. U.S. v. Kinder[21]
involved a charge of homicide arising from the killing
of a civilian prisoner, who was not resisting, violent,
attempting to escape or to commit any offence. Apparently
the order was given to discourage other local civilians
from entering the prohibited area in which the deceased
was killed and to boost troop morale. The Board of
Review considered that

the superior officer issuing the order was fully aware
of its illegality... and maliciously and corruptly
issued the unlawful order. ... [No justification will
lie if the homicide is the result of an order] manifestly
beyond the scope of the superior officer's authority
and ... so obviously and palpably unlawful as to admit
of no reasonable doubt on the part of a man of ordinary
sense and understanding .... [T]he accused was aware
of the criminal nature of the order, not only from the
palpably illegal nature of the order itself, but from
the surreptitious circumstances in which it was necessary
to execute it.... Of controlling significance ... is

the manifest and unmistakable illegality of the order.... Human life being regarded as sacred, moral, religious and civil law proscriptions against its taking existing throughout our society, we view the order as commanding an act so obviously beyond the scope of authority of the superior officer and so palpably illegal on its face as to admit of no doubt of its unlawfulness to a man of ordinary sense and understanding.... In our view no rational being of the accused's age [20], formal education [grade 11] , and military experience [two years] could have ... considered the order lawful. Where one obeys an order to kill ... for the apparent reason of making [the] death an example to others, the evidence must be strong indeed to raise a doubt that the slayer was not aware of the illegality of the order.... The inference of fact is compelling ... that the accused complied with the palpably unlawful order fully aware of its unlawful character.... [As to the defence argument] that the accused was mistaken in law as to legality of the order of his superior officer, the defense fails for a prerequisite of such defense is that the mistake of law was an honest and reasonable one and ... the evidence ... justifies the inference that the accused was aware of the illegality.

The war crimes court which heard the Einsatzgruppen case[22] had held that soldiers were not automata but reasoning agents, and the Review Board adopted this view:

... a soldier or airman is not an automaton but a 'reasoning agent' who is under the duty to exercise judgement in obeying the orders of a superior officer to the extent, that where such orders are manifestly beyond the scope of the issuing officer's authority and are so palpably illegal on their face that a man of ordinary sense and understanding would know them to be illegal, then the fact of obedience to the order of a superior officer will not protect a soldier for acts committed pursuant to such illegal orders...

Even before the My Lai incident drew attention to some of the infractions of the laws of war that were being committed by American forces - and probably not by them alone - in Vietnam, other Vietnam incidents had resulted in courts martial of United States military personnel. In U.S. v. Keenan[23] it was held that not even the fact that the actions involved were in keeping with the training received by the acccused would excuse

412

obedience to an order palpably illegal on its face.   It
was reiterated in U.S. v. Griffen[24]   that "the killing
of a docile prisoner taken during military operations
is not justifiable homicide", for an order to kill such
a person is "so palpably illegal on its face as to admit
of no doubt of its unlawfulness to a man of ordinary sense
and understanding."

The first of the My Lai trials was that of Sergeant
Hutto who was acquitted, but the statement of law in
the Instructions given by the presiding Military Judge
to the court members is of interest:[25]

... under the facts standing before this court, that
order ... was unlawful. ... Determination ... that that
order was illegal, does not resolve the issue ... whether
or not the accused was justified in his actions because
he acted in obedience to orders. You must resolve from
the evidence and the law whether or not the order ...
was manifestly illegal on its face, or if you are not
satisfied beyond a reasonable doubt that the order was
manifestly illegal on its face, whether or not the
order, even though illegal ... was known to the accused
to be illegal or that by carrying out the illegal order
[he] was committing an illegal and criminal act.

... [A] member of the United States Army is not and may
not be considered, short of insanity, an automaton,
but may be inferred to be a reasoning agent who is under
a duty to exercise moral judgment in obeying the orders
of a superior officer.

... [A]n order ... is unlawful if it directs the commission of a crime under United States law or under the
law of war....

... Acts of a subordinate in compliance with his supposed
duty or orders are justifiable or excusable and impose
no criminal liability, unless the superior's order is
manifestly unlawful or unless the accused knew the
order to be unlawful or that by carrying out the order
the accused knew he was committing an illegal act.

... [A]n order is 'manifestly unlawful', if under the
same or similar circumstances, a person of ordinary
sense and understanding would know it to be unlawful...
[U]nless you find beyond a reasonable doubt that the

order given to the accused ... was manifestly unlawful...,
you must acquit the accused unless you find beyond a
reasonable doubt that the accused had actual knowledge
that the order was unlawful or that obedience to that
order would result in the commission of an illegal
criminal act.

The fact that the law of war has been violated pursuant
to an order of a superior authority, does not deprive
the act in question of its character as a war crime,
nor does it constitute a defense in the trial of an
accused individual, unless he did not know and could
not have been expected to know that the order was
unlawful.

...[O]bedience to <u>lawful</u> military orders is the sworn
duty of every member of the armed forces; the soldier
cannot be expected in conditions of war discipline to
weigh scrupulously the legal merits of the orders
received and certain rules of warfare may be controversial.
Thus a subordinate is not criminally liable for acts
done in obedience of an unlawful order which is not
manifestly unlawful on its face, unless the subordinate
has actual knowledge of the unlawfulness of the order
or the unlawfulness of its demands. In the absence of
such knowledge the subordinate must be considered duty
bound to obey the order and he cannot properly be held
criminally accountable for acts done in obedience to
what he supposed was a lawful order.

Knowledge on the part of the accused ... may be proved
by circumstantial evidence.... The tactical situation
and pressures upon the soldiers of 'C' Company prior to
and during the incident ... are significant in consideration of the knowledge of the accused as to the legality
of the order only insofar as you are satisfied that he
was aware of these facts, a determination you should
make based upon your own training, experience and
common sense.... [T]he accused characterized this
shooting by stating 'It was murder'.... [H]e didn't
agree with all the killing but he was doing it because
he was told to do it; while he didn't approve all the
killings, he did because he was ordered to do it....

Sergeant Hutto was acquitted, but at a later date
Colonel Howard, the presiding Military Judge, stated[26]
that

while he had ruled that the order in question was
illegal, he had after labored consideration, stopped
short of ruling that it was <u>manifestly</u> so, even though

it was his opinion that such an extreme ruling as to the latter point would have been supportable at the appellate level.

This confirms how subjective may be the ultimate decision as to whether an unlawful act is 'manifestly' so, while the evidence as to the facts, including the accused's own opinion as to the nature of the killings and the refusal of some of his comrades to participate, indicates the difficulty involved in assessing any particular accused's knowledge of what is in fact illegal.

The most notorious of the My Lai cases was that of Lieutenant Calley, charged with acts arising out of the same sequence of events and based upon the same orders and, unlike Hutto, found guilty. The presiding Military Judge at the original trial was Colonel Kennedy who said:[27]

The conduct of warfare is not wholly unregulated by law. Nations have agreed to treaties limiting warfare; and customary practices governing warfare have, over a period of time, become recognized by law as binding upon the conduct of war. Some of these deal with the propriety of killing during war.... The law attempts to protect those persons not actually engaged in warfare, and limits the circumstances under which their lives may be taken.

... Summary execution of detainees or prisoners is forbidden by law.... I instruct you as a matter of law, that if unresisting human beings were killed at My Lai (4) while within the effective custody and control of our military forces, their deaths cannot be considered justified, and any order to kill such people would be, as a matter of law, an illegal order. Thus if you find that Lt. Calley received an order directing him to kill unresisting Vietnamese within his control or within the control of his troops, that order would be an illegal order.

The question does not rest there, however. A determination that an order is illegal does not, of itself, assign criminal responsibility to the person following the order for acts done in compliance with it.

Soldiers are taught to follow orders, and special attention is given to obedience of orders on the battlefield. Military effectiveness depends upon obedience to orders. On the other hand, the obedience of a soldier is not the obedience of an automaton. A soldier is a reasoning agent, obliged to respond, not as a machine, but as a person. The law takes these factors into account in assessing criminal responsibility for acts done in compliance with illegal orders.

The acts of a subordinate done in compliance with an illegal order given him by his superior are excused and impose no criminal liability unless the superior's order is one which a man of ordinary sense and understanding would, under the circumstances, know to be unlawful, or if the order in question is actually known to the accused to be unlawful....

.... Knowledge on the part of any accused ... may be proved by circumstantial evidence, that is by evidence of facts from which it may be inferred that Lt. Calley had knowledge of the unlawfulness of the order which he has testified he followed.... If you find beyond reasonable doubt ... that Lt. Calley actually knew the order under which he operated was unlawful, the fact that the order was given operates as no defense.

Unless you find beyond reasonable doubt that the accused acted with knowledge that the order was unlawful, you must proceed to determine whether, under the circumstances, a man of ordinary sense and understanding would have known the order was unlawful. Your deliberations on this question do not focus solely on Lt. Calley and the manner in which he perceived the legality of the order found to have been given him. The standard is that of a man of ordinary sense and understanding under the circumstances.

... Unless you are satisfied from the evidence, beyond reasonable doubt, that a man of ordinary sense and understanding would have known the order to be unlawful, you must acquit Lt. Calley for committing acts done in accordance with the order.

The most marked characteristic of this Instruction is the absence of any reference to 'manifest' unlawfulness, which was so basic a feature of the Hutto Instruction and was so fundamental to the reasoning of the Israeli court in the Melinki case. On this occasion it would seem that the Presiding Judge merely considered it

necessary for the accused, as a man of ordinary sense
and understanding, to know that in the circumstances
in which he was placed the order was in fact illegal.
The verdict of guilt indicates that the court accepted
this view, unless they considered Calley's subjective
knowledge of the illegality to have existed beyond any
reasonable doubt. The finding was confirmed by the
Court of Military Review:

Judge Kennedy's instructions were sound and the members'
findings correct. An order of the type appellant says
he received is illegal. Its illegality is apparent
upon even cursory evaluation by a man of ordinary sense
and understanding. A finding that it is not exonerating
should not be disturbed.... Appellant ... argues that
[Keenan, Griffen and Kinder] are all wrongly decided
insofar as they import the objective standard of an
order's illegality as would have been known by a man
of ordinary sense and understanding. The argument is
essentially that obedience to orders is a defense
which strikes at mens rea; therefore in logic an obedient
subordinate should be acquitted so long as he did not
personally know of the order's illegality. Precedent
aside, we would not agree with the argument. Heed
must be given not only to subjective innocence - through
ignorance in the soldier - but to the consequences for
his victims. Also, barbarism tends to invite reprisal
to the detriment of our own force or disrepute which
interferes with the achievement of war aims, even
though the barbaric acts were preceded by orders for
their commission....

Once again there is no reference to 'manifest'
unlawfulness, but merely to such 'illegality as is
apparent upon even cursory evaluation by a man of
ordinary sense and understanding', which is perhaps a
somewhat wider concept and one that appears to be less
technical and perhaps more readily understood by the
ordinary soldier.

The fact that a civil judge has overturned Calley's
conviction on the basis that pre-trial publicity made
it impossible for him to enjoy his right to due process

does not in fact affect the validity of the court
martial and the legal process, and especially not the
rightness of the law expressed. To accept the argument
of the civil court would be to impugn the Nuremberg and
Tokyo Trials as well as every other war crimes trial
which has taken place in recent years, and for that
matter any trial arising from crimes that have shocked
the public and been reported upon at any length or with
any emotion before an actual trial took place. In fact,
it would almost make it impossible for any such trial
ever to take place, for to a great extent such process
depends upon the publicity given to the allegations,
frequently before any person has been arrested.

The decision of the civil judge emphasises the contention that all persons accused of war crimes, whether
members of one's own armed forces or not, should be
tried by a tribunal specially created for this purpose
and applying international law in no way subject to
the peculiarities, procedural or substantive, of any
particular system of law. If the civil finding in the
Calley trial is allowed to stand, it will be obvious
to the meanest intelligence that justice has neither
been done nor been seen to be done.[28]

In some of the earlier cases, as in some of the
post-1945 war crimes trials,[29] there was a tendency to
point out that a serviceman cannot be expected to carry
Oppenheim,[30] the _Manual_ or other legal texts around
with him, particularly when on active service and
certainly not when in action, but it was nevertheless
assumed that any ordinary and reasonable man, even
including a soldier, would - or should - know automatically when an order was 'manifestly' unlawful. However,
the difficulties illustrated by the contradictory
findings in _Hutto_ and _Calley_ suggest that not only is
'manifestly' a controversial term, but the construction

of the same facts by different tribunals may well
lead to contrary results as a result of the use of such
limiting terms. Perhaps it is time to abandon not
only the word 'manifest', but also 'unlawfulness' and
'illegality'. These words are in themselves somewhat
vague and open to varying interpretations, and could
quite easily include non-punishable wrongs. The 'man of
ordinary sense and understanding' is presumed by the
law to know the law and, even though he is not expected
to carry copies of the Criminal Code or of leading
textbooks, interpretations and glosses around with him,
he is adjudged liable for acts which are criminal since,
as a citizen, he must have known that he was breaking
the criminal law. It is doubtless necessary for the
ordinary soldier to have some guide to enable him to
decide which of the orders directed to him by his
superiors are such that they are not to be obeyed and
would result in punishment were he to comply with them.
Since the standard is that of the ordinary man, it may
be proper for the ordinary man's concept of criminality
to be applied. In other words, it is suggested that the
test of lawfulness of an order should be measured by
whether the act consequent upon such order is one which
would involve the doing of something which is 'clearly
criminal'. That is to say, rather than the law providing
for the trial and punishment of 'an act in compliance
with an unlawful order', it should do so in respect of
'a criminal act in compliance with an order', whether
that order appears to be lawful or unlawful.

It would seem that this is in fact the line along
which the Judge Advocate General's Department of the
United States armed forces is at present moving,[31] even
though the 1969 edition of the Manual for Courts Martial
provides[32]

An act performed manifestly beyond the scope of authority

or pursuant to an order that a man of ordinary sense and understanding would know to be illegal or in a wanton manner in the discharge of a lawful matter, is not excusable,

while the suggested model instructions prepared by the United States Army Judiciary, Office of the Judge Advocate General, with the assistance of the Judge Advocate General's School of Law[33] still refer constantly to orders which are

'plainly unlawful' if, under the same or similar circumstances, a person of ordinary sense and understanding would know it to be unlawful ... [and] the burden is on the prosecution to establish the guilt of the accused by legal and competent evidence beyond a reasonable doubt that the order given to the accused ... was plainly unlawful, as I have defined the term...

This requirement of 'manifest unlawfulness' is to be found in a series of war crimes trials starting with the Llandovery Castle after the first world war and culminating in Nuremberg and the trials held by a variety of countries after 1945, as is to be seen by reference to any of the large collections of war crimes trials reports. But the comments that have been made with regard to the trials conducted by United States military tribunals of members of the United States armed forces are typical and of particular significance as national applications of the same principles. The problems confronting a soldier in deciding whether his action is criminal and may result in his trial are equally difficult whatever his nationality. The attitude of any tribunal that may try him is as subjective and likely to be as 'unique' as were those which tried Hutto and Calley after My Lai. These facts merely emphasise the need to seek some common form of rules of war that may be generally if not universally acceptable and which may be imparted to the ordinary soldier for his guidance. In fact, as a result of the Vietnam experience the United

States has sought to introduce model courses on the
international law of war and has prepared an outline[34]
for the guidance of those instructors whose task it is
"to familiarize military personnel with their rights,
duties and obligations under the Hague Conventions of
1907, the Geneva Conventions of 1949, and the customary
law of war ... [explaining] the obligation not to
commit war crimes [and] to report all violations of the
law of war." In addition to drawing attention to some
typical acts which would amount to war crimes, such as
desecration of the dead, including the taking of ears
to substantiate a body count, from the point of view of
our discussion perhaps the most important part of the
document is that relating to obedience to superior orders:

The legal responsibility for the commission of war crimes
frequently can be placed on the military commander as
well as his subordinates who may have committed the
crime. Since a commander is responsible for the actions
of those he commands, he can be held as a guilty party
if his troops commit crimes pursuant to his command, or
if he knew the acts were going to be committed even
though he did not order them....[35]

Illegal Orders and Individual Responsibility. In all
cases, the person who actually commits a crime is
subject to punishment, even if he acted pursuant to the
orders of a superior.... Acting under superior orders
is no defense to criminal charges when the order is
clearly illegal as is [for example] an order to kill a
prisoner of war. While an American soldier must obey
promptly all legal orders, he also must disobey an
order which requires him to commit a criminal act in
violation of the law of war. An order to commit a
criminal act is illegal.

It would appear from this statement that the United
States military authorities, while accepting the principle that orders involving the commission of a war
crime, or for that matter any other crime, should not
be obeyed, have adopted the same approach as one finds
in national criminal law, namely that members of the
armed forces like other United States citizens know

what the criminal law is, and should therefore know
when an order would entail the commission of a criminal
act.

   The 'Lesson Plan', reflecting the experience of Vietnam,
gives examples of the type of order that should be
disobeyed:

An order to execute a prisoner or detainee is clearly
illegal. An order to torture or abuse a prisoner to
get him to talk is clearly illegal. An order to torture
anyone is obviously illegal. These are orders whose
illegality is very clear [- although reports of what
happened during the Vietnamese hostilities would suggest
that the 'clarity' and 'obviousness' of the illegality
of these orders are perhaps matters of somewhat recent
enlightenment]. Is an order to dump a dead body into
a well also illegal? Yes. The order is illegal for
two reasons. A dead body in a well poisons the water
and the poisoning of wells and streams is a war crime.
Also it is mistreatment of a body which is a war crime.
What about an order to cut the ears off the enemy dead
to prove a body count? This order is illegal, too. As
we have seen the mutilation of bodies is a war crime,
and an order to cut off ears would therefore be illegal.
Equally illegal would be an order to take as souvenirs
valuables from dead bodies or from any prisoner. The
law of war requires that valuables of dead soldiers be
collected, safeguarded, and forwarded to the Central
Prisoners of War Agency. If you steal watches or money
off the dead and keep them, you are violating this law;
and no order or permission can make your action lawful.

There is always the question of what to do if it seems
to be a situation of 'my life or his'. For example, you
are on patrol with six men and capture an enemy soldier.
It's burdensome to take him with you. To turn him
loose would jeopardize the lives of the patrol. Your
partrol leader orders you to execute him. Do you do it?
[A number of alternative modes of action are suggested,
ranging from taking him along, evacuating by air, leaving
him tied and gagged to be found by his own forces, and
even] if the prisoner is willing, he can be given the
job of carrying medical or food supplies, or assisting
your own wounded....

... The decision to execute, to murder the prisoner is
an easy one. It is the wrong decision. It is also a
war crime and a violation of the Uniform Code of
Military Justice and under no circumstances will such an

act be tolerated. Even carrying out an order is not a
defense to a charge of murder. If you murder a prisoner
you can be tried and executed. There are always, in
actual combat, effective alternatives, which are legal,
humane and which fit the military situation. The
alternatives to murder are limited only by our imagination and generally will be a better aid in accomplishing
your mission. Any prisoner is important for intelligence
purposes.... So far we have discussed orders which can
never be justified. They would always be illegal, and
an American should always disregard such orders. If
you obey an illegal order you can be tried and punished.

In some cases, orders which could be legal in some
situations may be illegal in others. The rules of
engagement will guide your actions. These rules set
out the targets which you may attack. By knowing these
rules you will be able to act properly in different
situations. If you disobey the rules of engagement,
you can be tried and punished for disobedience of
orders. The disobedience may also be a war crime for
which you can be tried and punished.... An order to
shell enemy soldiers located in a village is legal even
though some civilians may be injured and their homes
and livestock destroyed. Suppose, however, that we are
conducting a cordon and search operation in the same
village. Orders to burn down all the buildings in the
village; to kill off all the livestock; to shoot
everything that moves - are illegal orders. You must
disregard such illegal orders [- shades of My Lai and
Calley].

You should not presume that an order is illegal. If you
think it is illegal, it is probably because the order is
unclear. For example, while on patrol we capture a
prisoner. On our return the patrol leader questions
him. When the patrol leader finishes the questioning
he tells you 'get rid of that man'. That order is not
clear. The patrol leader undoubtedly [?] means take
the man to the Detainee Collection Point. Similarly,
an order to clear an area of the enemy is not one to
kill everything you see. Rather [?] it means to find the
enemy soldier and destroy his ability and will to resist.
Such an order obviously does not include looting a store,
burning a farmer's house or murdering the women and
children. Rather than presume that an unclear order
directs you to commit a crime, ask your superior for
clarification of the order. Above all, remember that
if you are the leader make your order clear and understandable. Don't put your subordinates in the position
where they may think you are giving an illegal order.

But suppose you are given an illegal order: 'Shoot every
man, woman and child in sight'. Obviously that is an

illegal order. What do you do? First and most important
you should try and get the order rescinded by informing
the person who gave it that the order violates the law
of war [- did the writer of this directive ever come
into contact with a regular army sergeant?]. If he
persists, you must disregard such an illegal order. This
takes courage [!], but if you fail to do so you can be
tried and punished for committing a criminal act in
violation of the law of war. No one can ...[punish you]
for your refusal to obey. The lack of courage to
disregard an illegal order, or a mistaken fear that you
could be court-martialed for disobedience of orders is
not a defense to a charge of murder, pillage or any
other war crime. The Code of Conduct[36] states, 'I am
an American fighting man, responsible for my actions,
and dedicated to the principles which made my country
free'. The American soldier who follows that Code,
should have no problem with illegal orders. Further,
you have a second step to take if an illegal order
results in a violation of the law of war. You must report
such violation to the appropriate authorities....

... Usually, the soldier will report any known or
suspected violations of the law of war through his chain
of command.... Most commanders have established
reporting procedures by local regulations and directives
which require prompt, initial reports through the chain
of command. Failure to comply with these regulations
and directives may subject you to prosecution under
the UCMJ.

While a soldier should normally report through his chain
of command, you may hesitate to do so if someone in the
chain above you was involved in the alleged crime, or
if for some other reason you feel that such channels
should not be effective. At such times, there are other
officers to whom you can report or with whom you may
properly discuss any possible violations of the laws
of war....

... You may also discuss the problem with a Judge Advocate,
a military lawyer who knows the law of war and how it
applies. Many soldier prefer to discuss problems with
the Chaplain, and this is an accepted way to report
violations of the law of war.

These directives may sound perfectly reasonable

outside the heat of battle and particularly to those

who will not have to carry the brunt of actual fighting.

The procedures for protest and report are, however,

hardly practicable outside base camp, and suggest that

424

the entire document was drawn up by personnel aware of
what happened in Vietnam and anxious to avoid a
repetition, but the directive has a ring of what one
might expect from a civilian employed by the armed
forces or of a civilian in uniform who remains secure
in the safety of his office. There is no doubt that it
is a good thing that troops should be instructed in the
rudiments of war law and reminded that there are
restrictions on their freedom of action, and that they
should be enjoined to bear in mind that they are
rational beings and not automata and as such not merely
entitled but required to refuse to obey illegal orders,
that is to say orders which entail the commission of
criminal acts. However, these guidelines, at least in
their details, are frequently hardly practicable.
Unfortunately, soldiers remain human beings susceptible
to normal human emotions and ideological reactions.
Further, the document ignores the fact that modern
warfare is no longer what it was at the time of the Hague
Conference. In 1907 it was still possible to recognize
the enemy by the uniform or other identifying marks he
wore. Already during the second world war, with the
participation of partisan units and such bodies as the
French Forces of the Interior, it frequently became
difficult to distinguish fighting men from ordinary
civilians. One of the problems of post-1945 hostilities
centres on just this fact. It is easy to instruct men
that they are only permitted to search out and destroy
the fighting capacity of enemy troops, and must not take
any action which would directly cause the death of women
and children. But there is no attempt to tell the
soldier how he is to distinguish the non-combatant
child from a boy soldier, the civilian from an infiltrator
or saboteur, and the ordinary village population from
guerrilla units, when the latter are dressed in exactly
the same clothing as the former, as appears to have been

the case in Vietnam. Moreover, ordinary soldiers under the strains and stresses of modern warfare can hardly be expected to bear all these injunctions in mind when the enemy with whom they are faced has been denigrated by their high command, their political leaders and the media to the level of uncivilized sub-humans.

Most systems of municipal criminal law reject the idea that an accused can avoid liability by pleading ignorance of the law or that he was complying with the order of an hierarchic superior who, he had presumed, knew what the law is. In the same way, most military systems take the same approach, and one might refer in this connection to the summing-up of the 1970 Conference of the Société Internationale de Droit Pénal Militaire et de Droit de la Guerre. The Rapporteur pointed out[37]

For an order to contain in itself a feature that elimin-
ates its unlawful character it must in the first place
be legal both in form and content; an order which runs
counter to the law, or which is unlawful as such, cannot
be converted into an act possessing lawful character
by reason of the commission of an act in furtherance
of its execution....

Certain legislations recognize that in the exercise of
this power and duty of verification [of the legality
of the order] the subordinate may place an erroneous
construction on the situation; in such case the situation
is governed by the rules relating to mistake as to
subject matter.

If the subordinate does not even entertain any doubt
as to the incompetence of his superior or the unlawful
character of the order if this mistake can be regarded
as justified, i.e. if incompetence or illegality are
not manifest, execution does not lead to liability
because the subordinate can always raise the lawfulness
of an order received.

If on the other hand the subordinate does have doubts
on these points, he must express these doubts to his
superior. This may be done in various ways, but it is
recognized that a subordinate must bring his doubts to
the notice of his superior before carrying out an order
he regards as unlawful if the order has not been

cancelled. The mistake of the subordinate as to the unlawful character of the order will do away with criminal intent and prevent the subordinate from being punished.

Lastly, if the unlawful character of the order is obvious, the subordinate must not obey such an order and it is no longer open to him to raise the plea of mistake; when the purpose of the order is to cause an offence to be committed and when its unlawful character is obvious, the mistake of the subordinate - if it is a mistake - is henceforward a mistake of law that can exculpate no one; a subordinate, like all citizens and persons submitted to legislation, is presumed to know the law and he must know that no one, not even his superiors, is entitled by issuing orders to abrogate a provision of the law.

It must be borne in mind, however, that a particular national legal system may in fact permit named officers to amend or abrogate a particular legal provision. Thus, under the Canadian National Defence Act,[38] the Governor General, the Minister and the Chief of the Defence Staff may make law by regulation or order, so long as the change is not inconsistent with statutory law. Likewise, any change so effected that was inconsistent with the law of war would afford no defence to a member of the armed forces charged with war crimes.

Once again we are presented, in this Conference document, with a presumption of knowledge of the law, including the international law of war. But no suggestion is put forward to indicate how the soldier should be informed of the content of that law, or what his position is likely to be if the action he is about to take is considered compatible with that system by his own country, although rejected by other belligerents. However,since there are parallels in many of the municipal systems of criminal and military law, perhaps it may be possible to find a formulation that may be generally applied,[39] at least among those countries which possess a similar understanding and approach to the principles of criminal justice and of law in general.

Moreover, in view of the growing frequency of multi-national military exercises; of training manoeuvres held on friendly soil; of the secondment of personnel, particularly officers, of one nationality for duty with the forces of another nation; and of the employment of national units in operations under the umbrella of the United Nations, perhaps one might hope that such a general formulation might prove more readily acceptable than might have been thought likely shortly after the termination of the second world war. The fact that some countries, for example, the Federal Republic of Germany, Israel and the United States, have already applied the general principles of international law in this field as against their own nationals lends some support to this hope.

Since most countries, and certainly those within the western alliance system, generally accept the maxim ignorantia juris quod quisque tenetur scire, neminem excusat[40] it is suggested that these countries be encouraged to replace the concept of 'manifest illegality or unlawfulness', which is not readily understood by the ordinary man, by that of 'obvious criminality' - although this might face the courts with the invidious task of defining 'criminality' - which is more likely to be appreciated and place the international law of war on the same level as ordinary criminal law. This would also encourage the soldier to regard international law as having equal authority and being equally binding as his own system of national law, so that ignorance of the one would, in his eyes, be no more a defence than is ignorance of the other. But this means that steps must be taken to make the armed forces aware of what the law is, and the American directive is an indication, however primitive, of what can be done along these lines. At the same time there must be an abandonment of 'the

reasonable man of ordinary understanding'. This
individual is a man of peace living the ordinary life
of a citizen in an urban conurbation or a rural
encironment. He must be replaced as he has been in so
many non-English environments;[41] the man on the Clapham
omnibus must give way and the soldier must be measured
by the standards of the reasonable soldier in similar
circumstances to the accused. This may require
military manuals and directives to be revised in the light
of the experience of serving officers - especially in
the case of those, such as the British, which at present
appear to prevent the defence of superior orders or
ignorance of the law from ever constituting a justification, excuse or defence to a war crimes charge, even
though available by way of mitigation - with constant
updatings to recognize the changes that take place in
warfare and to ensure that what appears as guidelines
for the soldier does in fact reflect what he is likely
to find in reality.

* Based on a paper prepared for 4 Falk (ed). The
Vietnam War and International Law (1975).

1   See, e.g., Hookey, 'The "Clapham Omnibus" in New
    Guinea', in Brown, Fashion of Law in New Guinea
    (1969) 117; judgment of Bright J. in R. v. Gibson
    (1973), S. Australia Judgment No. 1810; and III
    above.

2   Green, 'Superior Orders and the Reasonable Man',
    (1970) 8 Can. Y.B. Int'l Law 61.

3   Prime Minister Trudeau, Press Conf., 8 Apr. 1970,
    9 Int'l Legal Materials 600.

4   Holland, The Laws of War on Land (1908) 1-2.

5   E.g., Cheng, General Principles of Law as applied
    by International Courts and Tribunals (1953);
    Friedmann, 'The Use of "General Principles" in the
    Development of International Law', (1963) 57 Am.J.
    Int'l Law 279; Green, 'Comparative Law as a "Source"
    of International Law' (1967) 42 Tulane Law Rev. 52;

Herczegh, General Principles of Law and the
International Legal Order (1969).

6
See III above.

7
U.S. Dept. of the Navy, NWIP 10-2, Law of Naval
Warfare (1955, amended 1959); see also U.S. Army
Field Manual on Law of Land Warfare (1956),
FM27-10, paras. 33, 34.

8
The Law of War and Neutrality at Sea (1957)45-6,48.

9
See, e.g., comments by Smith on 'War in Three
Dimensions', The Crisis in the Law of Nations (1947)
67 et seqq.

10
Part III, The Law of War on Land (1958) paras.113,107.

11
Para. 109, n.1.

12
Para. 111, and n.1(a).

13
See Stein, 'Legal Restraints in Modern Arms Control
Agreements', (1972) 66 Am. J. Int'l Law 255, 281.

14
10 Int'l Legal Materials 1300. The debate in the
Senate Committee on Foreign Relations, 93rd Cong.,
2nd Sess., 10 Dec. 1974, indicates that the U.S.
would now only use herbicides in conditions which
permit them in the U.S., i.e., for agricultural
purposes, and for control of vegetation within U.S.
bases and installations or around their immediate
defensive perimeters.

15
Ibid., 1304.

16
(1661) Kelyng 13.

17
(1960) 32 Int'l Law Rep. 563,565.

18
1958/9, Pesakim (D) vol. 17, 90 (S) vol. 44, 362 -
extracts from the decision are to be found in the
Eichmann judgments (36 Int'l Law Rep. 5).

19
15 Fed. Cas. 1235, 1240.

20
For some of these, see Green, loc.cit., n.2 above.

21
(1954) 14 C.M.R. 742, 770, 773-5, 776.

22
In re Ohlendorf (1948) 4 Nuremberg Mil Tribs. 470.

23
(1969) 39 C.M.R. 109, 117.

24   (1968) _ibid._ 586.

25   U.S. v. Hutto (1970/1) - a copy of these Instructions
was made available by the librarian of the U.S. Judge
Advocate General's School of Law (italics in original).
The relevant section of the Instructions is reproduced
in Norene, Obedience to Orders as a Defense to a
Criminal Act (1971 - unpublished JAG School thesis)
68-77.

26   Norene, _op.cit._, 78 (italics in original).

27   U.S. v. Calley (1969/71, 1973) - the texts here
used were made available by the librarian of the
JAG School, (the charge by the J.A. at the initial
trial is reproduced in 2 Friedman, The Law of War
(1972) 1703, the extracts quoted are at 1721-2,1723-4).

28   "It ... is of fundamental importance that justice
should not only be done, but should manifestly and
undoubtedly be seen to be done", R. v. Sussex
Justices, ex parte McCarthy [1924] 1 K.B. 256,259,
per Hewart L.C.J.

29   _Loc.cit._, n. 2 above.

30   International Law, 2 vols., 1st ed. 1905/6 - still
probably the best known text on the subject (now,
vol. 1, 8th ed. 1955, vol. 2, 7th ed. 1952).

31   Information given to the writer when visiting the
JAG School of Law, Virginia.

32   Para. 216d.

33   Norene, _op.cit._, 66-8.

34   'The Geneva Conventions of 1949 and Hague Convention
IV of 1907', Dept. of the Army, ASubjScd 27-1,
8 Oct. 1970.

35   Parks, 'Command Responsibility for War Crimes',
(1974) 62 Military Law Rev. 1.

36   Dept. of the Army, AR 350-30.

37   Recueils de la Société de Droit Militaire Pénal
et de Droit de la Guerre, Ve Congrès International,
Vol. 1, 1971, 371, 373.

38   R.S.C. 1970, N-8.

[39] See Draper, 'Objective and Individual Responsibility for the Application of Humanitarian Law in Armed Conflicts', in Instituto Internazionale di Diritto Umanitario, Norme Umanitarie é Istruzioni Militari (1973), 37, 45 et seqq.

[40] "Ignorance of the law, which every one is bound to know, excuses no one" - perhaps one might mention here Selden's explanation: "Ignorance of the law excuses no man; not that all men know the law, but because it is an excuse every man will plead, and no man can tell how to confute him", Table Talk: Law (1892 ed.) 99.

[41] See n. 1 above.

XI

STERILISATION, MARRIAGE AND THE LAW*

Man with all his wisdom toils for heirs
he knows not who (Nevison v. Taylor (1824)
8 N.L.J. 43, 46, per Kirkpatrick C.J.).

It is only within the last ten or fifteen years or so
that population problems have become a matter of international concern, inextricably tied up with issues of
ecology, over-population and the exhaustion of natural
resources. The interest in this matter has affected
writers, both lay and learned,[1] and reached its culmination with United Nations sponsored World Population
Conferences held in Belgrade in 1965 and Bucharest in
1974. The sociological aspects of the matter range
from migration[2] and the movement of populations to
population control, with some States seeking to achieve
zero-growth. State enforced policies of control are
not looked upon with favour for the main part, for they
soon revive memories of Nazism and the shadow of genocide,
for the Genocide Convention[3] includes in its definition
of this crime.

... (c) Deliberately inflicting on the group conditions
of life calculated to bring about its physical destruction in whole or in part;
    (d) Imposing measures intended to prevent births
within the group...

Before international interest became so marked,
population control was considered a matter essentially
private to the individuals concerned, although governments
did not hesitate to introduce legislative controls and

sometimes complete bans on the modes that might be
applied to achieve this end. In some Catholic countries,
for example, any form of contraceptive practice was
officially banned and the sale, supply or advertisement
of contraceptive devices was illegal. It was not until
the end of 1973 that the Irish Supreme Court confirmed
the woman's constitutional right to import contraceptives,[4] although their sale in Eire remained illegal.
Even in the United States it was only as recently as
1965 that the Supreme Court struck down as unconstitutional a Connecticut statute making the imparting of contraceptive information criminal,[5] while before the Canadian
Criminal Code was amended in 1968[6] their advertisement
or public sale was banned. On a more general level,
most municipal systems made abortion a criminal offence,
although the decisions of the United State Supreme Court
in Roe v. Wade and Doe v. Bolton,[7] which upheld the
right of the woman to seek, and of her doctor to perform
an abortion within a named period, while totally
ignoring any 'right' of the putative potential father,
introduced a series of amending statutes in a variety
of countries, though rarely recognizing the woman's
right to an abortion on demand.

Apart from abortion and mechanical aids to contracep-
tion, there remains sterilisation, in which surgical
aid is invoked by a man or woman in order to interrupt
reproductive capacity, although in some cases further
surgery can effect a repair. For a variety of reasons,
many countries have in the past forbidden or discouraged
resort to sterilisation, often because of the fear of
abuse - one often meets allegations that doctors in
hospitals catering to the needs of underprivileged
groups frequently perform unnecessary hysterectomies,
without always informing the woman of the nature of the
treatment which is being provided. Today, however, most

of the legislative restrictions have been raised, and
population experts, frequently with governmental backing,
advocate sterilisation as the most effective method of
population control. In some cases, however, unfortunate
personal complications have arisen when parties who have
been sterilised regret the finality of the operation
since they desire further children, perhaps because
their economic status has changed or because the sterilised party has formed a relationship with a new partner.

While a number of the medico-legal and social questions
relating to sterilisation may have been resolved by
reason of the change in social environment, many of the
original issues, especially those of a sociological
character, remain relevant in other connections. This
is particularly so in relation to recent genetic engin-
eering efforts[9] affecting, for example, sex changes -
thus Jan Morris,[10] formerly a man and now a woman, has
disclosed that his children now address him as an aunt.
Similarly, as a result of changes in life-style, attempts
have been made to regularize uni-sexual marriages with
consequent serious juridical problems.[11] Moreover, in
a different field, operations involving the implant of
a new heart raise interminable controversy as to the
moment of death, while proposals to recognize a right
to recover for pre-natal injury focuses attention on the
right not to be born.[12]

In a sense, sterilisation is, of course, nothing but
a surgical operation like any other and, on occasion,
has to be performed for straightforward medical reasons.
This, however, is not the case when a person wishes to
undergo sterilisation for ideological reasons, or
because his wife is physically incapable of further
confinement. But in this connection reference must be
made to the definition of health to be found in the

Preamble to the Constitution of the World Health Organization,[13] which has significance for both the doctor and the lawyer:

Health is a state of physical, mental and social well-being and not merely the absence of disease or infirmity. [Moreover,] the enjoyment of the highest attainable standard of health is one of the fundamental rights of every human being without distinction of race, religion, political belief, economic or social condition.

It is probably difficult to contend that this definition is not wide enough to cover both the individual who wishes to achieve mental peace for either egotistic reasons or out of consideration for the welfare of society, as well as the one who seeks the operation to save his partner from further childbearing risks.

The problem of what constitutes health confronted lawyers and doctors long before the establishment of the World Health Organization. It was brought to the forefront of public and professional consideration by the case of R. v. Bourne,[14] the decision in which has constituted a landmark in the development of the law. The charge arose from an operation for abortion and not sterilisation, and the defence revolved round the contention that mental health was equally important with physical health in order to legalise what would otherwise be an illegal operation. Under the combined effect of the Infant Life Preservation Act, 1929[15] and the Offences against the Person Act, 1861,[16] which then governed the situation, an induced miscarriage was only permissible if done in good faith for the purpose of preserving the life of the mother. The learned judge directed the jury that

those words ought to be construed in a reasonable sense, and, if the doctor is of opinion on reasonable grounds and with adequate knowledge, that the probable consequence of the continuance of the pregnancy will be to

make the woman a physical or mental wreck, the jury are
quite entitled to take the view that the doctor, who,
under those circumstances and in that honest belief,
operates, is operating for the purpose of preserving
the life of the mother.

The jury thereupon acquitted.

This view of the legality of a particular operation
draws attention to a fundamental issue underlying the
problem of voluntary or therapeutic sterilisation,
namely, the legality of any operation and the validity
of the consent given to its performance. The problem
of his liability for assault should be ever-present in
the mind of a doctor, for any operation performed without consent, even though it might be a legal, as distinct
from the generally understood idea of an illegal,
operation, may open the door to an action for damages
for civil assault. [17]

The Constitution of the World Health Organisation refers
to health as being dependent on a "state of complete
physical, mental and social well-being", and this may
well be considered by some as the authorisation for
socio-economic sterilisation and, for that matter, for
every kind of operation of a social character. This
aspect of the problem is of significance for the plastic
surgeon whose cosmetic operations might, from the legal
point of view, not fall within the classification of
those which may be described broadly as medical, in the
curative sense. The modern realisation of the importance
of physchosomatic conditions might well militate in
favour of the view that a young female suffering from
some facial or other physical disability should be
permitted to make use of surgical means in order to
remove the disability which is interfering with her
"state of complete physical, mental and social well-
being" - but does it also extend to the criminal on the

437

run, whose 'mental and social well-being' may well
depend on a cosmetic operation that completely alters
his facial characteristics?

In addition to the Constitution of the World Health
Organisation, there are one or two other international
instruments which are of relevance. In the first place,
there is the Universal Declaration of Human Rights,
1948,[18] whereby the General Assembly went on record that
everyone, regardless of race, culture, language or
religion, has the right to found a family[19] although the
Soviet Union, which abstained on the vote, has prevented
Soviet women from joining their foreign husbands abroad,
while Australia, which voted for it, refused to allow
Japanese wives to join their Australian husbands in
Australia, and the United States, which was a prime mover
in drafting the Declaration, in some of its states treated
marriages across the colour line as criminal.[20] This
right raises the problem of consent, particularly as
the Declaration also provides that no one shall be
subjected to cruel, inhuman or degrading punishment,[21]
and this itself touches a specific aspect of the legal
nature of sterilisation.

Finally, as already mentioned, there is the Genocide
Convention, which, unlike the Universal Declaration, is
a binding treaty. Broadly, it is directed against
organised crime the purpose of which is to deny the
character of a group qua group, and includes the imposition of measures intended to prevent births within the
group. The significance of this type of activity as an
international crime was made clear in the trial of
Adolf Eichmann.[22] Although Eichmann was not charged
with genocide per se, he was accused and found guilty
of a crime against the Jewish people, in that he

devised measures the purpose of which was to prevent

438

childbearing among the Jews of Germany and countries
occupied by her ... [and] for the sterilisation of
the offspring of mixed marriages of the first degree
among Jews in Germany and in areas occupied by her.

From the point of view of genocide, the essence of
sterilisation measures must be that they are directed
against the members of a group because they are members
of that group. This means that doctors practising
female or male sterilisation of patients coming to them
could not be considered as falling within the scope of
the Convention.

Apart from these international aspects of sterilisation,
there are four specific problems with which the lawyer
is concerned. One is the problem of punitive sterilisation for sexual offenders, which has been advocated,
and the concomitant legislation passed, in a number of
countries, particularly the Scandinavian, although in
the United States the tendency is to regard such
measures as unconstitutional. In some places it is
even advocated for the treatment of homosexuals.[23] In
so far as heterosexual misconduct is concerned, it must
be borne in mind that, despite popular misconceptions
to the contrary, sterilisation is no answer to the problem
of the mass rapist. With the possible exception of
brain surgery, the only surgical treatment for this type
of sexual offender is castration. As Sir Richard Burton
has pointed out in his footnotes to the Arabian Nights,[24]
from the point of view of the harem, ordinary sterilisation may have advantages rather than drawbacks! This
also appears to be the view of the Minnesota judge who
stated that male sterilisation "frequently improves the
health and vigour of the patient."[25]

Scandinavia has long been regarded as the group of
countries whose criminal policies are most progressive
and whose example is frequently cited by penal reformers.

Provision is made in some of the penal codes for the
compulsory sterilisation of dangerous sexual offenders.
This is the position under a Danish statute of 1935,
although the powers have never been used. On the other
hand, with psychopathic criminal detainees, voluntary
sterilisation is regarded by the courts as a justification
for release a short time after the operation has taken
place.[26] It would appear from this that the principle
of consent is preserved, just as it seems to have been
preserved in other medical experimental schemes conducted
in United States prisons and elsewhere, and portrayed
so effectively in a film like Kubelik's Clockwork Orange.
It is submitted, however, that when the temptation of
early release is offered to the 'volunteer', it is a
little difficult to regard his consent as being freely
given. The approach of the Norwegian criminal law is
somewhat different. Unlike the position in Denmark,
the Norwegian court can only recommend sterilisation or
castration as a matter of treatment, and not as a
punishment. Nevertheless, it may be carried out without
the individual's own consent. While provision is made
for voluntary submission to the operation, a statute
of 1934 gives an expert committee authority to order
the sterilisation or castration of persons with certain
mental abnormalities,'if there is reason to believe his
abnormal sexual instincts will lead him to commit
sexual offences'. The request to the committee must
come from the individual's guardian, the local chief
of police, or the director of the institution in which
he is detained.[27]

   In the United States, penal treatment is a matter of
state competence, and a number of state legislatures
have propounded sterilisation legislative measures,
which frequently include punitive sterilisation.[28]
28 of the states possessed such legislation, and in

only Minnesota and Vermont was it on a purely voluntary basis, although Maine, North Carolina and South Dakota contain provisions for both voluntary and compulsory sterilisation. In most cases the operation is directed against mental defectives detained in state institutions. A good example, although in this case mental abnormality is not an essential prerequisite, of such legislation is that of Oregon - Sterilisation is compulsory and mandatory at the instance of the State Board of Eugenics in the case of

all persons who are feeble minded, insane, epileptic, habitual criminals, incurable syphilitics, moral degenerates or sexual perverts; any person convicted of the crime of rape, incest, sodomy, the delinquency of a minor by sexual act or act of sexual perversion [- and this would seemingly include oral sex -], the crime against nature....

Somewhat similar legislation formerly existed in Ablerta, Canada, under the Sexual Sterilization Act,[29] permitting sterilization, sometimes without the patient's consent, of psychotics, mental defectives, epileptics, sexual recidivists, and the like. This was, however, repealed in 1972[30] as being contrary to the Alberta Bill of Rights.[31]

Sometimes, the attempt has been made to widen the scope of such punitive sterilisation far beyond the range of sexual crimes. Thus, in Oklahoma a 1935 statute provided for the sterilisation of those who had been convicted to two or more felonies involving moral turpitude. It was expressly made to apply to larceny, including larceny by fraud, but not to embezzlement. In Skinner v. Oklahoma[32] the Supreme Court had to consider the challenge to this statute lodged on behalf of an individual who had been convicted of stealing chickens in 1926, and of robbery with firearms in 1929 and 1934. He was in jail when the statute came into force in 1935, and in 1936 proceedings were launched for his sterilisation. The judgment was delivered by Justice Douglas, and appears to have been written against the background of what was becoming known of the conditions in Nazi Europe:

This case touches a sensitive and important area of human rights. Oklahoma deprives certain individuals of a right which is basic to the perpetuation of a race - the right to have offspring .... The power to sterilise, if exercised, may have subtle, far-reaching and devasting effects. In evil or reckless hands it can cause races or types which are inimical to the dominant group to wither and disappear. There is no redemption for the individual whom it touches.[33] Any experiment which the State conducts is to his irreparable injury.[34] He is forever deprived of a basic liberty.... Strict scrutiny of the classification which a State makes in a sterilisation law is essential, lest unwittingly or otherwise, invidious discriminations are made as against groups or types of individuals in violation of the constitutional guaranty of just and equal laws.

In the instant case, the majority were of opinion that to punish the man who had twice been convicted of larceny by sterilisation, while not treating in the same fashion one who had become a professional embezzler constituted 'invidious discrimination in violation of the constitutional guaranty of just and equal laws.' Chief Justice Stone and Justice Jackson agreed that the statute was unconstitutional, but both were concerned that legislative sterilisation was being used for social reasons without paying the slightest attention to the 'inheritability' of this type of criminal propensity. In fact, the latter almost went so far as to condemn any compulsory eugenic sterilisations as unconstitutional:

I think the present plan to sterilize the individual in pursuit of a eugenic plan to eliminate from the race characteristics that are only vaguely identified and which in our present state of knowledge are uncertain as to transmissibility presents other constitutional questions of gravity.... There are limits to the extent to which a legislatively represented majority may conduct biological experiments at the expense of dignity and personality and natural powers of a minority.

As distinct from the punitive sterilisation carried out at the discretion of State officials, there is therapeutic sterilisation conducted at the desire of the patient. In so far as the United States is concerned, some of the State sterilisation legislative measures expressly declare that

nothing in this act shall be construed so as to prevent the medical or surgical treatment for sound therapeutic reasons of any person in this state, by a physician or surgeon licensed by this state, which treatment may incidentally involve the nullification or destruction of the reproductive functions,[35]

and in 1974 it was announced by the Department of Health, Education and Welfare that sterilizations would in future be considered as family planning services, so that the Department would pay ninety percent of the cost for poor persons[36] - although the same would not apply to abortions, even though legal. The new law proposed for Sweden[37] provides for free sterilisation on demand for anyone over 25.

When sterilisation is lawful, there is an inevitable risk of abuse and legislation will often embody safeguards. It does not take much imagination to envisage a situation in which an unscrupulous mother, or other guardian, of an infant heiress suborns a similarly unscrupulous medical practitioner to perform an unnecessary salping-ectomy in order to evade the provisions in a will. Such an operation is obviously unlawful with the mother and doctor liable to prosecution.[38] Connecticut[39] has made express provision for this, stipulating that, except as authorised under the act,

any person who shall perform, encourage, assist in or

443

otherwise promote the performance of either of the operations described in [this legislation], for the purpose of destroying the power to procreate in the human species, or any person who shall knowingly permit either of such operations to be performed upon such person, unless the same shall be a medical necessity, shall be fined ... or imprisoned...

While consent is required to render such operations lawful, and the doctor will be protected if the patient voluntarily requests the operation, it does not follow that legal implications will not in any event arise. For example, the patient may be married and if he or she arranges for the operation without the consent of the marriage partner a matrimonial offence may be committed.[40] Consideration of this problem, however, is best postponed until after certain other medical implications have been examined.

In 1934 a Minnesota court came to the conclusion that it was not contrary to public policy for an individual to submit to therapeutic sterilisation on behalf of a third person. The problem in Christensen v. Thornby[41] arose from the fact that it was considered dangerous for the wife to have a further confinement and the husband therefore agreed to submit to vasectomy, being assured by the surgeon that he would thereby be rendered sterile. In fact, the wife became pregnant and survived the birth. The doctor was sued for breach of contract and the expenses involved in the confinement. The judge found for the doctor, pointing out that,

instead of losing his wife, the plaintiff had been blessed with the fatherhood of another child.

A somewhat similar case occurred in Auckland, New Zealand, in 1974. The claim failed, it being held that the doctor had performed the operation in accordance with medical knowledge available at the time - 1969 - there having apparently been a natural regeneration of the vas.[42]

444

More difficult from the doctor's point of view is the
situation which arises when, in the course of an abdomin-
al operation, he discovers that sterilisation of his
patient is medically advisable or that hysterectomy
is inevitable. In 1949 a Canadian doctor discovered,
while performing a Caesarian operation, that tumours
were present on the uterine wall and, having told the
husband that sterilisation might be necessary, he tied
off the woman's Fallopian tubes. Although the consent
certificate signed by the husband had referred to a
"Caesarian operation and any further surgical procedure
found necessary by the attending physician", when she
came out of hospital the woman sued the doctor. In the
view of the judge

the point is whether an emergency existed, whether it
was necessary that the operation be done, not whether
it was then more convenient to perform it.

Since he did not regard sterilisation as immediately
necessary to preserve the woman's health, he awarded her
$3,000 damages[43] - presumably, the patient should have
been sewn up and, after she regained consciousness,
informed by the surgeon that a further operation was
necessary, and a new consent secured. Three years later,
a Californian surgeon was faced with a similar problem.
During an operation he discovered that his patient's
Fallopian tubes were infected and, on his own initiative,
removed the diseased portions, rendering the woman
sterile. In Danielson v. Roche judgment for the doctor
was upheld on appeal.[44] In England the medical defence
unions decline to indemnify surgeons for performing
sterilisation operations.[45]

Closely akin to therapeutic sterilisation, and of
prime significance sociologically, is eugenic sterilisation. The major criticism of eugenic sterilisation
is that in the hands of a fanatical regime eugenics

and race purity can become the ideology under which
abominable crimes are committed. It is significant to
note that in the first year of operation of the Nazi
sterilisation statute of 1933, no less than 56,244
sterilisations were ordered,[46] and it was envisaged
that the Hereditary Health Courts (Erbgesundheitsgerichte)
would order some 400,000 persons to be sterilised. This
figure, which had nothing to do with the anti-Jewish
programme, was made up as follows: feeble-minded, 200,000;
schizophrenics, 80,000: epileptics, 60,000; manic-
depressive insane, 20,000; physically deformed, 20,000;
deaf-mutes, 18,000; chronic alcoholics, 10,000; victims
of St. Vitus's dance, 6,000; and blind, 4,000.[47]

As has been seen in connection with punitive sterilisation, eugenic sterilisation is provided for by legislation in most of the American states. The first
statute was enacted in Indiana in 1907, and by 1915
fifteen states had legislation permitting eugenic
sterilisation. This number had increased to thirty-two
by 1935, but was down to twenty-eight in 1961, but now
seems to be generally allowed. The majority of the
known sterilisations in the United States, and certainly
those performed in accordance with the statutes, are
compulsory, and in the fifty years from 1907 to the end
of 1957 60,166 persons had been sterilised. Of these,
31,038 were mental deficients, 26,922 were suffering from
mental illness, and the remaining 2,206 were epileptics,
criminals and the like. Of the total, 19,998 were
performed in California. Since the Second World War
there has been a gradual decline in the number of
compulsory sterilisations.[48] On the other hand, in the
last ten years or so there has been a vast increase in
the number of voluntary sterilisations throughout the
world, by young and old alike, for a variety of reasons,
contraceptive, ecological, fear of war, ideological,

but rarely eugenic.

In so far as the compulsory sterilisations were of
mental defectives or of persons thought likely to commit
sexual offences, and invariably of persons who had been
institutionalised, it might well be questioned whether,
particularly in view of the fact that ordinary sterilisation does not normally affect sexual potency, institutionalisation rather than sterilisation is not the correct
treatment. If mental abnormality warrants institutionalisation, the same condition will continue after the
sterilisation has been performed. If this is so,
institutionalisation should continue, when there is no
need for sterilisation.

At one time it was considered that compulsory sterilisation of the mentally unfit was contrary to the
Constitution of the United States. However, the
constitutionality of such legislation was upheld by
Oliver Wendell Holmes, one of the greatest common lawyers
of all time. In <u>Buck</u> v. <u>Bell</u>[49] he delivered the opinion
of the Supreme Court upholding the validity of a
Virginian statute which had been invoked to deal with a
feeble-minded inmate of an institution, who was born of
a feeble-minded mother and had herself given birth to
a feeble-minded illegitimate child. In words that have
become memorable, Holmes summed up the position thus:

It is better for all the world, if instead of waiting
to execute degenerate offspring for crime, or to let them
starve for their imbecility, society can prevent those
who are manifestly unfit from continuing their kind.
The principle that sustains compulsory vaccination is
broad enough to cover cutting the Fallopian tubes.
<u>Three generations of imbeciles are enough</u>.

It is difficult not to sympathise with the last few
words of Holmes's comment, but the implications of the
statement that "society can prevent those who are

manifestly unfit from continuing their kind" are, in
the light of Hitler's activities, terrifying. Nor does
it matter much that so enlightened a law-reformer as
Dr. Glanville Williams has expressed support for
legalised sterilisation, pointing out that

> there is a striking contrast between human fecklessness
> in our own reproduction and the careful scientific
> improvement of other forms of life under man's control.
> No rose-grower, pigeon-fancier or cattle-breeder would
> behave as men do in their own breeding habits.[50]

The prospect of State stud-farms, assisted by such
medical advances as sperm, eye and kidney banks makes
the imagination boggle, especially in view of the great
advances which have been made with transplants, including
the use of replacements from animals - which may eventually cause the conservationists to rise up in anger![51]

Eugenic sterilisation legislation exists in other
countries too and the question arises whether such
sterilisation may, from the point of view of the doctor,
be defended on similar grounds as therapeutic sterilisation. In the case of eugenic sterilisation it cannot
be argued that it is the health of the patient that is
involved. What is at stake is the alleged health of
the unborn generation and the interest of society in its
fitness. Generally speaking, save in such matters as
succession to property,[52] including a crown or a title,
or for damages in respect of a deceased parent, unborn
embryos have not generally speaking been regarded as
possessing legal interests. For one thing, there is no
guarantee that the unborn will ever be born alive. It
has been held, for example, by an Irish court that there
is no cause of action in a child who alleges that it is
deformed as a result of injuries suffered in a railway
accident while en ventre sa mère.[53] On the other hand,
a Canadian court has awarded a child damages in tort

in respect of a deformity held to have been caused by a negligent pre-natal injury to the mother[54], while in the United States damages have been awarded for the death of a viable fetus, defined as a legal 'person'[55], although normally a woman will not be awarded damages in respect of an embryo that she has lost as a result of an accident. In view of Dr. Williams' approach, it is perhaps not irrelevant to mention that a similar attitude is taken by the law in respect of the loss of cattle. Thus, if cattle die because, for example, their pasture has been poisoned by industrial fumes, damages will not be recoverable in respect of the first prizes they did not win or the calves they did not produce. At the next agricultural show there might well have been a better prize steer, while a cow might drop her calf prematurely. Similarly, damages will not be awarded for timber that does not reproduce itself, allegedly because of industrial fumes.[56]

In recent years there has been an increasing tendency, particularly in the common law countries,[57] to press for recognition of the rights of the unborn child in the widest possible sense. Thus, much of the campaign against abortion on demand has been conducted on the basis that the embryo is a life in being entitled to legal protection, and that this right to protection is on a higher level than the woman's right to decide not to have a child. In the field of tort, the argument to a great extent has gone on the basis of pre-natal injury resulting from, for example, traffic accidents. It has, however, been suggested that recognition of such a right has far greater implications. Difficulty will obviously arise in determining where to draw the line to distinguish between those causes of injury which give rise to an action and those which do not, and how far the liability will extend. The most notorious

instance of this kind is the series of actions that have
been brought in a number of countries as a result of the
tragedies arising from the use of thalidomide by their
mothers. An early instance of this kind is to be seen
in Sinkler v. Kneale[58] when an American judge awarded
damages for 'imbecile mongolism' held to have arisen
from the use of teratogenic agents during the first
month of pregnancy, although it has been stated[59] that

the chance of a succession of simultaneous chromosomal
changes in the cells of a one-month old fetus can almost
certainly be totally excluded.

The writer of this comment has, however, raised some
interesting issues that could arise if antenatal rights
were fully recognized. He enquires, for example, whether
a child could bring a claim against its mother as a
result of deformities traceable to the mother's smoking
during pregnancy; whether an action could be brought by
a deaf child whose mother had suffered German measles
and not had an abortion; whether a claim would lie
against one or both parents if the child were born
syphilitic; whether it would lie if the parents were
unmarried and the child were born into a society that
discriminates against bastards;[60] and, even, if such a
claim could be brought in the event of a miscegenous
relationship with the child being born a half-caste into
a society that rejects or discriminates against such
racial mixtures. It may be thought that many of these
suggestions are too far-fetched to warrant serious
consideration. It should be remembered, however, that
should the principle of the child having a right to sue
for antenatal injury be conceded, then such matters as
these might become very real, unless the legislation in
question was very strictly worded - and even more strictly interpreted and applied when actual cases present
themselves before the courts.

In the field of criminal law, there is often some
recognition of the unborn child as a person, so that to
inflict a prenatal injury upon a child capable of being
born alive, preventing it from being so born may amount
to child destruction, and a similar injury causing its
death after being born alive might amount to murder or
manslaughter.[61] To incite someone to murder a child
when born, if the inciting has taken place before birth,
has even been held to amount to soliciting to murder a
"person".[62]

Perhaps it is worth commenting here on the problem of
breach of contract. As has already been mentioned, it
was held in Minnesota in 1934[63] that a contract to
perform or submit to a eugenic or contraceptive sterilisation was not contrary to public policy, but that in the
case in issue the patient could not recover damages for
breach of contract in respect of an ineffective sterilisation as a result of which his wife bore him another
child. Had the wife died - for it was on account of
her weak health that the husband submitted to the operation - a different verdict might have been reached. On
the other hand, as recently as 1974 a New Zealand court
denied damages for breach of contract on the basis that
the operation, though unsuccessful, had been performed
in accordance with proper surgical practice.[64]

Problems may arise in the absence of permissive
legislation. The 1934 Report of the British Departmental
Committee on Sterilisation[65] considered sterilisation of
normal persons to be unlawful, and recommended enactment
of permissive legislation. While there has been no
English judicial decision on the validity of voluntary
eugenic sterilisation as such, in an obiter dictum
Lord Denning has expressed the view that sterilisation
to prevent the transmission of an hereditary disease
would be lawful.[66] In the same way, the Baltimore City

Circuit Court has upheld the lawfulness of a eugenic
sterilisation decree issued on the petition of a husband,
relatives and the Incompetent Committee in the absence
of any legislation relating to sterilisation.[67] This
decision is interesting since it is stated in Wharton's
Criminal Law that "consent cannot cure such operations
on women as prevent them from having children."[68]

Under the impact of the population explosion, perhaps
the most important problem relating to sterilisation
is that raised by operations performed for contraceptive
of socio-economic purposes. Generally speaking, in the
common law countries legislation tends to be absent, and
the matter has become confounded by references to the
common law offence of mayhem, although sterilisation
has now become popular with both married and unmarried
persons, and there appears to be no fear or threat of
prosecution.

According to Coke, "the life and members of every
subject are under the safeguard and protection of the
king," and he refers to a case at Leicester in 1604 in
which

a young, strong and lustie rogue, to make himself impotent,
thereby to have the more colour to begge or be relieved
without putting himself to any labour, caused his
companion to strike off his left hand[69]

- both were convicted of mayhem. In those days, it was
thought that castration would diminish bodily vigour and
thereby render a man less capable of fulfilling his
military duties, so that castration was explicitly held
to be a maim and a felony.[70] Blackstone described it as

an atrocious breach of the king's peace, and an offence
tending to deprive him of the aid and assistance of his
subjects. For mayhem is properly defined to be the
violently depriving another of the use of such of his
members, as may render him the less able in fighting,

either to defend himself or to annoy his adversary. And therefore the cutting off, or disabling, or weakening a man's hand or finger, or striking out his eye or foretooth, or depriving him of those parts, the loss of which in all animals abates their courage, are held to be mayhems. But the cutting off his ear, or nose, or the like, are not held to be mayhems at common law; because they do not weaken but only disfigure him.

It would thus appear that Blackstone provides a common law ground on which a cosmetic plastic operation might be defended. This does not, however, seem to be the case under modern French law, for

there is some doubt whether the cause is licit where a patient runs a bodily risk for aesthetic reasons actuated merely by a sense of coquetterie.[72]

Today, the general view is that sterilisation and castration do not interfere with a man's fighting potential, and this is likely to become more true the more the methods of warfare reduce the individual's participation to that of pressing a button. In fact, in Christensen v. Thornby[73] the Supreme Court of Minnesota expressly stated that sterilisation "does not render the patient impotent or unable 'to fight for the king' as was the case in mayhem or maiming." It may be relevant here to refer to the crisis of conscience that. was presented, in the course of discussion, to a medical practitioner in Singapore in 1962. A married man with a child asked the doctor to sterilise him, and was met by the response that, in the absence of good medical or contraceptive reasons, a need for psychiatric treatment was indicated. When it was explained that the man was worried by the risk of nuclear war and of children being born deformed because of the effects of gamma rays, or into a world polluted by radioactive fallout, the doctor indicated that, in such circumstances, he might be prepared to perform a sterilisation operation. In view of the strength with which one may hold pacifist views or conscientious objection to war, it may well be that the time has come to review the common law approach to mayhem. Perhaps with this in mind, another proposition was put before the medical practitioner in order to ascertain his reactions. He was asked whether he would be prepared to amputate the applicant's right arm[74] and indicated that in his view such a request merited immediate incarceration in a mental institution. The case of the pacifist was then put to him, and it was suggested that in view of the ideological divisions that now split the world there might be no place for a conscientious objector should a major war break out. In view of this, the only way in which one might be able to give effect to one's conscience might be by such incapacitation as would render the objector completely useless from the war point of view. Nevertheless the doctor maintained his objections to such an operation, wisely, since this would amount to "grievous hurt" under s. 320 of the Singapore Penal Code, and would probably be unlawful under any system of criminal law.[75] It is true that the example is far-fetched, but, theoretically, if it is justifiable for a doctor to perform a sterilisation operation in order to assist in preventing children from being brought into a nuclear world, it ought to be equally justifiable - and perhaps even ethical from the medical point of view - to assist a person who does not wish to take part in a war of which he does not approve. Some support may be found for this suggestion in s. 87 of the Code:

nothing which is intended to cause death, or grievous hurt [- and if artificial limbs can enable the person affected to live a full life other than serving in the armed forces, it may be possible to argue there is no 'grievous' hurt -], and which is not known by the doer to be likely to cause death, or grievous hurt, is an offence by reason of the harm which it may cause, or be intended by the doer to cause, to any person, above eighteen years of age, who has given consent, whether

express or implied, to suffer that harm; or by reason
of any harm which it may be known by the doer to be likely
to cause to any such person who has consented to take
the risk of that harm.[76]

There can be no doubt that a doctor performing a sterilisation operation does not intend to cause death or
grievous hurt, although this may ensue from any operation.
However, by s. 320 it is expressly stated that 'grievous
hurt' includes

> Firstly - emasculation; ...
> Fifthly - destruction or permanent impairing of the
> powers of any member or joint.

'Emasculation' has not been judicially defined, and
according to the Oxford Dictionary it means 'the action
of depriving of virility; the state of impotence;' while
in Ratanlal's Law of Crimes[77] - the Singapore Penal
Code is based on that of India, of which Ratanlal is
probably the leading commentary - it states that the
term means

the depriving a person of masculine vigour, castration.
Injury to the scrotum would render a man impotent.

Lest it be contended that this seems to confine the act
to a male, it should be pointed out that by s. 8 'the
pronoun 'he' and its derivatives are used of any person,
whether male or female,' and presumably this is equally
true of the commentary. Further, in 1860 when the
Indian Penal Code was promulgated and 1872 when it was
adopted in Singapore it is feasible that sterilisation
as we now know it was not envisaged, and therefore it
becomes necessary to define the terms that have been
used sufficiently widely to apply to modern practice too.
As regards the term "member", while this prima facie is
used to indicate the limbs, it is in law frequently
employed to indicate the male sexual organ.

The combined effect of sections 87 and 320 seems to be
that an operation performed for other than purely medical
reasons, in the narrow meaning of the term, with the
intention of "emasculating" the patient, or destroying
or permanently injuring the powers of any of his or her
members, is an illegal operation since it constitutes
"grievous hurt". As is the case with other illegal
operations, consent does not constitute a defence, as
is clear from section 87 itself. Ratanlal's comment
in this connection is that "where an act is in itself
unlawful, consent can never be an available defence."[78]

Section 88 of the Penal Code is also relevant to any
argument aiming to suggest that sterilisation is legal,
particularly if it is asserted that this does not
constitute "grievous hurt" within the terms of section
320. By section 88

nothing which is not intended to cause death, is an
offence by reason of any harm which it may cause, or
be intended by the doer to cause, to any person for whose
benefit it is done in good faith, and who has given a
consent, whether express or implied, to suffer that harm,
or to take the risk of that harm.[79]

This would imply that even an act constituting "grievous
hurt" does not amount to an offence if done with the
consent of the patient and for his benefit. There can
be no question that if the reason for the sterilisation
operation is therapeutic it would be protected by this
section. Eugenic sterilisation, however, is for the
benefit of the community at large and not for that of
the patient and would not be so covered. Contraceptive
or socio-economic sterilisation would also not be protected, especially "as mere pecuniary benefit is not
benefit within the meaning of this section."[80] This
would of course raise numerous problems in, for example,
India where for a time it appeared as if a person subjecting himself to sterilisation was being paid, as distinct

from receiving compensation for lost wages, while payment was also being made to 'social workers' who persuaded persons to become sterilised.[81]

The position under the Penal Code has now become somewhat historical since Singapore has enacted legislation permitting sterilisation, while India runs a government scheme in its support.

The problem just considered raises the whole issue of consent to mutilation and operations in general. Thus according to Lloyd's view of French law, while a

surgical operation which is reasonable and necessary having regard to the patient's condition would be perfectly lawful,... a submission to vivisection for reward would be illicit as incompatible with human dignity.

On the other hand, in English law an "agreement to perform a dangerous experiment in physiology might be lawful, at any rate unless the degree of danger is very great."[82] According to the Shorter Oxford English Dictionary "vivisection [is] the action of cutting or dissecting some part of a living organism" - a definition which would include both sterilisation and castration.

The term "illegal operation" is habitually employed to indicate an abortion which has been performed without any clear and present medical need. The fact that it has been performed upon a consenting woman does not render the operation legal and the consent is no defence to either the doctor or the woman, unless it falls within the terms of the local law which now, increasingly, permits abortion for socio-economic reasons if these are likely to endanger health, while in the United States the Supreme Court has virtually permitted abortion on demand during the first three months of pregnancy.[83] Similarly, if a masochist consents to an unlawful caning, then either because of the risk of bodily harm or because

of the potential public character of the place in which
it has been carried out, the caning remains an indecent
and unlawful assault.   In R. v. Donovan[84] the Court said
that the test of legality was whether the blows were
likely or intended to do bodily harm, which was defined
to include any hurt or injury calculated to interfere
with the health or comfort of the victim:

If an act is unlawful in the sense of being in itself a
criminal act, it is plain that it cannot be rendered
lawful because the person to whose detriment it is done
consents to it.   No person can license another to commit
a crime.

The result seems to be, as Glanville Williams points out,
that

a person cannot effectively consent to any blow, or
presumably to any incision or puncture, that is likely
to diminish his comfort.[85]

Here we come face to face with the fact that while one
may participate in a competitive boxing match fought
with regulation weight gloves, though the risk of permanent physical harm or even death is obvious, it is unlawful to take part in a prize fight since bare-knuckle
fighting is likely to endanger life and health and the
match constitutes a disorderly exhibition - a
description which may be equally applied to many recent
ice hockey matches, amateur and professional, national
and international.   In so far as masochism is concerned,
the rather more lax approach now taken to sexual deviance,
involving public advertisements, might suggest a more
lenient approach than that adopted in Donovan.

Apart from any problem relating to criminal liability
in respect of a possibly illegal sterilisation operation,
problems will obviously arise in the field of divorce,
particularly if the unsterilised spouse contends that
sterile intercourse involves sufficient cruelty to ground

an action for dissolution of marriage. It must be
remembered of course that natural sterility in one or
both spouses cannot afford grounds for dissolution. A
different rule would mean that a woman beyond the age of
child-bearing could never enter into a valid marriage.

Before considering cruelty and sterilisation, it is
useful to see what the attitude of the courts has been
to other forms of non-reproductive intercourse. The
starting point for any such discussion is Dr. Lushington's
judgment in D-e v. A-g in 1815[86] in which the wife had
no uterus and only a short vagina. A number of unsuccessful attempts at coitus had been made and eventually the
husband sought a declaration of nullity:

Mere incapability of conception is not a sufficient ground
whereon to found a decree of nullity. The only question
is whether the lady is or is not capable of sexual intercourse.... In order to constitute the marriage bond ...
there must be the power, present or to come, of sexual
intercourse. Without that power, neither of two principle ends of matrimony can be attained, namely, a lawful
indulgence of the passions to prevent licentiousness,
and the procreation of children according to the event
design of Divine Providence[87]... Sexual intercourse, in
the proper meaning of the term, is ordinary and complete
intercourse, it does not mean partial and imperfect
intercourse; ... if so impossible as scarcely to be
natural,... legally speaking, it is no intercourse at
all.... Certainly it would not lead to the prevention
of adulterous intercourse, one of the greatest evils to
be avoided.... If there be a reasonable probability
that the lady can be made capable of vera copula [by
medical or surgical means] - of the natural sort of
coitus, though without power of conception, I cannot
pronounce the marriage void.... In the case first
supposed, the husband must submit to the misfortune of
a barren wife, as much when the case is visible and
capable of being ascertained, as when it rests in
undiscoverable and unascertained causes. There is no
justifiable motive for intercourse with other women in
the one case, more than in the other. But when the coitus
itself is absolutely impossible, and I must call it
unnatural, there is not a natural indulgence of natural
desire; almost of necessity disgust is generated, and
the probable consequences of the connexions with men of
ordinary self-control become almost certain (sic). I am

of opinion that no man ought to be reduced to this state
of quasi-unnatural connexion, and consequent temptation,
and, therefore, I should hold the marriage void. The
condition of the lady is greatly to be pitied, but on no
principle of justice can her calamity be thrown upon
another.

It is difficult to tell from this judgment whether
Dr. Lushington was more concerned about the procreation
of children - 'the principal end of marriage' - or the
prevention of adultery. Later judges seem to have been
more specific about the procreation aspect of the problem.[88]

Almost 150 years later, when surgeons had affected
various methods of remedying natural deficiencies, including the creation of artificial passages, the English
courts were again faced with the problem of a woman
lacking a natural vagina. B. v. B.[89] concerned a female
hermaphrodite whose male organs had been removed surgically. She had no vagina and at the time of the marriage
the husband was aware that she could have no children,
but was apparently unaware that intercourse was impossible.
After marriage, the wife underwent an operation for the
provision of an artificial vagina, but since complete
penetration was still impossible, the husband left and
sued for nullity. The Divorce Commissioner held that
since this was a mere connection between the parties not
amounting to a vera copula there was no consummation.
By way of obiter, he expressed the view that there could
never be consummation with an artificial vagina.

This dictum was expressly disapproved by the Court of
Appeal in S. v. S.[90]. The wife here had no uterus and a
short vagina, and before marriage had told her fiancé,
who was already aware that coitus with her might be
difficult, that she could not bear children. Three years
after the marriage, the husband suggested that the wife
take medical advice. By now she had a vagina about an
inch long, which the gynecologist attributed to the

husband's attempts at coitus. The doctor pointed out
that an artificial vagina could be surgically created,
and the wife expressed willingness. Before the operation
could take place the husband left and sued for nullity
for non-consummation, although medical evidence confirmed
that, while there was an impediment to normal intercourse,
the woman was not a virgin. The Court accepted that the
marriage had never been consummated, since

it was not possible for the husband, owing to the abnormality of the wife's sexual organs, to achieve full
penetration, or anything like full penetration.... [But]
before relief can be granted it must be shown that the
wife's incapacity is incurable.... It is admitted
that absence of a uterus, and the consequent inability
to conceive, is of no significance, and the fact that
the cavity to be created would be a mere cul-de-sac
leading nowhere would not of itself be conclusive.

It was, however, contended on behalf of the husband that,
even if full penetration could be achieved, intercourse
by way of an artificial vagina would not constitute a
vera copula, although this would not be the case were it
a question of enlarging what was originally an inadequate
vagina. The Court was not convinced that there was no
vagina, since the doctors referred to vaginal inspection
and the absence of a 'normal vagina'. Willmer L.J.
pointed out that the fact that a doctor was of opinion
that consummation was possible by way of an artificial
vagina, did not mean that this was conclusive from the
point of view of the law,[91] and he found

it difficult to see why the enlargement of a vestigial
vagina should be regarded as producing something different
in kind from a vagina artificially created from nothing.
The operation involved in either case is substantially
the same.... In either case the resulting passage has
substantially the same characteristics, at any rate for
so much of its length as is artificially created. In
either case there is no more than a cul-de-sac, and
there can be no possibility of a child being conceived.
It is admitted, however, that inability to conceive a
child is no ground for saying that the marriage cannot
be consummated. It is also admitted that the degree of

461

sexual satisfaction that may be obtained by either or both of the parties makes no difference.... In either case full penetration can be achieved, and there is thus complete union between the two bodies. Counsel for the wife conceded (no doubt rightly) that an artificial cavity created in some other part of the wife's body, into which the husband's organ could be inserted, would not be appropriate. But there is no question of that in the operation suggested. What would be created would be a vagina, albeit an artificial one, and it would be located precisely where a natural vagina would be. In such circumstances, I do not see why intercourse by means of such a vagina should not be regarded as amounting to a vera copula. ... [Unlike the position when a condom was used,] in the case of intercourse by means of an artificial vagina, the husband's organ would at least be united, in physical union, with the appropriate part of the wife's body.... If it is to be held that a wife with an artificial vagina is incapable in all circumstances of consummating her marriage, it can only be on the basis that such a woman is incapable of taking part in true sexual intercourse. If that were right, the strangest results would follow. It would involve, for instance, that such a woman might be to a considerable extent beyond the protection of the criminal law, for it would seem to follow that she would be incapable in law of being the victim of a rape.[92] What is even more startling would be that a woman would be incapable in law of committing adultery.[93] Consequently, the wife of a man engaged in intercourse with such a woman would be left wholly without a remedy. I should regard such a result as bordering on the fantastic....

In this case it was indicated that had the husband been fully aware of his wife's disability before the marriage and had despite this contracted marriage, then he would have been considered to have approbrated her condition. All the members of the Court of Appeal were at one in dismissing the husband's plea, and it is perhaps to be regretted that leave to take the issue to the House of Lords was refused. Having held that the husband could not get a decree of nullity and that there was a valid marriage, the decision opens the way to the wife, should she so wish, to bring an action for divorce on the ground of desertion. In those countries where divorce is obtainable by reason of marriage breakdown, it is possible that the husband too could secure a dissolution for this reason.

There has, of course, been no case of an action for
nullity on the basis of non-consummation which has
involved an artificial penis, although impotency has
long been recognized as sufficient. In view of the fact
that penetration of the labia is sufficient for rape[94]
and also for adultery,[95] it might be considered that
the same would be true for nullity, especially as in
Dennis v. Dennis, Singelton L.J. said[96] that in his view
there was

> no distinction to be drawn between the words 'sexual
> intercourse' in the definition of 'adultery' ... and
> 'carnal knowledge' in the criminal law. In regard to
> ... a charge of rape, it must be shown there is some
> penetration

but, in the instant case, he accepted that the co-respondent was in fact impotent on the occasion cited. Hodson
L.J. also conceded that, while something less than
completion might suffice, 'there must at least be
partial penetration for the act of adultery to be proved'[97]
and he refused to accept that an attempt which might
result in impregnation because of contact and ejaculation
would suffice, even though in Russell v. Russell[98],
Lord Dunedin had said that, even in the absence of
penetration 'fecundation ab extra is, I doubt not,
adultery.' In view of the Dennis decision, it is somewhat
surprising to read the decision in W. v. W.[99], in which
Brandon J. held himself to be bound by Dr. Lushington's
view of 'ordinary and complete intercourse' in D-e v.
A-g and granted a wife's plea for nullity:

> ... on occasion, the husband was able to penetrate the
> wife for a short time, but soon after he got inside her,
> his erection collapsed and he came out. In my view,
> penetration maintained for so short a time, resulting
> in no emission inside the wife or outside her, cannot
> without violation of language be described as ordinary
> and complete intercourse. I do not think there is any

authority binding me to hold that, I do not see why I
should not make a finding of fact in accordance with
what seems to be the realities of the case. On these
grounds,... this marriage has not been consummated.

It would seem from his comments with regard to _ejaculatio
ante portas_ that, unlike Hodson L.J. who would not have
regarded this without penetration as sufficient to
constitute adultery, Brandon J. might have regarded
such emission after inadequate penetration as sufficient
for consummation. Before leaving this aspect of the
subject, it might be worth mentioning that, despite the
weight of modern technical comment by doctors, sexologists,
marriage counsellors and the like, with regard to sexual
activity short of intercourse, the English divorce court
has not yet shown itself willing to accept anything less
than sexual intercourse as sufficient to constitute
adultery. In _Dennis_ v. _Dennis_ it was agreed that adultery
might be inferred from the surrounding circumstances, but
in _Sapsford_ v. _Sapsford and Furtado_[100] Karminski J.
applied the traditional tests:

The wife masturbated the co-respondent. That, of course,
is an act of sexual familiarity which on any view of
marriage can hardly be thought to be consistent with the
duties of a wife towards her husband, but ... I have to
decide whether or not the behaviour between the co-respondent and the wife amounted to adultery. On the other
hand,... an act of adultery need not be such a complete
act of intercourse as is required to consummate a
marriage,... adultery need not be a _vera copula_....
There has to be intercourse in which both the man and
the woman play ... their normal role, and that mere
masturbation by itself cannot come within the ambit of
mutual intercourse

although in the instant case, he was of opinion that even
if there were not completely satisfactory coitus, there
was sufficient penetration, apart from the act of masturbation, to constitute adultery. In view of the constant
emphasis of the need for penetration of the female
genitalia one is compelled to ask what the attitude of
the judges would be if, instead of sexual intercourse,

464

the defendant and the co-respondent had indulged in
buggery, particularly in a case in which the defendant
spouse had preferred this form of relationship and had
been denied it by the marriage partner. It is hardly
feasible that in such a case any judge would today maintain that there had been no adultery. However, with the
trend to accept breakdown of marriage as sufficient to
ground a divorce it is unlikely that problems of this
kind will arise in future.

The above discussion suggests that, whatever might at
one time be thought to be the principal end of marriage,
the possibility of impregnation is no longer a sine qua
non for adultery. But what if impregnation is frustrated
as between husband and wife because of some action taken
by one of the spouses, bearing in mind that

mere abstention by the husband from intercourse could not
... amount to cruelty or give to the wife any remedy,
even though it might injure her health,[101]

although in Lawrance v. Lawrance[102] it was held that if,
the marriage having been consummated, either spouse
persistently refused intercourse so that the partner's
health is or is likely to be affected, a divorce might
be obtained on account of cruelty. This interference
with the possibility of conception may arise either because one of the parties has submitted to sterilisation
or because intercourse always takes place with a contraceptive or is frustrated by way of coitus interruptus.
In so far as contraceptive practices are concerned, it
might be thought difficult to argue that the marriage had
not been consummated. In Cowen v. Cowen,[103] however,
the English Court of Appeal held that where throughout
a marriage one partner had refused to have intercourse
except with a contraceptive or by way of withdrawal,
there was no consummation for, in the light of Dr. Lushington's test,[104] the Court was

of opinion that sexual intercourse cannot be said to be
complete when a husband deliberately discontinues the
act of intercourse before it has reached its natural
termination or when he artificially prevents that natural
termination.... To hold otherwise would be to affirm
that a marriage is consummated by an act so performed
that one of the principal ends, if not the principal end,
of marriage is intentionally frustrated.

This statement suggests that if one of the partners to a
marriage enters the marriage knowing that he is sterile
and keeps this fact from the other, then it should be
possible to hold that the marriage, despite intercourse,
could not be consummated due to the frustration, knowingly,
of one of its principal ends. However, as Horridge J.
pointed out in L. v. L.[105] "mere incapacity to conceive
was no ground for a decree of nullity of marriage." But
would it be possible for the other spouse to argue
that the contract was frustrated by mistake on his part
or fraud on the part of the sterile party?

   It only took a year before there was a retreat from
the reasoning in Cowen, for in Baxter v. Baxter[106] the
House of Lords took the opposite view. Although the
wife had refused to permit intercourse without the use
of a condom, it was held that there was a vera copula,
since there was a complete conjunction of bodies, and
therefore the marriage was consummated. Lord Jowett
declared that

it is indisputable that the institution of marriage
generally is not necessary for the procreation of children,
nor does it appear to be a principal end of marriage as
understood in Christendom

- does this mean that different standards might be
applied if the parties to a marriage are atheists or
non-Christians? Although a marriage in which intercourse
regularly takes place with the aid of contraceptives is
not regarded as null, it does not mean that a spouse
objecting to the persistent use of such methods is
without any remedy. Obviously, any other grounds for

divorce will still be available - and this is also true
if the practice is agreed to.

For coitus interruptus or the use of contraceptives
to be significant as a means to divorce, it is necessary
for the objecting spouse to prove that his or her health
has been adversely affected as a result of the practice
in question. Perhaps the starting point for this
discussion might be <u>Cackett</u> v. <u>Cackett</u>[107] since Hodson
J.'s judgment still hankers after some of the traditional
views. As the wife's parents were first cousins, the
husband refused to have a child and, objecting to contraceptives, employed coitus interruptus and the wife's
health suffered. The judge found that

penetration was effected and there was the possibility
of conception.... Seed was emitted by the man in close
proximity to the woman so that conception might have been
effected.... It seems to me impossible to determine
exactly where normal intercourse begins and ends. There
could be no legal standard laid down which would define
a matter of that kind.

Having refused a decree of nullity, he granted a divorce
for cruelty.

There are two cases in this connection which may be
compared, for not only are they the counterpart to each
other, but they were heard within the same week. <u>Knott</u>
v. <u>Knott</u>[108] was a case in which the husband insisted on
coitus interruptus, and

... in refusing to let his wife have children he was
'reckless' of the effect on his wife and his conduct
was 'inexcusable'... For the man deliberately and
without good reason permanently to deny a wife who has
a normally developed maternal instinct a fair opportunity
of having even a single child is of itself cruelty when
injury to her health results and when he adopts a course
which preserves to himself a measure of sex enjoyment....
The refusal to allow the wife to have a child, and the
conduct accompanying it, ... is a deliberate act contrary
to the laws of nature and one which any reasonable
husband must realise is likely to affect his wife's
health. Permanent and unreasonable starvation of the

maternal instinct may ... be of itself a cruel thing...
Even though both parties may obtain physical satisfaction,
yet, so far as the woman is concerned, the permanent
deprivation of having children [was sufficient, for her
health was affected] in a more direct manner than any
method of sex relationship which allows the wife to have
all satisfaction short of satisfaction of the maternal
instinct.... The course of conduct pursued by the
husband ... in relation to sexual matters was cruel.

In Forbes v. Forbes[109] it was the wife who refused to
have children and insisted on the use of contraceptives.
At first the husband complied, but later the wife
insisted on using a diaphragm, even though she knew it
disgusted her husband and affected his mental health.
In the judge's view

Quite apart from the exhortation in the solemnisation of
matrimony that, first, Christian marriage was ordained
for the procreation of children,... it is a natural
instinct in most married men to propagate the species
and to bear the responsibilities and to enjoy the
comforts of their own children. If a wife deliberately
and consistently refuses to satisfy this natural and
legitimate craving, and the deprivation reduces the
husband to despair, and affects his mental health,...
she is guilty of cruelty.

Denning L.J. had suggested in Fowler v. Fowler[110]
that the situation might be different if the wife's
refusal was based on a fear of the consequences for
herself and without any intention to injure her husband,
but this was not confirmed in P. v. P.[111]:

A spouse who was inhibited by a physical impediment known
to the other spouse and who made every effort to cooperate could scarcely be said to be cruel, even though in
the end it had a disastrous effect on the health of the
other spouse.... [But] if ... this wife was consistently
depriving her husband of the amount of intercourse which
she ought really to have been affording, and depriving
him of the opportunity of becoming a father, which she
knew that he wanted, and that these matters seriously
affected his health, ... then ... if the conduct becomes
unendurable in the sense that ...the husband should not
be called on to endure it, the court can and should help
him.

This discrepancy is explained by the fact that this

decision was rendered after the House of Lords had decided <u>Gollins</u> v. <u>Gollins</u>[112], which was far more in accord with social needs than earlier decisions, in that it decided that matrimonial 'cruelty' was to be measured by the reality of the injury done to the other spouse and no longer depended on the 'guilty' party's intention to cause harm to his health. The importance of this was shown by <u>Sheldon</u> v. <u>Sheldon</u>[113] in which the husband, after normal intercourse with his wife for a number of years, refused to indulge any more and refused her the child she wished. Lord Denning stated

... he has persistently, without the least excuse, refused her sexual intercourse for six years. It has broken down her health. I do not think she was called upon to endure it any longer.... No spouse would have any chance of obtaining a divorce on such a ground except after persistent refusal for a long period; and it would usually need to be corroborated by the evidence of a medical man who had seen both parties and could speak to the grave injury to health consequent thereon, for,   as Salmon L.J. pointed out, impotence is not a ground of divorce, and if in the present case the evidence was equally consistent with impotence as with a wilful refusal of intercourse, the commissioner would have been right in refusing a decree.... [But] this evidence establishes wilful refusal.... When a man knows that his young wife is being made ill through sexual starvation, it is indeed cruel for him wilfully to refuse her sexual intercourse.

So far we have been concerned with the problem of wilful refusal to perform a 'full and complete' act of intercourse likely to cause impregnation. It may happen that, although complete intercourse in the sense of a <u>vera copula</u> takes place, impregnation is impossible on account of the voluntary sterilisation of either spouse. In view of the comments that have been made with regard to the natural desire for children and the suggestion that procreation is the principal end of marriage, it is necessary to look at some of the problems inherent in the event of voluntary sterilisation, for this is becoming much more common and it may well be that the sterilized

person does not inform his potential spouse that a
sterilization has been performed, or he may undergo such
an operation after marriage without informing the spouse
of his intention.

In those countries where, as it was suggested in the
British Brock Report,[114] voluntary sterilization might
be regarded as illegal, it would mean that any doctor
performing such an operation was in fact committing a
criminal act and if his patient were to die, then,
regardless of the prior consent that may have been given,
the doctor would face a charge of manslaughter and
perhaps even of murder. But the possibility of such a
charge now being brought is radically reduced, so long
as the doctor has used all the precautions and skill to
be expected of one performing such an operation.[115]

As has already been indicated, marriage is a contract
and the parties to it have certain expectations. It is
perhaps not surprising, therefore, that in a variety of
American jurisdictions, for example, the concealment of
pre-marital sterilisation has been held good ground for
annulment.[116] In fact it may well be that this is one
of the situations in which any legislative measure
providing for sterilisation should stipulate that such
suppression is a ground of nullity, thus removing any
possible doubts. It might also go further and break into
the traditional concept of confidentiality between doctor
and patient. Sterilisation operations should, perhaps,
be notifiable so that a local authority might be required
to maintain a list which could be consulted under safeguards at the request of a person about to enter marriage
and seeking to confirm that his partner has not in fact
undergone any such operation. Should a person enter
marriage with one who has been sterilised and whose name
is on such a list, then, on this ground at least, it
should not be possible for a decree of nullity to be

obtained. As to sterilisation after marriage, a similar
list might be maintained so that spouses would have some
means of ascertaining whether the partner to the marriage
had since undergone such an operation. If this were in
fact the case and the partner's consent had not been
obtained, then the example of the court in Keyling v.
Keyling[117] might be followed and a divorce granted for
constructive desertion or, as is now more likely to be
the case, for marital breakdown.

There has been a series of English cases involving
similar problems. Thus, in L. v. L. (1922)[118] the wife
had undergone, prior to marriage, an ovarian operation
involving sterility, a fact of which she was aware.
The husband knew of the operation, but maintained that
he was unaware of the wife's inability to bear children,
and although intercourse had taken place he brought an
action for nullity alleging non-consummation. The claim
was dismissed on the ground that consummation was not
the same as conception, and "mere incapacity to conceive
was no ground for a decree of nullity of marriage."
Twenty-five years later, in J. v. J.[119] the court had
to consider a case in which the operation had been
performed, with the knowledge of the other party, before
marriage and in which the marriage had subsisted eleven
years. The man had promised his fiancée not to become
sterilised, but six weeks before the date of marriage he
had the operation. The woman felt that it was by then
too late to break off the marriage, and normal coitus
with emission by the husband took place. The wife did
not know that she might have grounds for nullity, and
when she brought her action it was held that the delay
was excused by her ignorance of her rights[120] and as there
was no insincerity on her part. In view of this it was
held that knowledge of impotence was not an absolute bar,
and that the husband

in having the operation, rendered himself incapable of
effecting consummation by reason of a structural defect
which he had himself brought about in his organs of
generation.

The English cause célèbre in relation to sterilisation,
and the one that is of most importance for the medical
profession, is Bravery v. Bravery.[121] The marriage
took place in 1934 and a child was born in 1936. Two
years later the husband had himself sterilised. Intercourse continued until the wife left in 1951. The wife
sued for divorce alleging cruelty, and it was held that
she knew of the operation, apparently never made any
strong objection, and really left because of his bad
temper and not the sterilisation. The decree was refused,
and this refusal was confirmed by the Court of Appeal,
with Denning L.J. dissenting. In the course of their
joint judgment, Evershed M.R. and Hodson L.J.[122]
commented that

as between husband and wife for a man to submit himself
to such a process without good medical reason ... would,
no doubt, unless his wife were a consenting party, be
a grave offence to her which could without difficulty
be shown to be a cruel act, if it were found to have
injured her health or to have caused reasonable
apprehension of such injury. It is also not difficult
to imagine that if a husband submitted to such an
operation without the wife's consent, and if the latter
desired to have children, the hurt would be progressive
to the nerves and health of the wife.... We feel bound
to dissociate ourselves from the more general obser-
ations of Denning L.J.... in which he expressed his view
(as we understand it) that the performance on a man of
an operation for sterilisation, in the absence of some
'just cause or excuse'... is an unlawful assault, an
act criminal per se, to which consent provides no answer
or defence. The court must, no doubt, take notice of
any relevant illegality which appears in the course of
any proceeding before it; but in the present case both
the general question, whether an operation for sterilisation is prima facie illegal, and the more particular
question whether the operation here performed was a
criminal assault, are alike irrelevant to the issue to
be determined.... We are not prepared to hold in the
present case that such operations must be regarded as

injurious to the public interest.... In our view, in
the circumstances of the present case, it is neither the
duty nor the function of this court to do more than draw
attention to the obviously grave potentialities of such
an operation for the parties to the marriage....

It is important to bear in mind that although the
majority of judges upheld the marriage, they did so on
its particular facts, finding the allegations of cruelty
not proved. They did not hold sterilisation operations
by consent were legal, since they were of opinion that
the matter was not in issue. Denning L.J., in the course
of his dissent, made a number of remarks that are of
significance from the point of view of the medical
practitioner.[123] In his view the fact that the wife did
not go to the surgeon and protest at the husband's
proposal to be operated upon was irrelevant:

It was not for her to approach the surgeon, but for the
surgeon to approach her.... There was no just cause for
this operation at all [- it appeared from the evidence
that the husband did it to spite the wife for showing
too much affection to the child of the marriage -].
If the husband had undergone it without telling his wife
about it beforehand, no one could doubt that it would
be cruelty.... When this husband was sterilised, the
effect of it was not over and done with at once, like
a blow with the fist or like an act of adultery. This
operation had an effect which continued, day in and day
out, year in and year out, throughout the marriage.
No act of sexual intercourse could result in a child.
The effect on the wife's health might not be immediate.
It might have a delayed effect.... An analogy is, I
think, to be found from the criminal law about surgical
operations. An ordinary surgical operation, which is
done for the sake of a man's health, with his consent,
is, of course, perfectly lawful because there is just
cause for it. If, however, there is no just cause or
excuse for an operation, it is unlawful even though
the man consents to it.... [The learned Lord Justice
referred to the Leicester case reported by Coke.124]
... Another instance is an operation for abortion,
which is 'unlawful' within the statute unless it is
necessary to prevent serious injury to health. Likewise with a sterilisation operation. When it is done
with the man's consent for a just cause, it is quite
lawful, as, for instance, when it is done to prevent
the transmission of an hereditary disease; but when it

is done without just cause or excuse, it is unlawful,
even though the man consents to it. Take a case
where a sterilisation operation is done so as to enable
a man to have the pleasure of sexual intercourse without
shouldering the responsibilities attached to it. The
operation then is plainly injurious to the public
interest. It is degrading to the man himself. It is
injurious to his wife and to any woman whom he marry,
to say nothing of the way it opens to licentiousness;
and, unlike contraceptives, it allows no room for a
change of mind on either side. It is illegal even
though the man consents to it.... If a husband under-
goes an operation for sterilisation without just cause
or excuse, he strikes at the very root of the marriage
relationship. The divorce courts should not countenance such an operation for sterilisation any more than
the criminal courts. It is severe cruelty. Even
assuming that the wife, when young and inexperienced,
consented to it, she ought not to be bound by it when
in later years she suffers in health on account of it,
especially when she was not warned that it might affect
her health....

It is clear from these statements that Denning L.J.
(now Lord Denning, Master of the Rolls) recognises
that there may be a "just cause of excuse" which would
render a sterilisation operation lawful. He would,
apparently, recognise that sterilisation for therapeutic
or eugenic purposes done with consent, although it is
not clear whether he regards the consent of the other
spouse as essential, would be a lawful operation. It
is equally clear that, in his view, sterilisation for
contraceptive or socio-economic purposes is unlawful,
and remains so whether consent is given or not. The
comment with regard to "licentiousness" is not really
of major significance. If it were, then, to be consistent, Lord Denning would be compelled to attack the use
of contraceptives, whereas earlier in the judgment he
indicated that the same effect could legitimately have
been achieved by the husband by their use.

Before leaving the Bravery case, mention should be
made of the fact that, despite Lord Denning's comments,
vasectomy can, as was pointed out in the case, be

reversed. Further, although this case as well as J. v.
J. dealt with sterilisation of the man, and the judges
made their comments in reference to the husband,
what they said is equally true of female sterilisation
and of the wife. On the other hand, since, at the time
the common law developed, women did no military service,
it may be doubted whether sterilisation of the female
would ever amount to common law mayhem.[125]

Divergencies of this kind among the judges inevitably
cause difficulties. Thus, the 1955 volume of British
Surgical Practice construed the decision as upholding
the legality of voluntary sterilisation, while the 1956
British Encyclopaedia of Medical Practice stated it
reinforced medical doubts as to the legality of such
operations,[126] and the 1955 edition of Sir Eardley
Holland's Obstetrics maintained that the operation was
only legal if undertaken to preserve the life of the
patient or to avert serious injury to physical or
mental health.[127] Lord Denning's view means that an
operation is legal only when there is a just cause,
and this has led one commentator[128] to suggest that

a medical practitioner, having received his training
largely at the public expense and by being put on the
medical register thus being put in a favoured position
to be able to handle dangerous drugs, etc., should not
use his privileges and skill for anything but a purely
therapeutic purpose. He therefore should not concern
himself with the making of money by carrying out face
lifting operations and other cosmetic activities. A
surgeon who charges high fees by persuading elderly
ladies to have their faces lifted or their noses
straightened may be said to be battening upon the foibles
and silliness of these women instead of practising
legitimately the profession for which he was trained
and given special privileges.... [On the other hand,]
it often happens that when the victim of a road accident
is claiming damages, among the items of special damage
is a sum to cover the cost of a plastic surgery operation to remove the scars due to the victim's face
having been badly cut by the glass from the windscreen
shattered in the accident.

In other words, we are back at considering when an operation is medically necessary.

In view of the population explosion and the strong pressures that now exist there is need in those countries where there is still some doubt as to the legality of voluntary sterilisation for some doctor possessing the courage of Bourne[129] to announce his intention to perform the operation, and rely upon the fact that there would probably be no prosecution, or no conviction if a trial ensued. Some countries have gone very far in recognizing the right to voluntary sterilisation. Long before the World Health Organization promulgated its definition of health, Swedish legislation acknowledged a woman's right to have herself sterilised for eugenic, social, medical, and medico-social reasons,[130] and in 1974 it was announced that Sweden intended providing free sterilisation for anyone over 25 seeking it. Such legislation, as well as the WHO definition, provides the justification for a doctor, whether the physical or mental health of the patient demands it, to perform a sterilisation operation on any grounds that he and his patient consider just. This is largely as it should be. Generally speaking, all operations should be the concern of the patient and his or her medical adviser, although the lawyer must be aware of the risks of abuse inherent in the situation, while the doctor must apply to this, as to any other operation, the normal skill to be expected in medical treatment.

While there are some who seek to avoid the possibility of conception by having recourse to sterilisation, there are some women who feel so deprived at the lack of a child that they have recourse to artificial impregnation. In view of the attitude that courts have adopted towards the parental instinct, one might be excused for assuming that, at least if the other spouse consents, such activities would be encouraged. Perhaps the earliest case in this connection is <u>Orford</u> v. <u>Orford</u>,[131] which arose in Canada and is probably a perfect example of the traditional approach to marriage and sexual activity. The judge believed offspring to be one of the main purposes of marriage, and he was of opinion that

had such a thing as 'artificial insemination' entered
the mind of the [Mosaic] lawgiver, it would have been
regarded with the utmost horror and detestation as an
invasion of the most sacred of the marital rights of
husband and wife, and have been the subject of the
severest penalties.... Adultery... involves the
possibility of introducing into the family of the husband
a false stream of blood.... The essence of the offence
of adultery consists, not in the moral turpitude of the
act of sexual intercourse, but in the voluntary surrender
to another person of the reproductive powers or faculties
of the guilty person; and any submission of these powers
to the service or enjoyment of another person other
than the husband or wife comes within the definition of
'adultery'.... What [the wife says] took place here
was the introduction into her body by unusual means of
the seed of a man other than her husband....

For these reasons, Orde J. held that artificial insemination by a donor was contrary to public policy and amounted to adultery. He even considered that A.I.D. without her consent would amount to rape. If this were so, and if it is the introduction of another man's seed into her body which constitutes the adultery, it would follow that the mere attempt to inseminate by way of a syringe should also constitute adultery. After all, the use of a contraceptive by a co-respondent does not mean that his intercourse with a wife does not amount to adultery, and what would be the position if the semen used had been taken - as is apparently medically feasible - from the vaginal passage of a woman with whom the donor had actual intercourse? Moreover, if A.I.D. constitutes adultery, if it has been carried out with the husband's consent it might be considered that there had been connivance and no matrimonial offence.

Since there is a presumption that the child born in marriage is a child of the marriage,[132] although this can be rebutted by evidence of male impotency[133] or of non-access,[134] one might presume that if the husband has consented to the A.I.D. of his wife, the child should be legitimate and the husband considered its father. However, in 1954 a Chicago court held[135] that artificial insemination by a donor

with or without the consent of the husband, is contrary to public policy and good morals, and constitutes adultery on the part of the father. A child so conceived is not a child born in wedlock and is therefore illegitimate. As such it is the child of the mother and the father has no right or interest in said child.

This decision should be compared with Strnad v. Strnad[136] in which a New York court held that where the husband consented it had the same effect as adoption, so that the child would be legitimate. However, in 1963 the New York Supreme Court held[137] the child to be illegitimate, although since the husband had consented he was liable to support it. As if to emphasise the type of confusion caused by the Bravery decision, the California District Court of Appeal shortly thereafter held that a husband who consented and held out the child thus born as his own would not be criminally liable for failing to support what was in fact somebody else's child.[138] The British courts have been no more consistent. In L. v. L.[139] the English Divorce Court granted a decree of nullity for non-consummation to a woman who had been artificially impregnated by her own husband. In Scotland, on the other hand, it was held[141] that a woman who, while separated from her husband, had conceived by artificial insemination from a donor had not committed adultery, because of the 'extraction of human relationship from the act of procreation'. The judge considered that to hold otherwise would mean that a mere injection without impregnation would suffice. In so far as New Zealand

478

is concerned, since 1963 artificial insemination without the husband's consent is a ground for divorce.

Artificial insemination, whether by a donor or a husband, involves certain problems for the doctor. In both cases he must ensure that every care it taken that the process is done hygienically and under proper supervision and conditions. When a donor is involved, perhaps ethics and morality demand that he be chosen in such a way that the offspring might have been born of the parties to the marriage. This is not to suggest that the doctor should seek out a 'twin' of the husband, but he should ensure that the donor is healthy; that the semen if stored has been stored properly and is unadulterated; that the donor had if not the same racial characteristics as the husband, at least the same pigmentation. If due to his carelessness things went wrong, the doctor might well be liable to the wife and possibly to the husband too; while if the suggestions made above with regard to the right of the embryo to a full life take effect, he might even be liable to the child as well.[141] This raises the question whether it is not time for legislatures to lay down the rules that are to apply when artificial insemination is resorted to, both for the protection of the parties, as well as for the medical practitioner.[142]

In recent years new problems have arisen affecting the marital relationship, some of which owe their origin to medical developments. As early as 1947 Mrs. Gardner who found that she was uncontrollably sexually attracted to women and who frequently wore male clothing, talked with her husband of undergoing a sex-change operation. Before this could take place, however, he sought a divorce for cruelty on the basis of her lesbianism and succeeded,[143] while in Spicer v. Spicer[144] a similar decree was granted, even though the female intervener had been dismissed from the suit, the wife having agreed

that 'her admitted persistent friendship with the
intervener had amounted to cruelty.' The implication of
this decision is that any friendship which is unpalatable
and causes pain to the other spouse could be held to
amount to cruelty sufficient to ground a divorce. Once
again, the concept of marriage breakdown would cover
any situation of this kind.

   The problems arising from a successful sex-change
operation are perhaps best illustrated by the English
case of <u>Corbett</u> v. <u>Corbett</u>.[145] The respondent had been
registered as a male at birth in 1935 and had joined the
Merchant Navy in 1951, when he was clearly male 'although
possessed of a womanish appearance with little bodily
and facial hair'. He had long desired to be a woman
and underwent surgery in 1960, whereby any male genitalia
he possessed were removed and an artificial passage
created resembling a vagina. He then met the petitioner,
who was a married man with children, but who himself
often wore female clothes. The petitioner became
interested in the respondent 'as a woman', and after
obtaining a divorce went through a form of marriage with
the defendant in Gibraltar. No sexual relations had
taken place before the marriage and the parties were
together for only fourteen days thereafter. Prior to
the marriage, although the respondent had been unable
to secure a new birth certificate, a female's national
insurance card was issued and 'he' acquired a female
name by deed poll. The petitioner sought a decree of
nullity for non-consummation - which would have meant
that the respondent was in fact a woman - or on the
ground that since the ceremony was between two men it
could not constitute a marriage. Medical evidence was
to the effect that the respondent was a 'male homosexual
transsexualist' or a 'castrated male' or 'inter-sex
[to be] assigned to the female sex'. Ormrod J. tended
to agree with the first opinion:

480

The respondent has been shown to have XY chromosomes and therefore to be of male chromosomal sex; to have had testicles prior to the operation and therefore to be of male gonadal sex; to have had male external genitalia without any evidence of internal or external female sexual organs and, therefore, to be of male genital sex; and, psychologically, to be a transsexual.... The body in its post-operation condition looks more like a female than a male as a result of very skilful surgery.... [But] the biological sexual constitution of an individual is fixed at birth (at the latest), and cannot be changed either by the natural development of organs of the opposite sex, or by medical or surgical means. The ... operation cannot affect the true sex....

The fundamental purpose of law is the regulation of the relations between persons and between persons and the State or community.... [L]egal relations can be classified into those in which the sex of the individuals concerned is either irrelevant, relevant or an essential determinant of the nature of the relationship. Over a very large area the law is indifferent to sex.... [T]here is nothing to prevent the parties to a contract of insurance or a pension scheme from agreeing that the person concerned should be treated as a man or as a woman, as the case may be. Similarly, the authorities, if they think fit, can agree with the individual that he shall be treated as a woman for national insurance purposes.... On the other hand, sex is clearly an essential determinant of the relationship called marriage, because it is and always has been recognised as the union of man and woman. It is the institution on which the family is built, and in which the capacity for natural heterosexual intercourse is an essential element.... [T]he characteristics which distinguish it from all other relationships can only be met by two persons of opposite sex. There are some other relationships such as adultery, rape and gross indecency in which, by definition, the sex of the participants is an essential determinant....

... The question [is] what is meant by the word 'woman' in the context of a marriage, for I am not concerned to determine the 'legal sex' of the respondent at large. Having regard to the essentially heterosexual character of the relationship which is called marriage, the criteria must... be biological, for even the most extreme degree of transsexualism in a male or the most severe hormonal imbalance which can exist in a person with male chromosomes, male gonads and male genitalia cannot reproduce a person who is naturally capable of performing the essential role of a woman in marriage... [T]he respondent is not a woman for the purposes of marriage but is a biological male and has been so since birth. It follows that the so-called marriage is void.

481

... [It has been submitted] that, because the respondent
is treated by society for many purposes as a woman, it
is illogical to refuse to treat her as a woman for the
purpose of marriage. The illogicality would only arise
if marriage were substantially similar in character
to national insurance and other social situations, but
the differences are obviously fundamental. These sub-
missions, in effect, confuse sex with gender. Marriage
is a relationship which depends on sex and not on gender.
... I would, if necessary, be prepared to hold that the
respondent was physically incapable of consummating a
marriage because I do not think that sexual intercourse,
using the completely artificial cavity constructed by
[the operation] can possibly be described ... as
'ordinary and complete intercourse' or as 'vera copula -
of the natural sort of coitus'[146]. In my judgment it
is the reverse of ordinary, and in no sense natural.
When such a cavity has been constructed in a male, the
difference between sexual intercourse using it, and
anal or intra-crural intercourse is ... to be measured
in centimetres.

I am aware that this view is not in accordance with some
of the observations ... in S. v. S.,[147] but ... those
parts of the judgment which refer to a wholly artificial
vagina, go beyond what was necessary for the decision...
and should be regarded as obiter. The respondent in
that case was assumed to be a woman, with functioning
ovaries, but with a congenital abnormality of the vagina.
... This is a very different situation from the one
which confronts me. There are ... certain dangers in
attempting to analyse too meticulously the essentials
of normal sexual intercourse.... The mischief is that,
by over-refining and over-defining the limits of
'normal', one may, in the end, produce a situation in
which consummation may come to mean something altogether
different from normal sexual intercourse....

... I hold that it has been established that the
respondent is not, and was not a woman at the date of
the ceremony of marriage, but was, at all times, a
male. The marriage is, accordingly, void....

It may well be considered that it is high time the

courts recognised the possibility that such a narrow

medico-legal definition of 'sex', even for the purposes

of marriage, is completely out of touch with modern

social needs. After all, had the respondent in this

case required medical treatment there is no doubt that

this would have been given in the woman's ward of a

hospital, just as it cannot be doubted that the individual him/herself would have always used public conveniences set aside for women, and had an attempt been made to use those intended for males would probably have been arrested. Switzerland appears to have taken a far more socially-minded view of this type of situation. In May 1974 the Swiss authorities recognized the civil status of a former male who had changed sex and

agreed to re-register the man as a woman provided that if she marries she informs her spouse beforehand about the operation.[148]

The Swiss, therefore, accept that a valid marriage may be contracted between a man and a man who has become a woman, and presumably would give such a person the full protection of the criminal law, recognizing that as a woman she could be raped even by way of her artificial vagina. This is in direct contrast to the view of Judge Crush in Cinncinnati who dismissed charges of rape and aggravated assault when it was discovered that the complainant was a man undergoing sex change operations. In the judge's view the plaintiff had not been raped, but was 'an obvious homosexual', whose creditibility was nil.[149] While it may be true that the witness's credibility was nil, there is no real reason why a person with an artificial vagina, be that person medically female or male, cannot be the victim of rape. Perhaps, this is but one further ground for agreeing with those who argue that rape is merely another form of assault, and that it would be more in keeping with the victim's dignity and protect her from cruel and unnecessarily suggestive cross-examination if the sexual aspects of this crime were removed.

Since society's attitude to homosexuality has changed and some homosexual couples have entered into more or less permanent bilateral arrangements; and since we

have accepted for many purposes that legal consequences
may flow even from an unmarried relationship between a
man and a woman;[150] are changing our attitude towards
illegitimacy; and no longer regard procreation as
essential to a valid marriage and allow sterilisation,
there appears to be no reason why we should not also
recognize that a permanent relationship between two
persons of the same sex can acquire legal recognition
and protection. In 1974, using very similar reasoning
to Ormrod J. in Corbett a Manitoban judge refused[151]
to recognise a ceremony entered into by two men before
a clergyman as creating a marriage. It may be that this
was not a marriage in the traditional sense. But we
have wandered far from tradition in both our sexual and
our family relationships. It may be asking too much
to expect a legislature or the mass of society to
afford the word marriage to such a liaison. Perhaps,
though, acceptance would be accorded if some other term
were evolved to give legal cognizance to what may after
all be an even more permanent relationship than is
often created in a 'proper' marriage. Such a development
would ensure for one thing that if the 'husband' or
earning partner of the relationship were to die without
leaving a will, the 'housewife' partner would be entitled
to succeed to the matrimonial house and property sooner
than the 'husband's' next of kin, who may as likely as
not have refused to have anything to do with such
'husband' from the moment he entered into his 'marriage'.

Ormrod J. said that 'The fundamental purpose of law is
the regulation of the relations between persons, and
between persons and the State or community.' Too often,
the law seems to lag behind what the public desires and
too often the law becomes out of date and out of accord
with social needs.[152] In so far as the personal lives
of individuals are concerned, particularly in their
most intimate relationships, it is high time that the

law took note of its 'fundamental purpose' and made an
effort to regulate 'the relations between persons, and
between persons and the State' in a manner that preserved harmony in those relations, recognizing that the
State, its institutions and the law are the servants
of the people and that people are not the playthings
of the law.

In 1929 Max Radin wrote[153]

If [the judge] shuts his eyes and averts his face and
cries out that he will not judge, he has already judged.
He has declared it to be lawful by not declaring it
unlawful.

In this area, too often the truth is exactly opposite.

* Based on an address to the 1962 Singapore conference
  on sterilisation held under the auspices of the
  International Planned Parenthood Federation.

1 See, e.g., Lee, Population and Law (1971), the first
  vol. in Duke University's Law and Population series.

2 Plender, International Migration Law (1972), vol.2
  of the Duke series.

3 1948, 78 U.N.T.S. 277, Art. 2.

4 The Times (London), 12 Dec. 1973.

5 Griswold v. Connecticut (1965) 381 U.S. 479.

6 S.C. 1968-69, c.41, s.13.

7 (1973) 410 U.S. 113, 179, resp.

8 See I above.

9 E.g., Taylor, The Biological Time Bomb (1968);
  Hilton & Harris, Ethical Issues in Human Genetics
  (1970); Stringer, Ethics and Judgment in Surgery
  and Medicine (1970); Newell & Simon, Human Problem
  Solving (1972); Fletcher, Ethics of Genetic Control:
  Ending Reproductive Roulette (1974); Friedmann,
  'Interference with Human Life: Some Jurisprudential
  Reflections' (1970), 70 Col. Law Rev. 1058.

10 Conundrum (1974); see, also, Corbett v. Corbett [1970] 2 W.L.R. 1306 (n.145 below).

11 See, e.g., Manitoba decision in North and Vogel v. Matheson (1974 - unreported).

12 See, e.g., Edwards, 'The Problem of Compensation for Antenatal Injuries', (1973) 246 Nature 54.

13 1948, 14 U.N.T.S. 185.

14 [1939] 1 K.B. 687, 693-4, per Macnaghten J.

15 19 & 20 Geo. 5, c. 34, s. 1.

16 24 & 25 Vict. c. 100, s. 58.

17 See, e.g., Murray v. McMurchy (1965) 381 U.S. 479.

18 Res. 217A (III); and see VII above, n.60.

19 Art. 16 (1). See Skinner v. Oklahoma (1942) 316 U.S. 535, 536, per Douglas J.

20 See, e.g., Green, 'Human Rights and the Colour Problem' (1950) 5 Curr. Legal Prob. 236, 245.

21 Art. 5.

22 Eichmann v. Att. Gen., Israel (1962) 36 Int'l Law Rep. 5, 277.

23 See, e.g., St.John-Stevas, Life, Death and the Law (1961) 227.

24 1 Supplemental Nights (Burton Club ed., 1887), 70.

25 Christensen v. Thornby (1934) 93 A.L.R. 570,572, per Loring J.

26 McWhinnie, Denmark - A New Look at Crime (1961), 6.

27 12 Int'l Rev. of Crim. Policy (1957) 13; for evidence of Nazi practices, see Nuremberg Proceedings, vol.10, 21, vol. 20, 238.

28 St.John-Stevas, op.cit., App.VIII-X.

29 R.S.A. 1970, c. 341.

30 1972, c. 1.

31 1972, c. 87.

[32] (1942) 316 U.S. 536, 541, 546.

[33] In fact, male vasectomy can be reversed in some cases. At the S'pore conference Dr. G. Phadke of Bombay reported on 18 cases, in which the vas had been rejoined. In 15, the semen showed sperm, and 9 of the 15 impregnated their wives.

[34] This seems to be confirmed by the Tuskegee Jail V.D. experiment in which some prisoners were denied treatment. In 1974 an out-of-court settlement was announced (Globe and Mail (Toronto), 16 Dec.1974).

[35] St.John-Stevas, op.cit., 296 (Arizona), 302 (Mississippi), 304 (New Hampshire).

[36] Globe and Mail, 9 Dec. 1974.

[37] Bull. of Legal Developments [1974] No.19, 3.

[38] For reference to such occurrences in the U.S., see Minty, 'Unlawful Wounding: Will Consent Make It Legal? (1956), 24 Medico-Legal J. 54, 61-2.

[39] St.John-Stevas, op.cit., 297; see, also, 300 (Kansas), 307 (Utah).

[40] Keyling v. Keyling (1942) 23 Atl. 800.

[41] (1934) 93 A.L.R. 570, 572.

[42] Globe and Mail, 6 Nov. 1974.

[43] Murray v. McMurchy [1949] 2 D.L.R. 442, 445 (italics in original).

[44] (1952) 241 P.2d 1028.

[45] St. John-Stevas, op.cit., 146, n.1.

[46] 29 Eugenics Rev. (1937/8), c. ibid. 161.

[47] Schuman, Hitler and the Nazi Dictatorship (1935)382.

[48] St.John-Stevas, op.cit., 174; for a state-by-state breakdown, see App.V, 291.

[49] (1927) 274 U.S. 200, 208 (italics added); see, however, Skinner v. Oklahoma, n.32 above.

[50] The Sanctity of Life and the Criminal Law (1958) 82.

[51] See Friedmann, loc.cit., 1073, n.49.

52 Winfield, 'The Unborn Child', (1942) 8 Camb. Law J. 76, 77.

53 Walker v. Great Northern Rly. of Ireland (1890) 28 L.R.Ir. 69.

54 Montreal Tramways Co. v. Leveille [1933] 4 D.L.R.337.

55 Hall v. Murphy (1960) 113 SE 2d 790,793; Fowler v. Woodward (1964) 138 SE 2d 42,44.

56 See, e.g., Trail Smelter Arb. (1938/41) 3 U.N. Rep. Int'l Arb. Awards 1905, 1929.

57 See, e.g., British Law Reform Comm., Working Paper No. 47 (1973).

58 (1960) 401 Pa. 267.

59 Edwards, loc.cit., 54.

60 Such a claim was rejected by an Illinois court in Zepeda v. Zepeda (1963) 190 NE 2d 849.

61 R. v. Senior (1832) 1 Moo. C. C. 346. See, also, Hong Kong trial of accused charged with stabbing pregnant woman, inflicting injuries upon her unborn child from which it died after birth: the accused was acquitted of murder, but found guilty of manslaughter, Straits Times (Singapore), 6 Jun. 1963.

62 R. v. Shepherd [1919] 2 K.B. 125.

63 Christensen v. Thornby (1934) 93 A.L.R. 570.

64 See n. 42 above.

65 (1934) Cmd. 4485 (The Brock Report).

66 Bravery v. Bravery [1954] 3 All E.R. 59, 67.

67 Ex p. Eaton (1954 - c, St.John-Stevas, op.cit., 163, n. 2).

68 12th ed., s. 182.

69 Coke on Littleton (1628) 127a, 127b.

70 Hawkins, Pleas of the Crown (1739) 107.

71 4 Commentaries (1768), ch.15, 1.

72 Lloyd, Public Policy (1953) 29.

73   Loc. cit., n. 63 above, 572, per Loring J.

74   See Minty, loc.cit., 58, for a similar request by Byron with regard to his club-foot.

75   See, however, Burmese case of Shwe Kin [1915] A.I.R. (L.B.) 101 - A claimed to be proof against edged instruments and invited B to test his claim; B cut A's arm inflicting a wound from which A bled to death.

76   See, however, R. v. Donovan [1934] 2 K.B. 298, consent no defence to an indecent assault (caning) likely to cause grievous hurt.

77   (1966) 864.

78   Ibid., 192; see also, 183 et seqq.

79   Italics added.

80   Ibid., 194 citing Stephen, Digest of Criminal Law, Art. 226.

81   See, e.g., plan of Assam branch of Indian Tea Assoc., News of Population and Birth Control (London), No. 108, Oct. 1962.

82   Lloyd, op.cit., 29.

83   See n.7 above.

84   [1934] 2 K.B. 498, 507, per Swift J.

85   Op.cit., 103.

86   1 Rob. Ecc. 279, 296, 299(Italics in original).

87   The Book of Common Prayer lists the causes for which matrimony is ordered: 'first, the procreation of children...'

88   See, e.g., G. v. G. (1871) L.R. 2 P. & D. 287, 291: "if the organs of the woman were so formed structurally as to render intercourse impossible, the marriage would be void. If is apparent enough that without intercourse the ends of marriage, the procreation of children, and the pleasures and enjoyment of matrimony cannot be attained", per Lord Penzance; G. v. M. (1885) 10 A.C. 171, 204: "The procreation of children being the main object of marriage, the contract contains by implication, as an essential term, the capacity for consummation", per Lord Fitzgerald - but consummation is no guarantee of conception and procreation.

89 [1955] P.42, 46, 47, _per_ Commissioner Grazebrook.

90 [1962] 3 All E.R. 55, 58, 59 (_sub.nom._ _S.Y._ v. _S.Y._ [1963] P.37).

91 At 62, 63.

92 See, however, _R._ v. _Lines_ (1844) 1 C. & K. 393, in which it was held that the question in issue was "whether, at any time, any part of the virile member of the prisoner was within the labia of the pudendum of the prosecutrix: for, if it was (no matter how little), that will be sufficient to constitute a penetration", which would imply that an artificial vagina might suffice.

93 See, however, _Dennis_ v. _Dennis_ [1955] 2 All E.R. 51, 56 - "there must at least be partial penetration for the act of adultery to be proved", _per_ Hodson L.J.

94 _R._ v. _Lines_, n. 92 above.

95 _Dennis_ v. _Dennis_, n. 93 above.

96 _Ibid._ 55.

97 At 56.

98 [1924] A.C. 689, 721.

99 [1967] 3 All E.R. 178.

100 [1954] 2 All E.R. 373.

101 _Walsham_ v. _Walsham_ [1949] 1 All E.R. 774, 775, _per_ Wallington J.

102 [1950] P. 84.

103 [1946] P. 36, 40.

104 See n. 86 above.

105 (1922) 38 T.L.R. 697, 698.

106 [1948] A.C. 274, 286.

107 [1950] 1 All E.R. 677, 678, 680.

108 [1955] 2 All E.R. 305, 309-10, _per_ Sachs J.

109 [1955] 2 All E.R. 311, 314, _per_ Commissioner Latey.

110 [1952] 2 T.L.R. 143, 148.

111 [1965] 2 All E.R. 456, 463, per Sterling J.

112 [1964] A.C. 644.

113 [1966] 2 All E.R. 257, 260-1, 264-5.

114 Op.cit., n. 65.

115 See, e.g., Minty, loc.cit., 59, who says of salpingectomy, 'It is about as serious as a simple appendicectomy, but there can be no absolute guarantee against complications and fatal results.'

116 Twiner v. Avery (1921) 113 At.1 710; Aufort v. Aufort (1935) 49 P.2d 620; Vileta v. Vileta (1942) 128 P. 2d 376; Stegianko v. Stegianko (1940) 295 NW 252; Osborne v. Osborne (1937) 191 A. 783.

117 (1942) 23 Atl. 2d 800.

118 Loc.cit., n. 105.

119 [1947] P. 158, 161, per Somervell L.J.

120 In C. v. C. (1961), however, a delay of 28 years was not considered too long (The Times, 30 Oct.1961).

121 [1954] 3 All E.R. 59.

122 At 61, 63, 64.

123 At 65, 66, 67.

124 See n. 69 above.

125 Minty, loc.cit., 59.

126 At 155, 112, resp.

127 At 361.

128 Minty, loc.cit., 62.

129 See n. 14 above.

130 Williams, op.cit., n. 50, 80.

131 (1921) 58 D.L.R. 251, 258, per Orde J.

132 Russell v. Russell 1921 A.C. 689.

133 R. v. Luffe (1807) 3 East 193, 202.

134 (Eng.) Matrimonial Causes Act, 1950, 14 Geo. 6,

c.25; see, also, Quebec Civil Code, 1973 ed., Art. 220, which permits husbands to renounce wife's child in case of 'l'impossibilité physique de se rencontrer avec sa femme'; see, also, Re B. and B. [1972] 26 D.L.R. (3d) 481.

135 Doornbos v. Doornbos (1954) (unreported, c. (1955) 41 Am. Bar Assoc. J. 263).

136 (1948) 78 NYS 2d 390.

137 Gursky v. Gursky (1963) 242 NYS 2d 406, 409-10.

138 People v. Sorensen (1967) 66 Cal. Reptr. 7, 13.

139 [1949] P.211.

140 Maclennan v. Maclennan [1958] S.C. 105, 113-4, per Lord Wheatley.

141 See Tallin, 'Artificial Insemination' (1956), 35 Can. Bar Rev. (Part I) 1, (Part II) 166, 175.

142 See ibid., 183 et seqq., for legislative suggestions.

143 Gardner v. Gardner [1947] 1 All E.R. 630.

144 Spicer v. Spicer [1954] 3 All E.R. 208.

145 [1970] 2 W.L.R. 1306, 1322-3, 1324-5, 1326-7.

146 See n. 86 above.

147 See n. 90 above.

148 The Times, 23 May 1974.

149 Globe and Mail, 27 Sept. 1974.

150 Thus, during the war, 'unmarried wives' of English soldiers received 'family' allowances.

151 North and Vogel v. Matheson (1974 - unreported) - Philp, C.C.C.J., Manitoba, adopted Ormrod J.'s comments in Corbett re purpose of law, and sex and marriage.

152 See I above.

153 'Permanent Problems of the Law' (1929) 15 Cornell Law Q. 1, 15.

Maccoby, S. 290
Maine, Sir Henry 83
Malaysia, law in 67,88-9
Man, primitive 8
Manifest illegality/unlawfulness 409-10,411-5,416,417,
     418-9,420,426-7,428
Mannheim, K. 296-7
Mansfield, Lord 46-7
Marriage 12-7,73-9,105,108-15,121-3,299,438,481-2,484
     Christian 12,13-4,108,121,459,466,468
     consummation 13-5,459-62,464,465-6,471,478,482
     miscegenation 438,450
     Native 76-9,105,108-15,121-2
     sterility and 459-62,466,471
     sterilization and 458-9,469-76
     unisexual 435,480-3,484
Mawedopenais 124
Mayhem 452-3,454,475
McCardie, Mr. Justice 61
McDougal, M.S. 137-8
McNair, Lord 302
McNaughten Rules 168
Military Law 159,399,400,427
Military objectives 402-3,405-6
Mill,J.S. 324
Minorities 249-55,271,273,287-93
Mis-tah-wah-sis, Chief 125
Monogamy 12-4,73,75,78,111,114-5,121
Montefiore, Sir Moses 245
Montesquieu, Baron de 321
Moore, J.B. 158,183
Moore, W.H. 157,159
Morality
     law and 1-52,123,127,173,210-1,265,314
     meaning of 3-8,102,106,314
     positive 4
Morris, Lt.Gov. 124-5
Morris, Mr. Justice 435
Morrelli, G. 312
My Lai 412,413-7,420

Namibia 148-9,187-8,267, v. also South West Africa
Nationals, treatment of 207-10,245-8,259,262,284-6,291
     296-7, v. also human rights
Native and common law 61-98
     customary law 76-9,81-3,84-5,89-91,104-13
Natural law, modern 70,222,300,310
Nervo, L. Padilla 267
Non-refoulement 328,350-1,353,354,355,368
Nuclear weapons 47-8,159,403
Nuremberg principles 186,219

Riphagen, W.   312
Rolin. H.   229
Roman-Dutch law   64-5,85-7,93
Rome, aliens in   63-4
Roosevelt, Mrs. E.   151-2
Root , E.   324-5
Rosenne, S.   160
Rousseau, J.J.   283
Roy, S.N.G.   210-1
Ruskin, J.   129
Russell, Lord, of Killowen   184
'Russian Wives'   299

Sachs, Mr. Justice   467-8
Sanction(s)   145,146,164-5
Sanctuary   335
Santos, A.   193
Satow, Sir Ernest   331
Schwarzenberger, G.   283,286,292,305,306,313
Scott, J.B.   146-7
Scott, Sir Wm.   286-7
Seijos, R.F.   196
Self-determination   51,127,140-1,190,208-15,218-20,221-2,
      227,230,242,270,306,356,392
'Separate but equal' doctrine   44-6,242
September in Quinze   37
Settlement of territory   100-3,113
Sex   6
      definition of   480-3
Sex change   435,460,479,480-3
Sexual intercourse   459-70,481,482, v. coitus interruptus
      contraceptives, with   462,465-8,477
      denial of   465,469
Shaw, G.B.   397
Simon of Glaisdale, Lord   389
Simonds, Viscount   41-2,43
Singapore, law in   67,69,74-5,454-6
Sissons, Mr. Justice   90,108-10
Slavery and slave trade   286-7,300,336,338-9
Smith, H.A.   246,296
Smuts, J.C.   257
Society   7
South Africa   49-51,188,206,209,213,218,246,252,258,261
      264,296,301-2
South West Africa   148-9,187-8,267, v. Namibia
Sovereignty   145,154-5,156,274,302,323
      U.N. Declaration on   201,214,225,270
Stable, Mr. Justice   35-7
State succession   170
Statelessness   242,244,254,255-6,297, v. refugees
sterilization   30-1,434-6,437,438-48,451-7,465,469-76,484
Story, Justice   287
Suffield, Lord   21
Suicide   23-6